AMERICAN
WINGS

Chicago's Pioneering Black Aviators and the Race for Equality in the Sky

SHERRI L. SMITH AND ELIZABETH WEIN

G. P. Putnam's Sons

G. P. Putnam's Sons
An imprint of Penguin Random House LLC, New York

First published in the United States of America by G. P. Putnam's Sons,
an imprint of Penguin Random House LLC, 2024

Visit us online at PenguinRandomHouse.com.

Library of Congress Cataloging-in-Publication Data
Names: Smith, Sherri L., author. | Wein, Elizabeth, author.
Title: American wings: Chicago's pioneering Black aviators and the race for equality in the sky /
by Sherri L. Smith and Elizabeth Wein.
Description: New York: G. P. Putnam's Sons, [2024] | Summary: "A nonfiction account of a group of determined Black Americans who created a flying club and built their own airfield on Chicago's South Side in the period between World Wars I and II"—Provided by publisher.
Identifiers: LCCN 2023022245 (print) | LCCN 2023022246 (ebook) | ISBN 9780593323984 (hardcover) | ISBN 9780593324004 (epub)
Subjects: LCSH: African American air pilots—Biography—Juvenile literature. |
Air pilots—United States—Biography—Juvenile literature. | Aeronautics—United States—History—20th century—Juvenile literature. | Private flying—Illinois—Chicago—Societies, etc.—History—20th century—Juvenile literature. | United States—Race relations—History—20th century—Juvenile literature.
Classification: LCC TL539 .S633 2024 (print) | LCC TL539 (ebook) |
DDC 629.13092—dc23/eng/20230705
LC record available at https://lccn.loc.gov/2023022245
LC ebook record available at https://lccn.loc.gov/2023022246

ISBN 9780593323984

1st Printing

Printed in the United States of America
LSCH

Design by Richard Amari
Text set in Sabon Next Pro

For my dad, who earned his wings in the footsteps
of these pioneers; and for my brother Derek,
the rocket kid with his eyes on the sky —S.L.S.

For Tim, for the wonder of our first flights together
in Africa, and all our flights ahead —E.W.

And for everyone who has ever dreamed they were flying, and
the brave ones who wake up and make those dreams come true.

CONTENTS

I shall never be satisfied until we have men of the Race who can fly. Do you know you have never lived until you have flown? Of course, it takes one with courage, nerve and ambition to fly. And, too, age and health are to be given great consideration. But I am thankful to know we have men who are physically fit; now what is needed is men who are not afraid to dare death . . . We must have aviators if we are to keep up with the times.

—Bessie Coleman, in an interview with
the *Chicago Defender*, October 8, 1921

PROLOGUE

A DREAM TAKES FLIGHT

Omaha, Nebraska, 1919

It was going to cost three dollars to ride—about $50 in 2023, but the work of several days, or even weeks, in 1919. Cornelius Robinson Coffey had the money from his side job running special deliveries for the Omaha post office. But the rule was white people first. He stood aside with the other onlookers in the cold Nebraska field and waited his turn, his eyes on the January sky.

Overhead, an airplane buzzed, boldly announcing man's dominion over the air.

Aviation was a fairly new craze, the Wright brothers having made their first flight barely fifteen years earlier, on December 17, 1903. But it hadn't taken long for the world to turn the airplane into a weapon of war. Today's barnstormer—one of those pilots who staged air shows in farmers' fields, selling tickets for quick plane rides and setting up shop in local barns—was a World War I veteran, recently home from Europe since the end of the Great War in 1918. Even the barnstormer's plane was a veteran of sorts. His Curtiss JN-4, a type nicknamed the Jenny, was one of the little two-seater biplanes that had been used to train American men to fly for the war effort.

White American men, that is.

Born on September 6, 1903, Coffey—as most people would call him in later years—was Black. And at only fifteen years old, he was the same age as the entire field of modern aviation. His home state of Nebraska had been a hub of aviation activity from the start, with the Wright brothers performing at the State Fair in Omaha in 1910.

While the Midwest wasn't the Deep South, segregation and racism still held sway. White customers went first. After waiting patiently for his turn to come, Coffey finally fished out the price for his first ride in a genuine airplane.

The pilot must have been astonished. This Black boy had the gall *and* the money to take a ride in the sky. The barnstormer turned to the other onlookers—undoubtedly white people—and said, "When I get through with him, that kid ain't going to even look at another airplane."

But Coffey's money was green, so the man took it, and let the boy climb up into the plane. The Jenny was built of fabric stretched over a wooden frame, a single-engine biplane with stacked wings and two open cockpits, one behind the other. Coffey most likely rode in the front cockpit, where the pilot could keep an eye on him.

The little wood-and-fabric Jenny rattled down the field and leapt up into the air.

In those days, there was hardly anyplace you could get a really smooth ride. Outside the city, scarcely any roads were paved. Inside the city, they were often paved with cobblestones, with embedded trolley tracks an extra hazard. Coffey knew what speed was like—he rode a Henderson motorcycle. But the silken speed of flight was something he could never have imagined. From the moment the Jenny's wheels left the ground, he loved it. It didn't bother him in the least that the pilot was doing his darnedest to scare the living wits out of the uppity little Black kid with his pocket money and his belief that he should be allowed to fly.

Everyone said Black people weren't made for flying. People said they were cowards. They were lazy. It took brains and guts to be a pilot.

But this kid seemed to have both.

With every loop and dive, Coffey just had more fun. The pilot upped his game, tilting the plane into rolls and spins. He might have even scared himself a little, flying upside down, or nosing the plane into a dive, only pulling up in the nick of time to skim the treetops.

"I think it was rougher on him than on me," Coffey said calmly afterward.

Three dollars bought fifteen minutes of thrills in the sky, and when they landed, the pilot had to admit he was impressed.

"Well, you know, if I was going to be here for any length of time, I'd probably teach you to fly," he told the boy.

Coffey had the feel for it, no doubt. But everyone knew Black people couldn't learn to fly. Cornelius Coffey had likely been told that, too.

So he hopped back onto his Henderson motorcycle and headed home. He wouldn't come near another plane for nearly a decade.

But when the time came, he would prove just how wrong everyone had been.

The teenaged Cornelius Coffey on his Henderson motorcycle.
KENNETH SPENCER RESEARCH LIBRARY, UNIVERSITY OF KANSAS

CHAPTER 1

PRE-FLIGHT, DETROIT, 1927

I'm goin' to Detroit, get myself a good job
I'm goin' to Detroit, get myself a good job
Tried to stay around here with the starvation mob

I'm goin' to get a job, up there in Mr. Ford's place
I'm goin' to get a job, up there in Mr. Ford's place
Stop these eatless days from starin' me in the face

—Blind Blake, "Detroit Bound Blues," 1928

DR. Ossian Sweet had a sweet ride. It was a beautiful Marmon luxury motorcar that he wouldn't let anybody touch except for a single mechanic in all of Detroit, Michigan—a town so full of car manufacturers that it would one day earn the nickname "Motor City."

So it was a bad day for Dr. Sweet when his Marmon broke down on Montcalm Street, in a neighborhood far from his preferred garage near where Ford Field Stadium stands today. Sweet had the car towed to a closer garage for safekeeping. But he told them not to touch it— *his* mechanic would come by and take care of it himself.

The mechanic on duty when Dr. Sweet's car arrived at that other garage was John Charles Robinson, a young Black man from Gulfport, Mississippi, known as Johnny to his friends. And he took immediate offense at not being allowed to touch that Marmon.

Johnny was a good-looking youth with a dark complexion and

thick black hair. He'd worked hard to elevate himself from a skinny little shoeshine boy to an automotive technician. He was a graduate of the famous Tuskegee Normal and Industrial Institute in Alabama, pretty much considered the best education available to young southern Black men. Johnny knew how to build an entire automobile from the ground up. So who was this fancy mechanic who was worth such a long wait, when he, John C. Robinson, was as skilled as anybody?

=====

Cornelius Robinson Coffey, the brown-skinned boy with a big name, was about ten or eleven years old when, in 1914 or '15, he looked up into the Arkansas sky and saw an exhilarating sight: a squadron of early flying machines passing overhead in the small river town of Newport. He realized then that people really could fly.

Coffey was the youngest of three kids born to Henry and Ada Wright Coffey. His mother seems to have died early in Coffey's young life, and by 1910, the young family had moved in with their grandma, Cyntha Wright, Ada's mother. Henry was a railroad man, able to hook a train together and drive a steam locomotive between the station and the roundhouse where it was stored—and no more than that. In 1915, America was only fifty years out from the end of slavery. Even in the North, segregation was commonplace, and in the South, it was the law of the land. The racism of the time would not allow Henry to become a full-fledged engineer.

With the dream of flight still years off, Coffey found a love of something closer to home—engines. He may have been inspired by the steam engines his father worked with on the railroad, but Coffey was most fascinated by the internal combustion engines that powered cars and motorcycles.

When he was only twelve years old, Coffey taught himself to drive a Model T Ford automobile. The Model T, created by Henry Ford in 1908, was sturdy and easy to drive; the boxy black car rode high on spoked wheels and resembled a horse-drawn buggy without the horse. It took a complex process of eleven steps to start the 1914 Model T, including winding a crank to turn over the engine, and turning the crank took more muscle than young Cornelius Coffey could muster. As he described it, "I'd climb up on the crank, hold on to the radiator cap and jump up and down until the engine kicked over." He used his new driving skills to get a job. "My spirit was kindled to go into a line of work where I wouldn't be bound by the limitations my father had to put up with," he avowed. "The car dealer in town hired me to show customers how to drive. Folks were so excited by their first car, they'd take lessons from a Black child."

Coffey's older sister, Vida, married a young man named Leander Walker, and in 1916 the couple moved three states away, from Arkansas to Omaha, Nebraska. Leander worked there in a packing house, and later, on the railroads as a porter. Henry Coffey seems to have passed away about this time, so Coffey's older brother, Vernon, took him to live with Vida and her husband in Omaha, where Coffey became the only Black student in his class. There, in 1917, fourteen-year-old Coffey somehow got his hands on a motorcycle, one of the popular Henderson four-cylinders. He'd already taught himself to drive a car; a motorcycle proved to be no challenge. He began earning a little money of his own doing special deliveries for the local postmaster for eight cents a letter.

In that same year, the armed conflict that had been raging in Europe since 1914 became the first "world war," reaching America in the form of a draft. Vernon joined the U.S. Army to fight in France.

Black men had served the young United States in integrated units as far back as the Revolutionary War. They served in the U.S. Navy throughout the nineteenth century. But after 1820, African Americans were banned from serving in the U.S. Army. That policy changed with the Emancipation Proclamation in 1863. But during the Civil War, Black men were only able to serve in segregated units, and the same became true in the Navy as well. The Navy wouldn't allow Black officers, and enlisted men were employed only in service as stewards, cooks, and deckhands. The Marines didn't accept Black recruits at all.

Segregation in the United States military had in fact grown steadily worse since the birth of the nation. One major reason for this was that most military training took place in the southern states, where the weather was milder during the winter. The white population of the South didn't like Black soldiers from the North, with their expectations of equal treatment and equal rights. When Black men from the northern states were sent to southern training camps, they couldn't believe the humiliating segregation laws they were expected to obey: having to drink from separate water fountains and use separate restrooms from the white population, having to line up for food at the back door of local diners, having to stand while riding public transport so white passengers could sit, not being allowed in public buildings—not to mention the verbal abuse from local residents. In Houston, Texas, the situation became so poisonous in August of 1917 that the city erupted in rioting as Black soldiers, white policemen, and local citizens shot and bayoneted one another. But the terrible training situation didn't stop African Americans from wanting to serve their country.

After the United States entered World War I in 1917, a universal draft was established for all American males aged between twenty-one and thirty-one with no specific reference to race. Black men like Vernon Coffey registered and were drafted for military service despite the snarl of hostility and red tape. Black combat units were formed, and were often sent straight to the fighting in Europe without training— just to avoid the conflict that might arise from a long stay on a southern military base.

As for aviation, there wasn't a chance that a Black man would be allowed to fly for the U.S. military. Eugene Bullard, a Black American who was in Europe when the war began, trained as a pilot and enlisted with France because the U.S. wouldn't take him. He became the only African American pilot to serve in World War I.

The so-called "Great War" raged on for over four years. An estimated twenty-one million people of all races died in the

Eugene Bullard in the uniform of the 170th French Infantry Regiment, 1917. He was the only Black American to fly in World War I, as a member of the French Lafayette Flying Corps.

Eugene Jacques Bullard (U.S. Air Force Photo)

war, but Vernon Coffey was not one of them. Vernon returned to the States in 1919 and moved to Kansas City, Missouri. He found work as a railway porter like his brother-in-law, managing luggage and assisting passengers, while, two states away, Cornelius Coffey finally got up close and personal with a real airplane for the first time.

But that year a wave of prejudiced rage and hatred swept the nation.

Overseas, African American soldiers had been treated with more respect than they were given back home. Many of them, returning from the victory of World War I like Coffey's brother, Vernon, quickly became the target of white supremacists, who feared the potential power of military-trained Black men seeking freedom and equality in the face of American racism. Across the country, eleven Black veterans—along with sixty-seven other African Americans—were lynched by white mobs. Horrifically, some people were even burned alive. There were race riots in twenty-eight American cities; homes and businesses owned by Black Americans were destroyed, churches were burned, and at least 250 people were killed.

The brutal period became known as the Red Summer for the shocking amount of blood spilled across America. It was named so by James Weldon Johnson, then a field secretary for the National Association for the Advancement of Colored People (NAACP). On a trip to Washington, D.C., that summer, Johnson saw for himself how "men and women of my race were being mobbed, chased, dragged from streetcars, beaten and killed within the shadow of the dome of the Capitol, at the very front door of the White House."

That September, in Omaha, where Coffey lived, a Black civilian named William Brown was arrested on trumped-up charges. A lawless mob set fire to the courthouse where Brown was being held, before dragging him out and hanging him. It took military intervention to disperse the crowd; two white civilians were also killed in the riot. No one was ever found guilty.

What could the future offer to a Black boy in a city that allowed such injustice?

"Why don't you go to school and learn a trade?" suggested Coffey's brother-in-law, Leander.

"Well, I'd like to be an auto mechanic," Coffey replied.

There were no such schools in Omaha. So, in 1921, when Coffey was seventeen or eighteen years old, he made a two-hundred-mile trek on his trusty Henderson motorcycle to scope out Kansas City. But when he arrived at the Sweeney School of Automotive Engineering, he was told they did not accept students of color. Coffey had biked all that way for nothing.

He returned to Omaha and graduated from Capitol High School in June 1923. By then, in a move toward adult independence, he seems to have left his sister's house to live at the local "Y," the Young Men's Christian Association or YMCA, a community center that provided dorms for young single men. It may have been there that he learned of automotive schools in Chicago that did accept Black students. After some time, now nearly twenty years old, Coffey transferred his Y membership to Chicago and headed to the "Windy City" for a new chance at learning his trade.

He found that chance at the Ogden Davis & Company School of Automotive Engineering, less than a mile from the Y where he was living on Chicago's South Side. A Frenchman named George Keon ran the place, and though "the little school only had about three or four cars, . . . he was really good," Coffey recalled.

Cornelius Coffey in his teens or early twenties, likely with family

KENNETH SPENCER RESEARCH LIBRARY, UNIVERSITY OF KANSAS

Coffey finished the course in eleven months, graduating on May 17, 1926, at the top of his class.

He was exactly the mechanic that Chevrolet dealer Emil Mack was looking for.

Emil Mack sold and repaired automobiles in the all-white north-west Chicago suburb of Elmwood Park. He called the director of Coffey's school one day, looking to hire Ogden's best mechanic, and demanded, "I want the student that finished [at the] head of the class." A businessman to the core, Mack added, "I don't care what color he is. If he's the young man I'm looking for, send him out and I'll interview him, and if we can make it, we'll come to an agreement."

Coffey took the job, and Mack was delighted with his skill and diligence. For a year, Coffey worked for the Chevy dealer in Elmwood Park, making a long two-hour round-trip streetcar ride every day between the Y on the South Side and the dealership in the northwest.

But Coffey's sister, Vida, now living in Detroit, Michigan, urged him to join her there. The lure of running his own garage in that booming industrial center of the motor industry was too much to resist. In 1927, Coffey found another mechanic to replace him at Mack's dealership, telling his boss it was only temporary. He headed to the Motor City to set up his own shop, and that's where he impressed Dr. Ossian Sweet enough to become the one and only mechanic for his beloved Marmon.

When Cornelius Coffey showed up to tend to Dr. Sweet's car, Johnny Robinson was less than impressed.

Coffey didn't cut much of a striking figure. Now twenty-three, he was soft-spoken and mild-mannered, and rarely went looking for a fight. Coffey tried to clear the air: he assured Johnny that Dr. Sweet hadn't meant to question his ability or qualifications.

"It isn't that," Coffey explained, when Johnny confronted him. "I've just been taking care of his car, and he don't like for everybody to fool with it."

That wasn't good enough for Johnny.

"Where did you get your experience?" he asked.

"In Chicago," Coffey told him.

That changed John Robinson's tune. Johnny was making plans to head to Chicago himself. It would be to his advantage to have connections there.

The two men got to talking and made a discovery: they both wanted to fly.

Johnny and Coffey were caught in the wind of an aviation craze that was sweeping the Black community in America—part of a surge in creativity called the Harlem Renaissance, named for the predominantly Black neighborhood of Harlem in New York City, where the movement was centered. The writers and artists of the Harlem Renaissance believed that by embracing their African roots and their American lives, they could create something uniquely American that was not beholden to classical European ideals. They believed that celebrating their unique experience as both Black and American was valuable and necessary to gaining equality. This new expression extended into other frontiers, like aviation, as well. But Harlem wasn't the only place seeing a boom in Black brilliance. Chicago was having its own awakening.

Things had changed for Black people in aviation since Coffey's first flight in 1919. This leap forward was in large part due to a Black woman named Bessie Coleman, who'd got her flying start in Chicago. "Queen Bess," as she was called, had opened the skies to her people. Like Coffey and Johnny, she'd been drawn to the glamour and excitement of flight. But she faced the double disadvantage of being a woman as well as being Black. Bessie couldn't find anyone in the United States who would even think about teaching her to fly.

Born in Texas, as a young woman Bessie had made her way to Chicago in search of opportunity. It was while earning her living there as a beautician that she was able to chat and gossip with many of the city's

Absolute classics: Bessie Coleman balancing on the wheel of a Curtiss JN-4 Jenny, circa 1923

SMITHSONIAN NATIONAL AIR AND SPACE MUSEUM (NASM 92-13721)

wealthy and influential Black entrepreneurs. Her winning personality and energy eventually got the attention of Robert S. Abbott, the innovative publisher of the weekly *Chicago Defender*, one of the largest Black newspapers in the country. Abbott was a determined and philanthropic businessman who used his newspaper to campaign for equal rights. He disliked using the color-coded words "Negro" or "Black" or "colored" to describe African Americans. Under his guidance, the *Chicago Defender* consistently opted for the terms "Race" and "the Race" in its reporting. In Bessie Coleman's desire for wings, Abbott saw a golden opportunity for the Race in the form of a hot news story that could be drawn out into installments.

Abbott and the *Defender* sponsored Bessie with both publicity *and* financial support.

With the *Defender*'s backing, she took a basic course in French. Then, like the Black combat pilot Eugene Bullard, she traveled to Europe and found flight instructors in France willing to take her on as a student.

On June 15, 1921, at the age of thirty, Bessie Coleman became the first Black female pilot—and the first person of African American and Native American descent—to hold an international pilot's license. In fact, she was the first *American* of any race or gender to hold an international pilot's license.

Bessie knew she'd need to have a few air stunts under her belt if she wanted to impress a crowd on the barnstorming circuit. So she did further training to learn some aerobatic finesse, tricks like loops and rolls. These flight maneuvers, passed on from combat pilots in World War I, would not only make her a flashier pilot, but might even save her life one day.

From the moment Queen Bess returned to the States with her international pilot's license in 1922, her exploits became popular reading not just in the *Chicago Defender*, but in Black newspapers all over the country. Her barnstorming campaign of flying shows, lectures, and even a short film she was able to play for local communities was all in service of a bigger dream: to open aviation schools across the U.S. for Black people longing to take to the sky.

Unfortunately, before that dream could come true, Bessie fell out of her plane and was killed during a trial run for an air show in Florida in April 1926. The ill-fated plane was a Curtiss Jenny, the same kind of aircraft in which Coffey took his first flight.

Bessie's body was returned to her home in Chicago for burial in Lincoln Cemetery in Blue Island, Illinois. Thousands of people attended her funeral. Queen Bess remained an inspiration to Black pilots everywhere, even in death.

Had she lived, perhaps Johnny or Coffey would have been able to attend one of her schools. As it was, they would have to forge a path for themselves.

So far, neither man was having much luck.

"I wrote to two or three places," Coffey said, "and they don't seem to want to accept us."

Johnny knew how that went. He'd been asking around just like Coffey, and with as little success. It seemed that no white pilot in America would willingly teach a Black man to fly.

———

They didn't know it yet, but Coffey and Johnny had other things in common besides both being talented automobile mechanics who longed for wings.

John Charles Robinson was born in Carrabelle, Florida, likely on November 26, 1903 or 1904. His father was killed in an accident working on the Carrabelle docks while Johnny was still a baby, and his mother, Celeste Huff Robinson, took her infant son and four-year-old daughter, Bertha, to make a fresh start in the boom town of Gulfport, Mississippi. There she met and married Charles Cobb, a member of Celeste's church who had a good job in the same line of work as the men in Coffey's family: the American railroads. Cobb was a porter for the George M. Pullman Company, the manufacturer that built sleeping cars.

Charles Cobb was warm, hardworking, and ambitious. He treated the young Robinson children with as much love as if they were his own. Celeste wanted them to keep their father's name, and they did, but it was Charles Cobb whom they called Daddy as they grew up. Soon after his marriage to Celeste, Charles decided his job as a porter kept him traveling away from his family too much. He found work with the Gulf and Ship Island Railroad in a locomotive shop at the terminal where timber and cotton arrived in Gulfport on its way to be sold overseas. By the time Johnny was two, Celeste and Charles Cobb had built a spacious house in Gulfport's Big Quarter and were able to supplement their income by renting rooms.

Johnny got his first sight of a plane at about six years of age. Aviation wasn't much older than him, and the experience was unforgettable. On the first day of winter in 1910, standing on Gulfport's East Beach in a huge crowd of Black and white spectators, Johnny watched the first airplane ever to fly into the town, a seaplane that landed on the Mississippi Sound.

That plane was a Curtiss "Pusher," so called because its engine and propeller faced *backward* and were located *behind* the pilot's seat. It resembled the Wright Flyer: the Curtiss had a fragile bamboo frame held together with wire and thin fabric, one high and one low wing, and a seat for the pilot up front and open to the air. There was a wooden float attached beneath the plane so that it could land on water.

This amazing aircraft was flown by a Canadian adventurer named John Moisant, who was in the middle of a barnstorming tour of the southern states with a group of flyers called the Moisant International Aviators. A sudden winter storm had come screaming down from the north and cut short one of their air shows, so Moisant, with some extra time on his hands and looking for a place to rest and refuel, decided that Gulfport was a fine place to stop for a while.

As the dashing aviator came soaring down from the sky in his thrilling new machine, Johnny told his stepfather, "I'm gonna fly in one of those things someday, Daddy."

But the only flying Johnny did in his teens was kite-flying. Even so, he did it with skill and smarts. His peer group was crazy about kites, coming up with elaborate designs and building each one themselves. They'd have kite fights, in which kids would attach broken glass or razor blades to their kite tails to try to cut each other's kite strings.

"Johnny designed a kite with wings like a bird and could make it dip and then go straight up," said his friend Harvey Todd. "He was considered the best."

Like Coffey, Johnny was an ambitious and enterprising teen. Outside of his attendance at the all-Black Gulfport High School, he held a series of jobs, from shining shoes at the train station to sweeping stockroom floors and delivering packages for the Bee Hive department store in Gulfport. At fifteen, after a few informal driving lessons, Johnny managed to get a job driving a truck and handling ship orders on the Gulfport docks. "We didn't know how in the world he could drive a truck," said another school friend, Henry Tartt.

Johnny graduated in 1919 after finishing tenth grade—that was as high as schooling went for Black students in Gulfport in those days. But Celeste and Charles Cobb were ambitious about their children's education. Johnny's older sister, Bertha, had graduated from Straight

Johnny Robinson (far left) as a teen, with a group of friends in Gulfport, Mississippi
MISSISSIPPI GULF COAST MUSEUM OF HISTORICAL PHOTOGRAPHY

College in New Orleans (now Dillard University). Johnny's parents and his minister all encouraged him to go to college at the Tuskegee Normal and Industrial Institute in Alabama.

The Tuskegee Institute—today known as Tuskegee University—was founded in 1881 and took the practical view that it was important to produce young African Americans who were employable as well as educated, offering classes in teaching, agriculture, and industry. In 1921 at barely sixteen, Johnny started a course there in automotive mechanical science. That was as close as he could get, he figured, to studying aeronautics, and a grounding in mechanics would lead to a well-paid job, in addition to standing him in good stead when he finally got a chance to work on aircraft.

In his three years at Tuskegee, Johnny learned how to take apart an engine and put it back together. He took courses in electrical and mechanical theory. He and his classmates had to build a working automobile from the ground up. At the same time, Johnny was studying English and history—and reading anything he could get his hands on that had to do with aviation. His future was looking bright.

But, in 1922, while Johnny was in college in Alabama, a Black man was lynched by a white mob in his hometown of Gulfport. Johnny had spent his summers working back in Gulfport during his years at Tuskegee. The lynching was a harsh reminder of the limitations placed on his dreams. By the time he graduated in 1924, he knew he wasn't going to stay in Mississippi. He wanted more than dead-end jobs, segregated living conditions, and the terrifying racism that the American South had to offer a young Black man.

So, again like Cornelius Coffey, Johnny Robinson headed north to Detroit, Michigan—the center of the new automobile industry. With his skills and mechanical education, Johnny was sure he'd be able to get a good job there. And he hoped, like so many others, that by making this move he'd be able to escape the legal and illegal horrors of the South, with its restrictive "Black codes," also known as Jim Crow laws, which took their name from the racist depiction of a lazy, unintelligent character played by a white actor wearing "blackface" makeup.

Working as a mechanic in a Detroit garage, with a little money of his own to spend, Johnny began asking around about places where he could get flying lessons. A weekend trip to the Detroit City Airport got him nowhere. The airport staff told him, "Not a chance." No one there was willing to let a Black man take control of an airplane.

Next, Johnny tried Ford Airport in nearby Dearborn. Here, he asked every pilot he met if he could get a ride in one of their planes. He went from pilot to pilot and kept coming up against the same word: No.

Finally, one of the white pilots gave him a tip. This man certainly wasn't going to risk his own reputation by taking a Black man up in his plane, but he told Johnny to go out to the countryside and look for barnstormers who flew at makeshift landing fields where government—and social—rules were more relaxed. Those pilots might be so ready to make an extra dollar that they wouldn't care what color the hand was that offered it.

So Johnny began to explore the fields and farmland outside of Detroit. At the end of a track, apparently near a town called Willow Run, he found a barn converted into a hangar containing double-winged biplanes. Two of these were the usual ex-military workhorse Curtiss Jennies, a common sight in the decade following World War I, all now a little worse for wear; but on this airfield there was also a beautiful new red-and-white Waco 9.

The Waco 9 was a state-of-the-art biplane first flown in 1925, hugely popular with barnstormers because the front seat was big enough to stuff in two paying passengers instead of one. Its frame was made of welded steel tubing, light and strong, a modern upgrade from the wooden Jenny. Even if the owner had bought it second-hand, this plane couldn't have been more than a year old.

Johnny knew he was likely to get the cold shoulder if he asked for a flight. But when he overheard one of the local pilots complaining about a faulty engine on one of the Jennies, Johnny saw his chance. He offered to fix the engine in exchange for a ride, and he got it—but not in the Jenny whose engine he'd fixed. It seems that an entire Sunday school class was also lined up waiting for plane rides that day, and the pilot Johnny had helped out didn't have the time to fit him in. So another deal was made. The owner of the new Waco 9, reportedly a man named Robert J. Williamson III, agreed to take Johnny for a flight in exchange for some future aerobatic training from the Jenny's pilot.

Johnny—again like Coffey—was into motorcycles. He was no stranger to thrill-riding: he sometimes even performed as a stuntman to make a little extra money. If he became airborne doing a bike stunt, it must have given him a taste, for a second or two, of what it was like to fly.

Now, as the Waco 9 took off, he was experiencing that feeling for himself, of being free from the ground, of silky smooth, unimpeded speed. From the sky above that farm strip, fields and woods would have stretched away beneath the small Waco 9 as its engine powered it into the sky. Detroit would have been a smear of smoke and haze in the near distance, Lake Erie a blue line on the horizon. At a few thousand feet above the ground, the wind would have been fierce and cold in that open cockpit, the noise of the engine a roar, and the wires connecting the wing struts would be humming. The genial pilot even let Johnny take the controls and get a feel for the plane. He was in his element at last.

When his feet were back on the ground, Johnny asked the owner of the Waco 9 if he'd give him flying lessons. The man seemed to have legitimate excuses for saying no: he wasn't a certified instructor, and he said he was about to move to Texas. Instead, he gave Johnny some advice. He suggested Johnny head to Chicago. They both knew he shouldn't have any trouble finding a decent auto mechanic's job there, and in Chicago, he could study at the American School of Aviation, a flight school in the city.

Johnny liked the idea. One of his uncles had relocated to Chicago, and so had his sister, Bertha. He began to make plans for a move.

=====

Now, because of Dr. Sweet's broken-down Marmon, Johnny was talking to a kindred spirit who knew Chicago, and who had the same goals he did.

"You know, Bessie Coleman had to go to Europe to learn to fly, and it look[s] like we're going to have to find some money or something to get over there," Johnny told Coffey.

"Well, maybe we can figure out something," said Coffey with determination.

"If you ever come back [to Chicago], look me up," Johnny said. "A good friend of mine at W. T. Brown Funeral Parlor between 39th and 37th, he'll always know where to find me, so stop in there and ask him."

In one short conversation, Coffey and Johnny had gone from being combative to being potential partners.

=====

In May of that year, 1927, a white U.S. Air Mail pilot named Charles A. Lindbergh astonished the world by making the first nonstop solo flight across the Atlantic in his plane the *Spirit of St. Louis*. The reaction from all the corners of the globe was aviation fever. With the same fire also driving him, at twenty-two, Johnny headed to Chicago.

In another year, Coffey would return to Chicago, too. There, Johnny Robinson, and destiny, would be waiting.

CHAPTER 2

GROUND SCHOOL, 1927-1929

> Hog Butcher for the World,
> Tool Maker, Stacker of Wheat,
> Player with Railroads and the Nation's Freight
>   Handler;
> Stormy, husky, brawling,
> City of the Big Shoulders ...
>
> —Carl Sandburg, "Chicago," 1914

CHICAGO! The "Second City"!

Nicknamed for its historical status as the second-largest city in the United States (Los Angeles surpassed it in 1982), Chicago had a population of about three million people in 1925, nearly three times the population of Detroit, and six times the populations of Omaha and Kansas City put together. Also known as the Windy City for the powerful winds whipping off Lake Michigan, Chicago's position on its western shore made it the gateway to the Midwest. The city had a growing Black population of over one hundred thousand, about double that of Detroit, as a result of the Great Migration, a vast movement of southern African Americans into the North. From 1915 on into the 1970s, over six million Black people, including members of both Johnny's and Coffey's families, left the South seeking a better life away from the deep-seated segregation and racism of Jim Crow.

Bronzeville, on Chicago's South Side, was a booming community of Black businesses, churches, cinemas, and restaurants, with its own political leaders and social elite. The recent surge in Chicago's Black citizens gave the neighborhood its colorful name, "bronze" being considered a flattering reference to skin color at the time. It was here, in the fall of 1927, that Johnny Robinson headed. He first found a job testing and repairing taxis for the Yellow Cab Company. But his plan was to open his own garage, which he soon did.

Having a day job was important, but what Johnny was really looking for was a flight school. He applied to aviation schools half a dozen times, including, no doubt, the Chicago-based American School of Aviation, but for unknown reasons, his applications were always rejected. It must have been frustrating when Black newspapers shouted the names of other highflyers, such as Jesse S. Samuels, "the only member of our race to complete a course in aviation in Illinois," according to a January 1927 article in the *Chicago Defender*.

It's unclear where Samuels got his training, but it probably wasn't at a well-known flight school. In those days, there was no standard curriculum to follow to learn to fly, no straightforward path to earning a pilot's license, and Johnny wanted something with structure. The aviation industry in the U.S.A. was only just beginning to be regulated; in 1926, the Air Commerce Act had established an Aeronautics Branch of the U.S. Department of Commerce, and the new organization was getting to work by introducing a system for numbering registered aircraft and by drafting clearer rules for conducting flights and licensing pilots. The first federal pilot's license was issued to William P. MacCracken, Jr., the head of the Aeronautics Branch himself, on April 6, 1927. Bessie Coleman's 1921 international pilot's license had been years ahead of the U.S. federal government.

The new Aeronautics Branch ruled that registered aircraft had to be flown by licensed pilots holding either a private or commercial license, with the commercial licenses further classified as either "transport" or "industrial." A professional aircraft mechanic had to hold an airplane mechanic's license. Everybody in aviation at the time—aircraft owners, pilots, and mechanics alike—had to apply for their licenses by the deadline of May 1, 1927. Anyone who didn't apply risked an eye-watering fine of $500 (about $8,500 in 2023).

But in spite of the threat of such a hefty fine, it took some years for the new regulations to really take effect. The feds didn't rush out to check up on things; there were still plenty of barnstormers with shady flight credentials willing to make a quick buck without attracting official attention, which must have given Johnny some hope. Before 1927 was over, Johnny invited a few other Black flight enthusiasts to join him in a group he called the Brown Eagle Aero Club. The group held lectures and discussions on aviation. Coffey would drive over from Detroit during weekends to join Brown Eagle meetings, and the club's growing membership gave Johnny and Coffey a social circle as well as an angle for raising awareness of aviation in their African American community. The two young men were both crazy about the sky, and they were fast becoming real friends.

Clubs like the Brown Eagle Aero Club, dedicated to the art and skill of flight, were part of the legacy left by Bessie Coleman, for the magic of Queen Bess's vision and personality was still felt throughout the nation. She was a particularly strong source of inspiration for an eloquent young Black man named William J. Powell, who'd grown up in Chicago and had a degree in electrical engineering from the University of Illinois. Powell may well have been among the thousands of mourners who'd attended Bessie's Chicago funeral in 1926. Despite his education and World War I veteran's status, he was rejected by flight school after flight school because of his race. But in 1928, the Los Angeles School of Flight accepted him to join an already international mix of students. It was there that Powell founded the Bessie Coleman Aero Club in honor of his hero.

Meanwhile, the non-flying citizens of Bessie's hometown in Chicago were also hard at work trying to honor her memory and keep her dream alive. A Bessie Coleman Charity Club began raising funds for a boys' home, and the Cooperative Business League donated a splendid granite tombstone and bronze plaque to be raised over Bessie's grave in Lincoln Cemetery. Hundreds of people attended an impressive dedication ceremony there, held on Memorial Day in 1928 at the graveside of the adored young flyer, with music provided by the Whitlow Brass Band, whose thirty members were all women. There were prayers and speeches, and both the governor of Illinois and the newly appointed assistant secretary of commerce for aeronautics sent moving and respectful messages to be read at the event. It's possible, if not verifiable, that Coffey and Johnny were there in the crowd.

There was one fly in the ointment at this memorial service. A flashy Black aviator and parachutist named Hubert Fauntleroy Julian had volunteered to participate in the ceremony by flying over Lincoln Cemetery and parachuting down to join the crowd there. He promised that he'd arrive overhead in an airplane at 10:30 a.m. on Memorial Day, in exchange for the minister taking up a collection to raise funds for a record-busting transatlantic flight to Rome that Julian wanted to attempt. The scheduled moment in the service arrived, and the audience that was gathered around Bessie Coleman's grave waited expectantly, watching the skies. The appointed time came and went. But there was no sign of an airplane or of Julian himself.

Born in Trinidad in 1897, Hubert Julian was dubbed the Black Eagle of Harlem after parachuting out of a plane over New York City while dressed in a crimson flight suit and playing the saxophone as he floated down to earth. A joyride with a famous Canadian airman led him to claim he'd learned to fly in Canada during the Great War. Julian had made a name for himself as a daredevil in the air, but he rarely pulled off his exploits successfully; he was much more accomplished as a

Hubert Fauntleroy Julian
BETTMANN / CONTRIBUTOR

showman than as an aviator. Nevertheless, wherever he turned up, he was big news, and the dedication for Bessie Coleman's memorial was no exception.

The service ended, and Julian still hadn't appeared. The audience, tired of waiting, began to drift away. It wasn't until five hours later, at 3:30 p.m., that he finally arrived—not by plane or by parachute, but in a rented army truck. It turned out he hadn't made the necessary arrangements—like hiring a plane. Apparently he was so chagrined that he was crying "like a baby" when he pulled up at the cemetery. "Julian Disappoints," the newspaper headlines blared; it would prove to be a prophetic slogan.

Though Hubert Julian didn't cross paths with Johnny Robinson and Cornelius Coffey on Memorial Day in 1928, these men would come together dramatically in the future. And it wouldn't be many years before both Johnny and Coffey would fly over Bessie Coleman's grave themselves, in a moving memorial tribute that became a tradition repeated even into the twenty-first century.

No one could have been aware of any of this at the time, though. In 1928, Johnny Robinson and Cornelius Coffey may have had their heads in the clouds, but their feet were still stuck firmly on the ground.

═══

Coffey soon decided to return to Chicago himself. He moved back into his familiar quarters at the Y, and went to see his old boss, Emil Mack, out at the car dealership where he'd worked before. It must have been the easiest job hunt ever.

"Hey, your job's waiting," Mack told him.

Coffey was immediately rehired, and in a happy turn of events, Mack hired Johnny as well. Every day, the two friends would commute from the South Side of Chicago out to Elmwood Park for work. And in between working and shuttling back and forth, the young men hatched a plot to take to the skies.

They set their sights on a Heath Parasol airplane kit. Created by the E.B. Heath Aerial Vehicle Company right there in Chicago, the kits provided materials and blueprints for building a small single-seat "parasol wing" monoplane. This meant the plane had one long wing mounted onto struts that held it across the top of the fuselage, or body, of the aircraft. The thing that intrigued Coffey the most was the Parasol's engine. It was the exact same type that powered his old Henderson motorcycle.

Coffey and Johnny pooled their money together and bought the Heath kit for $600, close to $10,000 in 2023—no doubt a big purchase, but about the same price then as for a car. The Henderson Motorcycle Company had a factory in Chicago; the two men visited the plant and were able to buy a rebuilt engine for around $150. Between them, they scrounged spare parts they might need. Then, even though neither one of them knew how to fly, over the next six months, working weekends and evenings in Johnny's garage, they built their first airplane.

And that wasn't all that was taking off.

County court records state that on September 24, 1928, one Cornelius R. Coffey married a stenographer named Jennie B. Davis in Allen County, Indiana. Just one state and a short car or boat ride away from Chicago, northern Indiana was the Las Vegas of the Midwest in the 1920s. Lots of happy couples flooded into the state because of its lenient marriage license laws. The rule was that men had to be at least twenty-one and women eighteen, or with parental consent, eighteen and sixteen respectively. And they had to be sober—which was open to interpretation. Quickie marriages were so popular that one story tells how a marriage magistrate, too sick to attend the courthouse, made money by having couples brought directly to his bedroom.

Coffey would have been twenty-five on his wedding day, and Jennie would have been nineteen. But it seems hard to believe Coffey had time for marriage. By all accounts, he was a shy, serious man, most comfortable when talking about mechanics and engineering. In 1928, he had a full-time job and an airplane to build—did he really take off to Indiana and meet up with a young lady? While there seems to be no record of divorce, a Jennie B. Davis with the same birthdate and particulars got married a few years later to a different gentleman. That marriage license claims to be her first. So perhaps it was a "weekend wedding" annulled before it could begin.

Johnny, too, may have been distracted by romance at this point—and his young lady is just as mysterious as Coffey's. She was probably Dora Earnize Tate, born in Alabama in 1907. She's referred to as "Mrs. Robinson" in newspaper reports from the mid-1930s, but she was still using her maiden name in 1932, and there's no evidence that she and Johnny ever formally tied the knot. Could they have been courting as early as 1928? Earnize may well have helped Johnny with the money and the organization to set up the independent garage business he'd opened, and she seems to have run the place herself when Johnny was busy with other things.

Distractions or not, Coffey and Johnny were both working hard on getting in the air. But there was a problem with the Heath Parasol: it only had room for one person. Without two seats, neither of them could fly; even if they found someone willing to teach them, they wouldn't be able to use the Heath Parasol as a training aircraft. So they began to look for a second plane, one that could fit a student or passenger, as well as a pilot.

Johnny came across an ad in the *Chicago Tribune*: a car dealership had accepted an airplane in trade for a car, and they were now looking to sell. Coffey and Johnny decided to check it out.

The plane was a Humming Bird, one of a handful of experimental biplanes built by Burd S. White, whose son Harold worked with him in Iowa, and it had room for three—a pilot and maybe both Coffey and Johnny at the same time. Happily, the dealer was willing to trade the unusual vehicle for something more useful to him, like a car.

Johnny just happened to have a Hudson brougham, a type of early automobile modeled after a stagecoach, where the driver sat up front in the open air and the passengers sat in the back in an enclosed cabin. Johnny was willing to give up his wheels for some wings.

With Johnny's car and two hundred dollars of Coffey's savings, they were able to make a deal for the Humming Bird. The dealer helped arrange for them to keep it at a small field called Akers Airport.

Located at Grand Avenue and Wolf Road in Elmhurst, Illinois, Akers was a few blocks south of Chicago's present-day O'Hare International Airport and close to where Coffey and Johnny worked in Elmwood Park. Like many early airfields, Akers was a former farm, still showing the bones of its past life. The airplane hangar and shop were in the farm's original barn. A rambling old farmhouse became the front office—and living quarters for the pilots, who were mostly single men.

Johnny and Coffey were the only two Black men at the site. But they could pull their own weight among the white aviators.

"When they found out there that we were mechanics at Elmwood Park, just four miles east of there, and that we were making a living every day repairing cars," Coffey said, "they began to realize, 'Hey, these guys can help us out.'"

Every weekend, Coffey and Johnny would head out to Akers Airport and do whatever they could to support their aviation dreams.

They paid the rent for their plane's parking by offering repair jobs on cars and motorcycles owned by the white aviators who flew at Akers. But their schemes didn't always end well. When Johnny insisted they could make a little extra cash by renting the Humming Bird to another pilot to use for flight instruction, a student wrecked it. Fortunately, some of the other pilots needed help with a plane engine, and they offered Coffey partial ownership in exchange for the work. Coffey got their plane up and running, only to have it go up in literal flames when a co-owner crashed it.

Frustrated and anxious to get in the air himself, Coffey began taking expensive flying lessons from a white pilot by the name of Red Clymon, who owned a popular new model of open-cockpit biplane called a Travel Air 2000.

"Back in those days, it cost you ten dollars an hour for flying time," Coffey said. Expensive though it was, $10 an hour was on the cheap end for flying lessons, and depending on the plane you went up in, it could cost as much as $20—or somewhere between $175 to $350 an hour in today's money. That was twice what a man needed then to support a family for a week with food and rent included. So flying expenses, plus the cost of shuttling back and forth to the airfield, added up quickly.

"Hey, you guys are commuting all the way to the South Side," the Akers aviators noticed. "Why don't you fix up a room out here and you'll be at the airport[?]"

"That made sense to us," Coffey said. What they'd save on rent and transportation could go straight into flying. Coffey moved out of the Y once and for all, and Johnny left his place in Bronzeville, returning every so often to collect his mail. Now they'd be able to fly before and after work, as long as there was light in the sky.

Spending so much extra time at the airport brought Coffey a big break, when Akers pilot Alex Sergeyev made him a proposition he couldn't refuse.

"You know, I got a Waco 9, but there ain't no engine in it," Alex told him. "You find an OX for this Waco 9, you can have the airplane." He meant a Curtiss OX-5 engine—a popular workhorse of early aviation, used in all the Curtiss Jennies as well as Wacos, and often repurposed in a new plane when an old one got smashed up.

The Waco 9 was a really exciting offer. This was the same kind of plane that Johnny had taken his memorable first flight in—easy to fly, great for barnstorming from farm field to farm field, and definitely big enough for an instructor and a student to fly together.

Coffey lost no time in finding the all-important engine, and with the Waco 9 ready to fly, he finally had his wings. He'd done four hours' flying with Red Clymon in the Travel Air 2000, and Red reckoned Coffey was ready to "solo" in his own plane, a huge step along the road to becoming a licensed pilot. So in 1928, Cornelius Coffey finally took the controls of an airplane alone for the first time.

The ability to fly solo, in his own plane, meant that Coffey was able to "build" his flying time in the Waco 9, without the expense of an instructor, allowing him to rack up the necessary flight hours needed to qualify for a license. The only things Coffey had to pay for now were gasoline and oil.

But he knew that he couldn't become a qualified instructor himself without the correct Department of Commerce certification, and he couldn't get that in the Waco 9, which was not an "identified," or Department of Commerce–certified, plane. Johnny didn't have as much flight experience as Coffey yet, and he wasn't anywhere near ready for solo flight. They both needed to up their game.

One day in 1929, they saw an ad in *Aero Digest* magazine: the Curtiss-Wright School of Aviation, newly established following the merger of the Curtiss and Wright aviation companies, was starting a "Master Mechanic's Course." Johnny had already received a pile of rejections from aviation schools. So this time, the two men decided to take a new approach, possibly inspired by a story that had been widely reported on in Black newspapers across the country, including the *Chicago Defender*, in May of that year.

One Miss Hazel V. Pleasant, an eighteen-year-old "popular society girl" from the "colored district" of Jacksonville, Florida, had applied for a place in a "Girls' Flying Club." Inspired as a high school student by a personal meeting with Bessie Coleman in Jacksonville just before her tragic death there in 1926, Hazel didn't say anything about the color of her skin in her written flying club application. She was one of thirty-six successful applicants, chosen from a pool of two hundred, to win flying lessons worth $300 (more than $5,000 today—essentially the equivalent of a full pilot's license course). Successful, that is, until they found out she was Black. A decision on whether she'd be allowed to accept the award was still pending at the time of reporting, and unfortunately the newspapers didn't follow up on what happened. But Hazel said that the other girls in the club were "very cordial, even inviting her to their homes to meet their parents."

Whether or not Coffey and Johnny knew about the tactics used by Hazel Pleasant, they agreed that the thing to do was to try to get accepted to the Curtiss-Wright School of Aviation on merit alone, without stating their race.

It worked. They both passed the application process for the Master Mechanic's Course. Ecstatic, they began mailing in weekly payments for their first semester. The final hurdle would come when they had to visit the school in person to receive their class assignments.

The Curtiss-Wright School of Aviation was located at 1338 South Michigan Avenue in the South Loop—Chicago's downtown area, named for the circle that the elevated train, or the "El," makes in the area. The school occupied an impressive seven-story building constructed in 1922, with a Classical Revival façade of terra-cotta brick and white glazed tile. It must have been an intimidating sight for two young men used to ramshackle garages and rural airfields. But their reception was all too familiar, taken straight from the pages of Jim Crow.

The school's director, Lewis M. Churbuck, would not let them enroll.

"Got to be some mistake," Churbuck told them. "We can't accept your money. We have to give you your money back."

Coffey and Johnny refused.

As Coffey said, "Unless we go through an approved school, we'll never get a mechanic's certificate."

The problem wasn't money, of course; it was race. Curtiss-Wright's students were white, and many of them came from the South. Churbuck was worried they wouldn't take kindly to sharing a classroom with African Americans. He apologized for the mistake, but Johnny and Coffey weren't interested in apologies. They'd paid their fees, they'd passed the application process, and they weren't going to give in.

Unfortunately, neither was Churbuck.

At a stalemate, the two aspiring aviators left the office disappointed. On their way out, Johnny noticed a sign on a wall advertising a vacancy for a janitor. In his experience, nobody cared what color a janitor was, and at least it would get him into the building. He walked back in and applied for the position. Remarkably, he got it. Apparently there was a place for Black people at Curtiss-Wright after all—just not in the classroom.

Ever persistent, Johnny had a clever plan for working at his new part-time job at Curtiss-Wright. "Always cleaning classroom floors at lecture time," as his old Gulfport school friend Henry Tartt recalled. For five months, Johnny cleaned up at the school during the aviation ground school courses. Polite and courteous, he'd quietly sweep the floor or wipe the windows at the back of classes full of white students. But Johnny was listening, perhaps even more carefully than they did. After class he'd copy formulas from the blackboard. If someone left lecture notes behind on a desk, or in the garbage, he'd make use of those, too, as well as the aviation manuals that the classrooms contained.

The lecturer, probably a man named Jack Snyder, grew wise to Johnny's interest in the classes. He knew perfectly well that Johnny was eavesdropping, but Snyder decided to indulge him. After all, Johnny could answer questions when none of the other students were able to.

"Isn't that right, Mr. Robinson?" Snyder would ask. Pausing in his cleaning work, Johnny would readily show off his knowledge.

The students, too, began to interact with Johnny. With aviation as a common interest, racial differences seemed to fall by the wayside. But a casual education was not the same as a diploma, and the payment situation for Johnny's and Coffey's applications to Curtiss-Wright remained unresolved.

Finally, Emil Mack, their boss at Elmwood Park, got wind of what was going on. Mack had grown to trust Coffey, who had learned all aspects of the Chevrolet dealership. When Mack left town, it was Coffey who ran receipts to the bank. So when Mack heard about the rejection from the aviation school, he called Coffey into his office.

"I understand you and Johnny [are] enrolled down at Curtiss-Wright and they won't accept you."

"That's right, Mr. Mack."

Mack wanted to know why.

"Just because we're colored." Coffey showed his boss the receipts for the tuition they had paid to date. "We been paying on the course since June," he explained.

It was a David and Goliath story—two young Black men up against a big institution. Fortunately, Mack sided with the little guys.

"Don't take any money back," he advised Coffey. "If they still insist on denying you . . . we'll get you a lawyer. I'll get you the best lawyer in the state of Illinois, and we'll sue them for enough money that you can buy your own school." Mack even offered to foot the legal bill.

Coffey told Johnny the good news. They agreed to stick to their guns.

———

Meanwhile, the two young men had found a use for their homebuilt Heath Parasol kit plane. At a Christmas party at the Dreamland Ballroom, they parked it on the dance floor where people could admire it and get a chance to sit inside. The occasion was likely one of many "pay parties," picnics, and social events that Coffey and Johnny

The Heath Parasol built by Johnny Robinson and Cornelius Coffey joins the party in a New Year's Eve toast. Coffey is in the middle of the kneeling row; Johnny stands at the far left.

KENNETH SPENCER RESEARCH LIBRARY, UNIVERSITY OF KANSAS

hosted as fundraisers through the Brown Eagle Aero Club. The plane made a great party guest, yet it raised a burning question: "But will it fly?"

Without official approval or certification, neither one of them was qualified to test the single-seat plane. Johnny got the idea of asking Jack Snyder, the Curtiss-Wright instructor he'd become friendly with, to come and take a look at the machine.

Snyder was curious to see the airplane that had been rigged up by a couple of Black auto mechanics before they'd even had any flight experience. He headed down to Johnny's garage and recognized the plane right away as a Heath Parasol. But, he asked, "What's this strange-lookin' engine?"

Johnny and Coffey confessed that it was from a motorcycle. What's more, they said, "We want you to fly it!"

Astonishingly, Snyder was game.

The plane was loaded onto a truck and taken to the racetrack at

Washington Park for the afternoon. The entire Brown Eagle Aero Club came along to watch, and to hear what Jack Snyder had to say.

Snyder gave the plane a thorough inspection. He commented on the motorcycle engine, and told Johnny and Coffey he'd like to start it up to see how it ran. The small crowd of aviation enthusiasts watched anxiously as Snyder climbed into the cramped, open cockpit. The homemade plane rumbled to life, and Snyder began to taxi across the grassy field.

The crowd's apprehension turned to astonishment as the little aircraft suddenly lifted from the ground—she was flying!

Snyder circled the airfield a few times before touching down again without any trouble. The seasoned pilot had obviously decided the plane was flyable. The first flight of the Parasol was a success.

Jack Snyder was hugely impressed. If Coffey and Johnny could pull off a stunt like this on the ground, he felt they should be able to get into the air, too. He offered to try to convince the administrators of the Curtiss-Wright School of Aviation to let them finally enroll in their classes.

And he kept his word. Snyder told the faculty of Curtiss-Wright, "If we don't teach them [to fly], they'll teach themselves."

The response? "Get 'em in here; one of 'em is filing a lawsuit against us anyway . . ."

═══

A couple of weeks later, Director Churbuck offered Coffey and Johnny a deal: drop the lawsuit, pass the ground school course exam, and they could join the classes.

But he washed his hands of what might come next. "You're going to be on your own, and if anything happens, it's going to be your own fault."

The school would accept no responsibility for any racist opposition the white students might instigate. It sounded like a threat, but Coffey and Johnny took it as a challenge.

They aced the exam. In 1929, they became the first two Black students at the Curtiss-Wright School of Aviation.

John C. Robinson

SMITHSONIAN NATIONAL AIR AND
SPACE MUSEUM (NASM 87-15491)

CHAPTER 3

TAKING OFF, 1929-1933

Ours is the commencement of a flying age, and I am happy to have popped into existence at a period so interesting.

—Amelia Earhart, *20 Hrs. 40 Min.*, 1928

EVERY Monday, Wednesday, and Friday after work, Johnny and Coffey made the fifteen-mile trek down to the Curtiss-Wright building. Classes ran from 7:00 p.m. to 10:00 p.m., and included shop work and a class called "Related Aviation." Their course would take two years to complete. And it would indeed be difficult. For one thing, in October 1929, just as the schoolwork was beginning, the stock market came crashing down, plunging not only the U.S. but the entire world into economic hardship and poverty that would last for an entire decade. During this period, known as the "Great Depression," savings vanished, unemployment skyrocketed, and everyone had to scrimp. It was hard to study when finding work was at the front of everyone's minds.

Johnny and Coffey were lucky to have jobs and a roof over their heads. They were excellent students and qualified auto mechanics. The real trouble, as Churbuck had predicted, came from their classmates.

"When we would go to the tool crib to draw our tools," Coffey said, "they'd get ahead of us and try to make us mess up." It was the same story outside of the classroom. "We'd go to the candy machine at recess, they'd get ahead of us"—and the candy would vanish before they arrived. But he told Johnny, "Look. We're going to make it regardless."

The school's director had told the two men that they were on their own when it came to race relations. But their instructor, Jack Snyder, felt otherwise. Snyder had been a World War I pilot and, according to Coffey, a flying ace—someone who has shot down at least five enemy aircraft in combat. Now the veteran pilot was watching another battle take place in his own classroom—a battle for civil rights.

One day, Snyder called his troublemaking students together.

"You know something?" he demanded of the group. "As far as I'm concerned, there's only two gentlemen in my class. That's Coffey and Robinson. I tell you fellows, I don't know how they put up with all this stuff. I'd have broke somebody's head."

This may have got their attention, but what he said next really impressed them.

"Now, I'm going to tell you about those two fellows. They own their own airplane . . . They're earning their living as auto mechanics. Now, at examination time, they probably won't need you. You'll probably need them, so you better be careful about how you treat people."

It was true. Coffey and Johnny were both building their hours in the air, as well as working and studying. Coffey was flying in the Waco 9; Johnny, though he hadn't soloed yet, was taking flying lessons in an Alexander Eaglerock biplane up at the Lake County Airport in Waukegan, north of Chicago, possibly making the long commute so he could get flight time with a certified instructor or cheaper rates. Though cash was scarce, both men were putting time and money into becoming licensed pilots.

As Jack Snyder told the bullies in their mechanics class, "Hey, they['re] flying every chance they get. They're working eight hours a day, and if they can get some daylight between their jobs, you know they fly even in the morning before they go on the job."

"After that lecture," Coffey said, "we couldn't spend our money." The line-jumping at the vending machine turned into rushing to fetch treats for Coffey and Johnny as the other students fell over themselves to get into their good graces. As Coffey put it, suddenly, "They wouldn't let you buy nothing."

———

Johnny finally soloed in Coffey's Waco 9, on a bitterly cold winter day, probably January 30, 1930. A Polish flight instructor named Warren Melvicke had coached him to this point. With the temperature hovering a few degrees below zero Fahrenheit, people warned Johnny it was too cold to fly—he'd risk frostbite from the bitter wind in the open cockpit at those temperatures. But Johnny was typically stubborn about doing what he wanted how he wanted.

He took off in the bitingly cold air, circled the airfield, and landed successfully. The event even made national news, being reported in the *Pittsburgh Courier*. But Johnny was so frozen by the flight that it took him several days to recover.

It was a hard lesson, but it didn't stop him from going up again, cold weather or not. On another bitterly cold day, Johnny got permission from the Chamber of Commerce to perform air stunts over the *Chicago Defender* building, which he used as an opportunity to shower a crowd of shivering spectators with leaflets advertising another Brown

Eagle Aero Club fundraising dance. Johnny's hands were so frozen after this flight that he damaged his plane when he landed—and unfortunately, a blizzard struck on the night of the dance, so it had to be canceled.

═══

Coffey and Johnny completed their aviation mechanics course in May 1931, finishing at the top of their class. With the Curtiss-Wright certifications in their hands, they were now qualified to take the Department of Commerce examination for official aviation mechanic's licenses. Johnny doesn't seem to have taken his test until at least 1932, but it was an immediate necessity as far as Coffey was concerned.

"I wanted to trade my experience as a mechanic to help pay for my flying," he explained.

He applied for the Department of Commerce test, and within two weeks he had received his license. Now, if only he could qualify for a commercial pilot's license—then Coffey could turn his childhood experience as a courier into a modern professional venture, flying people and packages to their destinations, not to mention becoming a flight instructor.

But already, a different kind of instruction opportunity presented itself. Lewis Churbuck, the director of Curtiss-Wright who had been so reluctant to enroll Coffey and Johnny in the first place, spoke at their graduation ceremony. Afterward, he approached the two men with congratulations, and a proposition.

"Now you two fellows have proven yourselves above average," he said. "You have proven yourselves gentlemen. If you know of any other colored students that want to take aviation, and if you'll get a sizeable group together, we'll enroll them. The doors are going to always be open to colored students, but if you get this group together, we'll make you assistant instructors."

It was an almost unbelievable opportunity, and an irresistible offer. The proposed aviation mechanics course would likely take one year to complete. They'd have use of the classrooms and modern facilities of the Curtiss-Wright building in downtown Chicago.

A "sizeable group" meant about twenty-five people, enough to form a full class. Finding them wasn't going to be easy. Though the economic brutality of the Great Depression affected everyone, it was especially hard on people of color, who were more likely to be turned away from good jobs just because of their race, and who often received lower pay if they were hired. In times like these, would any of them be willing and able to spend hard-earned cash on flight school?

But Johnny and Coffey were always up for any challenge. They accepted the offer, and started placing ads in the *Chicago Defender*. The paper's publisher, Robert S. Abbott, was the same man who'd sponsored Bessie Coleman in her quest to become the first Black female pilot and the first American with an international pilot's license. Abbott was more than happy to continue to promote the Race in new efforts to break into aviation.

Coffey and Johnny also hosted a screening of an aviation movie and gave lectures at churches and clubs, including their own Brown Eagle Aero Club. They reached out to all their friends, and even went door to door looking for candidates.

African American interest in aviation turned out to be stronger than they could have hoped. One evening, probably late in 1931, the

*Janet Harmon
Waterford, later Janet
Harmon Bragg*

SMITHSONIAN NATIONAL
AIR AND SPACE MUSEUM
(NASM 91-15485)

doors of Curtiss-Wright opened to a new class of about thirty Black aviation students.

Among them was a self-possessed young woman named Janet Harmon Waterford, later known as Janet Harmon Bragg.

———

Though the date varies in several documents, Jane Nettie Harmon was born on March 24, most likely in 1905, in a little house in Griffin, Georgia, about forty miles south of Atlanta. She was originally named after both of her grandmothers, but in the third grade, a teacher shortened "Jane Nettie" to "Janet," and it stuck. With medium brown skin, large dark eyes, and an attractive smile, at the age of twelve Janet stunned her parents when, just like Coffey and Johnny, she taught herself how to drive.

Her father, Samuel Harmon, was a brick mason. He'd bought the family a Model T Ford to take them to church on Sundays, but he didn't know how to drive it. Janet's six older siblings got to do the honors in exchange for using the car for dates or fun with their friends. One day when Janet's older brother Pat walked to church ahead of the family, her father turned to Janet and said, "Do you know how to drive the car?"

Janet had never driven a car in her young life, but she'd seen how it was done, so she said, "Oh yes, sir."

Her father cranked up the car—with the same kind of crank that young Coffey had had to stand on to turn himself—and Janet started the motor. Her mother, Cordia Batts Harmon, was horrified.

"Oh my God, Sam, you're going to kill my child!" Cordia exclaimed.

Janet didn't know how to go in reverse, but she didn't need to. She drove her father to church, shocking her brother Pat, who couldn't believe she'd figured it out.

When they got home, her mother told her father firmly, "Don't you ever do that again."

Janet would prove to be just as handy and resourceful at flying as she was at driving.

As a little girl, Janet was fascinated with birds in flight. As early as five years old, she'd lie in the grass looking up at the big fluffy clouds known as cumulus, with a church song in her head: "There's Not a Friend Like the Lowly Jesus." Janet had misunderstood the lyrics, and thought it was about the "long-legged Jesus." She pictured Him striding across the snowy clouds, and wondered what it would be like to see those clouds up close for herself.

When it came time for Janet to go to high school, her options were limited to one school in Griffin. Georgia, as a former slave-holding state, enforced segregation with Jim Crow laws that dictated where and how Black people could live, work, and go to school. Black and white students were not allowed to attend the same schools, and schools for African Americans were often miserably underfunded.

But Samuel Harmon wanted his daughter to have a good education, so he sent Janet to an Episcopalian boarding school in Fort Valley, about sixty miles south of home. There, Janet impressed the teachers with her abilities in math, physics, science, and sports. She also had to take "charm" classes. Janet was taught how to behave in polite company, and how to sit or stand quietly. It was "something I needed very badly," Janet confessed.

She graduated from high school in 1925, and enrolled at Spelman College in Atlanta. Spelman is a historically Black college, much like the Tuskegee Institute in Alabama, and Janet's older sisters had been to school there, too. With twelve other young women, Janet joined Spelman's challenging nursing program. Students worked in the college hospital for a six-month probationary period; if they couldn't cut the mustard, they were kicked out. Six months later, only two students from Janet's intake were left, and she was one of them.

The training was excellent preparation in nursing, but not for the shocking prejudice and disregard for life Janet faced in her first job. She worked in a white hospital in Griffin, in the basement where there was a small area for treating Black patients—if it could be called treatment. After seeing a neighbor bleed to death because of neglect from the hospital staff, Janet ignored protocol in order to save another patient from the same fate. The supervising nurse then tried to take credit for Janet's quick thinking. Janet decided she'd had enough. She quit the job and began to consider her prospects.

As chance would have it, her older sister Viola came to visit the family from Detroit, where she'd moved to teach. Viola and her husband, Fred, invited Janet to stay with them and try her luck up North. Janet took them up on their offer, and by 1932 she had moved from Detroit to Chicago, still working as a nurse. There, she met and married a man named Evans Tyree Waterford and became Janet Harmon Waterford, but their relationship only lasted two years before they agreed to a divorce.

Single, though still going by the name of Waterford, Janet was making good money even in the middle of the Great Depression, thanks to her nursing skills. One day, she was struck by a picture of a nesting bird on a billboard with the caption: "Birds Learn to Fly. Why Can't You?"

Janet's childhood fascination with birds and clouds came flooding back, and the message stuck with her. She started thinking about how she could get flying lessons.

When Janet read a story in the *Chicago Defender* about Coffey and Johnny's aviation mechanics course being offered at the Curtiss-Wright School of Aviation, she knew she'd found her chance. For the next year, every Tuesday and Thursday evening, she would head to the Curtiss-Wright building to learn how to follow the birds up into the sky.

═══

On Janet's first day, she stood out in the crowd. She was the only woman in the room.

"I didn't know one instrument from another," Janet said of those

early days. "Coffey was our instructor. I learned motors and just everything, the groundwork in flying. I didn't have an idea that all of this
was really before flying; I thought perhaps we'd just go get in a plane
and learn to fly and that was it. But it was different." It wasn't easy,
either. "I didn't know it was going to be as rough as it was," Janet admitted. Fortunately, she'd always been an exceptional student in math,
physics, and science. "After the classwork and the theory part of it,
I learned the rules and regulations, meteorology, navigation, and all
of these things, the different clouds that I'd never even thought
about." Those big clouds, which as a little girl she had imagined Jesus
striding along, were key to the science of flight. "Each class day it was
fascinating. I couldn't hardly wait for another day to come."

The class moved on from the basics to making model airplanes, in
order to understand all of their moving parts. The Curtiss-Wright students also worked on engines and state-of-the-art aircraft, brought in
from working airfields for overhaul before being sent back into service. Curtiss Fledglings, biplanes used as primary trainers by both the
U.S. Navy and the U.S. Army, were brought in for maintenance, as well
as American Eagle biplane training aircraft, and popular types like the
Travel Air 2000, the International, and the Heath Parasol—the kit aircraft that had been Coffey and Johnny's first plane.

Janet and the other students grew familiar with well-respected motors, such as the Wright Whirlwind, which powered Charles
Lindbergh's *Spirit of St. Louis* in his first flight across the Atlantic in
1927, and the Pratt & Whitney Wasp, which had been successfully
used in a record-breaking eight-day flight around the world. And they
worked closely with the Challenger engine. Designed by the Curtiss
company itself, the Challenger was a new engine frequently used in
light aircraft built in the late 1920s and early 1930s.

Coffey and Johnny had very different styles in manner and in teaching. Coffey was soft-spoken, whereas Johnny could command a room. Janet thought Coffey was the better instructor because of his sincerity: he paid attention to individuals and made sure that a student really understood what he was saying, whereas Johnny left that responsibility up to the student. But they both knew their business.

Just as life had been hard for Coffey and Johnny in their early days at Curtiss-Wright, things were difficult for Janet—for a different reason, this time. Even though the other students in Janet's class were Black, she was the only woman.

"I didn't know what tool to pick up," Janet said, "whether it was a sixteenth-inch wrench or . . . nobody would tell me." So Janet made a trip to Sears and bought her own shiny green toolbox, filling it with tools from a list provided by Coffey. "I became very, very independent," she explained. And it paid off. The men who had been too busy to help her before suddenly "were coming over and asking me, 'May I use your wrench?' No!"

It may have been rough going, but Janet received a boost from an unexpected visitor.

"One night after school Amelia Earhart stopped in and said hello," Janet recalled.

Earhart was a world-famous white female aviator, who in 1928 had been the first woman to fly nonstop across the Atlantic (as a passenger). A talented pilot who'd already set speed records and a huge advocate for women in aviation, Earhart was also the first president of the Ninety-Nines, an international organization for women pilots that she'd helped establish in 1929. By May 1932, she had become the first woman to fly solo across the Atlantic. The famous aviatrix knew just how hard it was to be a woman finding wings in a man's world.

"She encouraged me, too," Janet said. "She said, 'Stick with it.'"
And Janet did.

====

Coffey and Johnny's students didn't just learn and study—they also
socialized, becoming members of the Brown Eagle Aero Club, and
hosting social events to promote awareness of Black people in aviation. The Curtiss-Wright School of Aviation held a holiday dance and
bridge party on the school's premises at the end of 1931, an event that
was repeated annually and attended by both Black and white students.
And Johnny continued to publicly urge people to get training—
"Opportunities for young colored men in aviation exist and are going
to increase," he told newspapers.

But after a while in ground school, the aviation students began to
get antsy. After all, they were there to learn how to fly. One day, Janet
approached Coffey.

"When do we do some real flying?" she wanted to know.

"That's the question I've been waiting for a long time," he replied.

Though Coffey didn't yet have the credentials to teach flying him-
self, he knew the men who could. He brought Janet out to Akers
Airport and introduced her to a pilot instructor by the name of
Andrew "Dynamite" Anderson.

"And he was dynamite, really," Janet said. "So I went up with him.
He took me up for my first ride." Much like Coffey's first time in the
air with the barnstormer when he was a kid, "Dynamite did everything, I guess, maybe trying to discourage me. But each maneuver
he did, it became more fascinating to me. I'd say, 'Oh, heaven! This is
really flying!'"

Janet was hooked. "He was a good instructor, as well as a good friend of Coffey's. I paid $15 an hour, a lot of money in those days, but I was determined to start learning to fly."

In 1931, Akers Airport was sold to a land developer. Though flying seems to have continued there for a year or two after the sale, Akers was doomed to be subdivided. The Brown Eagles needed a new home.

Coffey and Johnny began checking out other Chicago airfields to try to find a place to fly. But again and again, "We were told that they just don't accept colored fellows at the field," remembered Harold Hurd, one of the students in Coffey and Johnny's first class at Curtiss-Wright. Hurd had moved to Chicago from Georgia as a kid, bitten by the aviation bug after spotting a crop-duster airplane winging its way overhead when he was young. In 1929, then a teenager, he first saw a Black man fly at an air show—most likely held at Yackey Checkerboard Airfield in Maywood, Illinois, a place where Bessie Coleman used to fly. As a student at Lane Manual Training High School in Chicago, now Lane Tech, he and three friends had built their own light airplane, fitting it with an engine from a used Chevrolet. Johnny and Coffey got wind of the three kids who were building their own plane and came out to see it—which is how Hurd ended up enrolled at Curtiss-Wright.

Being from Georgia, Hurd was likely familiar with the Jim Crow attitude they were facing as they hunted for a new place to fly. But this wasn't the South. The student pilots who'd been learning to fly at Akers were sick of the racial tension there and elsewhere. They decided it was time that they had an airfield of their own.

They set their sights on Robbins, Illinois, a small village on the southern outskirts of Chicago. Robbins had been incorporated as an all-Black community in December 1917, one of the first "race" villages of its kind in the nation. "They had a colored mayor out there. The police chief was colored. All of the officials were colored," Coffey explained. Robbins was thriving even in the lean years of the early 1930s, under a mayor named Samuel Nichols. If Robbins had a vacant field, Coffey and Johnny were certain they could persuade the people of Robbins to let their group use it.

When the men approached Mayor Nichols, he was keen on the idea of an airport for Robbins. The village was young and still underdeveloped, and the hard times of the Great Depression era encouraged self-help projects like this one. There was a grassy stretch of former prairie, just south of the village, that would make a decent landing ground. Coffey and Johnny's group could rent the land, as long as they provided the materials and labor.

Neither Johnny nor Coffey had the money to pay the rent for the field, nor to buy materials to build a hangar, but Janet came to the rescue. Her nursing experience had helped her to get a well-paid job as a health inspector for the Metropolitan Burial Insurance Association, a company that sold policies to cover the final expenses of its policyholders. Now Janet partnered with Johnny and Coffey as their financer.

The group settled on a site south of 139th Place that ran all the way to what is now Interstate 294. The plot of land formed a triangle between 142nd Street and Claire Boulevard, up to Ridgeway Avenue and 139th. While the space was suitable, there were some challenges.

As Coffey recalled, "It had a few trees in there, and they had some of these great big boulders. I don't know if you've seen a boulder almost the size of a car."

How on earth they would move these obstacles might have been hard to imagine for a different group of people. But Coffey and Robinson's group had imagination and talent galore. They also had help from the community. They rolled up their sleeves and got to work.

Robbins local Floyd Canter, Jr., lent equipment, machinery, and construction engineering experience. Bernard Childs, the son of the community's treasurer, also lent a hand. Janet said, "At times it seemed like we had help from the whole little village."

There was only room for a single runway, and the land had to be cleared before it could be used. Undergrowth had to be removed, trees cut down, ditches filled, rocks cleared, and the ground leveled. The weeds were taller than Janet.

Saturdays, Sundays, and holidays, the aviation students and other members of the Brown Eagle Aero Club met in Robbins to work. Janet often brought along lunch for everybody, consisting of "hot dogs, which we cooked over a fire, potato salad, lemonade or pop."

The trees were cut down, but that car-sized boulder was right in the middle of the intended runway. It just seemed to get bigger the deeper they dug. They didn't have the equipment to move anything that large. The club members gave up on ever lifting it out of the ground.

Finally, in a stroke of genius, they dug a hole even *bigger* than a car, and, as Coffey said, with a push they "let it fall into the hole, and that's how we got rid of [that] big [boulder]."

Once it was in the hole, they buried the rock and left it there.

After the holes were filled in and the ground smoothed over, another of Coffey and Johnny's students, Albert Cosby, volunteered his truck for trips to a nearby railroad yard to haul cinders, which were helpfully donated by Robbins's new mayor, Thomas Kellar.

"We used the cinders, the residue from coal burned by steam loco-motives of the period, for the runway," Janet explained. "These had to be spread, leveled, and tamped down." The job was complicated by the fact that Cosby's truck had a quirk: it often refused to go unless it was being driven in reverse.

The aviators were welcomed by the whole Robbins community. Restaurants gave them free meals; local people housed them when they needed a place to spend the night. Everyone's home was open to them.

"It was backbreaking work, but we all enjoyed it," said Janet.

=====

Janet was so smitten with the project that she bought a secondhand airplane, sight unseen, for about five hundred dollars, because she trusted Coffey's and Johnny's advice. It was an International with a Curtiss OX-5 50-horsepower engine. She described it as "a biplane, painted red, with two open cockpits and the barest of instrumentation . . . The fuselage framework was wood, covered with fabric." Like a Waco 9, the International could hold up to three people in its two cockpits. "It was a glorious day when Coffey and Robinson flew my plane to our new airport, but it also was getting cold, the end of the summer flying season," Janet said. "We would have to wait through the winter before we could actually learn to fly."

The coming winter also meant that the group's airplanes needed shelter. The International was about twenty-five feet long. With a thirty-five-foot wingspan, it would need a sizeable hangar. Johnny himself drew up the blueprints for the building work. That meant the hangar had to be built when Johnny was around, because no one else could figure out his notes.

With the Great Depression in full swing, everyone was used to money and materials being hard to come by. The group scrounged for lumber wherever they could find it. Much of the wood came from old railroad ties from the nearby Rock Island railroad line. Janet went along with Coffey in Cosby's truck to pick up used lumber from a helpful construction place on State Street, east of Robbins.

"We built the hangar, the roof, the sides, the back, and everything but the front doors. We didn't get those on," Coffey recalled. The hangar faced westward in a location that backed onto the property of Floyd and Helen White at 3627 W. 140th Place. The Whites had three children, and had taken a liking to Coffey, Johnny, and their crew; reportedly they even served as ad hoc security guards for the hangar when the pilots were not around.

The makeshift wooden structure had a tin roof, and was big enough to hold three airplanes. Though the old Heath Parasol kit plane seems to have been retired or moved on by this time, the building provided shelter for Janet's International, Coffey's Waco 9 from Akers, and a Church Midwing owned by one of the white pilots from Akers; some of them had joined the group in Robbins.

When the new airfield's runway was finally ready to use, probably in January 1932, Coffey and Johnny renamed their group of flyers. From now on they would be known as the Challenger Aero Club, after the Challenger engines that Curtiss produced and that they'd all had to work on in class.

An inspector flew out in a six-seater Stinson plane from the Illinois Aeronautical Commission to approve the field at Robbins. But he struggled to land his large plane on the small runway. When he finally touched down, Johnny told him humbly that the Challenger pilots "would not have a plane as large as his for a long time," and that they'd expand the field when they needed to.

But the inspector smiled and wished them luck. He had to try his take-off run twice before he was able to get the large Stinson up in the air again.

"Whew!" Johnny commented. "What a narrow escape."

It was official: they were approved as what Janet proudly called "the only accredited flying field owned and operated by Negroes in the United States."

═══

To celebrate their success, the Challenger Aero Club decided to acknowledge their roots with a special service dedicated to the memory of Bessie Coleman. They may well have been thinking of Hubert Julian's failed attempt to fly over her grave back in 1928, but it's also likely that they were inspired by the first air show ever performed entirely by Black pilots, held in September 1931 by the Bessie Coleman Aero Club led by William J. Powell in Los Angeles. That tribute to the L.A. club's namesake had included stunt flying and flowers being dropped from a Goodyear airship. Now the Challenger pilots wanted to stage their own tribute to Queen Bess; after all, she was buried in Lincoln Cemetery in Blue Island, about a mile from the Robbins airfield. The Challengers would be the first to honor Bessie Coleman with a real airborne display over her grave.

So on Memorial Day in 1932, people on the ground gathered by Bessie's resting place for a service of song and prayer. Janet gave a short speech describing Bessie's youth and the tragic details of the crash that led to her death six years earlier.

The highlight of the event was the moment when Johnny Robinson, flying Janet's plane, swooped low over the crowd and dropped a bouquet of roses over the grave of brave Queen Bess.

═══

That spring, Janet recalled, "I finally really learned to fly."

So did they all. "We started out in full force with my airplane. Coffey was one of my instructors." Janet remembered Coffey as a patient, detailed teacher. "To illustrate something, he would clear a spot on the ground with his shoe, then draw a chart of what I should do. You didn't forget what he told you."

The Curtiss-Wright School of Aviation had by now changed its name to the splendidly impressive "Aeronautical University." Eight students in Coffey and Johnny's class graduated with certificates for the Curtiss-Wright Master Mechanic's Course in aviation in June of 1932. That same year, Chinese students were also admitted to the course, and Coffey and Johnny even had white students learning from them. Contemporary photographs of the young people at work in Coffey and Johnny's practical classes show a mixture of Black and white faces side by side, universally focused on aviation engines. It wasn't long before a few more women began to join the course.

One of these seems to have been Earnize Tate, the woman who had helped Johnny set up his garage and who may have been married to him. She was later described briefly as "an aviation enthusiast" by the *New York Amsterdam News*. There is a photograph, published in the *Chicago Defender*, of Earnize and Johnny in flying gear in front of an airplane, apparently taken just after Earnize had a flight with him. She is looking at the camera with her mouth twisted in a tolerant half grin;

Johnny is smiling broadly, his eyes on Earnize. The caption reads: "The joy of being a licensed pilot is what Mr. Robinson must be thinking, if not saying."

Johnny probably received his private pilot's license on July 21, 1932, and at some point, possibly also in 1932, he seems to have received his Department of Commerce aviation mechanic's license. One of Johnny's business cards from this time, saved in a scrapbook by fellow Challenger pilot Dale White, proudly reads: "J.C. Robinson—U.S. Government Licensed Pilot and Mechanic—Instructor for Aeronautical University founded by Curtiss-Wright Flying Service." In addition to these duties, Johnny also acted as the airport manager for Robbins.

"Now that we have an approved flying field of our own, we have a hard task before us," he told the club, according to Janet. "We have got to work on a very strict basis because if any kind of accident happens, it will kill everything . . . Don't take anything for granted.

"Working on the planes here will not be any guesswork. When in doubt, ask me. There will be no acrobatic flying over the field. You have decided to go into aviation. It is nothing easy. You must make up your mind to put the necessary time and effort into it . . . you must learn to fly not passably, but well."

In the warm summer weather of that year, Robbins Airfield became a gathering place for aviation enthusiasts, both Black and white. The Challenger pilots also did quite a bit of touring and visiting other fields. In Oak Lawn, there was a white-operated airfield where the owners were cordial to the Challenger aviators. It was the perfect distance for a training flight. The airfield was owned and run by brothers Bill and Fred Schumacher, and the Challengers used it as a "rendezvous" airport; sometimes Fred came out to visit Robbins, too. Beacon

Airport in Gary, Indiana, was another easy hop of only twenty miles.

Janet was soon able to make flying visits to these other airfields. She had now earned enough hours to qualify for her first "cross-country" flight, meaning she was allowed to leave the vicinity of the airfield she was flying from without an instructor along.

"As usual, I was wearing my flying togs—leather helmet and goggles, leather jacket, riding breeches and boots," Janet said, describing getting ready for the big day. "Women didn't wear slacks in those days,

Janet Harmon Waterford modeling her latest design in "flying togs"

SMITHSONIAN NATIONAL AIR AND SPACE MUSEUM (NASM 99-154245)

so riding breeches became flying breeches, a sort of uniform." Coffey watched from the ground as Janet took off, buzzing the houses at the end of the runway. Following road maps and aeronautical charts, she flew southwest to Joliet, then northeast to South Chicago, before returning to Robbins.

She was unstoppable! In September, she flew as far as Cleveland, Ohio, with Johnny and a friend of Coffey's named Joseph Muldrow—who was also enrolled in the course at Curtiss-Wright—to enjoy the annual spectacle of the National Air Races there.

By the end of the year, Janet had earned what would later become known as a student pilot's license, which was similar to a private license in that it allowed her to fly where she liked as long as she didn't instruct other students or carry passengers for hire. Johnny's full private pilot's license didn't allow him to instruct students "for hire," but as long as they weren't paying him, Johnny was operating within the rules if he took a student up in a certified aircraft.

After a little over a year of teaching, it seems Coffey left his position as an instructor at Aeronautical University, though he continued to be involved in the activities at Robbins. Coffey still didn't have any kind of pilot's license, but now, for reasons unknown, he decided to return to his garage business in Detroit. Could his apparent marriage to Jennie B. Davis have had something to do with it? Court records from 1934 show a Jennie B. Davis living in Detroit. Perhaps Coffey returned there for his auto repair business, or for his marriage. But, given that those same records mark Jennie's marriage to another man, at least one of those ventures was destined to fail.

In the meantime, there were now ten other members of the Challenger Aero Club. Many of them eventually soloed in Janet's International. Janet and Johnny were the only two pilots in the group whose licenses allowed them to carry passengers or students, and apparently Johnny tended to hog the pilot's seat.

"Johnny Robinson was in charge of it, the flying," Janet recalled. "We would work all day, someone waiting to go up. Guess who would go up? Johnny Robinson would go up. Sometimes we would get so angry with him, you know, but yet we still had no other person that we could go and do this thing with."

Fortunately, Janet's work allowed her some flexibility with her hours, so if the weather was good, you could find her in the sky, too.

═══

As the Illinois Aeronautical Commission inspector had proven, the Robbins runway "was usable," Janet said. But "it was also fairly short, so we barely got off the ground in time to clear the houses bordering the field, no matter in which direction we took off."

Landing was just as much of a problem. In addition to being short, the runway was prone to crosswinds, and to try to keep the noise down, the aviators had to "slip" in fast and steeply when they were landing.

"Our white neighbors to the south, in Midlothian, really didn't like our flying so low over their homes, and often complained," Janet said.

Even today people complain about aircraft noise from small airfields. But in the white townships south of Robbins, it was the perfect excuse for covering up a racist objection. As if Black aviators somehow flew more loudly than white ones! What's more, if something went wrong with any of the Challenger planes—which happened a good deal in the early days of aviation—people didn't just complain about the noise, but also about emergency landings on their property. In fact, they did more than complain—they often called the police.

Charges were brought against Johnny, as the airport manager, for people flying too low, for noise, for planes coming too close to buildings, or for other air offenses. Even the mayor of Midlothian fussed about aircraft noise from planes flying straight over his house. More than once, white policemen from Midlothian and another town, Crestwood, issued warnings and went so far as to arrest the pilots. Local Robbins history has it that their own Mayor Kellar was often called upon to get the flyers released. But not even jail could keep them from climbing back into their planes the next clear day, ready to fly once more.

In December 1932, the second annual holiday dance and bridge party was held by the Challenger Aero Club in the beautiful ballroom of the Classical Revival Curtiss-Wright building in downtown Chicago, and according to a report in the *Chicago Defender*, it was "attended by students of both races." To the young men and women who'd built their own airfield and worked so hard all year to learn the mechanics and principles of flight, it must have felt as if things were really changing for the better. Life was going their way at last.

There is a famous photo of the Challenger Aero Club taken around this time. Dated January 30, 1933, it shows ten of its members lined up on either side of Coffey's Waco 9 in the snow in front of their homemade hangar at Robbins. To the left of the Waco's propeller, looking dapper in a long winter coat, suit, and tie, stands Paul G. Mitchell, who had come all the way from Maryland to join the group. His hands are stuffed in his pockets against the cold. Beside him, his fur collar popped up high against the wind, stands Albert Cosby—the owner of the truck that would sometimes only go in reverse. Clyde B. Hampton cuts a striking figure in a three-piece suit, trench coat, and rakishly tilted fedora; kneeling on either side of the wooden propeller are George Webster, decked out in flight gear, and Gerald Reed. Webster had a student pilot's license and was enrolled in the Master Mechanic's Course at Curtiss-Wright. Reed wasn't a pilot, but a fan of flying who frequented the airport.

On the right side of the propeller stands Janet Harmon Waterford in her "flying togs"—an all-white getup of wide-hipped riding breeches, boots, a close-fitting jacket, and a pilot's cap and goggles. Similarly dressed, but more sensibly bundled up in an overcoat, is one other woman, Doris Murphy Tanner, a Tuskegee graduate like Johnny. She would enroll in the Aeronautical University course later in 1933.

The Challenger Aero Club posing with Coffey's Waco 9 on Robbins Airfield in front of the hangar that they built themselves. Left to right: Paul G. Mitchell, Albert Cosby, Clyde B. Hampton, George Webster, Gerald Reed, Janet Harmon Waterford, Doris Murphy Tanner, Bill Jackson, Harold Hurd, Dale White, and Johnny Robinson

SMITHSONIAN NATIONAL AIR AND SPACE MUSEUM (NASM 87-15492)

Beside Doris Tanner stand Bill Jackson and Harold Hurd. The tall, slender Jackson mixes things up with a wool overcoat, dress shirt and tie, and a flying cap. Hurd wears the rest of the pilot's outfit—a leather bomber jacket and gloves. Beside Hurd stands Dale White, looking serious in his flying cap, aviator scarf, and double-breasted winter coat. Harold Hurd and Dale White, along with Clyde Hampton and Janet Harmon Waterford, had all graduated from Johnny and Coffey's class in 1932. Last but not least is Johnny Robinson, marked on the photograph as the manager of the Challenger Aero Club. Aviator cap, goggles, scarf, and leather gloves add a dash of the exotic to his pale trench coat.

One member of the club is noticeably missing from the photo: Cornelius Coffey.

———

Coffey's absence didn't seem to affect life for the rest of the Challenger Aero Club; Johnny and the others kept teaching and flying until Mother Nature herself stepped in.

On Monday, May 1, 1933, a few months after the Aero Club photo was taken, a tornado swept through the Chicago suburbs. Although it didn't touch down in Robbins, the terrible windstorm that came with it destroyed the Robbins hangar—and with the hangar went all three of the airplanes inside.

"It was our mistake by not putting up doors over the hangar, which left more vacuum for the wind to blow in and blow the [hangar] down," said Harold Hurd.

The storm apparently lifted Janet's beautiful red International off

Robbins locals and Challenger Aero Club members surveying storm damage to their hangar and aircraft, May 1933

SMITHSONIAN NATIONAL AIR AND SPACE MUSEUM (NASM 99-15503)

the ground and blew it over the roofs of a couple of houses on 141st Street. The wild wind finally flung the helpless little plane to the ground in an alley.

Incredibly, though Janet's International was severely damaged, it was repairable. But Coffey's Waco 9, and the Church Midwing owned by the young man who'd been friendly with Coffey and Johnny back at Akers, were both destroyed. The hangar was completely ruined.

Dale White, who served as the Challenger Aero Club's business manager, made a hopeful announcement to the press that they were going to hurry to rebuild the hangar in time for the exciting "Century of Progress" World's Fair that was about to open in Chicago at the end of the month. A handsome man with a friendly smile, Dale had been born in Minden, Louisiana, in 1899. He moved to Chicago in 1930 and, a couple of years later, joined Johnny and Coffey's class at Curtiss-Wright. Optimistically, Dale told the *Chicago Defender* that, despite the storm, the Challenger Aero Club was also planning an air show. Unfortunately, neither goal was met, though in July 1933 the Challenger pilots did make an appearance at the World's Fair, with an exhibit in the Travel and Transport Building of several aircraft engines they'd been working on in connection with Aeronautical University. Nettie George Speedy, reporting on the show, gave them a big splash in the *Pittsburgh Courier*, profiling many of the club members and their ambitions, and congratulating them for their persistence in attempting to rebuild the airfield at Robbins.

But there's no evidence that the Challenger aviators ever put up another hangar at Robbins. Not only were supplies scarce, but the pilots were discouraged by being "constantly molested by the police of the neighboring town," as Harold Hurd put it.

Getting back in the air no doubt felt like an exhausting and impossible task. With their headquarters reduced to rubble, and their flying machines reduced to wreckage, they had two choices: rebuild the little airfield, or quit.

But Johnny found a third option: a bigger, better opportunity, at an airport called Harlem.

CHAPTER 4

CLIMB, 1933–1934

Tuskegee, thou pride of the swift growing South
We pay thee our homage today
For the worth of thy teaching, the joy of thy care;
And the good we have known 'neath thy sway.

—Paul Lawrence Dunbar, "The Tuskegee Song," 1909

BACK in the summer of 1932, at Beacon Airport in Gary, Indiana, soon after Johnny received his own pilot's license, he had watched in horror as another Black pilot, Charles James, hurtled to his death in an out-of-control airplane.

When a reporter asked Johnny what he thought had caused the accident, he blamed it on the poor quality of the rented and unfamiliar aircraft that James was forced to fly. Across the board, whether due to race-based pay inequities or prejudiced suppliers, Black flyers often ended up having to make do with substandard equipment.

"A pilot, without a thorough investigation, is not ever sure that he is not embarking in a faulty machine," was Johnny's bitter contention. Having a place to park your own plane, and the ability to make your own decisions, was key to a successful flying club. And Johnny was determined to succeed.

Harlem Airport was located approximately seven miles north of

Robbins in the village of Oak Lawn, Illinois. The Challengers had often flown from Robbins to Harlem as a rendezvous point in training
exercises, and it was here that Johnny Robinson found a new home for
the Challengers Aero Club. The reason was Fred Schumacher.

Fred was a taxi driver with a high school education who had learned
to fly in 1927. His brother Bill had purchased the land for Harlem
Airport, and around 1929 Fred began to run it as its manager, helped
by his wife, Eleanor. The airport was named for one of the streets it ran
along, Harlem Avenue at 87th Street. Fred knew the Challengers from
their days in Robbins; he also knew that Oak Lawn wouldn't love the
idea of Black pilots in the area, but even so, he welcomed them to his
airfield.

"Don't bother to try to rebuild in Robbins," Fred told Johnny. "Move
here, and we'll give you a hangar."

Oak Lawn was quite a change from Robbins. Founded in the early
1800s on land taken from the local Potawatomi tribe, by 1930 the village had a population of 2,045 residents—2,043 of whom were white.
Two were Black. Oak Lawn frequently held minstrel shows as a form of
entertainment in the 1930s and '40s, featuring white actors in makeup
known as "blackface," performing racist stereotypes of Black people as
lazy and ignorant. How would the Oak Lawn community feel about a
group of talented Black aviators? Racial tension was inevitable.

"Look, fellows," Fred told the Challengers, "I'm going to put you at
the end of the field to save you from having any trouble with the other
guys."

"We went out there, but we had to operate on the lower end of the
field," Janet said. "[They] made it quite clear that we were not to be on
the northern part of the field, because there was no integration then."

This way, the only thing the white aviators would have to share with the Black newcomers was the sky. But that didn't stop the Challenger Aero Club from agreeing to the deal.

"We didn't care," Janet said. "The only thing we wanted was a little place to land."

Others might have felt differently. In a sinister turn of events, the hangar offered to the Challenger pilots burned down, possibly set on fire on purpose.

"Don't worry about it; we'll deal with it," said the Schumachers. Somehow a quiet truce was reached, and the Schumachers built a new hangar for Johnny and his crew.

Around this time, the Challenger Aero Club took on a patriotic duty, becoming a paramilitary or unofficial air guard. The aviation squadrons of World War I had made it clear that flight would play a leading role in modern warfare, and the United States Army Air Corps, which would eventually become the U.S. Air

Janet Harmon Waterford enjoying a day at Harlem Airport

SMITHSONIAN NATIONAL AIR AND SPACE MUSEUM (NASM 79-13664)

Force, was established in 1926. Civilian aviators of the 1920s styled themselves with military ranks such as "captain" and "colonel"; even Bessie Coleman had worn flying clothes that suggested a military uniform, with her own initials, "B.C.," embroidered on her cap in imitation of a designated rank. In those early years of aviation, an association with the military gave credibility and respectability to any flyer. The Challenger aviators knew this very well. But every one of them also knew that as Black pilots in America, the segregation of the United States armed forces would deny every one of them the right to fly and serve in any official military capacity at the national level.

A connection with a Black parachutist and aviator known as Major George Fisher gave the Challengers their new idea. Major Fisher was part of an organization known as the Military Order of Guard (MOG), set up during World War I and associated with the state of Illinois rather than with the federal government. If the Challengers couldn't join the segregated National Guard as an Air Reserve Squadron, why not join a state militia instead?

So the Challenger Aero Club pursued and won a charter from the state of Illinois as a "Military Order of Guard, Aviation Squadron." It was a small victory in a nation with a segregated military.

Although they weren't officially part of the National Guard, they were approved by the federal War Department, and as part of a state militia, both Coffey and Johnny were given the rank of lieutenant colonel. Johnny had command of the unit. Fellow Challengers Harold Hurd and Dale White were designated lieutenants, and Grover C. Nash was a second lieutenant. Nash was Harold Hurd's brother-in-law. Born in Dry Branch, Georgia, in 1911, he had learned to fly in St. Louis, Missouri, and graduated from Aeronautical University in 1933.

Once inducted, the group officially dedicated Challenger aircraft to MOG activities; they were allowed to display the Illinois MOG insignia on their planes, and the club members were able to wear military-style uniforms. The male members of the Challenger Aero Club were now the first Black paramilitary aviation unit in history.

———

The Challenger Aero Club moved to Harlem Airport late in 1933, and marked the occasion by officially changing their name yet again, this time to the Challenger Air Pilots' Association.

Meanwhile, probably with Earnize's help, Johnny found an old blacksmith's shed to use as his new home base at 47 East 47th Street. He converted it to an automobile shop, widening the doors and installing a workbench and tools for welding and cutting. The place was called Robinson's Auto Garage, and it doubled as Johnny's new home; the attic above the garage served as both bedroom and living room.

"They were doing some auto repair work to help finance the flying," Coffey said of the Challengers, though he was still in Detroit at the time, "and also it would give them a place to work on an aircraft. If they could pick up something that needed rebuilding, they could take it in there and rebuild it and then take it out to the airport." One of the vehicles they repaired was Janet's International.

They also built a club headquarters at the airfield.

"It was a new beginning—an airport with much better runway lengths," Janet said. "[Grover] Nash had bought a Buhl Pup, so now we had two planes."

Nash's Buhl Pup was a sleek-looking single-seat monoplane, which he named *The Little Annie*.

Just like that, the Challenger pilots were back in the air.

Curtiss-Wright's Aeronautical University was also growing. At the end of 1933, director Lewis Churbuck proudly boasted, "This school makes no discrimination against persons of any nationality." New classes for Black students would begin in January 1934, with Johnny as the only Black instructor.

The Curtiss-Wright company realized that Johnny's skills could be put to use in more ways than one, and hired him to deliver their Air Service planes to other states. The experience of professional flight and frequent visits to other airfields, not to mention the hands-on teaching of aviation and mechanical skills to eager young students, convinced Johnny that there was a deep need to connect flight training with an accredited Black educational institution.

Coffey shared Johnny's ambition for a college-based aviation program. The way many Black aviators saw it, there was a race for equality both on land and in the air. African Americans had to stake their claim to the sky before they were squeezed out of yet another opportunity. They needed to go bigger. And Johnny knew just where to start: his alma mater, Tuskegee Institute.

━━━

Founded in Tuskegee, Alabama, on the Fourth of July in 1881, Tuskegee Institute came into being when a white senator named W.F. Foster asked a formerly enslaved Black man, Lewis Adams, how to get the African American vote. Adams told him he'd like to see a school for Black people, who had long been denied an education by the appalling system of slavery in the southern states. The Tuskegee Normal and Industrial Institute began as a one-room shack with a single teacher—

the formidable educator and presidential advisor Booker T. Washington, who had himself been born into slavery. Under Washington's tutelage, in twenty-five years the school grew to 1,500 students and forty areas of study.

In 1934, Tuskegee seemed to Johnny and Coffey like the perfect place to start an aviation program for Black students. It already had an excellent mechanical and automotive department, and there was plenty of land around the campus that could be converted into an appropriate airfield to connect with a flight school. Tuskegee's southern setting meant that flying could take place year-round without having to deal with the hazards of northern winters.

Universities and colleges across the country, all of them traditionally white, were jumping onto the aviation bandwagon. Schools like New York University and the California Institute of Technology, which had received huge grants for aeronautics programs from the Guggenheim Foundation, had a head start. Coffey said, "They taught everything else at Tuskegee, and why not include aviation?"

As luck would have it, 1934 marked Johnny's ten-year class reunion at the renowned school. Johnny knew Tuskegee's registrar, Captain Alvin Neely, because he'd chauffeured for Neely during his college years. So through Neely, Johnny arranged a meeting with Tuskegee's president, Robert Russa Moton.

To make the visit newsworthy, Johnny and Coffey were going to fly to Tuskegee from Chicago. Coffey came back from Detroit to be Johnny's copilot and navigator. Though there's no record that Coffey applied for even a student license before October 1935, he was a competent and careful flyer, and it was completely aboveboard to have him along as a second pilot.

Coffey and Johnny would fly in Janet's newly restored International;

Grover Nash would also go along in *The Little Annie*, his single-seat Buhl Pup, "for the experience," Coffey explained. Nash was a handsome young man with a winning smile. He had a Curtiss-Wright Aeronautical University certificate, and he owned his own plane, all of which could certainly help in selling the idea of a flight program.

This would be the third-longest cross-country flight ever attempted by Black aviators. Their planned route would take two days, including refueling stops in Illinois and Tennessee and an overnight break in Birmingham, Alabama. After a last stop for fuel in Montgomery, Alabama, they hoped to finally make it to Tuskegee.

So early in the morning on Friday, May 18, 1934, the three men, in two aircraft, set off from Harlem Airport. Nash took off first in his Buhl Pup, and Coffey and Johnny followed in Janet's International. But just before the International reached the end of the runway, the engine suddenly shut down.

While Janet and the other Challenger club members watched, Johnny jumped out of the plane to swing the propeller around and start the engine again—a standard technique at the time, using the aircraft's propeller in much the same way a hand crank was used to start the engine on a Ford Model T car. Nash, already in the sky, circled patiently over the airfield, waiting for Johnny and Coffey to get going. But the International still idled on the ground.

It seems the two men were arguing over something. Janet thought it was about parachutes. Apparently, Coffey wanted to carry a couple for such long-distance travel, and they didn't have any. Whatever the reason, eventually they took off—without any parachutes.

This wasn't the first time Johnny and Coffey had disagreed about the preparations for the flight to Tuskegee. They'd also argued about the extra fuel tank the International was carrying, which had been Johnny's idea. Nash's little plane only had a seven-gallon tank, which meant the trio would have to land and refuel it every 175 miles or so, but the fifty gallons available in the International would help get them over long, empty stretches of open country without having to rely on white folks being willing to sell them additional fuel, especially in the southern states.

Unfortunately, the extra tank, when full of fuel, weighed 108 pounds—nearly as much as another adult passenger. Coffey was worried that the extra weight would make takeoff and landing more difficult, and he was right.

"Now, on our route down there, we had to stop [in] Decatur, Alabama," Coffey said. It wasn't one of the planned stops on their route; it seems that Nash was running out of fuel, and the International's tank didn't have enough in it to make up the difference. "There was no airport there, so observing the area, the only place that we could land was on a golf course."

The golf course was part of a country club outside of town. Both planes landed at about 11:30 a.m. on Saturday, May 19, in time for Nash to fill up. But once on the ground, they learned they could only get fuel delivered in twenty-five-gallon allotments. That meant paying for an extra eighteen gallons of gas Nash couldn't use.

Coffey was fine with the expense. Although they'd pay a bit more, Nash would be able to make it to Birmingham for that price. But Johnny saw it differently. Rather than pay for something they couldn't use, he insisted on putting the extra fuel in the International. That added weight that Coffey wasn't sure they could handle.

"We'll walk over the area that we're going to use for takeoff," Johnny said. "If the airplane don't feel light enough, when we get halfway, we'll abort the takeoff, and I'll tell Nash, give him a sign, and he'll come back and land."

It was a hot day, with ripples of heat rising from the ground: bad news for flying. Because hot air is thinner than cooler air, the warmer it is, the more power it takes to lift a plane off the ground. In practical terms, this means a plane needs a longer take-off run or a strong headwind to help it into the air on a hot day. Coffey said as much to Johnny. "Look. With that extra gas in there and with the heat and no wind, we ain't going to get off."

But Johnny still thought it would work.

So in his patient, methodical way, Coffey calculated how much of a take-off run they'd need. He stuck a wooden stick with a white rag tied to it into the earth at the spot where Johnny would have to lift the plane from the ground. If the International didn't have enough speed to take off by the time they reached that flag, Coffey reckoned they'd have to wait for more wind, or get rid of some fuel before they could take off. From the front seat of the plane, Coffey would have a clearer view of the runway than Johnny, so he told Johnny he'd call out when they reached the critical spot.

Coffey helped start Nash's plane, and gave him instructions to circle the golf course after takeoff, just in case he and Johnny had any problems.

Nash's Buhl Pup lifted off the green and into the air without any trouble. Johnny felt sure that he wouldn't have any trouble, either. He was worried about being late for his meeting with President Moton.

Coffey spun the International's propeller and clambered inside. The International was set up so that its two seats were one behind the other; the pilot sat in the back, where his weight would be more evenly distributed in solo flight, and his view wouldn't be obscured by the biplane's upper wing. Although there were flight controls in both seats of the International, only the pilot's cockpit had a full range of aviation instruments. Coffey had to trust Johnny to pay attention to the warning flag he'd set up on the golf course.

But Johnny ignored the flag. He also ignored Coffey waving frantically at him from the front of the plane.

They passed the flag and were still gathering speed on the ground. Coffey tried to warn Johnny not to try to lift off, but, as Coffey recounted, "He just kept right on going." Coffey braced himself and thought, "This is going to be good."

Exactly as he'd feared, the International didn't have enough power to take to the air—at least not safely.

And the golf course fence was coming up fast.

But somehow, Johnny pulled it off. He hauled the plane into the sky in the nick of time, and hung there with just enough speed to keep moving forward and up.

Johnny managed to get the staggering plane over the fence. But in doing so, he pulled the plane's nose up too high. That caused the aircraft to stall. This doesn't mean the engine stopped—in aviation terms, a "stall" is when the airflow beneath the wings is so disrupted that the plane hangs in the air just before diving, and in this position, the tail drags behind the rest of the aircraft.

"If we'd attempted a turn, anything, man, you'd fall right out of the sky," Coffey explained, shaking his head.

Now, although the International's nose was still hovering in the air, its tail was dragging. The next obstacle was looming—a house. And not just any house, but one with a big chimney.

"I never will forget. We hit that chimney on that takeoff and I felt the vibration," Coffey said. They hit so hard he thought they'd knocked the landing gear clean off.

Coffey loosened his safety belt so he could crane over the side to try to inspect the damage. To his relief, he saw that both wheels were still in place. It seemed they had simply bounced off the house—a stroke of incredible luck.

Then he looked back at the tail of the plane.

The whole back end of the plane had been nearly torn off, including the tailplane, which angles the aircraft up and down, and the rudder, which assists in turning. The only thing that still attached the International's tail end to the rest of it was a slender guide wire.

Miraculously, the International stayed in the air.

Coffey pointed frantically behind Johnny to make him look back. As soon as Johnny saw what had happened, he immediately cut the power to slow the plane down for an emergency landing.

But with the tailplane and rudder wrecked, the only possible way to control the plane was by adding or reducing engine power. Without power, the International plunged into a dangerous dive.

Using his own cockpit controls, Coffey hurriedly thrust the power back on—they'd have to fly a little farther to make a safe crash landing.

On the other side of the highway, just ahead of the limping International, was the answer. "I saw this cotton patch," Coffey said, "and everything was fine."

But it wasn't. As they got closer to the field, they realized there was a tree right in the middle of their path. The damaged plane was practically unsteerable and headed straight for it.

"We almost cleared that tree," Coffey said.

Almost. Their left wheel snagged the top of the tree. The plane had been moving so slowly that it could not break away. It swung around to the left, and cartwheeled into the cotton field.

The International lost its bottom wing, but miraculously landed upright. And that was the end of the flight.

Nash had watched helplessly from the sky while this drama unfolded. The crash kicked up so much dust that he thought it was smoke, and that the International had caught fire. He landed his Buhl Pup nearby and rushed to help his friends out of the wreckage.

But when the dust settled, Coffey was uninjured, and Johnny was able to walk away with nothing more than a cut from where his goggles broke and scratched his face.

The two men counted themselves lucky. That is, until the owner of the cotton field showed up.

Nash wasn't the only one who came dashing to find out what was going on. "People come across there with mules and bicycles and trucks, and I'm trying to stop them, see, because I knew if they ruined that man's cotton we had to pay for it," Coffey recalled. When the field's owner took in the damage the plane had done to his crops . . . "Sure enough, it cost us a hundred and twenty-five dollars to actually correct for that damage that was done."

So much for saving money on fuel: the crash ended up costing more than the three of them had between them. After a couple of days in Decatur dealing with the fallout from the crash, including taking Janet's broken International apart, shipping it back to Chicago for repair, and contacting the aero club back home for money to cover the damages, Coffey and Nash agreed that there was no way Johnny should miss his appointment at Tuskegee Institute.

So Nash loaned Johnny his Buhl Pup. He and Coffey would make

their way to Tuskegee by bus. Johnny flew the rest of the way to Tuskegee in *The Little Annie* through the May sunshine, without any trouble
at all.

=====

On Tuesday, May 22, 1934, Grover Nash's Buhl Pup became what was
probably the first plane ever to land at Tuskegee.

It was a couple of days later than planned, but still well in time for
Thursday's commencement ceremony. Johnny landed in an oat field
next to Tuskegee's School of Agriculture farm. Captain Neely was there
to greet him. The two men posed for a photo opportunity that appeared
in Black newspapers throughout America: Johnny sits smiling in the
cockpit of *The Little Annie* while Neely, smartly dressed in jacket, tie,
and boater hat, reaches up into the plane to shake Johnny's hand.

The newspapers all made it sound like the plane belonged to Johnny,
and it's hard not to wonder if that's exactly what he told the reporters.
The coverage of his eventful trip misleadingly and unfairly said that
"his" other plane had been "wrecked by a friend." Perhaps some at
Tuskegee had their doubts—Johnny was welcomed at the commencement events as a celebrity alumnus and a credit to the institute, but he
wasn't given as much special attention as he'd have liked.

Still, he kept his meetings. In addition to talking to Captain Neely
and President Moton, Johnny had a word with Frederick Douglass
Patterson, the director of Tuskegee's School of Agriculture, and George
L. Washington, the director of the School of Mechanical Industries.
They were all considering how to move forward with aviation as one
of Tuskegee's programs, but, unlike Johnny, they were moving with
caution.

Johnny Robinson in Grover Nash's Buhl Pup The Little Annie, *likely the first plane ever to land at Tuskegee University. Johnny is shaking hands with Tuskegee registrar Alvin Neely.*

Looking back, Coffey commented, "It might have been different ... if we hadn't have lost that airplane."

The Challenger flyers returned to Chicago, disappointed but not beaten, and Coffey went back to Detroit to run his auto repair business. Determined to keep building up his flight hours, he picked up his next airplane in Bay City, Michigan, a Great Lakes biplane in need of repair.

Coffey bought it, towed it to his automobile shop, and fixed it up. As for Janet, she was not pleased about the wreck of her only recently repaired International. Johnny also would need a new plane to keep the Challenger pilots flying.

He set his sights on a Command-Aire biplane that was being sold by a white owner. Johnny was nothing if not a smooth talker, and he managed to drive down the plane's price by pointing out all of its defects. Impetuous as always, when it came time to do the paperwork, he suddenly admitted, "I have no money!"

The man selling the aircraft was dumbfounded. "You mean you come in here and want a plane but have no money?"

"That's right!"

Johnny offered to pay the agreed price on credit. Apparently, the owner was so impressed with his audacity and sincerity that he let Johnny have the plane with no money down.

Johnny was happy to bend the truth if it cast him in a better light. But he wasn't a con man. Good to his word, he paid off the debt in due course. In the meantime, the Challengers had their new plane. They were once again scaling the heights of the sky.

Sometime that year, they also got a new member—someone who would help to take them to heights they couldn't yet imagine: the stunning and dynamic Willa Brown.

———

Willa Beatrice Brown was born in Glasgow, Kentucky, on January 22, 1906. Her father and mother, the Reverend Eric B. Brown and Hallie Mae Carpenter Brown, moved to Indiana when Willa was six, and raised their children in Terre Haute, where Willa graduated from Wiley

High School in 1923. Willa was pretty and petite, standing only five foot one, and became a strikingly beautiful young woman with movie-star looks that belied the grit and determination in her soul.

Like Johnny Robinson, she knew that the key to getting decent work would be continuing her education, and when she finished high school, she enrolled at the Indiana Normal School in Terre Haute (now Indiana State University). Her college courses were unusual and modern for a young Black woman: she chose to major in "commerce," what is now more or less known as "business administration." Willa learned typing and shorthand, the formalities of writing business letters, and accounting. In 1927, though she didn't yet have her degree, she landed an excellent job teaching typewriting to high school students in Gary, Indiana.

It's not obvious when Willa first got bitten by the aviation bug. She may well have seen the newspaper stories about Bessie Coleman, who was making headlines with her trips to France and her early flight achievements while Willa was in high school. No doubt, as a college student, Willa saw the reports of Bessie Coleman's death in 1926. Later, living in Gary, Willa probably saw small aircraft soaring regularly overhead in the neighborhood where she lived and worked, as planes took off and flew into Beacon Airport at 63rd and Broadway, only four miles south of the school where she taught. Beacon Airport hosted air shows by both Black and white performers (not, apparently, at the same time), and by women aviators, too. A headline in Gary's Black newspaper, the *Gary American*, on June 7, 1929, shouted, "Here's Your Chance To Go Skylarking For $5 If You Like Airplanes!"—while the article assured the timid passenger: "And if two engines die, the third will permit an extended glide to an absolutely safe landing."

So Willa Brown was surely aware of aviation and its attraction long before it occurred to her that she, too, could learn to fly, but she was also already very busy. As well as teaching, she had her own college degree to complete, commuting back to Terre Haute during the summers of 1928, 1929, and 1931 so she could finish her studies. She also threw herself into the social life of Gary's Black community, which is how she met one of Indiana's first Black firefighters, Wilbur J. Hardaway. Wilbur was loud, bold, confident, attractive, and full of life—"a likeable fella," according to Willa's brother Simeon. People who weren't annoyed by Wilbur's brash manner found him irresistible, and before long, Willa had fallen in love.

Like Johnny Robinson, Wilbur was educated at Tuskegee Institute. Also like Johnny, he was ambitious; he quit his job so he could run for the city council. In a race between eight Black and five white men, Wilbur's campaign was a success. On November 24, 1929, within three weeks of Wilbur's election as an alderman for Gary's Fifth Ward, Wilbur and Willa were married.

As a Gary alderman, Wilbur used his charm and personality to fight for diversity and equal rights, both locally and nationally. Meanwhile, Willa became head of the commerce department at the newly built Roosevelt High School, having completed her college degree in August 1931 with a bachelor of arts in education. The fabulous new Roosevelt complex at 25th and Harrison Boulevard had cost a million dollars to build, an astonishing amount during the Great Depression. It included a swimming pool, two gyms, and a huge auditorium. Two thousand students enrolled as the school opened its doors, and three hundred of them studied bookkeeping, shorthand, typing, and business training under Willa's guidance.

But there was a catch—the new school was segregated. There were no white students.

Wilbur used his position on the city council to join a groundswell of civic protest, but it didn't make any difference.

And—after less than two years—Willa and Wilbur's marriage wasn't working. Willa knew very well she wasn't ever going to be a model housewife, but that wasn't the only trouble. She'd fallen for Wilbur's charm, and now she was discovering his nastier side.

Wilbur had a reputation for violence. He was known as "The Fighting Alderman" and wasn't beyond getting into a fistfight at public parties; once he even took a swing at a political rival.

"We wrecked our apartment throwing everything handy at each other," Willa told friends later. "We fought like dogs, we threw dishes."

After Wilbur gave her a punch in the eye that bruised her so badly she had to hide behind dark glasses for a few days, Willa officially applied for a divorce. Ten days after she took out a protection order against Wilbur and applied for a warrant for his arrest, the Lake County court system granted her a divorce and legally gave her back her maiden name. She was once again Willa Beatrice Brown.

Willa was free of her abusive husband, she had her name back, and she had her college degree. She kept on teaching at Roosevelt for the rest of the school year. But she was ready to move on and to make a new life for herself. In 1932, at the age of twenty-six, Willa headed to Chicago.

When she arrived, always community-minded, Willa launched into social work. Her secretarial and business skills meant that she was never short of a paid job, even in the middle of the Depression. For a little extra cash, she also worked shifts in the Walgreens drugstore cafeteria at 47th and South Parkway—in the days before fast-food chains, almost every drugstore had a lunch counter where you could buy a cheap sandwich or a hot dog. And Willa made friends. Soon she was seeing a new young man, the handsome and accomplished John B. McClellan, Jr.

John was a graduate of Ohio State University and had been a chemist during World War I. He'd spent a year in Spain immersing himself in the language there, and now he taught science and Spanish at Wendell Phillips High School. Before long, John and Willa became close enough that Willa took him to Terre Haute for a Mother's Day visit to her parents in May 1934, just before Johnny's trip to Tuskegee.

On the drive back to Chicago afterward, John and Willa were involved in a tragic accident, likely with Willa at the wheel.

A local boy watched, screaming in horror as Willa's car vaulted a ditch and rammed into a tree. John was hurled fifteen feet into the air, landing hard and rolling another twenty feet before limply coming to rest.

The landing broke his neck and fractured his skull.

The boy and another person who lived near the spot managed to drag Willa from the wreckage with a broken arm, broken ribs, and a fractured vertebra. But John died in the ambulance on the way to the hospital.

The newspapers reporting the shocking accident predicted that Willa wasn't going to pull through, either.

But Willa was a survivor.

After a lengthy hospital stay, she began to stitch the torn pieces of her life back together.

In the aftermath of this terrible car accident, Willa was lonely and aching in body and soul. Her injuries prevented her from making the rounds in her primary job as a social worker, but she kept her second job at Walgreens.

The Walgreens drugstore cafeteria at 47th and South Parkway happened to be the place where members of the Challenger Air Pilots' Association sometimes went for lunch. Working at the lunch counter there in 1934, Willa overheard conversations about young Black people taking aviation courses and flying planes. Fascinated, she began to strike up conversations with the Challenger group, and that's how Willa Brown met Johnny Robinson.

Not immune to a pretty face, Johnny encouraged Willa to get into aviation. Since John McClellan's death, Willa had been yearning for a place to belong. She took Johnny up on the offer, and began to take flying lessons with him. In January 1935, she would enroll at Curtiss-Wright's Aeronautical University. The Challengers' efforts to expand Black aviation had added a passionate new convert to their number.

———

Willa's involvement with aviation came at a time when explosive international issues were about to raise the stakes for Black pilots in America, and for the Challenger pilots in particular. Throughout 1934, Italy was stationing soldiers, arms, and aircraft in its African colonies of Eritrea and Italian Somaliland (now Somalia), both of which bordered on the independent country of Ethiopia.

As a nation, Ethiopia predates the Bible. Landlocked by its neighbors Eritrea, Djibouti, and Somalia, it's a tropical place of mountains, rivers, and lowlands; its population speaks over one hundred languages. In 1934, Ethiopia was the only ancient African nation never to have been colonized by Europeans; an attempted invasion by Italy in the nineteenth century had been beaten back by the proud Ethiopians in a decisive victory at the Battle of Adwa in 1896.

Now, nearly forty years later, it was clear to the entire world that Italy's fascist dictator, Benito Mussolini, was planning another invasion of Ethiopia. The annexation of Ethiopia would enable Italy to unite its African colonies; Mussolini promised Italian citizens, suffering from the effects of the global Great Depression, that Ethiopia's rich resources and arable land would provide them with their "place in the sun." In December 1934, when a standoff between Italians and Ethiopians on disputed ground turned violent, Mussolini was sure to use it as an excuse to strike.

African Americans followed these events with breathless interest. They revered Ethiopia for its status as a free Black nation that had never been colonized. It was governed by the forward-thinking emperor Haile Selassie; in the four years since his coronation, he'd drawn up a constitution, established a parliament, and implemented so many modern programs for health, education, and public works that by 1934 Ethiopia had become a player in the world economy, exporting 25,000 tons of coffee every year. Haile Selassie so impressed the world with his innovation and nobility that he appeared on the cover of *Time* magazine twice—once in 1930 for his coronation, and again in 1936 as the recipient of *Time*'s "Man of the Year."

The fate of this charismatic African world leader and his country—the sole historically independent Black nation left in the world—would soon be bound inextricably with that of the Challenger Air Pilots' Association.

CHAPTER 5

ETHIOPIA, 1935

I am glad to know that they realize that Ethiopia is
fighting not only for herself, but also for Black men
in every part of the world and that Americans,
especially Black Americans, are willing to do
anything to help us to carry on and to win.

—John C. Robinson, January 4, 1936

AFRICA: the second largest continent on Earth, a collection of over fifty
nations, the ancestral lands of Black people everywhere, and, as scientists have discovered, the cradle of all humanity. This land has seen the
rise and fall of ancient kingdoms. But in the modern age, since the first
West Africans were dragged aboard the first slaving vessels, the nations
of Africa have been plundered by white Europeans. Colonized,
stripped of their wealth in gemstones, precious metals, and most precious of all, their people, the nations of Africa were torn apart by the
greed of other countries.

During the late nineteenth century, in a land rush known as the
Scramble for Africa, European nations conquered and divided Africa's
resources between them—so much so that by the end of World War I,
part of which was waged on African soil, there remained only two independent sovereign states in Africa. One of these was Liberia, a nation
established in the nineteenth century by the American Colonization

Society as an African homeland for formerly enslaved peoples from the United States and the Caribbean. The other was a single existing autonomous African nation that could trace its roots back for thousands of years: Ethiopia.

In 1935, as Italy's dictator Benito Mussolini threatened this ancient free Black nation, pitting modern tanks, bomber aircraft, and an arsenal of firepower against Ethiopia's foot soldiers armed with antiquated weaponry—quite literally spears and swords—Black Americans threw their support behind Ethiopia.

Their zeal was deeply inspired by the work, thoughts, and voices of three prominent Black men: Booker T. Washington, W.E.B. Du Bois, and Marcus Garvey.

Booker T. Washington, none other than the founder of Tuskegee Institute, had believed that the best way forward for African Americans was to give in to segregation. By creating their own community within the United States, Washington believed, Black people could support each other without harassment from white people. Washington died in 1915, but in the 1930s his ideas still held sway in some of the Black community.

His theory, however, was countered by the sociologist and historian William Edward Burghardt (W.E.B.) Du Bois, who, unlike Washington, had never been enslaved. Du Bois was born and raised in Massachusetts in a free Black family and was the founder of the National Association for the Advancement of Colored People (NAACP). He became the leading twentieth-century proponent of Pan-Africanism, the idea that people of African descent should unify and join their cultural forces. He argued that Black people in America, led by a small group of well-educated people like himself, which he called the

"Talented Tenth," should demand equal rights. Du Bois wanted this top 10 percent of African American society to lead the way into "a higher civilization," giving Black people power over their own lives.

Influenced by both Washington and Du Bois, Marcus Garvey offered a third path, one of uplift and complete separation. Garvey believed Black people should not only live apart from white people, but should leave America entirely. Garvey also promoted Black excellence and Black pride—messages that reached many people, though his extremism was frowned upon by Du Bois and other leaders.

Born Marcus Mosiah Garvey, Jr., in Jamaica in 1887, Garvey traveled and worked in Latin America as a young man before moving to London in the United Kingdom to go to college. When he returned to Jamaica in 1914, he founded the Universal Negro Improvement Association and African Communities League (UNIA-ACL); one of their most striking goals was to build a Black-governed nation in Africa, along the lines of Liberia, where African Americans could make a new home. Garvey found his most receptive audience for this "Back to Africa" movement in the Black neighborhood of Harlem, New York, where by 1919 he lived and had amassed around two million followers.

The Italian threat to Ethiopia was outrageous to all those who were trying to find a way forward for Black Americans. The NAACP, the Urban League (another organization devoted to achieving social equality for African Americans), Garvey, and newspapers around the country urged American support for Ethiopia. So did supporters of the Pan-African movement. In the spring of 1935, emotional feeling for Ethiopia ran so high that when a pair of Black student pilots who'd just received their pilot's licenses at New York's Roosevelt Field told reporters they were interested in commercial aviation and *not* in fighting against Mussolini's troops in Africa, they received a flood of abusive letters from angry Americans.

Indeed, Americans of all races were outraged by the actions of Italy's leader, and many white Americans were just as eager to volunteer to fight for the Ethiopian cause. "Italy would be whipped in short order if the American Negroes and American whites who wish to get to Ethiopia and take a shot at [Mussolini's] legions could obtain transportation and weapons to fight with," was the opinion of Robert L. Ephraim, who'd worked as an organizer for Marcus Garvey.

Ethiopia welcomed this support from the outside world. Emperor Haile Selassie needed a stronger military—and he wanted an air force.

=====

Ethiopia's forward-thinking head of state loved the idea of aviation.

Born in 1892, Ras, or lord, Tafari Makonnen ruled for several years as Ethiopia's Prince Regent before he was crowned Emperor Haile Selassie in 1930, it being a tradition dating to at least the fourteenth century for Ethiopian monarchs to take new official names when they ascended the throne. A small man but exquisitely regal, with high cheekbones, dark eyebrows, and a full beard, Haile Selassie wanted very much to modernize Ethiopia. His vision was to create the first Black air force in history.

Even before he became the emperor, he embraced the importance of aviation and recognized its military significance. Smitten with the idea of flight after watching a British Royal Air Force display in Aden in the south of Yemen in 1922, he convinced those pilots to give him a ride in one of their biplanes, becoming the first Ethiopian to take to the skies. As early as 1929, Ethiopia proudly issued postage stamps picturing their aircraft.

One of Haile Selassie's first acts as emperor was to start looking for a Black pilot to lead his air force and train young Ethiopians to fly. So in 1930, he enlisted the services of Hubert Fauntleroy Julian, the flashy showman pilot who called himself the Black Eagle of Harlem and who'd apparently burst into tears at Bessie Coleman's graveside when he turned up five hours late for her memorial service.

One of Julian's earlier uncompleted stunts had been a widely publicized attempt to be the first solo flyer to make a trip from New York to Ethiopia. The transatlantic flight went underfunded, but what little money Julian did raise left him open to accusations of fraud if he did not go through with it. So on July 4, 1924, in a seaplane dubbed *Ethiopia I*, Julian lifted off into the sky. The flight ended five minutes after takeoff, when his rickety plane lost one of the pontoons that allowed it to land on water, causing the plane to crash into the bay near Flushing, New York. Fortunately for Julian, the attempt was enough to clear him of legal worries. And it had an added benefit—the connection to Ethiopia led Hubert Julian's name to come to the attention of the then Prince Regent.

Six years later, in 1930, Julian was approached by a representative of Ras Tafari Makonnen. The Prince Regent was soon to be crowned as emperor, and he wanted the Ethiopian Air Force to perform at his coronation. His tiny air force of only three planes was then managed by France, whose colony in French Somaliland shared a border with Ethiopia. The Prince Regent wanted very much to have a Black pilot at the controls of one of these planes as his reign began. Would Julian be willing to perform?

Given how scarce money was during the Great Depression, it's no surprise that Julian jumped at the chance to be the honored guest of African royalty.

But his jump was even bigger than expected. While participating in a flyover in one of the planes flown by a French pilot, Julian parachuted out to land at the feet of the soon-to-be emperor. The daring move so delighted the Prince Regent that he bestowed Ethiopian citizenship on Julian and made him a colonel of the Imperial Ethiopian Air Force.

Unfortunately, though Julian's parachute stunts could be impressive, he often overestimated his own piloting skills. During the rehearsal for Haile Selassie's coronation, in an attempt to make an impression—but without permission—Julian took off in the emperor's brand-new private plane, a gleaming white de Havilland Gipsy Moth biplane that had been a personal gift from an upscale London department store. Almost immediately, Julian crashed the plane spectacularly, landing in a eucalyptus tree.

He'd made an impression, all right, as an incompetent pilot and an alleged thief. Julian was ejected from the country in disgrace.

By 1935, five years had passed since this unfortunate incident, and Haile Selassie had built up a small fleet of about ten aircraft as the core of his infant air force. His instructors were still mostly French, though, and the Ethiopian emperor longed to be able to give native Ethiopians their flight training from Black instructors. As Italy threatened invasion, he was again looking for a Black pilot to lead his air force—this time, one who could be relied on to lead men into battle. Fortunately, Hubert Julian was no longer so unusual in being a Black flyer with a pilot's license.

"Look, here's Hubert Julian went to Ethiopia and messed up," said Johnny. "Maybe they can use our experience over there."

Coffey still didn't have a pilot's license of his own, but he was a licensed mechanic, and Johnny was qualified to fly.

Their credentials had to be in shining order for Haile Selassie to take a risk on another American aviator, but it was worth a try. In 1935, Black aviators across the United States felt ready to rush to Ethiopia's aid. In New York, a group of licensed pilots volunteered to form a squadron. Eight of them posed for a propaganda photograph, standing at attention and dressed smartly in matching uniforms, flight helmets, and goggles. One of the group, a young woman named Lola Jackson, said that she intended to form a women's corps of flying nurses. They began to explore their travel options.

The Challenger pilots, like the New York pilots, knew they had skills they could offer in Ethiopia's hour of need. They started to make plans for a small number of their group to travel to Ethiopia to come to the emperor's aid. Feeling that Johnny was their most experienced and talented representative in the air, the Challengers agreed that he should go on his own to clear the way for the rest of them.

"I am going to try to get jobs for some American Negroes of proven ability," he vowed. "I told my fellow pilots [in Chicago] that I would do everything I could to get them in the air force."

Coffey made some arrangements of his own. "I sold my garage in Detroit, brought my airplane and car and tools to Chicago," he said. "I was to pick up the group of the most advanced students so that when [Johnny] gave the word, we could meet him in Ethiopia."

This plan wasn't without risk even at home on American soil, as a group of twelve white American aviators discovered when they announced their own intention to fight for Ethiopia against Italy. "We are willing to fight for an ideal," said Major Granville Pollock, one of their number, who'd flown and fought in World War I. But a national radio commentator named Boake Carter deplored the idea of Americans fighting for Ethiopia, and demanded that the United States government revoke the citizenship of these men—and of anyone else who wanted to go fight in a foreign country.

Since the end of World War I, there had been widespread national anxiety in the United States about getting involved in another war on foreign soil. In the summer of 1935, government leaders were pushing a law through Congress that would guarantee the U.S.A.'s neutrality, forbidding the export of arms and ammunition to warring foreign nations, requiring American arms manufacturers to hold export licenses, and warning people who entered foreign war zones that they were traveling at their own risk.

Were the Challengers willing to risk losing their American citizenship to fight for their ideals?

———

There was another hitch in the plan to send Johnny to Ethiopia.

Tuskegee Institute was slowly continuing to build an interest in aviation. When the Tuskegee General Alumni Association met in Chicago for their annual convention in August 1934, one of their discussion topics had been "the establishment of a course in aviation at Tuskegee." Johnny had participated with enthusiasm, giving a speech about "Opportunities in the Field of Aviation."

Early in 1935 came a change in leadership at Tuskegee itself, as President Moton retired, and Frederick Douglass Patterson, who'd been the director of the School of Agriculture when Johnny met with him in 1934, took over. Rather than launch an aviation program right away, under President Patterson the institute decided to offer courses in aviation through its existing School of Mechanical Industries.

They decided that Johnny Robinson should teach those courses.

In the spring of 1935, George L. Washington, the head of the School of Mechanical Industries, made an informal offer to Johnny to become part of Tuskegee's faculty.

Johnny was hugely tempted. But a different Tuskegee connection was tugging at him at the same time—one that was about to attract the attention of the Ethiopian emperor.

Claude A. Barnett was a Chicago-based journalist who, like Johnny, was a graduate of Tuskegee Institute, and who, as the *Encyclopedia of Chicago* puts it, was "deeply influenced by the self-help/service-to-the-race philosophy of Tuskegee's founder, Booker T. Washington." Barnett had founded the Associated Negro Press (ANP) in Chicago in 1919. Like the Associated Press of white newspapers, the ANP created a network of Black newspapers and journals across the United States, allowing them to share stories, photographs, comics, opinion pieces, and, most importantly, connections. It provided a united outlet for Black voices in the fight for equal rights in the United States.

In January 1935, Johnny spoke about the Ethiopian situation at a meeting sponsored by the Associated Negro Press in Chicago. Barnett heard him speak, and suggested Johnny get in touch with a young man he knew, Malaku E. Bayen, a medical student at Howard University in Washington, D.C., and a cousin of Emperor Haile Selassie. Barnett made the introductions, and Johnny let Malaku know he'd like to fly in Ethiopia.

Malaku did a bit of checking up on Johnny's reputation, including an assurance from Barnett that Johnny held a valid Department of

Commerce pilot's license, which he did. Eventually, Malaku Bayen mentioned Johnny to Haile Selassie himself, and in April 1935, Johnny received a telegram from Ethiopia offering him a one-year commission in the emperor's armed forces. He was the only Black American flyer actually invited to Ethiopia.

With the coveted offer in front of him, Johnny had a big decision to make—and not just his citizenship was at stake. Now Johnny had to choose between teaching the aviation program at Tuskegee, which he'd worked so hard to promote, or fighting for Ethiopia's freedom.

Johnny had never been to war. He hadn't even had any formal military training. Ethiopia was absolutely the unknown, thousands of miles from home, with a complex official language, Amharic, that he couldn't find classes for the way Bessie Coleman had done with French before she'd gone to France.

But the invitation from the charismatic Ethiopian leader Haile Selassie must have felt like destiny, and the opportunity of a lifetime. Johnny simply couldn't resist. Johnny Robinson, that kite-flying shoeshine boy from Gulfport, Mississippi, would be stepping onto the world stage in style.

He asked George L. Washington to postpone his placement at Tuskegee for a year, and started making travel arrangements. Johnny got a passport, key for international travel—Malaku Bayen probably pulled strings to hasten the process—and wrapped up his teaching job at Aeronautical University. Earnize Tate would take care of the garage that Johnny still operated, and Coffey would stand in for him as president of the Challenger Air Pilots' Association.

Johnny left Chicago by rail on May 2, 1935, making his way to New York City, where he boarded a ship bound for Europe. He'd broken his arm just before leaving Chicago, possibly while cranking the propeller of a plane to get it started (always a tricky and dangerous business), which added the inconvenience of a cast to contend with during the trip. Johnny sailed for nearly a month before arriving at the port of Djibouti in the colony of French Somaliland. From the Red Sea coast, Ethiopia and its highland capital of Addis Ababa was still a three-day train ride away across hot, empty wilderness and mountains.

Along the way, Johnny had his first meeting with the Ethiopian emperor.

At Dire Dawa, one of the dusty stops during the railway journey, Johnny was informally presented to Haile Selassie. The visit was unofficial and unexpected, and must have come as a real surprise to Johnny. Johnny appears to have been awed by the occasion. He bowed to the emperor and was led away again without anyone saying a word. It must have seemed a strange start to his career in the Imperial Ethiopian Air Force.

=====

Addis Ababa, established as a city by one of Haile Selassie's imperial predecessors in 1886 and declared Ethiopia's capital in 1889, was and is a bustling and complex mix of traditional huts and brand-new government buildings, poverty and wealth, the ancient and the modern mingling side by side. Johnny arrived there on May 29, 1935. His arm was still healing, causing him quite a bit of discomfort; the broken arm also meant he wouldn't actually be able to do any flying for the first couple of months in his new home. Instead, he set about getting the lay of the land.

"I arrived here last [Wednesday] and found things much different than I expected," he told Claude Barnett in a letter. "In some cases much better and in other cases 100 percent [worse]."

Johnny found Ethiopia to be so different from the U.S. that it was overwhelming. He struggled with the heat, and was shocked by the medieval level of contradictory poverty and pageantry he saw all around him.

"I can really see for an American Negro to succeed here he must possess the following qualifications—First a strong Stomach—A Silent tongue—A Kind Heart,—An Iron hand—The Patience of [Job], and above all things Know his line of work," he observed.

Johnny felt that "the white 'civilized' nations" were purposefully doing everything within their power to keep modern weapons out of the hands of the Ethiopians and other Africans so they could take advantage of that lack of military strength. He also felt that white Europeans and white Americans in Addis Ababa, who lived alongside the Ethiopians without the restrictions of American laws and prejudices, were influencing Ethiopians and making them hostile toward Black Americans. Before Johnny left the States, his Ethiopian supporter Malaku Bayen had warned him not to talk publicly about his involvement with Haile Selassie's military. Malaku also cautioned Barnett not to publish any news of Johnny's intentions before he'd arrived safely in Ethiopia, to avoid any unexpected administrative delays to his travel.

"Robinson has slipped quietly into the country," a staff member of Barnett's wrote to E.G. Roberts, one of George L. Washington's colleagues in the School of Mechanical Industries at Tuskegee. "He is to be attached to the Ethiopian air corps. But it has been wise not to let that be known. He is registered as a mechanic. The Ethiopian government paid his transportation and will pay him a salary."

Although Johnny's arm kept him from flying for the time being, as an experienced teacher and mechanic, he was able to give ground school instruction to the emperor's young student aviators right away. A dozen Frenchmen made up the expert members of the emperor's air force, in addition to about thirty Ethiopians who'd mostly been trained in England and France. Johnny had to rely on the French pilots to help translate his English into Amharic, the language of the Ethiopian student pilots. Wary of his own reception in the emperor's air force, and anxious not to be associated with Hubert Julian, Johnny cautiously told people he met in civilian life that he was a tailor, and that he'd been born in Ethiopia and was returning for the first time after twenty-five years.

It wasn't until three weeks after Johnny came to Addis Ababa that he finally had a real interview with Haile Selassie.

It was over nearly as quickly as the first one back in Dire Dawa during the rail journey to Addis Ababa, with Johnny just as much in awe as he'd been then. The emperor asked him how he liked the work he was doing, and Johnny answered politely that he liked it, adding virtuously that he'd like any work he did if it helped Ethiopia.

When the emperor pressed him to elaborate, even smooth-talking Johnny Robinson couldn't think of anything else to say, and another awkward meeting came to an end.

═══

While Johnny entered the whirlwind of impending war in Ethiopia, life continued for the Challenger pilots without him. Coffey, with his

quieter personality, lacked Johnny's flair; but he'd always been a charismatic leader in his own right, and the Challengers were glad to have
him back.

One of the Challengers' first big events after Johnny left for Ethiopia was to continue the annual tradition of a ceremonial Memorial
Day flight over Bessie Coleman's grave. But this time there wasn't just
one plane involved in the flyover—there were five.

"This year the club boasts of five ships owned and operated by pilots from Harlem Airport," the *Baltimore Afro-American* reported. The
count likely included Johnny's Command-Aire, Grover's Buhl Pup, a
Travel Air owned by a successful dentist named Earl Renfroe, Coffey's
Great Lakes, and Janet's plane, flown by Nash.

Coffey led the Memorial Day flight to Lincoln Cemetery, taking
off through haze and drizzle from Harlem Airport. Dale White, Earl
Renfroe, Grover Nash, and another pilot named William MacFar-
land all flew in formation behind him. Once there, the five planes
circled over hundreds of people gathered below, and scattered flowers over the grave sites of Bessie Coleman and wartime veterans.
Beside Queen Bess's grave, Willa Brown gave a speech that celebrated
the deeds of both Johnny and Coffey, describing how together they'd
broken down barriers at Curtiss-Wright, and commending their
deep commitment to encouraging other Black people to take to the
skies.

The ceremony must have been particularly poignant, as the expec-
tation was that the Challenger pilots circling overhead would soon be
joining the ranks of Ethiopia's air force.

Willa Brown was mentioned in several newspapers in connection
with the Bessie Coleman flyover. Now, as chair of the Challengers'

A formal portrait of the Challenger Air Pilots' Association members who were involved in the Bessie Coleman flyover in May 1935. Cornelius Coffey is far left in the middle row, Dale White far right. In front of them, second and third from left, are Willa Brown and Janet Harmon Waterford.

KENNETH SPENCER RESEARCH LIBRARY, UNIVERSITY OF KANSAS

education committee, one of her roles was to establish an aviation club for younger teens and children—"junior birdmen," as the *Chicago Defender* dubbed them, who would "study the principles of flying, make model planes and make weekly trips to the Municipal airport and listen to the talks of outstanding air pilots." Willa was also working on her Master Mechanic's Course certificate at Aeronautical University, which she appears to have completed by December 1935. In Johnny's absence, she'd been taking flying lessons with Fred Schumacher, the white Harlem Airport manager. She was issued a student pilot's license on March 6, 1935.

The number of women who were involved with the Challenger

club was one of the things that made the organization and their activities interesting and attractive to people.

"Negro women are proving again their ability to meet the people of any other race in skill and technical knowledge," Lillian Johnson commented with enthusiasm. She wrote a weekly series called "The Feminine Viewpoint" for the Norfolk, Virginia, *New Journal and Guide*; soon she'd work for the *Baltimore Afro-American* as the world's first Black female sportswriter. Johnson showcased the Challenger women in her story "Women in the Air" in May 1935, pointing out that both Willa and another young Black woman, Lola Jones, were enrolled at Aeronautical University and taking flying lessons. Lillian also mentioned Billie Renfroe, who flew from Harlem Airport in her husband Earl's plane.

Janet Harmon Waterford, too, was inspiring the younger generation to get in the air. Though busy with her nursing work, in April and May of 1935, Janet churned out a series of articles for the *Chicago Defender*, all designed to make young people aware of aviation. Her stories covered a range of subjects including the history of flight, different engine types, and, ominously, the influence of war on aviation development. Janet would soon set about organizing the Chicago Girls' Flight Club for air-minded young Black women in the Chicago area, drumming up sponsorship and hoping to raise enough money to buy a club plane.

With her limitless energy and big heart, Janet also seems to have spent some time during the summer of 1935 caring for her sister, who moved in with her while recovering from a serious illness. These responsibilities may well have kept Janet from signing up with the other Challengers preparing to make the journey to join Johnny in Ethiopia.

Johnny, meanwhile, in addition to adjusting to his new home, was getting his first serious taste of what it was like to be a press correspondent. Right from the beginning of his journey to Ethiopia, he sent regular letters to Claude Barnett giving his frank impressions, along with his permission for the ANP to quote him. Johnny's stories would be published under the pseudonym "Wilson James." This seems to have been Barnett's idea. "Wilson James's" articles were really nothing more than Barnett and other ANP correspondents crafting reports almost verbatim from the personal letters that Johnny addressed to them, which he signed as "Official Foreign Associated Negro Press Reporter." The experiences he described were clearly far more difficult and frustrating than he'd bargained for.

In July 1935, as a result of Barnett's mostly unfiltered transcriptions, Johnny's always opinionated and often provocative stories began to appear in Black newspapers across the United States. Tuskegee Institute took in the news of his Ethiopian adventures with admiration, and proudly talked about his association with Tuskegee in their campus newspaper. The press, both Black and white, including the *New York Times*, romantically began to refer to Johnny as "the Brown Condor." The name was partly in homage to the Black heavyweight boxing champion Joe Louis, known as the Brown Bomber, and partly, perhaps, to keep Johnny clearly disassociated from Hubert Julian, the self-proclaimed Black Eagle of Harlem.

Despite being thrown out of Ethiopia in disgrace, Julian returned to Ethiopia in the summer of 1935. He, too, wanted to offer his services to help this African nation fight against Italy. Wary this time of Julian's aviation ability, Haile Selassie gave him a commission as a foot soldier, not as a pilot.

Though they were both aviators fighting for the same cause, there was no love between Julian and Johnny. Julian had once visited the Challengers in Chicago to try to get them to finance one of his exploits—which they'd refused, "because of his reputation," as Harold Hurd put it.

Julian and Johnny crossed paths within a week of Johnny's arrival in Ethiopia, and when Julian tried to talk to him, Johnny warily told him he "had never seen him before and never heard of him in America."

Needless to say, Julian wasn't impressed by the Brown Condor.

He also bitterly resented the fact that Johnny had quickly become so highly placed in the Imperial Ethiopian Air Force. By August 1935, Johnny had been given the rank of colonel and put in charge of the emperor's small air fleet, ranking higher than the experienced Frenchmen. Now when Johnny wrote home to Claude Barnett, it was on fancy Imperial Ethiopian Air Force stationery bearing Johnny's full name beneath Ethiopia's symbolic crowned Lion of Judah. Julian tried to save face by going so far as to tell people that he'd actually sent for Johnny himself, to help train Ethiopian pilots.

Johnny certainly didn't help to improve their relations when he listed his grievances against Julian in a letter to Barnett. "I wish you would write some articles concerning these things because [Hubert Julian] is going to run a racket when he comes back to America saying he is employed to get people to bring back here, it will be a racket for him to raise more money," Johnny warned. He called Julian a liar who beat his servants and didn't pay his debts.

Barnett published this exposé under Johnny's pen name, Wilson James. It was like setting a match to a short fuse.

On August 8, 1935, Julian confronted Johnny in the lobby of the Majestic, Johnny's hotel in Addis Ababa. Julian shoved copies of the Wilson James stories from the *Pittsburgh Courier* and the *New York Amsterdam News* in Johnny's face.

"You, you dirty so-and-so, you did this," he snarled—and took a swing at Johnny.

The two men went at it, exchanging blows in front of everyone in the hotel lobby.

Johnny emerged as the winner in more ways than one.

Hubert Julian, once again in disgrace, was transferred to a remote area four hundred miles away, where he was assigned, as the *New York Times* put it, to "drilling native recruits." He left Ethiopia a few months later.

The reports describing the encounter all painted Johnny in an extremely favorable light, making it hard not to wonder if "Wilson James" was responsible for the "special dispatches" that provided *that* information to the ANP as well.

———

Johnny was undoubtedly a good mechanic and instructor, and capable in a fistfight, but he had no experience or training whatsoever as a fighter pilot, or with war.

At its height, Haile Selassie's Imperial Ethiopian Air Force had about twenty planes. None of them were warplanes, or any kind of match for the new Italian fighters and bombers they would be facing if Italy's invasion came to pass. In 1935, Haile Selassie could count on about fifty pilots at best, most of them with little flight experience. So as the head of Ethiopia's air force, Johnny wouldn't be a combat pilot but a courier, flying messages, Red Cross supplies, and sometimes the emperor himself, across distant stretches of difficult terrain between Ethiopia's cities.

Once his arm healed, Johnny spent his first weeks of flying in Ethiopia memorizing the mountainous landscape and landmarks until he knew the rugged, empty terrain like the back of his hand.

"There were no war maps, no plans, but Col. Robinson learned the country," said historian and journalist Joel Augustus Rogers, who worked for the ANP at the time as a war correspondent in Addis Ababa. Jamaican by birth and naturalized as an American citizen, Rogers was the correspondent who'd covered Haile Selassie's coronation, and he soon had good reason to appreciate Johnny's navigation skills when Johnny took him for a flight over Ethiopia's towering mountain ranges.

"There are no towns and the Ethiopian huts blend into the landscape," Johnny warned Rogers as they flew. "There are only the mountains and from up here they all look alike. One must learn his way as if he were traveling through a jungle."

Toward the end of September, Johnny was flying patrols to the border of the Italian colony of Eritrea, where Italy's forces were gathering. His aircraft was a slow, outdated French Potez biplane that he didn't much like. But he also didn't have much choice.

"Everyone here is of the opinion that war will start about the middle or the last of [October]," Johnny reported. "If we have to face the Italians in our present planes, airworthy though they are, it will be no less than murder." He added, "We have planes capable of flying and flying well . . . but they are of ancient vintage and as slow as snails in comparison with modern Italian planes."

By the time his report was printed in the American newspapers, this disparity had borne bitter fruit. Italian troops and warplanes had already swooped down from Eritrea into northern Ethiopia.

On a courier mission with messages to deliver, Johnny arrived in the Ethiopian town of Adwa on Wednesday, October 2, 1935, and spent the night at the Swedish Red Cross hospital there. And at daybreak on Thursday, October 3, Italy invaded Ethiopia.

Adwa was the site of Ethiopia's historic victory over the Italian army not quite forty years earlier in 1896, when Italy had attempted to colonize the country during the Scramble for Africa. Now Italy retaliated for that humiliation in full force. Four large Italian planes flew over the town and started to drop bombs.

Johnny was one of thousands caught unaware in the sleeping city. Awoken by the noise, he stumbled out of bed and ran to check on his plane—without it, he'd be stranded hundreds of miles north of Addis Ababa. In the streets, people clutching their belongings were running toward the hospital, seeking shelter.

"They were mistaken about being safe [there]," Johnny reported bitterly. "The bombing was indiscriminate and it also was inaccurate. I saw a squad of soldiers standing in the street dumbfounded, looking at the airplanes. They had their swords raised in their hands."

By October 6, 1935, Italy would conquer the town. The image of Ethiopian soldiers attacking modern Italian armaments with their traditional weaponry of swords and spears would become a symbol of the devastating war that was to follow.

"I will never forget that day, and the day after," Johnny wrote to Barnett. "I really had the closest call I ever had in my life (and I have really had some narrow escapes in my lifetime)."

Johnny couldn't take off from Adwa while bombs were exploding all around him. He spent the day struggling to keep his outmoded Potez biplane under cover so that it wouldn't become a target. When at last he was able to take off, he had no idea how many people had been killed in the raid—estimates were in the region of fifteen hundred. Johnny set out for Addis Ababa to bring news of the destruction directly back to Haile Selassie.

On his way, he ran into even fiercer trouble—his first real taste of aviation warfare.

As Johnny flew south over the unforgiving mountainous terrain of the Ethiopian highlands, two modern Italian fighter aircraft roared down on him, fiercely firing their guns.

Johnny had a machine gun mounted on the Potez. But the plane was so much slower than the Italian fighters that he couldn't possibly outgun them—any shot he lined up they could evade almost before the bullets left his gun.

His only hope was to outmaneuver them.

Now Johnny's flight experience and his familiarity with the harsh Ethiopian landscape came to his rescue. He guided the Potez to twist and turn in the air, dodging the Italian planes. Using what he knew of aerobatics, he pulled out all the tricks in his barnstorming book. He dove down low so that his plane was camouflaged against the ground. Finally, he managed to get ahead of his pursuers—but they were joined by others.

Dodging and weaving, rising and diving, desperately adjusting the flight controls and struggling to fly as fast as he could without overheating the Potez's engine, Johnny was chased by six enemy fighter planes almost the entire way back to Addis Ababa.

At last he managed to lose them. Still in one piece and, perhaps more importantly, still carrying the documents and information to be delivered to the emperor, Johnny was finally able to land on the airfield at Akaki outside Ethiopia's capital city.

No doubt sweating and breathing hard, Johnny got out and checked his plane for damage. "One part of the wing ... had ten holes in it," he later wrote to Claude Barnett.

It was the first time Johnny had a narrow escape from Italian fighter aircraft, but it would not be the last.

———

The outbreak of war in Ethiopia was outrageous to many Americans. Johnny's account of Italy's attack on Adwa even featured in *Time* magazine's coverage of the conflict on October 14, 1935. Haile Selassie tried to take advantage of this international sympathy, pleading with Europe and America for donations of modern medical equipment, medicine, and volunteer doctors and nurses, as well as airplanes and pilots who could provide an ambulance service to and from the front lines.

"Every red-blooded Negro who is anxious to help Ethiopia in her struggle against imperialistic rapacity and international gangsterism now has his or her opportunity to do something specific and concrete," the *Pittsburgh Courier* declared, exhorting readers to donate to the cause.

H. Murray Jacoby, who'd been the United States ambassador to Ethiopia, scrambled to work with the American Red Cross and arrange transportation of ambulances and supplies. In Chicago, at a conference promoting Ethiopia's independence, a thousand Black and white supporters together decided to name their fundraising effort the John Robinson Defense Fund for Ethiopia.

Under imperial authority, Johnny tried to order six new planes for the emperor's small fleet, intending for them to be used by the Challenger team when they arrived. But the U.S. wouldn't sell him the planes. With the first U.S. Neutrality Act in place since August 31, 1935, to be renewed in February 1936, it was illegal for any American manufacturer to sell planes to a country at war. Ethiopia—and the Challengers—would have to find another way.

====

In November 1935, Johnny was again involved in an aerial duel. This time, he was returning from a special mission for the emperor when he was attacked in the air by three Italian Caproni bomber aircraft. He managed to take a shot at one of them, but he knew his small reconnaissance craft was no match for the huge warplanes.

"He was able to escape only by sensational handling of his craft," reported Joel Rogers, the ANP correspondent from Addis Ababa. Johnny was lucky enough to be able to fly into clouds where his aircraft couldn't be seen. "The invaders were twice in position to bomb him," Rogers wrote, "but he got away both times."

The incident made it clearer than ever that the Imperial Ethiopian Air Force needed new planes. Since the U.S. wouldn't help, Johnny tried to change his tactics. He put in an order to the United Kingdom for six British aircraft. To his dismay, the British manufacturer insisted that the planes be flown and serviced in Ethiopia by British pilots and mechanics, and it didn't look like that support would get there any-time soon. Though he didn't like the deal, Johnny accepted it. The planes were too important to lose to pride.

Now that Johnny had seen active combat, together with the hope-lessness of the situation, he seems to have had second thoughts about getting the other Challenger aviators out to Ethiopia. No other Black American aviators had made it there; Johnny was seriously sobered by what he saw going on, and maybe even frightened. He'd seen firsthand how antiquated and inadequate the Ethiopian weapons were. He tried to discourage the other Challenger pilots from joining him.

"I shall stay here and deliver everything there is in me, but there is no reason for you to go down to death with me," he told them. "It will be better for you to remain in America and carry on the good work which we have begun in interesting our people in aviation."

Oddly, when Johnny's own warnings appeared to work, he felt be-trayed. Apparently having had a change of heart, he went out of his way to try to get the Ethiopian government to issue visas and to cover the cost of transportation for the Challenger pilots whom Coffey had chosen to make the trip. But when he sent Coffey a fast and expensive message by telegram saying he was ready to cable the money for six of them to come to Ethiopia, and asking for an immediate reply, Johnny was met with silence.

"Every one [of the Challenger group] have failed me so far, which means the last time I will ever ask [t]he Emperor permission to send for [anyone] else . . . [T]he boys there [in Chicago] can't say they [didn't] get a chance because the door was thrown wide open to them and they failed to walk in," Johnny commented sourly.

His bitterness at the silence from his friends might have been un-derstandable, but it was also unfair. The contradictory nature of his messages aside, his own letters sometimes took two months to get back to the U.S.A. He'd mailed a letter to Earnize in June—it arrived in August. Telegrams depended on a series of people relaying messages, and the Ethiopian infrastructure, as Johnny knew perfectly well, was extremely unreliable. His message may have been delayed, or the Challengers' response may have been delayed, or their response may have come after Johnny had already expressed his frustration to them.

Though Johnny didn't realize it, back home in Chicago, the Challenger pilots were anxious to join him. Coffey had applied for and received his student pilot's license in October. Photographs of Willa, "all togged out in aviator's togs, looking quite nifty," as Barnett put it, appeared in newspapers under the headline "Wants To Fight Italian Bombers," with a proud caption stating that Willa was "ready to answer the call to Ethiopia." Both Willa and Coffey had visited Barnett to make plans for the trip. All the pilots picked by Coffey had applied for passports.

But the U.S. government was dragging its feet on issuing those vital documents. Since Johnny had arrived in Ethiopia, the first of what would eventually become three Neutrality Acts had been established. Though Claude Barnett pulled what strings he could, the Challengers were essentially being held hostage by federal government politics. In the race for control over Ethiopia, the Italian army moved much faster than the U.S. bureaucracy.

"I came within six months of a trip to Ethiopia myself," Coffey later wrote, "but Italy invaded Ethiopia and the trip had to be canceled. I often think about how close I came to making that trip. But God had other plans for me."

CHAPTER 6

THE AIRWAYS PART, 1936-1937

We'll sing Ethiopia, proud of her blood—
All Afro-Americans, one brotherhood.

> —Rev. William Lloyd Imes,
> "We'll Sing Ethiopia," 1936

"PLEASE let Mr. Washington at Tuskegee know . . . that if I be able to live through this little war, I would still like to get my job at Tuskegee," Johnny wrote to Barnett in November 1935.

Johnny had definitely *not* "renounced his American citizenship to fight for Ethiopia," despite the rumors appearing in some American newspapers. He was planning to come back to the States when his year-long commitment in Ethiopia finished in May 1936. And he was still hoping that when it was over, his next career move would be teaching aviation at Tuskegee Institute.

"Don't be afraid about the job at Tuskegee," Barnett assured Johnny. "When I was there in October at Dr. Patterson's inauguration, Mr. Washington told me that your job was safe whenever you returned. However, I am writing him today and sending him your message."

That was on New Year's Eve, 1935. In the middle of January 1936, Barnett went to Tuskegee again and mentioned Johnny's potential job to Dr. Patterson in person. Patterson replied that there was no need for

Johnny to worry, that "he was interested in pushing the department" whenever Johnny got there.

With his formidable media clout, Barnett also worked actively to persuade Dr. Patterson of the benefits of an aviation program at Tuskegee. Ideally, the program would also hold special appeal for young people born in Africa, to prepare them for scientific and engineering work on the African continent. Barnett was aware that the Ethiopian emperor was eager to replace qualified white Europeans in his government and industries with qualified Black Americans. He pointed out to Dr. Patterson that William Powell's flight school in Los Angeles— formerly the Bessie Coleman Aero Club, and now called the Craftsmen of Black Wings—had seventy-five students enrolled; the school apparently had some government funding, enabling students to receive free flight training. "It occurred to me that you might get some aid of that sort to start a similar school at Tuskegee," Barnett encouraged.

Tuskegee was enthusiastic, and willing to wait for Johnny to come home from the war.

===

Johnny was in the thick of it now. As 1936 began, he was acting as the emperor's personal pilot, flying Haile Selassie over the long stretches of rugged mountainous terrain to the warfront in the newest and fastest plane of the Ethiopian fleet, a Beechcraft Staggerwing. Reaching speeds of 175 miles per hour, the Staggerwing was the only aircraft in service in the Imperial Air Force that could outrun Italian fighter planes. Adorned with the red, gold, and green national colors of Ethiopia, it was also recognizably the emperor's aircraft. That meant Johnny was a target.

The Italian forces in Ethiopia had not counted on the unforgiving mountains and the huge distances between cities across the landscape. Nor had they expected the desperately fierce resistance of the Ethiopian foot soldiers, who didn't hesitate to attack tanks with their spears. It took Mussolini's troops longer to push into Ethiopia's capital city, Addis Ababa, than they had hoped. But with a change of leadership in the Italian high command, their bomber aircraft began using poison gas against the Ethiopians. A form of chemical warfare dating to World War I, the gas was so damaging that it had been internationally banned. The Italians were using it in defiance of that ban, and in combination with their other modern weapons. Ultimately, the Ethiopians didn't stand a chance. And neither did Johnny.

As he sped through the skies between the front lines and Addis Ababa, Johnny endured three attacks with poison gas. Eventually he was injured by gunfire as well.

In April 1936, when it became inevitable that the Italians would march into the capital, people began evacuating the city. Johnny rightly guessed that the conflict would extend into a lengthy battle of occupation and guerrilla warfare. With the rainy season coming on and the Ethiopian government preparing to go into exile, there was very little a single American pilot could do to help. It was time for Johnny to go home.

Anticipating Johnny's return, the Challenger pilots ran a series of articles in the *Chicago Defender*, telling the story of Johnny's life and his battle to overcome racial prejudice and become a pilot. Janet wrote the essays herself, and they appeared on a weekly basis beginning on April 4, 1936. These enthusiastic pieces covered a range of topics, starting with Bessie Coleman's story and moving on to Johnny's, using his presence in Chicago as a way to describe the Challengers' history. Janet whipped up a frenzy of interest for Johnny's homecoming, and for the cause of Black aviation, by singing Johnny's praises for fascinated readers. Up until nearly the last possible second, the *Defender* made dramatic claims that Johnny was leading an attack for a special bomber squadron on a mission to destroy the Italian invaders. But that never happened.

On May 1, 1936, Johnny Robinson fled the besieged country. The next day, Emperor Haile Selassie himself departed on the last train out of Addis Ababa. The emperor would spend the next five years in exile in the United Kingdom. Though guerrilla resistance from the Ethiopians and Italy's lack of an organized colonization program doomed Italian rule of the country to fail, Mussolini's troops would occupy Ethiopia until 1941, when World War II would give the British an excuse to go to war with Italy and to assist the Ethiopians in taking back control of their nation.

As the Ethiopian emperor escaped to England, Johnny headed home to America.

By the time he had made the slow journey up the Red Sea and the Suez Canal, across the Mediterranean Sea, and overland from the French port of Marseille to Paris, he was out of money.

"I got a cable from Johnny telling me he was stranded in Paris," Coffey recalled.

Johnny asked Coffey to sell his Command-Aire airplane for the funds, but Coffey had a better idea.

"I had already had a group of fellows that wanted to buy my Great Lakes, and I knew it wasn't going to be too hard to sell it," Coffey said. "The three hundred dollars I got for that airplane, I sent to Johnny to come home on."

"Mrs. John C. Robinson, wife of the Chicago aviator . . . said last week that she was overjoyed to learn that her husband is returning home," ran a story about the elusive Earnize in the *Baltimore Afro-American*. "Although her husband taught her to fly a plane when they were first married, Mrs. Robinson is not fond of the air. Until recently, she managed the colonel's garage here, during his absence."

Another report, this one in Kansas City's *The Plaindealer*, commented that "[w]hile she has shrunk from the limelight during the Colonel's stay in Ethiopia, she has been in constant touch with him by cable and letter and has followed with keen interest his every move."

Indeed, Claude Barnett had been checking in with Earnize through-out Johnny's absence, usually by telephone, and knew that she was being very careful about what she said to the press. She confided to Barnett that Johnny had written to her on his way home. They were both excited about the idea of Johnny teaching at Tuskegee.

This fact somehow slipped to the press. The story about Earnize in the *Baltimore Afro-American* speculated that Johnny "may become an instructor in aviation at Tuskegee Institute, a plan he was considering before going to Ethiopia." Other newspapers, including the *New York Times*, announced with confidence that Johnny was going to be teaching aviation at Tuskegee in the fall.

Claude Barnett knew that Johnny's homecoming would make an incredible news story—and that it would reflect well on their shared alma mater. In May 1936, he contacted Tuskegee's president, Dr. Patterson, again, this time to arrange a publicity campaign and to make sure that Johnny's position there was still open. Dr. Patterson assured him that it was.

Barnett was working tirelessly to get press coverage for both Johnny and Tuskegee, not just in Black newspapers across the continent but also in white ones. The *New York Times* gave Johnny brief but regular mentions, and the *Waukegan News-Sun* in Wisconsin boasted that Johnny had once been a "local" flyer at Lake County Airways. Black newspapers jockeyed for exclusive coverage of Johnny's exploits. Now the *New York Amsterdam News*, along with the Associated Negro Press, the African Patriotic League, and other organizations, worked with Barnett on planning a welcome-home celebration.

"Robinson is not spectacular," Barnett warned Dr. Patterson. "What I fear is that as his wife fears, he will slip into the country without any announcement and proceed about his business."

To make the most of Johnny's arrival, Barnett helped arrange a huge press reception to meet Johnny when his return ship docked in New York; there would also be a banquet in his honor.

On Monday, May 18, 1936, Johnny arrived back in New York on the German steamship *Europa*. He was met with more fanfare than he could have ever imagined. The ship flew the flag of Hitler's government, an ominous black swastika against a blood-red background, a stark and ironic contrast to what the *Philadelphia Tribune* described as a freedom-loving "small forest" of American Stars and Stripes and the red, gold, and green tricolor of Ethiopian flags being waved by an excited crowd of hundreds of people who'd gathered at the docks to welcome Johnny home.

David W. Kellum of the *Chicago Defender* managed to get aboard Johnny's ship before it docked by hitching a ride on a Coast Guard cutter. He was able to get an exclusive interview and photographs with Johnny even before customs and immigration officials fast-tracked him off the ship. Johnny looked smart and official on arrival, wearing

*John C. Robinson
aboard the SS* Europa
*on his return from
Ethiopia in May 1936*

U.S. NATIONAL PARK
SERVICE

a leather flying jacket emblazoned with the emblem of Ethiopia's proudly crowned, high-stepping "Conquering Lion of Judah," over a sweater with a red, gold, and green winged lion's head, also wearing a crown, representing the Imperial Air Force. Johnny had grown a beard while he was in Ethiopia, a neat goatee, in an effort to fit in. "Everybody there has a beard," he told reporters. "Before I grew a beard they thought I was a boy. I'm going to keep it if my wife will let me."

But the beard and the impressive clothes could not hide the effects of his injuries. The poison gas had left him with breathing difficulties that would trouble him for months; Johnny mentioned that he thought he might need hospitalization. Percival Prattis of the *Pittsburgh Courier* commented to Claude Barnett, "Johnny looked like he had been used up. I almost felt like crying for him I was so struck by his appearance and the indications of what he had been through."

The moment Johnny set foot on American soil again, women sobbed and struggled to get close enough to kiss him, and a group of men carried him on their shoulders to the car in the motorcade that Claude Barnett had waiting. An air show was held in Johnny's honor at Roosevelt Airport; Lola Jackson, the only Black woman aviator on the East Coast, escorted him among a crowd of twelve hundred spectators. *Five thousand* people welcomed him home at the public reception held at the Harlem YMCA—a famous site in African American culture, at the heart of the burgeoning Harlem Renaissance. The event was hosted by a fundraising group called United Aid for Ethiopia, emceed by their treasurer, Dr. P.H.M. Savory. Joel Rogers, the ANP reporter who'd flown with Johnny in Ethiopia, was also there as a speaker, as well as Claude Barnett. But the crowd only had eyes for Johnny.

When he arrived, they cheered him for a solid quarter of an hour; whenever his name was mentioned they let out a roar. Johnny made a heartfelt plea to the crowd for aid to Ethiopia, urging doctors and nurses to join its fight for freedom.

He was the toast of New York—but that was nothing compared to the welcome he would receive in Chicago.

———

It was here that Willa Brown proved herself to be a force of nature. With her background in business administration, her newfound interest in aviation, and her flair for the dramatic, she and the Challenger pilots turned Johnny's homecoming into a hero's welcome such as the city had never seen.

"When he took the ocean liner to New York, we also arranged and scrapped up enough money so that he could fly from New York to Chicago," Coffey said. "We figured that by having him do that, then we could have a parade from Midway Airport—was Municipal Airport then—to the South Side."

So on Sunday, May 24, 1936, Johnny flew home from New York as a passenger on a TWA Douglas airliner, with Barnett as his companion. Instead of the typical "back of the bus" treatment most Black travelers received on commercial flights, Johnny and Barnett were treated like celebrities. The pretty young white flight attendant, Adela Jenkins, paraded among the fourteen other passengers so she could show them the silver trophy presented to Johnny at the reception in New York. The white pilots even insisted Johnny take a seat up front so he could watch them chasing higher altitudes around storms over Pennsylvania.

And then they approached Chicago.

Vera B. Slaughter, a reporter for the *Chicago Defender*, described the crowd's excitement as the TWA flight arrived overhead at Chicago's Municipal Airport. "Heads swing upwards! In the distance a tiny speck that looks like a sparrow, appears on the horizon. It grows and becomes a giant eagle, and finally as it slips closer in view it shows itself to be the giant twin-motored plane bringing the 'Brown Condor' home."

Three thousand people of all races had turned out to greet the returning hero. Among them, Cornelius Coffey, Willa Brown, Janet

Harmon Waterford, and the other Challenger pilots were ready and waiting to welcome Johnny home. The crowd roared as the plane came into view; people waiting in cars leaned on their horns and let out a cacophony of honking.

Challenger club member Earl Renfroe, whose wife, Billie, was also an aviation enthusiast, had just received a limited commercial license from the U.S. Department of Commerce. Renfroe flew over from Harlem Airport, probably in his Travel Air, so that he could join formation with the airliner like a military escort as the big TWA Douglas approached.

When the Douglas finally landed and Johnny emerged, Willa and Janet were there to greet him. They posed with Johnny on the airstair at the door of the plane, along with the flight attendant Adela Jenkins, everyone's arms full of peonies.

Congressmen, members of the Chicago Tuskegee Club, and the Illinois National Guard were all waiting to give him another welcome. Robert S. Abbott, the *Chicago Defender* publisher who'd sponsored Bessie Coleman fifteen years earlier, was also part of the reception committee.

"This daring young man . . . taught us greater respect for our race," Abbott told reporters. "We must fight for our rights, not crawl on our bellies."

After forty-five minutes of interviews, photos, newsreels, more flowers, and more women trying to kiss him, Johnny was whisked off the airfield in a brand-new open-topped Lincoln automobile draped with flags. It drove up Michigan Boulevard accompanied by fifty policemen, a motorcycle escort, and five hundred cars in a procession that was two miles long. When Johnny's Lincoln reached its destination at the

Johnny Robinson arrives in Chicago in May 1936 after his year in Ethiopia. With him on the airstair are (left to right) Mayor of Bronzeville W. T. Brown, Janet Harmon Waterford, flight attendant Adela Jenkins, and Willa Brown.

THE TUSKEGEE UNIVERSITY ARCHIVES, TUSKEGEE UNIVERSITY

Grand Hotel on South Parkway, a marching band of First World War veterans escorted him inside. Traffic was closed off for two blocks around the hotel as Johnny stood on a flag-draped balcony, expected to give a speech to a frenzied audience of about eight thousand people (some estimates were as high as twenty thousand).

Even after the welcome he'd had in New York, Johnny was stunned by Chicago's wild excitement at his return.

"I'm simply overwhelmed," he told the crowd.

He spoke of his disappointment in the way the war had ended. He bitterly criticized the international community and the League of Nations, an international organization established after World War I to try to maintain global peace, for their failure to give Ethiopia any assistance in its time of need.

A range of dignitaries and aviators also gave speeches, including both Willa and Janet. By the end of the day, Johnny was already taking bookings to give speeches in Philadelphia, Washington, and Kansas City about his adventures in Ethiopia, and more requests were pouring in.

Where was Earnize in this melee of activity and excitement? There's no trace of her relationship with Johnny after his arrival back in Chicago. Census records and a much later news story connected with her brother indicate that she probably continued to live in Chicago, as a divorced single woman under her maiden name—but nothing is mentioned about her former husband. And she isn't mentioned once among the hundreds of friends and officials who welcomed Johnny home.

===

Whether or not his wife was in the picture, Johnny's first couple of days back in Chicago were completely full. He gave a speech at a local high school and attended another banquet hosted by the Challenger group to raise awareness of aviation in the community, as well as some much-needed funds for their cause.

"Now Willa Brown, she had arranged for the catering service, and it was a very swanky eat shop, Morris's Eat Shop on 47th and King Drive," Coffey remembered. "He agreed to cater the outfit and get his money out of the profit that we would make. We not only paid for the food and the hall, we had six hundred and eighty-some dollars left to put down on this Taylor Cub." The Cub was a workhorse of a plane that Coffey put to good use out at Harlem Airport, and the Challengers' profit was ably managed by a new young Black pilot acting as their treasurer, Charles Johnson.

Meanwhile, Claude Barnett, with the assistance of the United Aid for Ethiopia group, helped Johnny to set up the John C. Robinson Aviation Fund so that he could buy a new plane for his own use.

In June, soon after Johnny's return, Dr. Patterson and George L. Washington drew up an agreement for employing Johnny and establishing an aviation course at Tuskegee, including plans for an airfield there. Tuskegee did not own an airplane, but if Johnny had one, they were excited about the prospects of him adding flight instruction to his ground school aviation program. Johnny visited Tuskegee in July, addressing a crowd of five hundred summer school students, and Dr. Patterson announced that Tuskegee's aeronautics course was being planned for the following year, with Robinson in charge.

At this point, Johnny either got tired of being micromanaged, or possibly his ego got the better of him. The Challenger Air Pilots' Association had been holding more banquets and rallies in Chicago to raise the funds to buy him a new plane; he was traveling all over the country, being greeted with brass bands and meeting local mayors, while accompanied by police escorts everywhere he went. He had even been honored with the key to the city of Cleveland, Ohio, and gave speeches about his adventures to both white and Black audiences. It must have been a heady experience, a far cry from his initial hopes of being a mere schoolteacher in a small southern college.

Johnny complained to Barnett that he wasn't satisfied with how his affairs were being handled at Tuskegee, saying that he had more experience in the air than the people who were doing the planning. He wanted control over the funds that had been raised in his name—more specifically, he really wanted to buy a new airplane, and he didn't want to have to wait for it. Bold newspaper headlines suggesting "Tuskegee May Buy Plane for Robinson" probably didn't help matters. Johnny insisted that he wanted to handle his own affairs from now on.

This meant not signing the agreement with Tuskegee. Johnny felt they weren't showing enough confidence in him, and they weren't fully committed to the new aviation program. Incredibly, he didn't just want a program—he wanted Tuskegee to establish a separate "J.C. Robinson School of Aviation," and he wanted to have complete control not only of its management, but also of its income. It's possible his hopes had been raised, and no doubt his ego inflated, by the suggestion of Clarence Wilson, an assistant federal attorney in New York, that a monument to Johnny's "heroic deeds" in Ethiopia should be set up in his name, and even by Claude Barnett's own proposal of a John Robinson flying school.

Johnny's demands proved to be a mistake. He badly overestimated the amount of clout he had with Tuskegee Institute. Washington very diplomatically responded that they could not change their plan to suit his, though Johnny was still welcome to join them on the terms that they'd originally offered.

But Johnny was convinced that he had the name and the knowledge to run his own aviation school. Instead of taking up the offer at Tuskegee, he decided to open his own school in Chicago—called, unsurprisingly, the John C. Robinson National Air College and School of

Automotive Engineering. With Willa in charge of his paperwork, Johnny would rely on his contacts in the city to help equip himself in style.

Mrs. Annie Malone, one of the guests at Johnny's welcome banquet in Chicago, had been a neighbor of Johnny's before he went to Ethiopia. Malone had built an African American beauty empire in St. Louis, Missouri, starting with a "Wonderful Hair Grower" product in 1900; in 1930, she'd moved her operation to Chicago, where she opened Poro College, a school for cosmetology with its main office at 4401 South Parkway in Chicago. A wealthy philanthropist who poured her fortune into uplifting her race, Malone saw another good cause in supporting African American aviation. She offered Johnny the use of a coach house behind Poro College, where he'd be able to hold classes for his new school.

Annie Malone and Johnny were so friendly that he appears to have stayed with her when he first returned to Chicago. He was her guest from the day of his arrival home, and used her address as the place where he could be contacted for lecture requests, later listing her address as his home address for his pilot's license. Annie Malone was nearly forty years older than Johnny, so it seems unlikely they were romantically involved; but it's possible that Earnize got fed up with living in Mrs. Malone's shadow, which may be why Johnny and Earnize went their separate ways at this time.

Johnny set up shop in the coach house behind Poro College, and proudly announced the opening of his new aviation school in September 1936. He promised a glittering array of mechanical and aviation courses, with practical flight instruction "under the supervision of a government-approved instructor using new, standard [airplane] equipment owned and operated by the Air College." Ambitiously, Johnny also announced that "[e]very student will be required to study French or Spanish, with the view of preparing for international commercial flying," though it's not clear if he intended to provide this instruction through his program or if the students would have to find their own language classes. Johnny told his friend Joel Rogers, the ANP reporter who'd been in Addis Ababa with him the year before, that he had twenty students, of whom fifteen were white, and that he was ready for them with a new training aircraft. Cornelius Coffey was listed on his faculty.

The John C. Robinson National Air College and School of Automotive Engineering officially opened its doors on Monday, September 28, 1936, at the Poro College location, with flying lessons to be held at Harlem Airport. The new students threw Johnny a surprise launch party, giving speeches and presenting him with baskets of flowers.

"This has been my whole life's dream to build a school," Johnny told them in gratitude.

The school received additional support from Coffey and the other Challenger pilots—with Coffey now teaching some night classes there.

But it seems Johnny may have regretted striking out on his own. In November 1936, he wrote to Tuskegee again, offering to move his entire school to Tuskegee if they'd agree to pay the transportation costs. Not surprisingly, Tuskegee's president, Dr. Patterson, rejected the offer.

━━━

The winter of 1937 was a difficult one for the states bordering the Mississippi River. Heavy rains in January and February forced the mighty river to overflow its banks, causing intense flooding to devastate communities in a dozen states. The American Red Cross called the Flood of 1937 the greatest disaster on record, outside of World War I. Many of the flood's victims were farmers and sharecroppers, and many of them were African American.

The *Chicago Defender* hired Johnny to fly down to Mississippi and Tennessee on a relief mission, touring in a new Curtiss Robin C owned by the *Defender*, a four-seater high-winged monoplane with a Challenger engine. When Johnny returned from the mission, he purchased the Robin from the *Defender* outright with the money he received from them for making the tour.

The new plane ran into trouble on the trip south, and Johnny had to land for emergency repairs in Dwight, Illinois. Once again, he called on Coffey for help, and his old friend drove down to make repairs

Johnny Robinson's Curtiss Robin at Harlem Airport. Johnny used this plane for flood relief in 1937, then purchased it from the Chicago Defender.

KENNETH SPENCER RESEARCH LIBRARY, UNIVERSITY OF KANSAS

behind the scenes, while the newspapers sang Johnny's praises for the good deeds he was doing.

Cornelius Coffey was never a man to hold a grudge, or to resent helping out a friend or colleague. He also wasn't one to waste time waiting for fortune to come to him. He'd spent the past year building hours of flight time toward the commercial pilot's license that would allow him to instruct students in the air. The full commercial license required both written and practical exams, plus a minimum of two hundred flying hours—an expensive proposition. But Coffey was good at finding solutions—and he was a mechanical genius. He even invented and patented a way to heat an aircraft's carburetor so that ice forming in the engine's air intake wouldn't block the engine; a similar system is still used in aviation today. These same mechanical skills would provide the solution for building his flying hours.

The north end of Harlem Airport was off-limits to Black pilots—but not to Black mechanics. The all-white OX-5 Club kept two planes, a Taylor Cub and a Lincoln-Page, in the hangar there, and they needed a mechanic.

"They said to me, 'If you keep these airplanes up, you can get all the flying you want,'" Coffey recalled. "At that time, I needed flying, because I'm trying to get that two hundred hours or better." Burning someone else's fuel in someone else's plane was definitely a cheap way to build flying hours. Ever the cautious fellow, Coffey overprepared. "If I went up there with a bare two hundred hours, I'd be turned down," he surmised. "I went to three hundred. And I went right on through without any problems."

By 1937, the commercial license was his. By "right on through," he may have meant that he even skipped the step of taking a private pilot's license on the way—existing records seem to jump straight from Coffey holding a student license to him being a commercial pilot.

While Coffey had been racking up his flight hours, one young white man named Charles Ecker had been anxiously awaiting the results, because he wanted to be Coffey's first student.

"When you get your transport license, I'll take off," he kept saying.

On the day Coffey took his final test for the commercial license, Ecker was waiting at the airfield to find out how he'd done.

"Did you get it?" he asked.

"Yes I did," said Coffey.

"I'm ready to take the lesson." The young man had asked his boss for fifteen minutes off so that Coffey could fly him as his first student.

In a wonderful reversal of Coffey's first flight with the barnstormer who thought he could scare a young Black kid out of the sky, Coffey

Cornelius Coffey, 1939

KENNETH SPENCER RESEARCH LIBRARY, UNIVERSITY OF KANSAS

took up a young white man and promised to teach him to fly—a small triumph over the racism that the Challengers had been fighting against for so long.

======

In July, Johnny entertained Annie Malone and her staff on a special Poro College aviation outing. Malone and forty-five of her employees spent a day at Harlem Airport, and Johnny took fifteen of them flying in turns before Malone herself was convinced it was safe to go up.

Johnny knew a good opportunity when he saw one, and soon he had convinced Malone to invest further in aviation. To keep up with her nationwide business, she bought Johnny a Stinson Reliant. These were typically single-engine high-wing planes of varying configurations—some could carry up to five passengers.

"I never questioned Johnny too much," Coffey said, "but I believe he sold Mrs. Malone on the idea of purchasing a private airplane so anytime she decided to make a trip—and as you remember, she had branches in St. Louis and Kansas City and around—he agreed to fly her on those trips."

Although, likely inspired by Coffey, Johnny had applied for a commercial license in 1937, he still hadn't passed the test. Technically, he could only carry passengers or teach students if he wasn't doing it for pay. But, unlike Coffey, Johnny never let the rules get in his way.

Now he hatched a scheme for a barnstorming tour of the South, flying from place to place, giving rides to spectators, and sharing his adventures with excited audiences. And since Coffey had his commercial license under his belt, Johnny proposed a joint tour. He would do the lecturing if Coffey would do the flying.

Coffey recruited one of his students, Jimmy Rainer, to come along for crowd control. "You know, people get so excited and all, they run into the airplane," Coffey said.

As they went from airfield to airfield, while Johnny was busy giving his talks about Ethiopia, Coffey would sit in the plane with the engine running and eat his lunch. The plane had to be started by hand-cranking the propeller, which was dangerous and took strength and skill. Coffey could do it himself, but sometimes it was easier just to keep the engine going while he waited. It was just the sort of back seat he was used to taking with Johnny. But far from being in the Brown Condor's shadow, Coffey was also having adventures of his own.

Coffey tells one story of a flight he made to Meridian, Mississippi, where he ran into trouble with his plane's oil pressure. He had to make what's called a "dead stick" or forced landing without power. When he landed, the Black airport attendant, a Mr. Crawford, was stunned to see that Coffey was Black, too. Mississippi's Jim Crow laws made it almost impossible for Black men to get into the air; Crawford loaded mail and freight, gassed up planes, and took care of the airfield, but he certainly wasn't a pilot. And now here was a Black flyer right in front of him.

"I'm going to have to repair this engine," Coffey said.

"You meant to say you gonna fix it?" Mr. Crawford asked in surprise.

Coffey went to work, and soon a crowd gathered.

"These white folks say, 'Where'd you come from?'" Mr. Crawford told him. "They never seen nobody like you."

The crowd would shout, "Hey, call the junkman! You'll never get that back together," as over several days they watched Coffey dismantle the plane to make repairs. "Boy, you ain't got enough knowledge to put that together. Where did you get your experience?"

"Chicago," Coffey would reply patiently.

The good folks of Meridian didn't trust this uppity Chicagoan. They chased off any other Black people who dared watch him at work, for fear they'd get uppity ideas, too.

But Coffey didn't let it get to him. Four days later, with the plane repaired, he offered to give Crawford a ride. The man politely declined. But he'd learned more about the mechanical aspect of aviation in those four days than in all the rest of his time in Meridian.

=====

Chicago was now leading the rest of America in sheer numbers of Black aviators. By the fall of 1937, a count of qualifying students and licensed pilots put Chicago ahead of both Los Angeles and New York. And out of twenty-six pilots in the area registered with licenses or student licenses, five of them were women. The Challenger Air Pilots' Association had really lifted off at Harlem Airport, even with Johnny in Ethiopia, and now it was thriving. Coffey was a capable leader, and Willa Brown was an inspired second-in-command.

Willa's skills as a secretary kept her in a number of day jobs, first working for the Chicago Social Security Board, then as a lab technician and a private secretary to Dr. Julian H. Lewis, who was an associate professor of pathology at the University of Chicago and a supporter of aid to Ethiopia. In September 1937, she enrolled in a business administration program at Northwestern University, taking courses in economics that she hoped would lead to a master's degree. But aviation was quickly becoming the focus of Willa's life.

Now, in addition to working, flying, and studying, Willa began a food service at Harlem Airport. When the pilots hanging out there got hungry, she started serving them hot dogs through the clubhouse window, and ended up operating a concession known as Brown's Luncheonette—also known as just the Clubhouse. Willa's younger brother Simeon, who was living in Chicago now and also taking flying lessons, handled the cooking. He had come to Chicago after high school in Indiana, looking for work like so many others during the Great Depression in the 1930s, and helped out at the airfield—including slinging hamburgers. Cheerful and well-liked by everyone, Simeon later confessed, "I spent about ten years of my life hanging around Harlem Airport."

Under Fred Schumacher's tutelage, Willa had soloed for the first time in June 1936. When Coffey earned his commercial license, he'd taken over most of her flight training. The Taylor Cub purchased with the money made from Johnny's welcome-home banquet after his return from Ethiopia was just the sort of workhorse plane the group needed so they could earn money giving lessons; Willa

The Taylor Cub purchased by the Challenger Air Pilots' Association with the money raised to welcome Johnny Robinson home from Ethiopia

KENNETH SPENCER RESEARCH LIBRARY, UNIVERSITY OF KANSAS

probably flew most of her solo hours toward her pilot's license in this plane.

"We put it into service, and we was charging six dollars an hour, dual, four dollars an hour[,] solo, and we made money," Coffey recalled.

The workhorse was proving itself to be a moneymaker, but it would also deal the final blow to Johnny and Coffey's friendship.

Banking on Johnny's fame, the Challengers had raised enough money to make a down payment of $668 on the Taylor Cub, with another $1,000 to be paid over the course of a year. According to Coffey, they had purchased the plane in Johnny's name, with the understanding that it would be put in both of their names once it was paid off. After all, Coffey had sold his Great Lakes to pay for Johnny's journey home from Paris.

But the joint ownership papers never materialized. When Coffey questioned Johnny, "he couldn't explain it, so I said, 'Well, if that's the way it's going to be, we just dissolve our association.'"

=====

An airplane falls from the sky.

Perhaps there is an explosion, a shower of flaming debris. Or a catastrophic disintegration. A collision. A silent fall. Witnesses run for help and notify authorities. Rescuers scramble through the wreckage to rescue survivors—or to retrieve the dead.

Since it was founded in 1967, the National Transportation Safety Board (NTSB) has been responsible for investigating crashes. A designated "Go Team" is immediately sent to the location of the crash, and the site is treated much like a crime scene. The first piece of evidence they hunt for is the so-called "black box" containing the flight data recorder and an audio recording from the plane's cockpit. These allow them to understand what was happening with the airplane, and to hear the conversations that took place between the pilot and copilot in the cockpit while the last moments of the flight were unfolding.

A lot of things can go wrong when flying. The Federal Aviation Administration lists the "ten most frequent causes for general aviation accidents involving pilot error" as:

1. Inadequate preflight preparation and/or planning.
2. Failure to obtain and/or maintain flying speed.
3. Failure to maintain direction control.
4. Improper level off.
5. Failure to see and avoid objects or obstructions.
6. Mismanagement of fuel.
7. Improper inflight decisions or planning.
8. Misjudgment of distance and speed.
9. Selection of unsuitable terrain.
10. Improper operation of flight controls.

After these causes, alertness and "giving way"—making room for other planes in the sky—are additional pitfalls.

Unfortunately, flight recorders didn't exist until 1953. And they have never existed for friendships. So, there is no recording of the fallout and aftermath of the Coffey/Robinson crash. Working together, the two friends had been soaring to greater and greater heights. It's hard to know whether their collaboration lacked adequate preparation, lost speed, or simply ran out of gas. In the end, failure to "give way" was a likely factor. Both men had grown in parallel, and it was time to spread their wings. But they could not do that in the same patch of sky.

There is little to indicate the moment of the break in the public record. Johnny's name simply disappears from Challenger documents. Coffey's name reemerges as he opens his own school down the line. Some researchers speculate on a love triangle between Coffey, Johnny, and Willa Brown. Whether or not these speculations are true, it's undeniable that the two men had grown apart. Johnny seems to have felt betrayed and alone in Ethiopia. Coffey appears to have felt unfairly treated in their partnership in the States. Years later, Coffey still referred to Johnny as his friend, but time and tide had softened the rift.

In 1937, it remained sharp and contentious.

The two men would take off again, but never in the same direction.

Clockwise from top left: Janet, Willa, Coffey, and Johnny, together at Midway Airport, Chicago, May 24, 1936

CHICAGO HISTORY MUSEUM, ICHi-021506

CHAPTER 7

THE *DEFENDER* FLYERS, 1938

Lift every voice and sing
Till earth and heaven ring,
Ring with the harmonies of Liberty;
Let our rejoicing rise
High as the listening skies . . .

—James Weldon Johnson,
"Lift Every Voice and Sing," 1900

CORNELIUS Coffey and John Robinson had gone their separate ways, but the legacy of their partnership, the men and women of the Challenger Air Pilots' Association, were soaring from height to height in their achievements.

The past couple of years had firmly established Coffey as the group's capable leader. While Johnny struck out on his own, in 1938 Coffey was finally able to begin his air transport business, the Coffey Flying Service. He invested in a yellow-and-red J-3 Piper Cub plane, an update on the Taylor Cub, apparently sharing its cost with a fellow by the name of Eddie Cyplis, who delivered groceries for Schumacher's grocery store.

Coffey wasn't the only one gaining ground for the Challengers. Around this time Janet Harmon Waterford also bought "a brand-new Piper Cub in the traditional yellow, with a bear cub depicted on the

Cornelius Coffey with a Piper Cub, likely around the time he started the Coffey Flying Service

KENNETH SPENCER RESEARCH LIBRARY, UNIVERSITY OF KANSAS

tail. It was a cabin plane, a three-place aircraft with dual controls," she recalled. "It had a two-way radio, which was something special at the time." Harold Hurd and Grover Nash were the only others she trusted to fly it. In fact, in May of 1938, Grover Nash became the first Black pilot to fly for the U.S. Mail service, as Janet proudly reported in the *Chicago Defender*. Of the 146 pilots selected for this trial run, only Nash was Black. He told reporters that "nowhere did anyone seem to notice his color"—he said he was welcomed everywhere he landed. Domestic air mail was a completely new innovation at the time, and it seemed incredible to people that their mail could arrive so quickly between small towns in the large state of Illinois.

Of course, Nash also flew in that year's annual Memorial Day flyover of Bessie Coleman's grave at Lincoln Cemetery, along with Earl Renfroe, Dale White, and the unstoppable Cornelius Coffey.

Although no women were involved in the Memorial Day flyover that year, by this time there were plenty of young Challenger women able to take wing, too. The Chicago Girls' Flight Club organized by Janet in 1936 could boast that all their members, including Willa and Janet, were flyers with official student licenses, all of them Black, and all of them taking off daily at Harlem Airport. In the past year, Willa

Flying members of the Chicago Girls' Flight Club at Harlem Airport in 1938. Left to right: club president Lola Jones, Willa Brown, Doris Murphy, Janet Harmon Waterford, and Dolores Jackson

SMITHSONIAN NATIONAL AIR AND SPACE MUSEUM (NASM NASM.1993.0060-M0000015-00020)

herself had spent about ten times as many hours in the air as she'd managed in 1936. Now, with Coffey as her flight instructor, she was qualified to take her private pilot's examinations.

On June 22, 1938, Willa Brown became the first Black woman in America to receive a full U.S. Department of Commerce private pilot's license. She took the written test along with fourteen other hopeful applicants, all white men, and received a score of 96 percent, the highest mark in the group. After she completed the flight test, Willa and Coffey beamed for photographers as he shook her hand in congratulations.

"I shall work next fall toward getting a limited commercial license," Willa told reporters. "That will permit me to take up passengers for pay. And I'm dreaming of the day when I'll be able to own a plane of my own . . . [with] speed to burn. I'll have one some day," she vowed.

Willa had always been in her element managing the Challenger activities at Harlem Airport. Now she had a fantastic new angle for drumming up publicity—her own success. In her inimitable way, she took full advantage of the limelight that her new qualifications offered. Black newspapers all over the country celebrated her achievement, and many of them included dazzling pictures of the petite and lovely young aviatrix. One of these was a full-length shot of Willa in classic aviation gear, including boots and white jodhpurs, a short leather flying jacket, a neat tie, and an airman's helmet with the goggles pushed back. She cut the perfect figure of an accomplished flyer.

Donning this striking aviator's outfit, one day Willa marched unannounced into the editorial office of the *Chicago Defender*. Elegant and dazzling, she looked as if she were about to take off in an air show.

"Pretty Aviatrix Sets Pace" is how newspapers captioned this picture of Willa Brown, triumphant after receiving her pilot's license in 1938

SMITHSONIAN NATIONAL AIR AND SPACE MUSEUM (NASM NASM.1993.0060- M0000018-00060)

When she walked into the room, the clacking of typewriters stopped; the whole place went silent as everyone caught sight of her.

Willa announced firmly that she wanted to talk to Enoch P. Waters, Jr., then the city editor for the *Defender*. Someone pointed him out.

"I'm Willa Brown," she said to Waters, and took a seat without waiting to be invited.

Waters was intrigued, impressed, and charmed. He listened, all ears, as Willa introduced herself as one of the Challenger pilots and told him their history. She explained that she hoped he'd be willing to support the Challengers with publicity in the *Chicago Defender*, the way its founder and publisher Robert S. Abbott had supported Bessie Coleman.

Like Willa, Waters believed in going big or going home. Of course the *Defender* had long been an advocate of Black aviation, but it was an eye-opener to Waters that there was a vibrant and growing local group of men *and* women flyers right there in Chicago. He agreed to come out to visit Harlem Airport and see it for himself. Willa offered him a free flight—a five-dollar value, worth about one hundred dollars in today's money. That sounded like a good deal to Waters.

When they took to the air at Harlem, Willa pulled out all the stops, flying figure eights and flipping the plane. These were the same basic aerobatics skills that student pilots were now taught to get their licenses. Elementary aerobatics helped pilots handle airplanes under all sorts of duress, and of course they helped barnstormers earn money at air shows. They could also be fun—Waters found the experience exhilarating—and a little terrifying.

"I wasn't convinced of her competence until we landed smoothly," he confessed.

But by the end of the day he was hooked on aviation, and committed to providing news coverage for the Challenger pilots' activities.

The timing was perfect, because the Challengers were planning a spectacular event for Black aviators in August, and in addition, the white airfield managers at Harlem Airport were planning a September event that would be the biggest they'd ever held.

The "Mammoth Air-Show" organized by the Challengers, held in Chicago on August 28, 1938, was a thriller. To avoid stealing thunder from the air show being planned by the managers at Harlem Airport

*Poster advertising the
Challenger air show
held August 28, 1938,
at Markham Airfield in
Harvey, Illinois*

SMITHSONIAN
NATIONAL AIR AND
SPACE MUSEUM (NASM
99-15426)

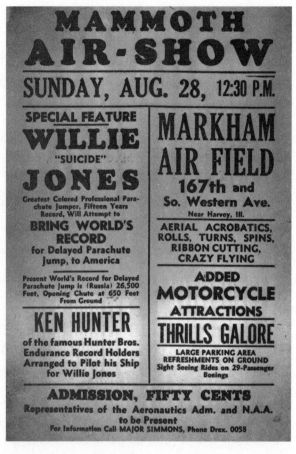

for the following month, they staged the event at Markham Airfield in
Harvey, Illinois (later expanded as Rubinkam Airport), a short hop of
about fifteen miles southeast of Harlem. The main feature of the show
was a parachute jumper known for his death-defying stunts as Willie
"Suicide" Jones. Jones was attempting to break a world record for
height by leaping from 29,400 feet; the previous record had been set
by a Russian two years earlier. Although Jones's achievement wasn't
official (allegedly due to an instrument failure), he ended up smashing
the previous record to smithereens.

In addition to this showstopper, Willa led a parade of twenty planes, all flown by Black aviators, in a stunt flight demonstration. The extravagant aerial displays were watched by an estimated ten thousand spectators, eight thousand of them white. Word was sure to spread: Black people certainly could fly!

And that event was nowhere near the scale of the enormous air show planned by the white managers of Harlem Airport for the last week of September in 1938. Around a hundred flyers from states all over the Midwest were expected to fly to Chicago to participate. Though the competitions were restricted to planes whose engines didn't exceed 40-horsepower, there were to be exhibitions, stunts, planes flying upside down, precision bombing with sacks of flour, women competing against men—all this just for a chance at a trophy, as no cash prizes would be awarded. The *Chicago Defender* declared that the entire show would be free to the public, in the name of encouraging people "to develop interest in flying and to serve as a demonstration for students of aviation."

In another sensational innovation for an American air show, it was one of the first—if not *the* first—to encompass both Black and white flyers. It wasn't unusual for Black and white pilots to work together at Harlem Airport these days, especially once Cornelius Coffey established his flight training there; by September of 1938 he was instructing around thirty-five students to learn to fly, of whom one-third were white. Now the white chairman of the air show contest committee, Robert A. Morrow, invited Coffey and a dozen of the other Black pilots who flew at Harlem to participate in the air show, including two of the women. Willa Brown and Lola Jones planned to compete, along with Cornelius Coffey, Earl Renfroe, Grover Nash, Dale White, Harold Hurd, and several others.

When the big day came, for the first time in history, forty-eight Black and white aviators participated together to entertain a crowd of at least twenty-five thousand spectators, of which three to five thousand were Black. It was probably the largest mixed crowd that had ever turned up to watch an air show.

One of the most thrilling stunts of the show was a parachute race between two student pilots, one of them a white man and the other a dashing young Black flyer named Chauncey Spencer.

Chauncey sported a debonair mustache over a winning smile. And he was working hard to keep himself in the air. Born to a well-off African American family in Lynchburg, Virginia, Chauncey had struggled to find a place for himself down south. "Our family was not poor, but not rich—working people," he would later say. His father and grandfather were businessmen; his mother, Anne Spencer, was a librarian, an educator, and a poet of the Harlem Renaissance. Her connections to the upswell of creativity in arts and literature in Harlem, New York, meant that the Spencer household was a gathering place for some of the great names of the movement. It also meant Chauncey was exposed to a world of possibility.

At the suggestion of a family friend, he headed north to Chicago around 1936, with the express goal of learning to fly. Unfortunately, once he reached the Windy City, that same friend now told him, "Oh, you came at the wrong time. Things are bad now. [The] Depression, you know."

The Great Depression was indeed crushing the nation. To make matters worse, in 1934, an agricultural crisis had blown up in the central United States. The region became known as the Dust Bowl because of drought and a series of devastating windstorms that destroyed much of the farming in the nation's so-called breadbasket. Displaced farmers of all races hit the road looking for work, food, and opportunity—and finding little of anything. It was in this time of need that Chauncey had also hit the road looking for his own opportunities. But he was not to be deterred.

"I went to visit the John Robinson School of Aviation," he recalled—Johnny had just established himself at Poro College. "I sensed something was wrong when I walked into the garage. There were two car engines, an aircraft [propeller], but nothing that resembled an aircraft school. Colonel Robinson seemed eager for my nine hundred dollars that my father had given me to study but, leary of the school, I left."

Dr. Earl Renfroe—a new acquaintance and a well-established member of the Challenger Air Pilots' Association—told Chauncey about Aeronautical University, formerly Johnny and Coffey's old Curtiss-Wright stomping grounds. Chauncey found the administrators there discouraging, but again, he was persistent.

"I finally persuaded the administrator to accept my one hundred dollars in exchange for permission to begin the classes," Chauncey later wrote. "The next day, I had attended classes for only two hours when I was called to the office and was told that it wasn't working out, that the white students in school had objected, and that they threatened to leave school if I returned to any more classes."

Race relations had clearly changed since Johnny and Coffey had stopped teaching there. But fortunately, the folks at Aeronautical University were able to refer Chauncey to the Coffey Flying Service.

"If they would give me instructions, Aeronautical University would give me their seal of approval upon completion of satisfactory work," Chauncey explained. "I was willing to eat the cheap meals at North Shoreline Restaurant and skimp on the money my father sent to me. The important thing was that I was beginning—in more ways than one—to get off the ground."

Chauncey secured a dishwashing job, which over three or four weeks let him scrape together the $25-an-hour flight instruction fee. And that was how Chauncey Spencer earned his wings and came to join the Challengers.

By the time of the 1938 Harlem air show, Chauncey was still only a student pilot, but he was making a name for himself as a daredevil parachute jumper. With his handsome looks and rakish mustache, he earned the nickname "Chauncey 'Clark Gable' Spencer." And like the famous actor Gable, he was a true performer. He loved to get a crowd's attention and sympathy by messing with their minds.

During one jump, Chauncey leapt out of a plane at five thousand feet, allowing himself to fall a thousand feet before opening his chute while the crowd watched below. After floating gently down for another thousand feet, he purposefully let go of the parachute and let it float away between his legs. Even from that height, Chauncey said, "You could hear them say, 'Oh, he definitely is gonna kill himself!'" There he was, plummeting toward the ground unchecked—but Chauncey had a trick up his sleeve. "They didn't know I had a seat parachute underneath me." At only eight hundred feet from the ground, he pulled his second chute, and drifted the last distance to safety. The crowd went wild.

In the Harlem air show, Chauncey competed against a white student pilot, Sidney Ruben, in a parachute race to reach the ground first.

"The pilot took us up ten thousand feet and we bailed out," Chauncey remembered. "It was thrilling to hurl down from the plane at a rate of one hundred fifty feet per second."

As the *Chicago Defender* later reported, "Spectators held their breaths as Spencer hurtled downward, his body describing thin tiny arcs in the course of the fall. It was not until the chute blossomed out above

Spencer barely 1,200 feet from the ground that watchers found their voices and let go with lusty cheers."

Parachutes in the 1930s were nowhere near as steerable as they are today, and the two competing young men both landed so far away from the airfield that no one could tell who reached the ground first— though naturally the *Chicago Defender* awarded the win to Chauncey.

"The crowd loved us all the same," said Chauncey. When he touched down in the backyard of a local residence at 54th Street and Carson Avenue, he was mobbed by a crowd of people who'd seen him coming down and who were so excited about getting his autograph that they nearly tore his clothes off.

The rest of the show was a huge success for the Challenger pilots. The Challengers' treasurer, Charles Johnson, came second in precision

Chauncey "Clark Gable" Spencer after his parachute race at the Harlem Airport air show in September 1938

SMITHSONIAN NATIONAL AIR AND SPACE MUSEUM (NASM 99-15424)

flying. Lola Jones also participated in this competition, later describing her flight tricks: "I did my snap rolls, my slow rolls, and I did my [three hundred and sixty] degree." Willa, Coffey, and Dale White were among those taking part in precision landing, in which the contestants had to land their planes in a tight circle only forty feet across. There were even students participating from Johnny Robinson's flying school.

The show, and the huge promotional splash that the *Defender* gave the Challengers and their participation, was fantastic publicity. Enoch Waters kept on promoting them throughout the rest of the year, running stories about local pilots and celebrating an air performance by Willa and Coffey on Armistice Day, as Veterans Day was then known. Word was spreading about the organization and its accomplishments.

But Waters knew that the Challenger Air Pilots' Association could go even bigger. At his suggestion, they would undergo another transformation—they were going national.

CHAPTER 8

THE MOONSHOT, 1939

We choose to go to the moon in this decade and do the other things, not because they are easy, but because they are hard, because that goal will serve to organize and measure the best of our energies and skills, because that challenge is one that we are willing to accept, one we are unwilling to postpone, and one which we intend to win . . .

—President John F. Kennedy, Address at Rice University on the Nation's Space Effort, Sept. 12, 1962

In 1969, the United States did something impossible. It sent men to the moon. Before that moment, the moon had been the stuff of fairy tales, made of green cheese, inhabited by the Man in the Moon. Early filmmakers and novelists had dreamt of the possibility of setting foot there. Scientists had looked at the distance between Earth and its satellite, and considered the gap untraversable. In fact, the idea of reaching the moon had been so preposterous that the actual achievement became a euphemism for a pie-in-the-sky impossible goal—a moonshot.

And, in 1939, the Challengers needed to achieve a moonshot of their own.

Throughout the second half of the 1930s, under the administration of Franklin D. Roosevelt, the United States had been growing increasingly worried about the possibility of war in Europe. In 1933, the National Socialist German Workers' Party began rising in power in Germany under a new leader named Adolf Hitler. Germany had lost a previous bid for power in World War I, and the National Socialists— or Nazis—were determined to reclaim the nation's standing on the world stage by force, if necessary.

Despite the U.S. federal government's policy of global neutrality, in 1937, the War Department drafted the "Protective Mobilization Plan," which they'd use if the country found itself facing a national emergency, or in other words, an armed conflict.

The new Protective Mobilization Plan guaranteed that Black American men would make up at least 9.5 percent of the mobilized troops—proportional to the population of eligible males in the U.S.— and recommended that this ratio should be maintained across all service units. It was a plan easier to put on paper than to put into practice. The U.S. military was a Jim Crow operation—segregating Black and white soldiers, and usually appointing white commanders for Black regiments. Outside of impressive units like the Harlem Hell-fighters of World War I, Black soldiers were typically given labor roles. As late as 1940, Black Americans only made up approximately 1.5 percent of the Army and 1.5 percent of the Navy, and as one writer put it, "The Marines and the Air Corps were completely off-limits." In the event of the U.S. going to war, the 1937 mobilization plan would suddenly increase the number of Black soldiers nearly tenfold every-where—*except for* in the Army Air Corps. Early in 1938, Black newspapers across the nation seized on this omission and launched a scathing critique of the War Department for its failure to commit to giving Black airmen a chance to serve their country in the sky.

The Challengers believed the sky belonged to everyone, too. But the government had played into a longstanding stereotype, fed by a lack of facts and imagination. Simply put, it did not believe Black people could fly.

Despite all of the evidence, historical and contemporary, to the contrary, hateful racial stereotypes that arose during slavery and the post-Emancipation period known as Reconstruction had deeply ingrained slanderous beliefs about Black people in the minds of white Americans. *Unintelligent, lazy, dirty, cowardly*—all of these words were associated with skin color and the narrative of white supremacy.

During Reconstruction, wealthy southern landowners were worried that poor white farmers might join forces with newly freed African Americans. The fear was that together, poor Black and white farmers would have a collective power greater than the former slaveholders. And so a campaign of difference was begun to keep the two groups separate. No matter how poor a white person might be, the narrative went, it was still better than being a Black person. Sadly, this dehumanizing story became ingrained across the nation. Even in the North, in non-slaveholding states, the stereotypes against African Americans came to hold sway.

In 1925, the United States government commissioned an Army War College report on the suitability of Black people for military service. The paper—based on conjecture and not fact—deemed Black men too cowardly to be trusted as soldiers. These stereotypes were reinforced by unscientific surveys and interviews. The renowned white aviator Charles Lindbergh even wrote impassioned articles specifically against the employment of aviators of color—all despite the fact that Black American soldiers had served with honor and bravery since the American Revolution, and as recently as World War I.

But wherever there is tension, there is a chance for change.

The Roosevelt administration was looking for new ways to stimulate the American aviation industry, just in case war did break out. New pilots couldn't qualify fast enough in the Army Air Corps, with some cadets taking as long as an entire year to complete their training. On September 17, 1938, the federal government authorized funds to initiate a new aviation program that would ramp up pilot training—and, in doing so, ramp up aircraft production by increasing the number of pilots needing planes. The initiative would be called the Civilian Pilot Training Program (CPTP).

The really wonderful thing about the CPTP was that the government was going to pay for it. The training would be administered through high schools, colleges, and universities across America, which would receive federal funding to help supply them with aircraft and instructors. It would make flight training available to lucky young people around the country at very little cost, creating a pool of qualified civilian pilots ready to enlist for wartime flying should the need arise.

Unfortunately, no Black colleges or universities were to be involved in the plan—making it almost impossible for any Black students to be selected for the CPTP. A training prototype was rolled out at thirteen colleges, supported by funds from the National Youth Administration. Three hundred and thirty trainee pilots joined the program; only one African American, a student at the University of Illinois named Roderick Williams, was allowed to participate.

The same exclusionary thinking that infected the War Department's use of Black soldiers had infected the government's decision to keep Black Americans out of the Civilian Pilot Training Program. Those who bothered to make excuses said there would be white people who would object to training side by side with Black Americans. The military believed Black men had their uses—as janitors, waiters, and laborers, always under white supervision. There was no provision in the 1937 mobilization plan for creating Black officers. The military remained segregated; and so, very nearly to the point of complete exclusion, was the planned CPTP.

The Challenger pilots were not alone in realizing that with government support, white Americans would soon be flocking to the skies, and Black Americans would once again be second-class citizens cut out of yet another American dream—unless they did something about it.

Back in 1936, when Claude Barnett had been trying to persuade Tuskegee Institute to open a flight school, he'd sent the Washington correspondent for the Associated Negro Press to rustle up a story on "why colored men are not permitted in the Army Air Corps," even though the Air Corps was actively recruiting white cadets. Now with Nazi Germany threatening war in Europe, and Japan at war with China, patriotism in America was running high. Several important national aviation bills were being pushed through Congress, including the Civilian Pilot Training Act and Public Law 18. The former would establish funding for the CPTP, while the latter would expand the U.S. Air Corps. It seemed there was a new opportunity to change the fortunes of Black pilots.

It was time for the Challenger moonshot.

When Willa Brown had made her daring move at the *Chicago Defender*, she'd been hoping that Enoch Waters could provide the Challenger aviators with a boost in free publicity. But the *Defender*'s advertising manager wasn't so sure "free" made sense to the paper's bottom line. So Waters appealed to the newspaper's publisher, Robert S. Abbott. Abbott had seen what Bessie Coleman's exploits had done for both his paper and for the race as a whole and, ever civic-minded, he agreed with Waters. Promoting Black aviators would be great for public relations.

But Waters took it a step further. He went to Willa and Coffey with a proposal. He felt that the Challenger pilots were perfectly placed to take advantage of the groundswell of media and public outcry against the prejudice underlying the 1937 mobilization plan. He suggested that the Chicago-based pilots establish a *national* association for Black aviators. If they could put together an organization that united Black aviation enthusiasts across the United States, Waters argued, the *Defender* would promote it. That way other newspapers couldn't accuse them of giving free advertising to a few random pilots; instead, they'd be pulling together information about flying events and activities all over the country, and the *Defender* would be able to broadcast their goals and achievements. What better way to educate the public, and the U.S. government, on what Black flyers could do?

Also, a national organization would unite Black pilots all over the United States with a single voice that could urge Congress to get inclusive language inserted in their pending aviation bills. And it would give clout and credibility to their bid for integration in the Air Corps and the Civilian Pilot Training Program.

Waters was the catalyst who brought this organization together and made it work. As Challenger Harold Hurd later stated, it would be the Black press that really gave African American aviation its wings, beginning a campaign of manifest change. "We've got to give Mr. Waters credit," Coffey acknowledged, "because he knew the connections, the *[New York] Amsterdam News*, the *Pittsburgh Courier*, the *Defender*." Also invaluable was the support of Claude Barnett and his international news-gathering service, the Associated Negro Press, with its attendant newspapers.

At the head of the media onslaught, as early as January 1939, the *Pittsburgh Courier* published a splashy photograph of Willa being harnessed up by Coffey before heading skyward to practice tailspins for an advanced flight rating. She was working on getting a limited commercial license of her own. The *Courier* used the photo op to tell readers that "President Roosevelt will name a Negro college as one of the several schools selected to train 20,000 pilots annually" as part of the Civilian Pilot Training Program. There wasn't any guarantee that this would actually happen; it was more of a hoped-for self-fulfilling prophecy. But the Challengers were going for that moonshot, and doing everything they could to ensure that it succeeded. In fact, guessing that Tuskegee might be the lucky institution, Coffey wrote to Tuskegee's President Patterson himself in January 1939, offering his services as an instructor there if the legislation went through.

Less than a month later, Earl Renfroe, the Challenger pilot who at the time, along with Cornelius Coffey, was one of four Black aviators in the country to hold a commercial license, wrote an impassioned editorial for the *Pittsburgh Courier*. "Now is the time for a terrific campaign in Congress and all colored newspapers to see to it that at least one Negro college of good standing is included in the new civilian flying program to be promoted by the Federal Government. We must get busy!" he declared. "Let's start right now to lay the groundwork for our first Negro squadron by getting our share of the appropriations for the President's Civil Aeronautics Program. Will our leaders select a school?"

On Friday, March 17, 1939, a group of pilots including Cornelius Coffey, Willa Brown, Janet Harmon Waterford, Dale White, Chauncey Spencer, Grover Nash, another female Curtiss-Wright student named Marie St. Clair, and Charles Johnson, as well as the non-flying newspaper editor, Enoch Waters, met to set up a board of directors for their new national airmen's organization. They elected officers for their group, with Coffey as their president and Waters officially designated a sponsor.

"The first name that we thought about was going to be the Negro National Airmen's Association of America," explained Chauncey. But under the guidance of Claude Barnett, the organization decided to drop the word "Negro," and with it, any Jim Crow limitations. "We are fighting segregation, why should we discriminate?" Chauncey pointed out.

And so the Challenger Air Pilots' Association now became the National Airmen's Association of America, or NAAA.

In this first official meeting, the NAAA laid the groundwork for planning the first national aviation conference for Black pilots, to be held in Chicago in August that year. Preliminary ideas included an air show, an aviation exhibit, and a gala dance. In the meantime, they'd have to work to reach out to Black flyers and flying clubs around the country to encourage them to participate.

Their meeting couldn't have been timelier. Only one week earlier, the Schwartz Amendment to the Air Corps expansion bill had been passed by the U.S. Senate. Created by and named for white Democratic senator Harry H. Schwartz of Wyoming, the amendment allowed "that at least one colored school shall be lent flying equipment for the training of colored pilots." No school had been selected yet, but the top contenders were Howard and Wilberforce Universities, along with Hampton and Tuskegee Institutes.

It was a huge and exciting victory in an ongoing conflict. In their new roles as members of the National Airmen's Association, Willa, Coffey, Earl Renfroe, and other airmen from the former Challenger group met with Chicago's mayor, Edward J. Kelly, to enlist his support in a bid for this proposed "colored" Air Corps training center to be located in Chicago. Coffey had hopes that the Coffey Flying Service would be selected.

The idea of Chicago as a training center had been suggested by Edgar G. Brown, a civil rights lobbyist and the president of the United Government Employees Union. Edgar Brown had been a fierce advocate for the Schwartz Amendment to the Air Corps bill. Enoch Waters described him as "a tense, stern-visaged man, ready to spring into action against racial discrimination at the slightest provocation. His most distinguishing feature was a Vandyke beard that he stroked from time to time," earning him the nickname "Billy Goat." But to Waters, Brown was "God's angry man."

When President Roosevelt signed the Air Corps bill into law on April 3, 1939, Army Air Corps officials requested that the Schwartz Amendment be changed to remove the specific reference to a "colored school." But still the law clearly stated that Air Corps training given to civilians would be required to include one or more schools "designated by the Civil Aeronautics Authority for the training of any Negro pilot."

Even altered, the Schwartz Amendment made the Air Corps bill something of a triumph for pilots of color. The military was still segregated, but there was hope.

Now that the Air Corps bill had passed into law, there was another battle to fight: the Civilian Pilot Training bill was still making its way through the House of Representatives.

Building on the achievement of the 313 trainees who'd successfully made it through the experimental program, this bill proposed to provide flight instruction for 15,000 civilian pilots between the ages of eighteen and twenty-five in the coming year. "Whether or not colored youths will be accepted for such training has not yet been determined," warned the Norfolk, Virginia, *New Journal and Guide*. "But the policy of the War Department is to exclude them from both the Army Air Corps and its training facilities for mechanics as well as pilots."

For the Coffey Flying Service, another stumbling block was the fact that, if and when the bill passed, the CPTP was going to be run through colleges and universities. Such academic affiliations had the dual benefit of making use of established facilities and also ensuring students had a certain level of education. Without the backing of an academic organization, Willa and Coffey had their work cut out for them. Several schools were putting in applications, and the Chicago aviators of the National Airmen's Association felt they had a right to apply as well, with as good a chance as any at being accepted.

Their secret weapon was "God's angry man," Edgar Brown.

"He being in Washington, every time any bill came up for

consideration, he let us know," Coffey said. "We'd start right away getting together to see what strength that we could advance, and we'd start writing to our congressmen and our senators and whatnot." Coffey also wrote to the governor of Illinois. "We never lost any time trying to get to people that could help us."

Edgar Brown also advised them to send formal petitions to President Roosevelt, the U.S. War Department, and the newly formed Civil Aeronautics Authority (the CAA was the precursor to today's Federal Aviation Administration). Mayor Kelly said he would present the petition to the president himself, insisting that "the training school be interracial so colored students could be assured the same advantages and facilities as whites."

Willa, too, threw body and soul into making noise about the National Airmen's Association of America, with the help of Enoch Waters and his camera crew. One of the NAAA's schemes for raising awareness and showing off the abilities of Black pilots was to host a series of events, including the offer of free flights to prominent Chicago citizens. The unofficial mayor of Bronzeville, Robert H. Miller, got taken for a spin by William Paris, the youngest Black aviator to hold a pilot's license. Willa Brown took Horace B. Cayton, a professor of anthropology at the University of Chicago, for his first ride in an airplane.

Meanwhile, Waters mailed an announcement about the NAAA's formation to a dozen Black newspapers. Willa tirelessly wrote letters to aviators all over the country inviting them to join. She promised that she'd fly to other cities and states in person to help them with promotion and organization for local chapters. Coffey said of Willa, "As an administrator I have never yet seen anybody that was any better. I'll put it that way."

The group was doing everything it could, but would it be enough?

Perhaps not, but for God's angry man. At the insistence of Edgar Brown, publicly representing the National Airmen's Association, Illinois congressman Everett M. Dirksen swooped in with an amendment to the CPTP bill specifically stating that "none of the benefits of training or programs shall be denied on account of race, creed, or color."

It was the change they needed. Despite opposition from the bill's original author, the House passed the amendment.

Now the Civilian Pilot Training bill was about to go to the Senate for a vote. It was crucial for the public to put pressure on the lawmakers in Washington in order to win this battle against racism.

Here, Enoch Waters, as city editor for the *Chicago Defender*, was again invaluable, as was the national Black press at large. Waters made a suggestion that would change not just the course of the Chicago aviators' lives but, in time, that of the nation: representatives of the National Airmen's Association should fly to Washington, D.C., and plead the cause of Black aviation in the halls of government itself.

====

The National Airmen's Association had already been planning a tour to drum up attendance for their August air meet, with Dale White and Chauncey Spencer doing the flying. The NAAA decided to combine the two different publicity tour ideas into a "Goodwill Tour" that would take Dale and Chauncey to D.C., where they would be hosted by Edgar Brown himself, as well as to a number of Black colleges and flight schools along the route.

MEMBERSHIP CARD

THE
NATIONAL AIRMEN'S ASSOCIATION
·AMERICA·

PIONEER
_____ BRANCH
THIS IS TO CERTIFY THAT

Dale L. White
_____

Is a Member of the N. A. A. A. for the Year ___1940___

C. R. Coffey   Willa B. Brown
639   President   Secretary

*Dale White's "Pioneer Branch" NAAA membership card for 1940, signed by
Cornelius Coffey and Willa Brown*

SMITHSONIAN NATIONAL AIR AND SPACE MUSEUM (NASM 9A12583)

Dale White was one of the first graduates of Coffey and Johnny's Curtiss-Wright class. He'd been the Challenger Aero Club's business manager back in their Robbins days, and he'd flown in formation behind Coffey in the air display over Bessie Coleman's grave. Chauncey "Clark Gable" Spencer was of course the dashing young student pilot known for his daring parachute jumps. Dale and Chauncey had become friends as they both worked on rebuilding the Travel Air plane owned by the dentist and accomplished pilot Earl Renfroe, who'd recently become an inspector for the Illinois Aeronautical Department.

A three-thousand-mile cross-country round trip was still a tremendous achievement in those days, and would be newsworthy. Dale and Chauncey were both photogenic, and Chauncey was good in the spotlight. Their stunt would get media attention for the NAAA that would alert Black people all over the country to the possibilities offered by aviation, as well as grab the attention of the nation's lawmakers who were voting for Black schools to be included in the Civilian Pilot Training Program. The long-distance flight would demonstrate Black flyers' proven ability in the air, and on arrival in the nation's capital, the two young men would deliver what the *Chicago Defender* called a "message of appreciation from the National Airmen's Association, sponsors of the flight, to congressmen and government officials in Washington who supported the fight for the inclusion of members of the Race in the federal air training programs."

The only barrier was the expense. The Goodwill Tour pilots would need a reliable plane, and funds to pay for fuel and room and board as they traveled.

They found an owner willing to rent them a Lincoln-Page biplane for $500. Chauncey had that money ready through his savings, but as Janet pointed out, "What about fuel, hotel expenses, food, and incidentals? They needed a minimum of $2,000. Mission impossible?" She added, "Heck no!"

All of the newly minted National Airmen's Association pilots contributed to the tour fund, but they were still coming up short. Outside help was needed.

"Chauncey, with tears in his eyes, told one of his coworkers, Queenie Davis, his sad, sad story, that we didn't have enough money," Janet said. By this point, Dale and Chauncey were both working with the WPA, or Works Progress Administration, a government-run program to help employ American citizens during the Great Depression. Queenie came up with a brilliant, if sketchy, suggestion. Why not ask the Jones brothers?

The Jones brothers—Edward, George, and McKissack, who was known as Mack—were businessmen in the truest sense. They ran the Ben Franklin department store on 47th Street in Bronzeville, reportedly "the world's only Black-owned department store," but their side hustle—perhaps their biggest moneymaker—was running a game called "Policy." Policy was an illegal lottery-style game that was a big part of the financial life of the African American community at the time. A recent article about Policy on the website maintained by Chicago's PBS channel, WTTW, explains that "People played every day, sometimes several times a day, in the hopes of 'hitting the numbers' and winning big." In 1938, a local Chicago paper estimated that Policy had become an eighteen-million-dollar business. The Jones brothers were at the top of the game. Undoubtedly, they had money to spare.

Sure enough, the Jones brothers donated a thousand dollars to the flight. A few months later, Chauncey would fly over the Jones estate and drop a bouquet of flowers with a thank-you note for their support.

But first, he and Dale had a trip to make.

———

The sky was overcast when Dale and Chauncey set out from Harlem Airport just after dawn on Monday, May 8, 1939, flying the cream-and-red painted Lincoln-Page biplane that they'd nicknamed *Old Faithful*. The words "National Airmen Assn. of America—Sponsored by *Chicago Defender*" were proudly painted on the side.

The first few hours of flying were beset with problems for the NAAA airmen. Almost right away, in Avilla, near Auburn, Indiana, Dale and Chauncey had to land to fix a broken gas line. They thought they'd dealt with it, but when they tried to take off, the engine gave them the same trouble. Six hours later and with the sky still covered in clouds, after some more tinkering and a telegram to Enoch Waters back in Chicago to let him know what was going on, they finally got on their way again.

After only twenty minutes, they realized they were off course. They landed in Fort Wayne, Indiana, to replan and refuel. This time when they took off, they made it across the state line into Ohio. But after another twenty-five minutes of flying, they watched nervously as their gauges showed that the Lincoln-Page's oil pressure was falling.

Suddenly there was a vibrating *bang*.

"The plane started bucking," Chauncey reported, recalling their alarm.

Dale, the more experienced pilot, made an immediate forced landing in a farmer's cornfield in Sherwood, Ohio.

"We swerved and slid and finally rested within a hundred yards of the farmer's barn," said Chauncey. "The farmer stared in disbelief at the cream-and-red plane sitting in his field."

The inauspicious arrival drew a crowd of curious men, women, and children, all peppering the two men with questions.

"Where were you going?"

"How did you become a pilot?"

"Can only two people fit in there?"

And the inevitable—"Can I have a ride?"

Dale and Chauncey climbed out of the plane and discovered that they had a broken crankshaft.

Fortunately for the two men and their limited budget, they'd landed among "a gracious group of people who paid all our expenses while we were there," Chauncey recounted. "To show our appreciation, Dale White and I returned a few months later to spend the day giving the townspeople plane rides and taking their picture in the plane."

But for the moment, they had a mission to complete. Dale and Chauncey sent back to Chicago for money and replacement parts.

"It took two days . . . to raise fifty-four dollars for a new crankshaft," Chauncey recalled.

Coffey and another man, most likely a fellow named Ben Hall, drove out to Ohio with the crankshaft and repaired the plane. Three days after they started out, Dale and Chauncey were in the air again. Next stop, the nation's capital, Washington, D.C.?

The journey was not as smooth as that.

On Thursday, May 11, the duo landed in Cleveland, Ohio, then

On to Washington! Chauncey Spencer (left) buckles on his flying helmet after the Goodwill Tour's extended mechanical delay. Dale White is beside him, ready to go, with able mechanics Ben Hall and Cornelius Coffey all set to see them off.

KENNETH SPENCER RESEARCH LIBRARY, UNIVERSITY OF KANSAS

headed onward to Morgantown, West Virginia. They planned to spend the night in Morgantown; it was already getting dark when they arrived.

And that's where racism reared its menacing head.

West Virginia had separated from the southern state of Virginia in the middle of the Civil War to join the Union. It had no Jim Crow laws. In theory there was no legal segregation there. But there were plenty of segregated businesses and practices, and there was plenty of prejudice. Now the airfield staff at Morgantown refused to rent a space in their hangar to the two Black pilots who wanted to park their plane.

"You can't stay here overnight," the ground crew told them. "Pittsburgh is only 55 miles away."

Dale and Chauncey managed to get the Morgantown airfield staff to sell them some fuel. Their plane was not equipped for night flying, but what else could they do? With no lights, they took off in the dark and headed for Allegheny County Airport in Pennsylvania.

The airfield there had a beacon light that let them know they were in the right place. But just as they started their landing approach, they noticed a Pennsylvania Central Airlines transport plane ahead of them. Keeping a safe distance so that the air turbulence caused by the bigger aircraft wouldn't upset them, Dale and Chauncey followed the white taillight of the big plane down to the landing strip.

There, they were immediately grounded for unsafe flying—as if they'd had a choice.

They spent the night in Pittsburgh. The next day—Friday—Robert L. Vann, the outspoken publisher of the Black newspaper the *Pittsburgh Courier*, joined them for a meeting with the airport manager and an inspector for the CAA. Vann got them cleared to continue their trip to D.C. He also made a generous $500 contribution to the flight.

The unlucky duo had to make yet another forced landing somewhere in the Allegheny Mountains of Pennsylvania, but the incident didn't delay them for long. They made it to Bennett Field, New York City's first municipal airport, on Saturday morning. On Sunday afternoon, after a stop in Philadelphia and another in Baltimore, they finally arrived in Washington, D.C.

═══

On maps, the aerial view of the streets of the nation's capital forms a broken diamond. When the city was first planned, the nation's first president, George Washington, envisioned the District of Columbia, or D.C., as a perfect gem, a square set on end with the points like a compass signaling due north, south, east, and west. And so it stood for the first fifty years of its existence.

In 1790, the bordering states of Virginia and Maryland had each given land to the new District of Columbia. But then, in 1846, the area now known as Alexandria, Virginia, changed its mind. Congress wanted to ban slavery in the capital. But the slave trade was an institution in Virginia. And so the diamond shattered, with a large chunk removed from the west side.

Soon afterward, the Emancipation Proclamation and a bloody civil war would abolish slavery across the nation. But the missing land would never be returned, and the flawed gem of racial discrimination against the formerly enslaved would remain set in government policy for another hundred years.

It was at this broken diamond that Chauncey Spencer and Dale White arrived in *Old Faithful*, determined to make that jewel shine bright enough to reflect all races in the sky.

The *Chicago Defender* reported that, in contrast to their greeting in Morgantown, in Washington the NAAA pilots "were assured that the plane would be in good hands during their stay in this city."

The halls of the Capitol must have been buzzing on Monday morning, May 15, 1939. Two months earlier, Nazi Germany had begun invading the nation of Czechoslovakia. In Europe the drums of war were growing louder. But in America, so were the voices of Black aviators.

Chauncey and Dale were met by a delegation headed by Edgar Brown. "God's angry man" proved to be the group's guardian angel. After a meeting with the Black press and multiple congressmen, Brown took them on the United States Capitol subway system, built in 1909 to connect the Capitol building with congressional offices. "As we were getting off the electric car," Chauncey recalled, "Harry S. Truman, then a senator from Missouri, came walking down the corridor."

Brown introduced Dale and Chauncey to Truman, and explained that they'd flown from Chicago to Washington to try to get Black aviators included in the Civilian Pilot Training Program that the Senate was about to vote on.

"Why aren't you in the Air Corps?" Truman asked, surprised. "Can't you get in?" He grilled them on whether or not they had tried.

"We'd like to try but we'd also like for you to help us open the door. We haven't been able to break down the barriers ourselves," Dale White said. "Mr. Truman, you don't know what it means to be embarrassed. I've tried these things before. There's just no use."

When Truman contended he had indeed been embarrassed before, Dale replied, "Not like this, Mr. Truman. Not like we are."

The statement must have resonated with Truman. At least his curiosity was piqued. He asked to see the airplane they'd arrived in, and made a trip out to the airport to look at it that very afternoon. Like the onlookers in Sherwood, Ohio, Truman was full of curious questions as he climbed on the wing to peer into the cockpit. "How much gas can this carry? How much did it cost to rent? Do you have insurance?"

"He was enthusiastic, though he didn't want a plane ride," Chauncey later said.

Evidently Truman found the men more impressive than their machine. He finished up by stating, "If you had guts enough to fly this thing to Washington . . . I've got enough guts to see that you get what you are asking for."

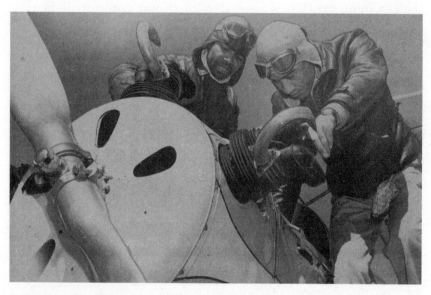

Dale White (left) and Chauncey Spencer checking their aircraft before takeoff, May 1939
COURTESY OF THE AFRO AMERICAN NEWSPAPERS ARCHIVES

===

Dale and Chauncey left Washington buoyed by their meetings, not just with Truman but with Senator James Slattery from their home state of Illinois, and Illinois congressman Everett M. Dirksen, who'd been responsible for the anti-discrimination amendment to the CPTP bill.

The two flyers spent the rest of the week completing their successful tour of Black schools, including a visit to West Virginia State College, drumming up publicity and interest in the National Airmen's Association and inviting local pilots to attend the air meet planned for August in Chicago. They returned home via Sherwood, Ohio, on purpose, to make a flying salute to the folks who had treated them so well when they were grounded.

The Miller children and their mother posing with the NAAA Goodwill Tour plane. The family hosted Chauncey Spencer and Dale White during their breakdown in Sherwood, Ohio, in May 1939.

Anthropologists St. Clair Drake and Horace Cayton directed a federal project to study urban Black life in Chicago, employing both Dale White and Chauncey Spencer. At Harlem Airport on May 18, 1939, Drake and Cayton helped to welcome Dale and Chauncey home after their Goodwill Tour to Washington, D.C. Marie St. Clair stands fourth from the left, next to Willa Brown; Horace Cayton is third from the right. St. Clair Drake kneels at left; third from the right kneeling is Dale White, then Enoch Waters, Jr., with Chauncey Spencer kneeling on the far right.

SMITHSONIAN NATIONAL AIR AND SPACE MUSEUM (NASM NASM.1993.0060-M0000026-00470)

The media drive for inclusion didn't slow down. As the time neared for the Senate's vote on the CPTP bill, the *Pittsburgh Courier* pushed for a guarantee that funding be set aside specifically for the training of Black aviators. Edgar Brown made an impassioned plea in Congress, mentioning the petition delivered by Dale White and Chauncey Spencer in his argument.

In Chicago, the Harlem aviators once again performed their Memorial Day flyover tribute to Bessie Coleman at Lincoln Cemetery. Then on Friday, June 16, 1939, the NAAA held a planning session as they set to work on the ambitious, and historically significant, National Air Meet that they were going to host from August 25 to 27, 1939.

With Coffey acting as their general chairman, everyone took on jobs for the air meet. Enoch Waters would arrange the program and was also in charge of publicity. In April, he'd sent nearly two hundred questionnaires to Black aviators across the nation, asking people to commit to fly to Chicago for the event. By this time, responses were coming in from aviators in other states who were hoping to join the August gathering, either in their own aircraft or in rented planes. Waters used the *Defender* to publish a weekly series of profiles of these pilots, including photographs and interesting notes about their lives and their individual struggles for wings.

Dale White would plan the air show; Chauncey Spencer was in charge of "ways and means," which meant he'd be looking after the budget; Marie St. Clair was responsible for entertainment for the guests; and Grover Nash was responsible for organizing exhibits. An NAAA member named Walter Evans would look after concessions. Their off-airfield base and headquarters would be the Wabash Avenue YMCA.

In addition to flight demonstrations and a dance, the group planned to put on an exhibition of the latest aviation designs and equipment, to hold business sessions, and to give visiting aviators instructions on setting up their own local NAAA branches. It was truly going to be a national conference, and according to the *Chicago Defender*, it would "mark the beginning of a new day in aviation so far as members of the Race are concerned."

The NAAA's meeting that June day must have been a joyful one. They had a reason to celebrate. Earlier that same day, Willa Brown had passed the grueling test to receive a limited commercial pilot's license, the highest flight rating ever achieved by a Black woman at the time. The rating allowed her to fly any type of licensed aircraft and gave her limited instructor's capabilities. Only four other Black pilots held this rating, all men. Four more held commercial ratings without limitations, and two of those were Willa's friends and peers at Harlem Airport: Earl Renfroe, and her teacher, Cornelius Coffey.

The NAAA would soon have something else to celebrate: on June 19, 1939, the Civilian Pilot Training bill passed in the Senate, with Everett M. Dirksen's anti-discrimination amendment intact. The following week, on June 27, 1939, President Roosevelt signed the bill into law. At long last the U.S. government was beginning to recognize the potential of Black aviators.

Willa Brown ready for takeoff, likely May 1939
SMITHSONIAN NATIONAL AIR AND SPACE MUSEUM (NASM 7B01167)

After a summer of touring, advocacy, and fundraising, Willa and Coffey flew cross-country to Louisville, Kentucky, where Willa was greeted with a motorcade and given the key to the city. "A throng of over two thousand persons greeted the flyers on their arrival," the *Chicago Defender* crowed. Ever the star attraction, Willa perched on the open back of an automobile, waving like a beauty queen at the crowd in a mile-long parade. She made appearances at the town's annual cooking school and home show, was interviewed on the local radio station, and was the guest of honor at a tea held by her old college sorority, Alpha Kappa Alpha.

High on these successful sorties, that same month, August 1939, the National Airmen's Association applied for a charter from the state of Illinois, changing their status from a club to an official business organization. Then, on August 16, the newly formed group gathered at Coffey's old stomping grounds, the Wabash Avenue YMCA in Bronzeville, and drew up guidelines with a set goal "to further stimulate interest in aviation and to bring about a better understanding in the entire field of aeronautics."

The initial members of this newest iteration of the NAAA were Cornelius Coffey, Dale White, Harold Hurd, Willa Brown, Marie St. Clair, Charles Johnson, Grover Nash, Edward Johnson, George Williams, Enoch Waters of the *Chicago Defender*, Janet Harmon Waterford, and the enthusiastic young Chauncey Spencer. They used the *Defender*'s offices at 3435 South Indiana Avenue as their mailing address.

Notably missing from the group was Johnny Robinson.

Like Coffey, Johnny had written to Tuskegee's President Patterson earlier in 1939, hoping that Tuskegee would be accepted for a CPTP course and once more offering to his alma mater his services as a flight instructor. He'd even gone so far as to suggest that they could use his Chicago flight school at Poro College as the northern base for their flight training. But Tuskegee, whether from past experience with Johnny, or because they had other plans, simply wasn't interested.

With that door closed to him, Johnny hoped that his own school would be accepted to the CPTP program. Unfortunately for Johnny, according to Edgar Brown, "Under the ruling of the War Department, the school operated by Col. Robinson is not qualified to teach flying: First, the Civilian Aeronautics Authority has to inspect and approve all private schools. The Robinson school does not exist in the minds and files of the Civilian Aeronautics Authority." Apparently the technicality was that Johnny's school was too far away from a flying field.

Johnny was outraged. He wrote a defensive press release, referring to Edgar Brown only as "a well-known man of question from Washington," and claiming to have "trained practically every Negro pilot in Chicago."

Edgar Brown issued a splendid and mostly gracious apology, ending with a sweeping general statement: "No one seems to know the exact status of the aviation program and Chicago's possibilities for participation in it." He finished up evasively, "Such information should be supplied by the CAA and the War Department."

═══

The last weekend of August finally arrived, signaling the start of the National Airmen's Association air meet. Aircraft began to touch down at Harlem Airport, flown by Black pilots visiting from six states. Other attendees came by train and automobile. The final program for the three-day event included a sightseeing tour, a public party, a catered breakfast, and even a special church service. Though he hadn't been involved with the planning, on Sunday morning before the service, Johnny Robinson hosted a breakfast event attended by the visiting aviators, family, and friends, all welcomed to the gathering by Janet Harmon Waterford. Despite his falling-out with Coffey and Willa, Johnny and Janet remained friendly.

"This air meet has fulfilled one very great need," Johnny said. "It has brought all of our leaders in the field of aviation together. They will go home and form strong local units as a result, out of which to build a stronger national unit."

That is exactly what the National Airmen's Association set out to do at the conference. In their business meetings, the number one item on the agenda was the establishment of local chapters and nationwide guidelines for the NAAA. The group adopted a constitution and elected national officers, with Coffey as their president and aviators from visiting states as vice presidents. Willa was to be the national secretary, with assistant secretaries corresponding from other states; the other national officers were all based in Chicago, with Enoch Waters acting as their advisor.

Finally, the group adopted three resolutions: they officially endorsed West Virginia State College as one of the sites they hoped would be chosen for training Black flyers under the new Civilian Pilot Training Program; they resolved to ask the Civil Aeronautics Authority to appoint at least one qualified Black inspector; and lastly, they planned to insist that Black instructors be employed by the CAA in the new training program.

To top off the weekend's festivities, the Chicago hosts awarded a

Dr. A. Porter Davis, Willa Brown, and Cornelius Coffey, posing with a Piper Cub
at the 1939 NAAA air meet at Harlem Airport

SMITHSONIAN NATIONAL AIR AND SPACE MUSEUM (NASM 91-15483)

glittering array of enormous trophies to the pilots who arrived first
and who had flown the farthest to get there, as well as to the youngest
and oldest visiting pilots. Dr. A. Porter Davis of Kansas City, Kansas,
won the prize for being the oldest—he claimed he'd flown to Chicago
exactly ten years earlier for an event planned in 1929, only to discover
that he was the only flyer who'd turned up. In fact, he was the Black
aviator who'd inspired the teenage Harold Hurd. Davis, who'd earned
his license in 1928 and run an aviation school for Black pilots for a
time, also received recognition in the form a new award, the Dwight
Green trophy. Donated by Illinois governor Dwight H. Green, who'd
been an Army pilot in World War I, the award recognized an
"outstanding contribution to [the] advancement of aviation."

Other well-known award winners at the conference were Dale White and Chauncey Spencer for the "outstanding flight of [the] year." Coffey received the award for "outstanding work in [the] organization," and Willa the award for the "outstanding flight of [the] year made by a woman." One other woman, Mrs. Abram D. Jackson, was honored for being "the only woman to fly to [the] conference."

The awards were presented by Chauncey Spencer's mother, the Harlem Renaissance patron and poet Anne Spencer, who told the *Chicago Defender* she hoped that her young man would go on to do even finer and bigger things.

The National Airmen's Association of America was now well staffed, well trained, confident, and ready for the next stage of the moonshot: the establishment of flight schools under the new Civilian Pilot Training Program. And the Coffey Flying Service was right there in the running.

CHAPTER 9

THE LOVE STORY OF CORNELIUS R. COFFEY, 1939-1940

Blivens—I see Miss Headstrong is taking aviation lessons.
Givens—That so? Always had an idea that girl was flighty.

—James M. Harrison, "Stray Thoughtlets,"
Norfolk, Virginia, *New Journal and Guide*,
January 14, 1922

On July 8, 1939, in Lake County, Indiana, about an hour's drive from Harlem Airport, Cornelius Coffey and Willa Brown tied the knot. It was not your conventional romance, if indeed there was anything romantic about it at all. According to Enoch Waters, the arrangement was purely practical.

The NAAA had established chapters in cities from Chicago to the East Coast. Thanks to the work of the press, more and more curiosity seekers visited Harlem Airport every weekend.

"Business increased to the point that Coffey found it necessary to buy a house trailer which he parked at the airport. This saved him from having to drive back and forth from home to field," Waters recounted. It was a move reminiscent of his days in the farmhouse at Akers Airport—a bachelor's life, through and through. Not so for the bachelorette.

Willa was also commuting, and working long hours for the school and the NAAA. She and Coffey were determined to turn this rise in fortunes into participation in the Civilian Pilot Training Program. But a single woman was not allowed to simply be roommates with a man in 1939—not unchaperoned. And so, in a true marriage of convenience, Waters believed, Willa married Coffey so she could share his trailer without scandal.

"I put it that way because I don't think Coffey was anxious to marry, though it was apparent, he was very fond of Willa and realized that she was the best thing that ever happened to him," Waters surmised. "They both decided and I agreed that marriage was a wise step. We didn't want to jeopardize our projects by providing fodder for gossip."

Although it might not have led to the gossip they feared, there is

Willa Brown, family, and friends at Paul Cox Field in Terre Haute, Indiana. Left to right: Eric B. Brown (Willa's father), Ione Sloss, Hallie Mae Carpenter Brown (Willa's mother), Ephraim Brown (Willa's brother), Willa Brown, Cornelius Coffey, Lola Jones, (?), Herman Sloss, Evangeline Harris, Mrs. Simeon Brown, and Simeon Brown (Willa's brother)

VIGO COUNTY HISTORICAL SOCIETY & MUSEUM

some mystery surrounding Coffey and Willa's marriage. Courthouse records show a second marriage license in the city of Chicago between Coffey and Willa dated February 7, 1947—nearly a decade after they first wed. What could this mean? Did the couple have a falling-out, only to remarry at a later date? Unfortunately, divorce records are harder to come by. What is known is that their marriage did not last. Later in life, both Willa and Coffey went on to marry other people.

But for now, the newlyweds got to work upgrading the facilities and equipment at Harlem so that they could apply for a grant to join the Civilian Pilot Training Program.

═══

Senator Truman had been as good as his word, with the presidential signing of the Civilian Pilot Training Act into law. But the moonshot wasn't finished, the battle not yet won. It remained to be seen just what resources the federal government was going to commit to Black aviation schools, and how many schools would be allowed to participate in the program. The good news for the Coffey Flying Service was that there was a requirement that at least 5 percent of the trainees were to be non-college students. Since Willa and Coffey were not affiliated with a college, this meant they had a fighting chance of being able to benefit from the program.

Then, on September 1, 1939, the world changed.

On that day, Adolf Hitler's Nazi army invaded Poland. In retaliation, Poland's allies, the United Kingdom and France, declared war on Germany. World War II had begun.

But the U.S. refused to join the fray. It declared its neutrality—let Europe handle its own problems, the thinking went. The nation was still reeling from the Great Depression. Its military was pitifully small, not up to the task of being spread thin across the ocean.

While the war seemed a world away, the United States also recognized its vulnerabilities. War in the U.S. was unlikely, but it would be wise to prepare against future conflict. And so, that same month, the CAA began making announcements about which Black schools would receive CPTP funding. The first two awards went to West Virginia State College and North Carolina Agricultural and Technical College. Hampton Institute, in Virginia, soon followed. The *Chicago Defender* and the National Airmen's Association were delighted to hear that they were directly responsible for West Virginia State's acceptance into the program. According to the college's president, John W. Davis, it was Dale White and Chauncey Spencer's visit to the college the previous spring that had inspired the school to apply.

The CPTP initially consisted of three phases: ground school, flight training, and advanced training. Ground school meant seventy-two hours of classroom work learning aviation fundamentals. To qualify, students had to be U.S. citizens between the ages of eighteen and twenty-five; there was a $40 fee for materials and instruction, and the government would foot the rest of the bill. The ground school would be delivered to college students as part of their course offerings, and all the students had to take a competitive examination when they'd completed the classroom instruction. The top ten in every group of fifty students would go on to the flight training section of the course.

A minimum of thirty-five hours of flight training (and a maximum of fifty) would take place at local airfields where students could finally get behind the stick and up in the air. Advanced training would be available for students who wanted to learn more complex aviation skills beyond those required to earn a basic pilot's license. Additional phases would be added as the nation tipped toward a war footing, but at the moment, those clouds were far on the horizon.

For now, flying schools applying to the program would have to meet certain government standards—the schools had to be within ten miles of an airport, the landing strips at those airports had to be of a certain length and width, and so on. The guidelines had high qualification requirements for all aviators; even instructors had to undergo recertification tests with the CAA, and all CPTP facilities required a permit granted by a CAA inspector.

The Coffey Flying Service held its breath. It was such a strong contender that an article appeared in *Time* magazine on September 25, 1939, voicing a national hope for a "School for Willa."

But there were a few challenges that Coffey and Willa were going to have to overcome to align with the requirements. They'd have to upgrade some of their facilities, and they were also going to have to hire another qualified instructor. Fortunately for them, one showed up on their doorstep in the nick of time.

Lewis Jackson was a Black aviation enthusiast who'd grown up in Angola, Indiana, and now owned a Piper Cub. Like so many aviators, Lewis fell in love with flying at an early age; he'd been obsessed since grade school, making model airplanes and reading all the aviation technical books he could get his hands on. He managed to get his first flight in 1927 at the age of fifteen, and two years later he designed *and flew* his own hang glider. When he was seventeen, Lewis tried flying a partially finished monoplane with a friend. They "taxied a great deal but never took off," as he recalled. By 1939, still in his twenties, he was a qualified flight instructor.

One fateful day that same year, Lewis was taking a passenger for a ride when suddenly his engine quit. Though he landed the plane safely, he had to make a special trip to Chicago to get the part he needed to fix the engine. While he was in town, he went out to Harlem Airport just to check it out. There, he met Coffey, Janet, and Willa.

"Mr. Coffey, I understand you're going to start a civil pilot training program," Lewis said.

"That's right, Lewis," Coffey told him. At the very least, they were going to try.

"I'd like to become a part of it," Lewis said.

Here was the second instructor Coffey's school needed.

But there was still a problem. The program allowed ten students for every two airplanes, but, at 40-horsepower, Lewis's Piper Cub didn't meet the CAA's baseline engine specifications.

"Lewis, they will require a 50[-horsepower] Cub," Coffey told him. "Now, I know Mr. Schumacher pretty well . . . we'll go to him[,] and if you agree to buy a 50[-horsepower] Continental-engine Cub, I'll try to get him to sell you one of his."

Fred Schumacher wasn't part of the CPTP, but he was willing to sell one of his qualifying aircraft, a J-3 Piper Cub, for Coffey and Lewis to use. In the meantime, Lewis borrowed Coffey's plane to get retested for the CPTP instructor's rating, flying out of Curtiss Field at Glenview, Illinois, for the exam. Glenview had been Chicago's premier civilian airport in the early 1930s, and the U.S. Naval Reserve had established a base there in 1937, which soon became the Navy's largest primary flight training program.

Lewis's new J-3 Cub checked one box for the CPTP. But the hangar that Fred Schumacher had built for the Challenger Air Pilots' Association when they'd first arrived at Harlem did not. The hangar was built on a hill, which made the hard-packed dirt floor uneven. Coffey's team had to grade, or level, the ground themselves and replace the dirt with cement in order to get CAA approval. Fortunately, Coffey and company were never afraid of a little hard work. At least there were no boulders in the way this time.

Once those requirements had been met, Coffey, Willa, and Enoch Waters filed the paperwork to turn the Coffey Flying Service into the Coffey School of Aeronautics and waited to hear from the CAA.

Finally, on October 16, 1939, the Coffey School was granted its own Civilian Pilot Training Program under the institutional title of the National Airmen's Association of America.

It was a time of triumph. Willa proudly announced, "The CAA air pilot course at Harlem Airport, Chicago . . . will be one of the schools opened next week at Government expense, to young men and women of the race without college training for aviation instruction."

Ultimately, the CPTP would be offered by six Black colleges and universities: West Virginia State College, North Carolina Agricultural and Technical College, Delaware State College, Hampton Institute, Howard University, and Tuskegee Institute. The Coffey School of Aeronautics was the only participating Black flight school not affiliated with a higher education establishment.

Johnny Robinson's school at Poro College wasn't given CPTP funding, but it *was* given funds from the National Youth Administration—the same program that had supported the experimental rollout of the CPTP in 1938. As part of the National Defense Program, which oversaw military production, Johnny was to conduct air mechanics training for young people through the Poro school.

It was a CPTP requirement that one woman be included in every group of ten students taking to the air. In the second week of December 1939, the program went into action at West Virginia State College, with Rose Agnes Rolls, a senior in business administration, becoming the first young Black woman to participate in CAA-sponsored flight training. Nine young men rounded out the first class.

But things didn't get moving in Chicago quite so quickly. Because of the complex situation in the area, with training often shared between different airfields and flight schools, the CAA and the Air Corps organized a special conference to address the distribution of Black aviation students among the several organizations involved. On January 15, 1940, officials from the city of Chicago, its school board, and the Black National Guard regiment, along with Harold S. Darr, who owned the Chicago School of Aeronautics at Glenview, gathered to hear their plans.

Five familiar members of the National Airmen's Association of America—Cornelius Coffey, Willa Brown, Earl Renfroe, Enoch Waters, and "God's angry man" Edgar Brown—were also there. And so was Johnny Robinson, invited along by Darr, as Johnny now operated the flight portion of his school through Glenview and kept three of his own planes there. Understandably, it was a tense reunion.

"I did not want to go because I had split up with the Willa Brown Coffey crowd and the National Airmen's Association," Johnny admitted. "Edgar Brown was running the show and they wouldn't let me say anything even if I went."

Dr. Midian Othello Bousfield, a successful physician who'd recently become the first Black man to serve on Chicago's school board, chaired the meeting. Dr. Bousfield readily admitted that he was unfamiliar with the situation, so he probably had no idea how tempers were about to flare.

First off, Enoch Waters demanded that Black aviators be given their constitutional rights to join the Air Corps.

The Air Corps representative, Major R.M. Webster, retorted, "I know as much about the Constitution as you do."

Major Webster went on to complain that the NAAA members were so concerned with the bigger picture that they weren't focused on the matter at hand—the distribution of the Civilian Pilot Training Program for Black aviators in Chicago. The talk grew heated, but, thanks to Edgar Brown's considerable diplomatic skills and experience as a lobbyist, the meeting settled down.

By the end of the day the group had agreed that the Chicago School of Aeronautics would provide a CPTP course for twenty college-educated students, drawn from the local community, and give them flight training at Glenview using Black instructors—including Johnny. The NAAA would be responsible for a CPTP course for ten non-college students, and the Coffey School of Aeronautics, operating as the National Airmen's Association of America, would provide their flight training from Harlem Airport. The ground school classes for both the college students from the Chicago School and the non-college students from the Coffey School would be held together at a location to be determined.

Harlem Airport wasn't equipped with classroom facilities, so Coffey and Willa turned to Dr. Bousfield, the Chicago school board member, for help. His wife, Dr. Maudelle Brown Bousfield, was the principal at Wendell Phillips High School. The Bousfields gave Coffey permission to use the classroom and machine shop at Dr. Bousfield's school. On an early visit to Wendell Phillips, Coffey also met Clifford Campbell, the assistant principal. "I tried to sell him on my idea of aviation," Coffey recounted, pushing the importance of aviation training as a trade for young Black people. He punctuated his pitch by giving the assistant principal a ride in his airplane.

And so, on February 5, 1940, the Coffey ground school course, "Aviation Mechanics," moved into the basement at Wendell Phillips High. Willa was named the director of flight training for the CPTP at the Coffey School, and became the instructor for the evening classes, three hours a night, four nights a week. By the middle of February there were sixty-nine students enrolled, six of them young women, and Willa continued to accept new students until March 4.

Later that month, Robert S. Abbott, founder and publisher of the *Chicago Defender* and Bessie Coleman's sponsor, passed away. The NAAA paused in their CPTP efforts to honor Abbott and his legacy with a flyover at his burial at Lincoln Cemetery. Dale White was at the helm, with the NAAA's assistant secretary, Marie St. Clair, in the passenger's seat. The duo dropped a bouquet of roses over Abbott's grave, which were then handed to his widow as a final thank-you for Abbott's contribution to Black aviation.

And then the group returned to the work that Abbott would have undoubtedly delighted in—the promotion of the NAAA's involvement in the Civilian Pilot Training Program. With the location at Wendell Phillips secured, Willa Brown and Enoch Waters again threw themselves into gear, this time with a national publicity campaign advertising the aviation opportunities offered in Chicago.

"Thirty Flight Scholarships For Government Training!" shouted the headlines and leaflets. The effort was a great success. Of the forty-seven students who took the ground school exams that spring, thirty-one passed the final test. The highest grade was earned by Simeon Brown, Willa's younger brother. The top ten candidates went on to form the Coffey School CPTP's first elementary flight class—Simeon, eight other young men, and one young woman (as required by the program)—taking to the skies with CAA funding at Harlem Airport.

—————

The CPTP setup in Chicago was considered experimental as far as the CAA and the War Department were concerned. The *Chicago Tribune* described it as a means for young Black flight students "to prove their worth in the field of aviation." From the start, the section for training college students was referred to as a "demonstration unit." "[The] purpose of the demonstration school is to test whether Negroes can qualify as acceptable pilots and deserve membership in the United States Army Air Corps," the *Tribune* explained.

Coffey's flight training unit for non-college students went a step further. "Every ten students that I took, I had one white student and one girl student in that unit. What I was trying to do is prove to our government that we not only could teach white students and they could fly together—see, they always told you that you couldn't integrate them. I said you could, because [Charles Ecker,] my first student after I got my [commercial license,] was a white student," Coffey said. "They had no excuse."

And prove it he did. The first non-college group of students included

Cornelius Coffey gives a young woman hands-on instruction in the dangerous work of starting a plane by swinging its propeller. Another woman is seated in the back of this Piper Cub, ready for a flight lesson.

KENNETH SPENCER RESEARCH LIBRARY, UNIVERSITY OF KANSAS

a young white man named Chester Krups. Within a year, the Wendell Phillips ground school class was 70 percent Black and 30 percent white, all of them working side by side. In a program where all the instructors were also Black, it was a powerful demonstration of successful integration in action.

"The field is not and never has been a Jim Crow airport," noted Howard Gould, a Chicago Urban League official, writing about Harlem Airport in a letter to the U.S. War Department. He went on to compliment Coffey's mandate of teaching both Black and white, male and female students. "This is as it should be and we are sure you will agree that Negroes can best advance in aviation where they participate equally with and have the same interests and same opportunities as white citizens."

In June 1940, the CAA sent officials to inspect both the ground school at Wendell Phillips and the flight training at Harlem Airport, and they were full of praise for what they saw. By this time Lewis Jackson had already soloed four students, and was waiting for decent weather to solo four more. The CAA inspector was impressed with the selection of students as well as the instructors, and told Willa that as the CPTP expanded, she would continue to be able to offer students financial aid.

Willa organized an open house at Harlem Airport on Sunday, July 7, offering airplane rides to the public and inviting them to meet the Coffey School's CPTP students. When the second round of ground school classes began at Wendell Phillips High School in August 1940, over a hundred young people, including several girls, turned up to enroll.

It was clear skies for the Coffey School. Coffey and Lewis Jackson were soon training ten students each. They "went through that program in about three and a half weeks, 350 hours, and never had a hang[-up], or any difficulty," Coffey said.

CHAPTER 10

THE TUSKEGEE TUSSLE, 1940-1941

> We do feel that if you will just give us a chance to prepare to fight, bleed, and die for our country, because we know no other, that we will do the job better than anybody else.
>
> —Statement to Congress of J. Finley Wilson,
> May 26, 1939

IN Europe, World War II was exploding.

In April 1940, Germany invaded Denmark in the shortest campaign of the war. The Northern European nation had never even declared Nazi Germany to be an enemy. The Danish military stood down, and within six hours, the Nazis were in control. By June, the Nazis occupied neighboring Norway, Belgium, and the Netherlands. French troops, assisted by units of the British Expeditionary Force from the United Kingdom, fought desperately as the Nazi invaders stormed across France. The cooperating European nations, known as the Allies, were on the run, pressed by the German onslaught until they were fighting with their backs to the sea along the shores of France.

In the French coastal town of Dunkirk, British troops gathered in a last-ditch attempt to flee across the waters of the English Channel home to safety in the United Kingdom. In a miraculous display of patriotic service, the British military rallied civilian boats and ships to join the rescue efforts. Operation Dynamo gripped the world. And it was a success. Despite heavy fire and casualties, over 338,000 troops were evacuated. They and other exiled refugees from the occupied European nations would regroup in the United Kingdom and brace for Germany's next wave of attack, for the Nazis now controlled mainland Europe—and they would not stop there. The new and untested leader of the United Kingdom, Prime Minister Winston Churchill, called on the United States for aid.

The answer was: No. America remained isolationist and neutral in its policies. It still refused to enter what it considered a foreign war.

But it was getting harder to ignore the possibility of future threats. The Civilian Pilot Training Program had become more important than ever to the security of the American nation. And for the Coffey School, a new battle was about to begin.

Early in June of 1940, around the same time as the evacuation of Dunkirk, George L. Washington, the director of Tuskegee Institute's School of Mechanical Industries, came to Chicago to give a speech at the Tuskegee Club there. He described the CPTP training that was going on at Tuskegee, and while he was in the city, he visited the Coffey School of Aeronautics.

"I had heard much about the [Coffey] operation, and it was an inspiration to see Negroes conducting flight training," he enthused.

When Tuskegee had joined the CPTP, there hadn't been any qualified Black pilots teaching in Alabama. Tuskegee's president, Dr. Patterson, had had to reach out to a white pilot as their first flight instructor.

Willa treated Washington to a flight over the city. "She impressed me as a well-educated and most progressive and aggressive advocate of the Negro in aviation," he later wrote.

The CAA had by now announced that it was ready to launch the

CPTP's advanced flight training initiative. As well as providing elementary flight training to forty-five thousand students in 1940 (from the ground up, as it were), the government would give secondary training to another nine thousand students who already had their basic pilot's licenses. The secondary training program was rolled out in July, with a further cross-country training course available for experienced pilots.

Back in Tuskegee, George L. Washington got a call from the regional director of the CAA, letting him know that "an institution in Chicago" was working at getting approval for the advanced flight training course—and that only one of the accredited Black CPTP organizations would be eligible to take on the program at this time.

Washington thought immediately of Willa, and the brilliant training center he'd seen at Harlem Airport. It was no secret that Coffey was hoping to offer the CPTP's secondary course in September—he'd told the national newspapers as much back in June.

Washington had seen his rivals in action. Coffey's school was impressive, but Tuskegee would not accept defeat.

Tuskegee wasn't as well equipped as Willa and Coffey's organization, nor did it have as many qualified personnel, but the advanced program was too big a prize to lose. So, in his application for the secondary training course, Washington played to Tuskegee's strengths: it had a well-known and respected institutional name with a reputation going back to the nineteenth century; it was positioned in the South, where cold winters wouldn't stop flight training; and, as Washington later observed, as an institution in a state where Jim Crow laws were in effect, "it could, as a partner in a segregated project, be quite relieving and comforting."

The U.S. military followed many of the same practices of segregation as the Jim Crow South. No doubt the Air Corps would be relieved to extend this standard to CPTP operations. It was a bald-faced way of pandering to the white CAA and Air Corps bigwigs who'd have to give approval for the program—not taking into account the African Americans who'd be learning to fly there. And it was in clear opposition to the Coffey way of integrating the skies.

In July 1940, Tuskegee won the bid for the first rollout of advanced CPTP training. Out of ninety-three flight schools, Tuskegee was the only Black flight school accepted to the secondary training program. If Black pilots wanted advanced training, they would also get a lesson in segregation, no matter where they were from.

It was the beginning of a frosty relationship between Chicago and Tuskegee.

Willa Brown, Cornelius Coffey, and the National Airmen's Association weren't just disappointed that they hadn't been awarded a secondary training program: they were also bitterly frustrated by Tuskegee's acceptance of a segregated program. They'd struggled long and hard not just for the right to be in the air, but also for the right to fly side by side with white aviators, for the right to share the sky.

———

For his part, George L. Washington now had to scramble to find qualified Black flight instructors for Tuskegee. Of course he immediately thought of the two accomplished pilots most closely associated with Tuskegee in the past decade: a powerhouse of aviation named Charles Alfred Anderson, and John C. Robinson.

Like Cornelius Coffey and Johnny Robinson, Charles Alfred

Anderson had been turned away from flight school after flight school because of his race. He learned to fly by working as ground crew, and with the help of a small flying school in his native Pennsylvania where other pilots agreed to give him aviation "tips"—as long as he used his own airplane. And that's exactly what he did, buying a plane and teaching himself to taxi. He learned to take off and land the hard way: by crashing into a tree the first time he tried it. Still, he managed to get his pilot's license in 1929, eventually taking lessons from a German man who'd been a combat pilot in World War I. In 1932, Anderson became the first Black pilot to get a commercial license.

Anderson went on to teach other Black flyers, one of whom was Dr. Albert Ernest Forsythe, a well-to-do physician from New Jersey who was a Tuskegee alum like Johnny. Together, Anderson and Forsythe had flown a record-busting trip in the summer of 1933, becoming the first Black pilots to fly coast to coast and back again across the United States, and they'd followed this up in 1934 with a sweeping "Pan-American Goodwill Air Tour," visiting ten Caribbean destinations in a plane christened *The Spirit of Booker T. Washington*, after the founder and first president of Tuskegee Institute.

Charles Alfred Anderson and Johnny Robinson each had unique and impressive accomplishments in the sky in addition to a cordial connection to Tuskegee, and either or both men would be a prize for Tuskegee's fledgling advanced flight training program.

Washington made phone calls to both pilots so he could personally proposition the two. Anderson was thrilled at the invitation, and agreed to do a training course at the Navy air base at Glenview to upgrade his commercial license with complex aerobatic flying in order to qualify as an advanced flight instructor for secondary training.

But Johnny, though enthusiastic over the phone, waffled yet again about signing a contract with Tuskegee. Apparently Johnny *still* didn't have that commercial license he needed in order to take legal payment for flying lessons.

Anderson completed his own certification, and took on Tuskegee's workload alone for the rest of the summer while they waited patiently for Johnny to get his commercial rating. And it appears he did get it at the end of July in 1940, possibly realizing that he was jeopardizing his own school by not having the correct credentials. But when Washington wrote to Johnny again about the offered job and received no immediate response, he gave up on Johnny's indecisiveness and looked around for another candidate.

The man who drew his attention was someone he'd met earlier that summer—Lewis Jackson, currently employed by the Coffey School of Aeronautics.

And so began a trend of poaching, or hiring away, of Coffey's staff.

Tuskegee had been awarded the first CPTP bid for secondary training, but that wasn't stopping the Coffey School from applying for their own advanced course as the program expanded. The catch for them wasn't a lack of instructors: it was that secondary training required yet another airplane, one that could do advanced aerobatics. At the time, Coffey knew, those cost a minimum of $7,500—nearly $140,000 today.

"That is when Willa came into the picture again," he said.

Willa set to work getting both the airplane and the secondary course secured. Unfortunately, Lewis Jackson was unfamiliar with Willa's skills of persuasion.

"Lewis got a little bit anxious and he didn't believe that we were going to get these airplanes on loan," Coffey said. And of course, George

L. Washington was waiting in the wings. Lewis decided to leave the Coffey School and go to Tuskegee.

To qualify as a secondary flight instructor, Lewis did the necessary training out at the Glenview Navy base in August, just as Anderson had done. But he stayed with the Coffey School until the end of September so that he could finish up instructing the summer session for the CPTP group there. He started at Tuskegee in time to join their fall program in 1940—and thus missed out on Willa's magic.

Willa made a trip to the Chicago School of Aeronautics at Glenview, where she talked to Harold S. Darr, the school's owner. He was sympathetic to the battle being waged by Black aviators. By the end of Willa's meeting with Darr, he'd agreed to lend two airplanes to the Coffey School.

═══

The scramble for planes and instructors didn't stop the National Airmen's Association from celebrating and sharing their successes, and in August 1940 they held their second national convention. "Fifty-six pilots and thirty-eight others registered for the three-day conference that had to be extended to five days to fully cover the agenda," Enoch Waters recalled. As he put it, "The NAAA had become a national functioning organization."

And what a month it was for Chauncey Spencer! At the conference, he and Dale White were awarded the second Dwight Green trophy for an outstanding contribution to the advancement of aviation, in recognition of their Goodwill Tour and their mission to Washington, D.C., the previous year. The immeasurable success of that trip was visible all around them.

But Chauncey wasn't just being showered with grateful praise—he was also in love.

Anna Howard was a vibrant young woman who'd just graduated from DuSable High School in Chicago. Her stepfather was an aviation buff; the whole family spent their weekends picnicking at Harlem Airport and watching the planes, and that's where Anna and Chauncey met. It's also where they got married, on Sunday, August 18, 1940, the same week as the NAAA air meet. The daring parachute jumper was giving new meaning to the words "happy landings."

Throughout that fall, Coffey and Willa continued to tackle their own requirements for offering a CPTP secondary training program. They had fantastic credentials: the college students in their consolidated ground school were examined in September and scored an average of 90. The non-college students reportedly also scored a high average. Two of the college students had come from Tuskegee Institute itself so that they could do their CPTP flying in Chicago.

In October, the CAA made plans for a commencement ceremony sponsored by the National Airmen's Association in which seventy-five flight graduates would receive their certificates, and by now there were over 150 new students enrolled in the ground school course. Not only that, Willa and Coffey had Edgar Brown arguing their cause in Washington—with special attention to ensuring that any bills authorizing new funding for the CPTP included the words "without regard to race, creed, or color." CAA funding continued to roll in.

"We must have done a pretty good job because they gladly gave us a secondary [training unit]," Coffey was at last able to say with satisfaction.

In addition to the aerobatic-capable planes Darr had loaned him,

The aviation mechanics class in the basement machine shop of Wendell Phillips High School in Chicago, part of the Civilian Pilot Training Program as run by the Coffey School of Aeronautics. Coffey's Boeing P-12 is in the background at the upper right.

SMITHSONIAN NATIONAL AIR AND SPACE MUSEUM (NASM 99-15431)

Coffey also managed to procure a damaged Boeing P-12 to begin training mechanics as well as pilots, with Harlem Airport owner Fred Schumacher's brother Bill as one of Coffey's students.

Writing to another interested prospective student, Wesley Hudson, Coffey gave a taste of what a "young [person] sincerely interested in [aviation]" could expect from the course at the Coffey School. At the time, Coffey's CPTP program was full. To pursue training out of pocket, he estimated, it would take six months and cost a total of $1,000 to gain a commercial pilot's license, the hourly rate in a Piper

Cub trainer being $6 dual (with an instructor) and $5 solo. That was nearly half what it had cost Coffey himself fifteen years earlier— though still not something most minorities could afford on second-class wages. In fact, in his reply to Hudson, Coffey included a CPTP application for the next round of scholarships, just in case.

But the student pilots were just as determined as their instructors. The young people scraped pennies from their budgets for food and clothing. Transportation to the airfield from wherever they were staying was always a challenge; some took the bus partway and were met at the stop by a car sent from the airfield, while others traveled in dilapidated cars or by motorcycle. One young man bicycled back and forth early in the morning and got his flight lessons in before going to work.

With the loss of Lewis Jackson, Coffey was still the school's only qualified advanced flight instructor. With two aerobatic planes at his disposal, and twenty students, he needed help. One day he was approached by one of Fred Schumacher's elementary instructors, a white man by the name of Homer Carrick.

"Mr. Coffey, I understand you got two airplanes and you['re] only able to fly one of them," Carrick told Coffey. Although he wasn't qualified to teach advanced flying, Carrick added, "But if you help me get an advanced instructor's rating, I'll take the other airplane and fly the other ten students."

"In two weeks' time," Coffey recalled, "I had Homer qualified."

———

The heady challenges of the CPTP training and advocacy that absorbed Coffey and Willa meant that some of the former Challenger aviators, still based at Harlem Airport but not involved in the CPTP, found themselves with few planes and no leadership.

The spirit that had brought them into the sky in the first place stirred them to action. Janet Harmon Waterford still loved the adventure and companionship that aviation offered. When William Paris and Charles Johnson flew to Ohio together to represent Harlem Airport at the Afro-American Air Derby in Cleveland at the end of August, Janet joined them in another plane, flying with two Texan aviators who'd stopped in Chicago to pick her up. The trio then headed to New York so Janet could get some cross-country practice. It was a hair-raising ride.

"In Pennsylvania, over the Allegheny Mountains, we ran into a terrific rainstorm," she said, and described how for half an hour their open-cockpit Waco had "pitched on the edge of eternity."

The eventful flight from Cleveland took a full four and a half hours. It was the longest Janet had ever been in the air at a single stretch.

For some women, such a rough ride might have seemed like a good opportunity to call it a day and hang up her wings. Most women in their early thirties would be married—or remarried—with children. Janet had a full-time career in nursing, and her mother now lived with her. But the domestic life was never enough for Janet. The question on the billboard that had inspired her all those years ago still inspired her: "Birds Learn to Fly. Why Can't You?" Only, this time, she'd be the flying bird inspiring new fledglings to take wing, as the operator of a new flight school.

Janet's latest endeavor was in partnership with Charles Johnson, the former Challenger pilot who'd made headlines by placing competitively against white aviators in one of the flying events held at the huge

Harlem Airport air show in 1938. Theirs would be a school for people who did not qualify for the CPTP—mostly women, and those outside the required age range of eighteen to twenty-five. Like the Coffey School, Janet's school took both Black and white students.

Based out of Harlem Airport, they called their project the Johnson Flying Service. Johnson owned two Piper Cubs, and Janet now had a Piper Cruiser.

"Chicago's winter weather, however, made it difficult to fly when there was snow on the ground, as in those days runways were not plowed and, anyway, ours were sod," Janet recalled. "So once snow time came we did little flying."

But in the winter, Janet kept busy in other ways. Janet, unlike Willa and Coffey, was still friendly with Johnny Robinson, and along with Johnny and Claude Barnett, she became an advocate for Tuskegee Institute's airport fund. For although Tuskegee had their secondary CPTP course, they still didn't have a local airport.

In the early days of Tuskegee's flight training, hands-on instruction took place forty miles away from the campus, at the municipal airport in Montgomery, Alabama. By the spring of 1940, the school began leasing Kennedy Field, south of Tuskegee, where the students—in an echo of the work the Brown Eagles had performed in Robbins—provided the labor to bring the rented field up to CAA standards.

But the institute still craved an airfield that they could own outright.

Both Janet and Johnny spoke publicly at a fundraising event in November 1940 to support the building of an airfield at Tuskegee within walking distance of the campus. The evening's entertainment, which the *Atlanta Daily World*'s correspondent Daniel J. Faulkner enthusiastically called "Tuskegee Institute airport hysteria," was held at Poro College and led by Tuskegee's president, Dr. Patterson.

According to Faulkner, Patterson emphasized in his own speech "that the Negro should be integrated into all phases of American democracy."

Those words may well have haunted him throughout the coming year.

But Janet's loyal support for Tuskegee, at a time when many of her friends felt betrayed by the school, would pay off for her own aviation goals down the line.

———

The Civilian Pilot Training Program had gone a good way toward opening the sky to young Black Americans. But if they were going to serve as military pilots they would need military training, and that still wasn't available to them. What's more, none of the recent legislation contained any clause that the Air Corps felt *required* them to actually admit Black pilots, regardless of the lawmakers' intent. Roderick Williams, the African American student who'd received his pilot's license in the initial experimental phase of the CPTP beginning in 1938, was turned down when he attempted to sign up with the Air Corps.

"Shall we ever be given the chance to fly for our country?" demanded James L.H. Peck, an accomplished Black aviator who, in addition to being a correspondent for the *Pittsburgh Courier*, was the author of a book on aviation. With the unrest in Europe, it was folly to deny military training to talented and qualified pilots; Peck pointed out in frustration that no amount of civilian flight experience actually prepares a pilot for combat flying, and that the Army Air Corps still wasn't accepting Black aviators.

Yancey Williams had a similarly frustrating experience. Williams was a twenty-four-year-old senior in the mechanical engineering program at the historically Black Howard University in Washington, D.C. He had completed primary CPTP training at Howard, and even passed an Army flying physical. On November 20, 1940, he applied as a flying cadet in the U.S. Army. Three days later, he was informed by the Air Corps that "appropriate Air Corps units are not available at this time, at which colored applicants can be given flying cadet training." Thanks to the military's segregationist policies, no airfield or flight school was equipped and willing to accommodate Black cadets. In other words, the Air Corps was closed to Black Americans.

After several appeals, Yancey Williams decided to sue the U.S. military with the legal aid of then NAACP lawyer Thurgood Marshall, who would go on to become the nation's first Black Supreme Court Justice, and his associate, W. Robert Ming, Jr.

Coincidentally, this lawsuit blew up in parallel with the Army wrangling a plan to deal with the surplus of Black soldiers that a military draft would lead to in the event of war. The 1937 mobilization plan called for 9.5 percent of the military to be made up of Black men, in proportion to the eligible population—a small percentage, but a large number, approximately 1.8 million men. Under segregation, the U.S. military would be required to provide separate housing, mess halls, and even medical care for these men. The Army had been working out a scheme to put the Black recruits to use as menial labor. But, in December 1940, it was proposed to develop an airfield dedicated to training Black Air Corps fighter pilots—a pursuit squadron—in connection with one of the Civilian Pilot Training Programs.

The plan was made public the same day Yancey Williams's lawsuit was filed in federal court. It's speculated that word of the impending lawsuit forced the military to speed up its plans. Needless to say, after the announcement, the lawsuit was dropped. Yancey Williams had, in effect, won.

The Army Air Corps considered Tuskegee the frontrunner for training the new squadron, even though it still didn't have its own airfield. Willa and Coffey, with their setup at Harlem Airport in Chicago, made for fierce competition. Nevertheless, on January 16, 1941, the War Department announced that it had chosen the Tuskegee Institute as the aviation training center for its Black pursuit squadron. At long last, the U.S. military would have a Black Air Corps—just not in Chicago.

Willa, Coffey, and Enoch Waters were outraged.

So was the NAACP, which complained directly to the secretary of war, Henry L. Stimson.

That the Air Corps training for Black pilots, for which they'd been fighting for so long, was to take place in the segregated South went against everything they'd been working toward.

———

Despite having grown up in the North, Willa Brown was no stranger to the effects of segregation.

When Willa was twenty-one years old, barely a month into her teaching career, she'd found herself in the center of a high-tension battle over segregation in the Gary schools. In September 1927, when eighteen Black elementary school graduates entered the almost-all-white Emerson High School in Gary, six hundred white students staged a protest by walking out of school and marching in a spontaneous parade carrying makeshift signs that said, "We won't go back until Emerson's white." With parental support, and as the administration looked the other way, the students involved in the Emerson School strike carried on their walkout for four days.

The city council, even though it included three Black members, sent all of Emerson's Black students to a temporary high school in a set of portable classrooms known as the Roosevelt Annex, where the young Willa Brown had just begun teaching. Three senior girls got the NAACP to fight their cause in court, arguing that they were about to graduate and needed Emerson High School's facilities such as labs and libraries—and they lost their battle. Outraged citizens called the commitment to segregation "discriminatory, un-American, prejudicial, unfair, and unjust"—even stating that it was a violation of the Constitution—but their protests were ignored.

The fallout of the strike was a classic example of the twisted notion "separate but equal" at work. The city agreed to spend $600,000 (equivalent to about $9,000,000 today, a huge sum of money) on a fantastic new school for Gary's Black students. Ultimately investing a million dollars in the project, the city delivered on its promise to build the beautiful facility, which opened as Roosevelt High School with Willa heading their commerce department in 1931 and 1932. Black and white teachers even received equal pay in the Gary school system—but school segregation in Gary remained firmly in place for twenty years to come.

Willa no doubt remembered this outcome as she actively joined the battle against segregation in the Army Air Corps. This time, however, she wasn't twenty-one and barely a month into her first teaching job. This time, she had the support of the media and of aviators all over

America. In January 1941, Enoch Waters and the National Airmen's Association of America sent furious press releases to the national newspapers, fully prepared to follow up with a campaign against the Air Corps's segregated training policy.

But Claude Barnett of the ANP agreed with Tuskegee's Dr. Patterson.

"Here we have what we have been yelling for, a chance to get into the Army Air Corps," he said, "and they want to give the Army a chance to go back on its program by starting opposition to it."

It was a common story for Black Americans—being told to take an unequal compromise and be grateful for it.

Barnett tried to calm Willa down, but he was too late to stop Enoch Waters's press release. The best he could do was to warn Dr. Patterson about what was going on, and to advise him not to worry about it.

"A strong resolution condemning the War Department's plan to establish an all-Negro pursuit squadron as a part of the United States Army Air Corps was adopted by the National Airmen's Association here [in Chicago] Friday," Waters announced in newspapers on January 25, 1941. The press release stated in no uncertain terms that the NAAA was determined "to intensify its campaign to have Negroes integrated without regard to race into the United States Army Air Corps which presently bars Negroes."

Equally outrageous to the NAAA was the plan for the squadron to be commanded by a white officer. Even during World War I, one all-Black Army unit—nicknamed the Buffalo Soldiers Division, a name intended to inspire strength and determination—had allowed educated African Americans to serve as officers leading Black troops.

"Our fight for entrance into the Air Corps has been long," Coffey said. Contrary to Barnett's assurances, he added, "We don't intend to compromise here . . . We'd rather be excluded . . . than to be segregated."

A photograph in the *Baltimore Afro-American* from February 1941 captioned "Proof That Races Can Mix in Aviation Training" shows Willa in a packed classroom at Wendell Phillips High School, demonstrating the construction of an aircraft engine to an attentive crowd of both Black and white faces.

"There is no segregation in the CAA programs," Willa declared proudly, "and there have been no race riots or violence because of this fact. [We] think the War Department is attempting to inject the racial issue where none has existed in the past . . . I don't see why this same spirit of interracial cooperation cannot be carried over into the Army Air Corps."

Claude Barnett worked hard to smooth over the relationship between Tuskegee and the National Airmen's Association. Meanwhile, Dr. Patterson managed to work around the issue of a white commander by requesting that Benjamin O. Davis, Jr., who'd been the first Black man to graduate from the United States Military Academy at West Point in over forty-five years, be transferred from Fort Riley, Kansas, to command the Air Corps unit at Tuskegee. Davis was an officer, not an aviator, though he'd long had an interest in flying. Now he would learn to fly alongside his men.

On March 19, 1941, the 99th Pursuit Squadron came into existence, with pilot combat training beginning at Tuskegee Institute. Even with the forced segregation, it was a victory. Tuskegee Institute would go down in history as the birthplace of the Tuskegee Airmen, the first pilots of color in the United States military.

The new Tuskegee-based Air Corps unit was exciting, but the Army had another word for it: "experimental." At this point, the military still had plenty of doubts about the program's prospects. But one prominent American who believed it would be a success was none other than the First Lady, Eleanor Roosevelt.

That same spring, Mrs. Roosevelt was traveling in the South on a tour to meet ordinary Americans struggling with daily living. The First Lady had a radio program in which she featured the folks she met. As a member of one of Tuskegee's funding boards, she spent a week in Tuskegee, and she took the time to watch the aviation activities and talk to the flight students. There she met the first of Tuskegee's CPTP flight instructors, Charles Alfred Anderson, soon to be known to everyone as "Chief."

"She said, 'I'm going to take a flight with you.' Of course everybody objected to it, you know. 'No, you can't do that, Mrs. Roosevelt. You can't go up with him.' But she was . . . the type of person [who] did what she pleased," Chief recalled.

She also insisted that the flight be photographed, as proof of her support. The iconic photo shows Chief and the First Lady smiling broadly from their seats in the front and back of a small Piper Cub training aircraft, with Lewis Jackson grinning as he holds the plane's window open so that the faces of pilot and passenger are plainly visible. Mrs. Roosevelt wears her customary little black hat decorated with flowers—and she looks delighted.

"Mrs. Roosevelt was willing to risk her life with one of us," Chief later said, "because she saw no reason why Blacks could not fly."

Eleanor Roosevelt seated in a Piper Cub on April 11, 1941, with Charles "Chief"
Anderson in the pilot's seat. Lewis Jackson stands below the wing, holding the window
open for the photographer to get a good shot of the First Lady.
U.S. AIR FORCE SAF, DRUs, AND FOAs

The photo ran widely in the press on both sides of the color line. It did much to raise the visibility of capable Black pilots and the Tuskegee "experiment" as a whole. Mrs. Roosevelt's stamp of approval even led to the Tuskegee Institute obtaining a substantial loan from the Rosenwald Fund, a charitable organization of which she was a board member. That loan provided enough money to enable the school to finally build its own airfield. Construction began on July 23, and although according to George L. Washington it was still a "muddy, congested situation" three months later, flying began there on November 8, 1941. It was named Moton Field, after the school's second president.

Throughout the spring of 1941, Johnny Robinson had been in contact with Tuskegee. He'd been elected president of the Chicago Tuskegee alumni club in December 1940, and had openly defended Tuskegee against the accusation of accepting a Jim Crow air squadron.

"I am opposed to segregation and discrimination not only in the defense forces, but in all other phases of American democracy," Johnny told a meeting of the Chicago Tuskegee club. "[But] I sincerely believe that in this, the early stages of this training, an all-Negro unit will enable the trainees to progress more rapidly, prove [their] ability, and establish [themselves] in this service." In February, Johnny published a scathing attack in the *Atlanta Daily World* against an unnamed "small group of Negroes [who] for selfish motives and personal gain" were "trying to gain public support in an attempt to block this forward step." It was a thinly veiled reference to Johnny's former comrades; the gulf between Johnny and Coffey seemed to be widening.

In addition to supporting Tuskegee's fundraising efforts, Johnny had been encouraging them to move his aviation mechanics training program to the institute, bringing with him his National Youth Administration sponsorship and government equipment. He and Janet Harmon Waterford flew to Tuskegee in April so Johnny could discuss "plans for courses in aviation mechanics" with President Patterson and George L. Washington. In May, Johnny called up Washington at Tuskegee and offered his services as commander of the 99th—or as the manager of Tuskegee's aviation program—or as their head of instruction in aviation mechanics—whichever they preferred.

Then he took time off his work for the National Defense Program to fly to Tuskegee again to discuss these possibilities in person. It appears that his employers weren't pleased, and threatened to dismiss him as an instructor. Johnny raced back to Chicago to save his job.

George L. Washington, faithful and generous as always to Tuskegee's alumnus hero, sent Johnny a telegram with an offer of employment. But Johnny told him that the salary Tuskegee was offering through the Alabama Department of Education was too low. Washington wrote back to explain patiently that all the managerial positions Johnny had suggested were already filled and that this was the top salary offered to flight and aviation mechanics instructors. They would be delighted to offer him a more senior job when a vacancy came up. Of course, all of this depended on his being correctly licensed—a constant lack, it seemed. Johnny didn't take Washington up on the offer.

This time his decision did little to slow the progress at Tuskegee. On July 19, 1941, the Civilian Pilot Training Program at Tuskegee Institute in Alabama officially became a military training school.

All eyes were on Tuskegee, waiting to see what it could do.

The answer was: its very best. Many of the civilian pilots trained at the Coffey School would eventually join the 99th for combat training. Even institute administrators George L. Washington and Dr. Patterson were given ten hours' subsidized flight training. Both eventually made it to solo level.

The "Tuskegee experiment" had begun.

———

Willa Brown and Cornelius Coffey were bitterly disappointed about the segregation in the 99th Pursuit Squadron, but it didn't stop them from continuing to promote the National Airmen's Association and to further build the Coffey School. Now that they had been granted their secondary training course, they were gearing up to teach the next levels, cross-country and instrument training. By the middle of June 1941, they owned a fleet of ten planes—a far cry from the little Heath Parasol with which Coffey and Johnny had begun. Willa and Coffey flew to Lockhaven, Pennsylvania, with Willa at the controls, to collect their latest brand-new Piper Cub. When they landed back at Chicago, the Coffey School students were waiting for Willa with a bouquet of flowers. If the sky was a kingdom, some of the newspapers noted that Willa was undeniably the race's new queen.

She was also now president of the Chicago chapter of the NAAA, and the belle of the aviation ball. Willa was a true role model for women in the field. The proof was in a stream of young Black women taking fresh instruction, flying solo, and graduating from the Civilian Pilot Training Program in Chicago: Alice Charlton, Leon Joy Gurley, and Rachel Carter, to name a few who made the newspapers in 1941. Rachel Carter, who was the only woman in the first class Willa had taught at Wendell Phillips, deeply admired her. "She had a sternness too and was businesslike," Carter observed. "She was serious and thought it important that the 'youngsters' succeed."

And Willa found other ways to help young women succeed. She gave Gurley paid work as her secretary; she gave Marie St. Clair free flying lessons. "She was a mentor to me," said St. Clair. "She took me under her wing, she was such a nice person."

Willa also continued to promote aviation for Black communities. She'd gone to Washington, D.C., in April with a delegation from Chicago, meeting with government department heads such as Robert H. Hinkley, chairman of the CAA, and asking specifically "that members

Willa Brown proudly posing with two Piper Cubs from the Coffey School of Aeronautics fleet, summer 1940

SAN DIEGO AIR & SPACE MUSEUM

of our race be completely integrated in the U.S. Air Corps." On August 17, 1941, Willa appeared on a nationally broadcast radio program, *Wings Over Jordan*; the show, based in Cleveland, Ohio, and emceed by a minister by the name of Glenn Settles, aired Sunday mornings and featured a choir and a conversation with a prominent person in the Black community.

To make her radio appearance, ever the show-woman, Willa flew to Cleveland and arrived over the city early so that she could plan a big entrance. Waters traveled with her.

Instead of landing, Waters explained, "we flew back to Oberlin, [Ohio,] noting the time carefully. We landed and Willa changed into the white outfit she had worn when I first met her and freshened her makeup." Willa then flew them back to Cleveland, landing, as Waters tells it, "at the exact time scheduled for our arrival. The assembled crowd was surprised at our punctuality and overwhelmed when Willa hopped out of the cockpit to the cheers of several hundred persons. A band struck up 'Lift Every Voice and Sing,' popularly known as the Negro National Anthem." Everybody posed for pictures, and then a motorcade of cars drove Willa and Waters to the radio station. "It was sensational," Waters declared.

Willa gave an eloquent speech about the history of Black aviation, beginning with Bessie Coleman, and finishing with—as well as taking the credit for, on behalf of the National Airmen's Association—the formation of the 99th Pursuit Squadron at Tuskegee Institute (whose name she didn't mention). Though she celebrated the acceptance of Black Americans into the Army Air Corps, Willa would never be happy about the military's choice to segregate the unit.

"Those who had worked hardest for admittance of Negroes to the Air Corps, though, were bitterly disappointed when the War Department announced that it would admit Negroes only into a separate unit," she told the nation over the radio. "In spite of bitter protest, the War Department has remained adamant in its insistence upon a separate squadron."

Willa's flight home with Waters was also sensational. Bad weather forced the duo to divert to a field in Angola, Indiana, Lewis Jackson's hometown. Witnesses to the plane's emergency landing were "dismayed as we gradually descended and two Negroes hopped out," Waters said. But dismay turned to awe when they saw Willa, resplendent in her white jodhpurs and flying cap. "They told us no Negroes lived there, so we were novelties of a sort.

"They treated us royally, rounding up a mechanic to take care of our engine and inviting us into their homes and feeding us. Willa was so impressed, she told the mayor she was going to put on an air show to express our gratitude. Three or four hundred people watched us take off," Waters recalled. True to her word, a few weeks later, Willa returned with some other pilots and put on a flight display that, according to Waters, "resulted in a flood of letters from the little town."

═══

In September 1941, a hundred pilots from all over the nation converged on Harlem Airport for the third annual National Airmen's Association conference. The event was growing. This time, it was Cornelius Coffey who was awarded the Dwight Green trophy "for meritorious contributions to Negro aviation."

The report in the *Chicago Defender* stated, "On the strength of his having supervised the training of a large number of students during the past year and the unselfish assistance he gave many, financial and otherwise, Coffey was voted the trophy unanimously." Whether because of his naturally retiring nature, or the solemnity with which he viewed the attention, the accompanying photo shows a serious-faced Coffey receiving his due.

In November, at a meeting at the historically Black Hampton Institute in Virginia, instructors from all the participating Black schools offering Civilian Pilot Training Programs came together, along with airport operators and government representatives. They joined forces for the first time as the Aeronautical Association of Negro Schools, agreeing to throw their support behind Tuskegee and the Coffey School as advanced training centers in a bid to ask the CAA to enlarge their student quotas. The group also began to plan a national air meet for all the Black CPTP flight schools to be staged in Washington, D.C., later that winter.

George L. Washington, the director of the Tuskegee Institute's School of Mechanical Industries, was elected president of the new association, and Willa Brown was elected vice president.

The two great powers in Black aviation had called a truce, it seemed. The NAAA and Tuskegee agreed to work together for their common cause. With every act of effort, skill, and goodwill, African Americans were claiming their place in the sky together.

═══

A highlight of the year for the Chicago aviators no doubt came on Monday, November 24, 1941, when Dr. Mary McLeod Bethune, the magnificently respected civil rights activist and advisor to President Franklin D. Roosevelt, visited the aviation classrooms at Wendell Phillips High School. There, she was given an introduction to aircraft engines by Willa Brown.

Perhaps it was this visit that inspired Willa to attempt another moonshot. Less than two weeks later, on December 6, 1941, she wrote a letter to First Lady Eleanor Roosevelt, well known for her dedication to equal rights for African Americans, and whose attention had done so much for the Tuskegee program. Willa told Mrs. Roosevelt about the National Airmen's Association of America, as well as the newly formed Aeronautical Association of Negro Schools. She politely and hopefully requested a personal meeting with the president's wife, either in Chicago or in Washington, D.C., asking that the famous

woman might hear her out on some unnamed "difficulties" these asso-
ciations encountered, difficulties Willa considered "far too great for
me to master."

One had to wonder what the mood was in the White House that
December. Throughout the year, war in Europe and Asia had been
rising to a fever pitch. But the United States was determined to stay
neutral. In the early days of Franklin Roosevelt's presidency, the country had been struggling to lift itself out of the Great Depression, and
most Americans had been content to deal with their problems at home
and not get involved with a war overseas.

But they would soon discover they had no choice.

Willa didn't get her meeting with Eleanor Roosevelt. Back in July,
Japan had invaded Indochina, threatening British and Dutch colonies
in the region. The United States had retaliated by freezing Japan's as-
sets—including access to imported American oil, on which it
depended. On December 7, 1941, the day after Willa sent her letter, the
Japanese Imperial Army attacked the U.S. Naval base at Pearl Harbor
on the island of Oahu, Hawaii, even though the Japanese ambassador
had been in peace talks with the United States up until the morning
of the attack. Battleships in the harbor were badly damaged, 169 U.S.
aircraft were destroyed, and 2,403 Americans were killed, both military and civilian. President Roosevelt called it "a date which will live in
infamy."

The next day, the United States declared war on Japan. Three days
later, on December 11, they declared war on the two major nations
supporting Japan, known as the Axis forces, Germany and Italy.

In an instant, America went from uneasy preparation and a decade-
long policy of staying out of foreign wars and the troubles in Europe,

to one of all-out global conflict. The United States had entered World War II.

Over the next months and years, the U.S. military would grow from one and a half million soldiers to over six million. And to reach that number, the country would have to call on all of its citizens, including people of color.

CHAPTER 11

WINGS OF WAR, 1941-1945

The negro does not perform his share of civil duties in time of peace in proportion to his population. He has no leaders in industrial or commercial life. He takes no part in government. Compared to the white man he is admittedly of inferior mentality. He is inherently weak in character.

—"Notes on Proposed Plan for Use of Negro Manpower," U.S. Army War College, 1925

Nor since the Civil War ended in 1865 had there been a war fought on U.S. soil. And that had been a war fought by Americans against Americans. For ninety-three years the United States had been at peace with its neighbors, Mexico to the south and Canada to the north, even as conflicts raged across the sea. With the attack on Pearl Harbor on December 7, 1941, the day that President Roosevelt said would "live in infamy," that sense of security was shattered, along with the lives of over 3,500 people killed or wounded in the attack.

In the days after the bombing of the naval base at Pearl Harbor, the Library of Congress—the national library of the United States— conducted "man-on-the-street" interviews, recording the thoughts of everyday Americans. In front of a pool hall in Washington, D.C., the oral historian Alan Lomax interviewed Black men and teens. A sixteen-year-old boy who worked the counter at a nearby restaurant told him, "When I first heard about the war I said to myself, I hope the United States will fight until the last man go down . . . Negroes . . . are proud of [the] United States and they will fight until the last man go down." When Lomax asked him what his friends thought of the attack on Pearl Harbor, the youth replied, "Many Negroes' lives will be lost in the war, as was before. And after this war . . . I hope the Negroes will have much more freedom than they have now."

Now that the United States had entered World War II, young Americans of all races expected to be recruited into the military. The determination to fight for freedom both abroad and at home was something that this unnamed sixteen-year-old restaurant server shared with Black Americans throughout the nation. Their patriotism ran high, but so did their frustration.

In an eloquent and impassioned letter to the *Pittsburgh Courier*, twenty-six-year-old James G. Thompson asked, "Would it be demanding too much to demand full citizenship rights in exchange for the sacrificing of my life?" Thompson was understandably outraged. He worked in an aircraft factory, but not assembling aircraft. Because he was Black, he was only allowed to work in the cafeteria. Thompson insisted that while the nation's first priorities were defense and victory, he warned that Americans should not "lose sight of our fight for true democracy at home."

Ever since the American Revolution, African Americans had served in the military on the promise of attaining their freedom. After Emancipation in 1863, the fight was for equal rights with white Americans. World War I, too, had been fought with this goal in mind. Although

Black Americans served bravely then, the fight for equality continued, and this new war could emerge as the catalyst for the changes that would deliver those rights.

"Those who perpetuate these ugly prejudices here are seeking to destroy our democratic form of government just as surely as the Axis forces," Thompson argued passionately.

On the back of the wartime "V for Victory" campaign launched by the United Kingdom in July 1941, which had been picked up by the United States even before it entered the war, Thompson suggested a name for this dual battle for freedom at home and abroad: the "double victory," or "Double V."

The *Pittsburgh Courier* popularized Thompson's suggestion in another sweeping national campaign beginning in February 1942. The newspaper proudly proclaimed: "The 'Double V' stands for victory against the enemies abroad and for victory against the forces at home who would deny the Negro full and free participation in every phase of national life." The Double V would be a triumph over the hatred and evil spread by Nazism, together with a triumph over racism and segregation in the United States.

Hawaii lies two thousand miles southwest of the United States mainland, and four thousand miles from Chicago. But Chicago felt the aftermath of Pearl Harbor as keenly as the rest of the world. Even before the Double V campaign took hold, the Black pilots at Harlem Airport would have agreed with that young counter boy from Washington, D.C. African Americans were ready to fight the evil of Nazism just as fiercely as they'd been fighting against racism for so long. And they were determined to win both victories, not just on the ground, but also in the air.

Now that the United States was at war, Americans were deeply fearful of being attacked on North American soil, and the threat was real. German U-boats slunk under the sea right up to the shores of the East Coast, and in Germany's Operation Drumbeat in the early months of 1942, those enemy submarines preyed on American shipping from the Gulf of Mexico right on up to the chilly waters of New England. On the ground, a spy who managed to enter the country could potentially get access to an American plane and study it for its abilities and weaknesses, then pass that information back to enemy pilots with ideas for how to most easily defeat the Americans and the other Allied nations. Hawaii had been vulnerable because it was an outlier, two thousand miles away from the rest of the country. But could something as terrible as Pearl Harbor happen on the mainland?

Late one night at a small airfield outside of Cleveland, Ohio, a few weeks after Pearl Harbor was bombed, a man named Earle L. Johnson decided to find out.

Johnson was white, a civilian pilot, and an American. He was also Ohio's state director of aeronautics. But tonight, he was a saboteur.

He loaded his own plane with three small bags and took off from his farm airstrip into the night sky, heading for a group of factories on the edge of the city—factories that manufactured supplies for the war effort.

Nobody paid any attention to the little plane puttering through the night. Dropping to five hundred feet, Johnson leaned out of his aircraft and dropped the loaded bags—one—two—three—onto the buildings below.

He returned home unmolested. In the morning, he contacted the factories to let them know: they had been "bombed."

There had been no explosions—no loud booms or flashes of light. In fact, no one on the ground had taken any notice. Fortunately, the bags only held sand, but Johnson had made his point.

Single-handedly, Johnson had managed to destroy the mainland United States's sense of security.

For his part, Johnson ordered a ban on all unauthorized civilian night flying in the state of Ohio. Then he sat back to see what the rest of the country would do.

The CAA immediately brought in a raft of new regulations for civilian pilots. For a while all flights were grounded. Then pilots had to prove their American citizenship, and get a photo ID with fingerprints; eventually they also had to get a radio license, as now all authorized planes were required to be fitted with two-way radios. Everyone had to file flight plans. Security at all airports tightened up—airplanes could not be left alone.

"After Pearl Harbor, every airport had to have armed guards," Cornelius Coffey explained. "We had to have lights on the airport and [areas] around all buildings had to be lit. I went to work and got all of my instructors deputized. They had sheriff deputy badges, and that gave them permission to carry arms. We had to arm all our personnel twenty-four hours a day."

Now if a careless Coffey School student ran out of fuel in the air and had to land in a field or on the highway, someone had to immediately drive out to the downed plane, bringing a few gallons of fuel along in a can just to get it into the air again and home safely. Otherwise, someone would have to stay and stand guard over the plane, or else it would have to be disabled so it was unflyable.

===

Security on the home front was something that American civilian pilots knew they could help with. They had a practical skill that could be used to protect their country. And thus the Civil Air Patrol (CAP) was born. This national paramilitary organization was the brainchild of Gill Robb Wilson, an aviation veteran of World War I, who'd made a trip to Germany in 1936 and had come home very alarmed by what he'd seen there. Long before the United States entered the war, Wilson had proposed that the U.S. government organize a home guard made up of civilians flying light aircraft who could keep an eye out for enemy threats on U.S. soil. By 1941, Wilson had the backing of the Office of Civil Defense, and a national headquarters was established on December 1, 1941. Exactly one week later, on December 8, the Civil Air Patrol was poised to make a public announcement for recruits. That same day, the United States declared war on Japan.

Earle L. Johnson, the farm strip flyer who'd "bombed" the factories in Cleveland, was one of the CAP's founders—and later, its commander. Other civilian pilots were quick to sign up, hot to help out on the home front. Less than a year later, there was a wing command in every state. CAP pilots flew their own planes, or rented aircraft; eventually, civilians flying for the CAP were allowed to bear arms, like Coffey's deputies, and by the end of the war, civilian pilots had reported 173 enemy submarines and even sunk two. They also reported shipwrecks and floating mines. Further inland they were responsible for patrolling pipelines and power lines, reporting forest fires, assisting the military with target practice, and keeping a secure patrol over airports.

The Coffey School, like other civilian flight organizations, was anxious to join the Civil Air Patrol, and not just because they were feeling patriotic. America's entry into World War II threatened the school's very existence.

Within a week of the United States entering the war, the Civilian Pilot Training Program had been drastically restructured as the CAA War Training Service (WTS), though it didn't take this new name until the following year. On December 13, 1941, President Roosevelt signed Executive Order #8974, "Control of Civil Aviation," declaring that all CAA pilot training facilities would from now on be solely devoted to training men destined to become military aviators. Women would no longer be accepted in the program; and though it wasn't expressly stated, the implication was that neither would Black men, since there was little prospect available to them in military aviation.

As valuable as the Coffey School had proven itself to be, they could now lose everything, and they needed to prove their worth.

On behalf of the NAAA, Cornelius Coffey and Willa Brown sent their state senator and representative in a delegation to their sympathetic governor, Dwight H. Green, to urge him to let them form an integrated unit of the Civil Air Patrol. They got their wish. Their officers were sworn in on March 20, 1942, with Cornelius Coffey as the squadron commander of Group 613-6 of the Illinois Wing, Civil Air Patrol. William Paris, now a flight instructor at the Coffey School, was the newly formed squadron's executive officer, and Willa Brown its adjutant (assistant to the commander).

The squadron was expected to patrol the skies, keeping a watchful eye over anything that might become a strategic target for attack or sabotage: airports, factories, warehouses, bridges, railroads, and the like. Group 613-6 pilots participated in such activities as target training and the surveillance of coastal areas, presumably the twenty-two-mile-

Swearing-in ceremony for the Civil Air Patrol, March 20, 1942. Cornelius Coffey is at left, Willa Brown third from the right. At right stands CAP Wing Commander Jack Vilas.

KENNETH SPENCER RESEARCH LIBRARY, UNIVERSITY OF KANSAS

long Lake Michigan shoreline in Chicago; they ran patrolling and navigation exercises that were precisely timed to the minute. Members also had to take their turn at overnight guard duty in the hangars on the ground so that no more saboteurs—real or civic-minded—could get the drop on U.S. property ever again. The group, including Willa, participated in a sham "bombing" of Chicago under the supervision of the city's supportive Mayor Kelly, who was now also the coordinator of civilian defense for the city.

In addition to the obvious skills their unit exhibited, Coffey and Willa were hugely proud of the fact that Group 613-6 of the Civil Air Patrol was an integrated, not a segregated, unit. The War Department had called it "impossible," according to the *Chicago Defender*: "an aviation squadron made up of Negro and white flyers under the command of Negro officers." Yet again, Coffey, Willa, and their team had managed to make the impossible happen.

But national security was a constant battle. Harlem Airport was shut down for just over an entire week in the middle of June 1942—losing prime flying weather for the 150 Black students enrolled in the CPTP/WTS course at the time—because a CAA inspector named Walter A. Storck decided that the airfield wasn't providing enough armed guards at their buildings. Storck had flown over Harlem, circled the airfield several times, and was surprised that nobody had signaled him to land. After he did land, he walked into a hangar without anyone trying to stop him.

It wasn't necessarily Coffey's fault, nor was his school the only flight training affected: Fred Schumacher, who was operating at Harlem Airport under two government contracts to teach civilians, was also affected. Schumacher brought the entire airport in line with federal regulations and increased the number of guards, bringing the total to nineteen, before the airfield was allowed to reopen.

═══

That summer, thousands of miles from Chicago, Japan continued to invade the countries of Southeast Asia with the goal of becoming a superpower in the East. If the Japanese Imperial Army could secure Midway Island, they would have a launchpad for further attacks on Hawaii. In June 1942, the U.S. struck back in a massive naval confrontation. The Battle of Midway decimated the Japanese navy. The United

States was gaining ground in the Pacific theater of war, named for the ocean on which it was waged, but the fight was far from over.

Wartime posed challenges both big and small to the Coffey School, including one that continually threatened their very existence: the battle for money. It was bad enough that, under the new wartime regulations, the CPTP/WTS no longer offered training to women. But with its new war footing, the government had begun to divert funding to focus on the men already in the program. While this change seems to have been program-wide, it was a particularly hard blow for Black students. So far, the Coffey School had retained its funding, but since the start of the war, other civilian training programs—especially those for Black students—were shutting down left and right. Willa had to be on her toes about anticipating that they might be next.

"Because of the reorganization of the Civilian Pilot Training Program now under supervision of the War Department, all ten Negro colleges throughout the country have had to fall out of the program," she told Illinois congressman Raymond S. McKeough in August 1942. She begged McKeough to present the matter to Henry L. Stimson, the secretary of war, citing patriotism, and the establishment of Tuskegee's 99th Pursuit Squadron as the great success of the Chicago "experiment." "Only one Negro school is left," she warned McKeough. "That is the Coffey school in Chicago, and unless the government feels the need of retaining at least one Negro school in [the] Civilian Pilot Training Program it is not known how long this one will continue to operate."

Willa's appeal worked. In the summer of 1942, the Coffey School received a loan for $25,000 through the federal government, and in the middle of August they announced that they were going to completely expand and reorganize. From now on, their entire establishment would be located at Harlem Airport—dormitories would be erected to house the students, the ground school would move there from Wendell Phillips, and in addition to the hands-on flight training in the air, throughout the coming winter they would be able to offer advanced flight instrument training in a Link Trainer simulator loaned to them by the War Department.

Between September 1, 1942, and July 1, 1943, the school would be expected to train sixty students in the elementary flying course, and another seventy-five students in whatever advanced courses the War Department designated, including secondary, cross-country, and instrument training. Another seventy-five young pilots would be assigned to advanced training at Tuskegee. Indeed, any young Black pilot who completed the Coffey course could expect to head straight to Tuskegee for military training with the 99th Pursuit Squadron.

In August 1942, Willa proudly attended the swearing-in ceremony as four young graduates of the Coffey School's CPTP/WTS course joined what was now known as the Army Air Forces. All four of them—Alexander Bright, James Brothers, Edward Flowers, and Porter Myrick—were off to Tuskegee.

Willa was hugely relieved at the results of her efforts. She called it a partial victory "in freeing the bottleneck which prevented the training of Negroes as pilots."

But Tuskegee was also a challenge to the Coffey School. The program at Tuskegee was growing by leaps and bounds; by the summer of 1942, they'd produced so many qualified aviators that the U.S. military decided to form the 332nd Fighter Group, which would include several new Black squadrons made up of all types of personnel who trained at

Tuskegee—including ground and support crew, not just pilots. The 99th Pursuit Squadron remained separate from this group, and were deployed for combat in North Africa in March 1943, going on to fight in Italy by the end of that year. The big operation at Tuskegee was constantly in need of fresh instructors, and the instructors at the Coffey School were always a little *too* good—which meant Tuskegee wanted them. Just as they'd done with Lewis Jackson, Tuskegee quickly snapped up Coffey's competent flight teachers.

"The funny thing about that was . . . we had not only the problem of trying to teach students, but we had to actually develop our own instructors," Coffey said. "And every time we'd get an instructor qualified, you know where he'd go": Tuskegee. Even Homer Carrick, the white pilot who Coffey had put through the advanced training course, didn't stay long, though Carrick, being white, didn't end up at Tuskegee. "When we finished the first group, the Navy grabbed him and sent him to Pensacola, Florida," Coffey complained.

Nevertheless, due to Coffey's determination and foresight, by September 1942 the Coffey School had fifteen instructors. Willa's brother Simeon was one of them, having qualified as a ground instructor in March. And fortunately, Coffey had learned from his experience. He started keeping new instructors ready and waiting, with his eye always on likely students and other pilots that he could train to teach.

The dormitories were also a new venture for the Coffey School. "We had to come up with a program of developing a barracks building," Coffey said. "We had to come up with obtaining uniforms for the students." With Willa's able assistance, Coffey managed to get hold of olive-green trousers with tunics and overcoats, surplus uniforms from the Civilian Conservation Corps, a program established in 1933 by the

Roosevelt administration to maintain the country's forest and parks. "We not only got uniforms for the cadets, but we had flying suits for winter operations. We had to get the fur-lined boots. We had to get the fur-lined helmets, and by the way, I'm talking about below-zero flying in an open cockpit," Coffey explained, a venture that required a leather face mask to protect pilots from the freezing wind. Unlike in the early days of the Challenger Aero Club, they couldn't allow Chicago's cold winters to stop CPTP classes, because they only had five weeks for each training session. "Many times, we would get rain that would stay in the runways, and we couldn't use them . . . [S]ometimes I had to transfer my operation to [Rubinkam Field, Markham Township, Illinois] or Joliet [Illinois]." The Coffey program used the Joliet airfield for night flying as well, because the sod and dirt runways at Harlem Airport lacked lights.

======

In July of 1942, a law was passed that amended the Civilian Pilot Training Act to also provide for the training of civilian aviation mechanics. Johnny Robinson, who'd been instructing aviation mechanics from his setup at Poro College under the National Defense Program, now became an instructor at the Army Air Forces Technical Training Command School at Chanute Field, about 120 miles south of Chicago.

The technical school at Chanute had become a hugely important training center for the U.S. Army on the ground. In fact, it was their hub for mechanical training on aircraft. Approximately forty of Chanute's instructors were Black men, including Johnny Robinson, while most of the young mechanics taking instruction from them were white—a truly unique arrangement in the Army at this time. The situation developed because the 99th Pursuit Squadron at Tuskegee was going to need mechanical and technical support for its segregated combat unit. In a segregated squadron, both soldiers and staff were Black—including doctors, nurses, secretaries, and mechanics. And just like every other U.S. Army Air Forces squadron, they had to be trained *somewhere*. Rather than set up an inadequate separate facility, the ground crew training for the 99th was rolled into the technical school at Chanute.

The school even boasted five Black women as instructors, teaching subjects ranging from basic aircraft and engine structure to instrument reading and parachute rigging. Johnny was considered one of the real stars of the show, and was featured in a couple of national radio broadcasts showcasing activities at Chanute.

The classes at Chanute were all mixed in terms of race. Enoch Waters, visiting the school so he could complete a series of articles about Army camps for the *Chicago Defender*, was impressed with how much the students seemed "for the moment unaware of the differences of color" because they were so absorbed in their assignments. "A white soldier from Texas pauses in the corridor between classes to discuss with a fellow student, a Negro civilian, a point which has them both scratching their heads," Waters observed.

Unfortunately, Enoch Waters finished off his positive report on a sinister note, mentioning that a separate training school for Black technicians was planned for Missouri.

"Exactly what will happen to the Negro instructors at Chanute Field under this new setup is still not determined," Waters warned. "If they are pulled out and all sent to Missouri under the new Jim Crow setup, Army democracy will suffer a bad setback."

He had reason to fear. The technical school at Chanute was up against the same fragile balance of power as the Coffey School at Harlem Airport. It was clear that the U.S. Army Air Forces weren't prepared to integrate their fighting squadrons; in December 1942, the War Department announced that Black pilots in the Army Air Forces would not be able to serve in bomber units, because these larger aircraft required multiple crew members, and the military did not want to have to integrate them.

Undeterred as 1943 began, the National Airmen's Association of America submitted a boldly ambitious business plan to the War

Department. After the poverty of the Great Depression in the 1930s, the war was bad news for peace but good news for the economy, creating jobs and production lines all over America. In this time of opportunity, the Coffey School wanted to establish and open a whole new airport at Rubinkam Field in Markham Township, where they had held their big air meet back in 1938, broadly expanding their flight training ability. Willa prepared a detailed report and requested $750,000 in federal funding to purchase land and equipment for the new flight center, figuring in costs for twenty-two planes, another Link Trainer, buildings, transport vehicles—right down to details such as seventy-five parachutes and fifty pairs of goggles, winter gloves, and flying boots.

The bid was rejected in March 1943, on the grounds that there was no military need or justification for such a big new operation in Chicago. However, in the same month, the CAA promised to provide the Coffey School with aircraft for the cross-country course, and discussed expanding the courses there to include training for instructors and for liaison pilots, who did courier and reconnaissance work. The CAA assured Coffey and Willa that they would be able to continue with the school's present training program "at least until the end of this fiscal year when our money runs out"—an ominous but distant deadline.

———

Meanwhile, Janet Harmon Waterford was keeping busy with the Johnson Flying Service, which offered flight instruction to women and any men who didn't qualify for the CAA's War Training Service. One day, one of Janet's white female students came to her with news, and an application.

"I want you to fill this out," the student said, giving the application form to Janet, "and I'm going to see it is mailed, because I'm going to mail it myself."

Janet was intrigued.

When the U.S. military expanded its capabilities in 1942, it had begrudgingly allowed two women, Jacqueline "Jackie" Cochran and Nancy Harkness Love, to create two female civilian flying units. In August of 1943, these two units merged to form the Women Airforce Service Pilots, or WASP. These were civilian women who would be trained to fly military planes in the United States to free up men to fight in combat overseas. WASP duties would range from observing weather conditions, to flying new airplanes from factories to the coasts for shipping to the European and Pacific theaters of war, to, perhaps most dangerously, test-flying repaired airplanes and towing targets so that soldiers on the ground could practice shooting at them in the sky.

Janet was more than qualified for the job. She submitted her application and, a couple of weeks later, was invited to the Palmer House hotel in downtown Chicago for an interview with a woman named Ethel Sheehy. Janet's three white female students had applied and received similar invitations. Elated, they all arranged to meet at the hotel.

"When he saw me, the Black elevator starter at the hotel directed me to a rear elevator—one for servants, although I didn't realize at first what he had done," Janet recalled.

When she figured out his mistake, she went back to the man and explained she was there for an interview. The elevator operator apologized and brought her up in the main elevator.

When Janet arrived at the interview suite, two of her students were in the waiting area. The third was being interviewed. Janet waited her turn. When she was called into the room, Mrs. Sheehy looked up in surprise.

"Are you Janet Harmon Waterford?"

"Yes," Janet replied.

"And do you fly?" the woman asked in astonishment.

"Yes," Janet assured her.

"Oh no! I don't know what to do," Sheehy exclaimed.

Janet asked what she meant.

"I've never interviewed a colored girl," the woman replied.

The WASP program was already facing the challenge of introducing women into a men's army; racial integration was not something it was prepared to tackle. In an attempt to dissuade Janet, Sheehy pointed out that the WASP training facility was in Sweetwater, Texas—not a friendly place for Black people, and under existing Jim Crow regulations, certainly not a place where any kind of integration could be expected.

None of this frightened Janet. She could see which way the wind was blowing, but stood her ground. At last Sheehy said she would refer Janet's case to Jackie Cochran, the female director of the WASP program. The reply, some time later, was not a surprise. "Whatever Mrs. Sheehy told you still stands," Cochran telegrammed.

Though they hadn't said so directly, Janet was shut out of the program on the basis of her skin color. The white student who had recommended that Janet apply, who had less experience, was accepted by the WASP without challenge.

The experience was hurtful, but Janet was not deterred. When her mother pointed out an article in the *Chicago Tribune* citing the desperate need for thousands of nurses to join the military nurses' corps, Janet filled out another military application. Once again she was rejected, this time on the grounds that "the quota for colored nurses" had been filled.

"Now I had made two attempts to serve my country, the only country I knew, and had been refused—not because of any physical or mental condition, but because I was Black. At this point I thought I needed a psychiatrist," Janet quipped.

Rather than accept defeat, Janet decided to increase her qualifications by getting her commercial and instrument certificates. She had already taken the exam for her commercial license, but had been grounded by Chicago's heavy winter weather.

"I thought, 'I will never get them here. What can I do? Where can I go?' I realized I already knew where I needed to go—to Tuskegee, where the weather was more reliable [and] the Army was teaching Black pilots . . . And to do that I needed to contact 'Chief' Anderson, the head of [training] at Tuskegee."

Janet had a good relationship with Tuskegee. She'd advocated for their airport fund and campaigned on their behalf; she'd met Tuskegee's President Patterson on several occasions, and she'd flown down to Tuskegee with Johnny when he visited in 1941. She'd supported the 99th Pursuit Squadron when it was formed. Now she turned to them for help.

Charles Alfred "Chief" Anderson was Tuskegee's first Black CPTP flight instructor and the man who'd taken Eleanor Roosevelt for a ride in a Piper Cub. Janet had first met Chief when he was receiving advanced flight training at the Chicago School of Aeronautics along with Coffey and Lewis Jackson. She wrote to him about coming down south to Tuskegee to get her commercial license.

"Dear Janet," he replied, "I will give you all the assistance I can."

Janet was still working as a health inspector for the Metropolitan

Burial Insurance Association. It paid well and she felt it was important work, but so was flying; the commercial license would make her invaluable as a flight instructor. So she went to see her bosses.

"I told them I wanted a leave of absence for four to six weeks to go to Tuskegee for advanced flying lessons. They were much impressed and interested, but worried about how I would survive. Really, though, I had not thought of much but getting to Tuskegee. I was willing to spend my last cent for the privilege of flying for 'Chief.'" Fortunately, she wouldn't have to spend that last cent. Her bosses spoke to the rest of the nursing staff, and they each volunteered to share Janet's duties for a month so she would still receive a paycheck. Fuel was rationed because of the war, but "they gave me gas coupons and sent me off in grand style," Janet later said. Her business partner, Charles Johnson, would stay behind to run things at their flight school. Janet was ready. "Tuskegee, here I come!"

On a cold February morning, Janet took off in Charles's red Piper Cub with flight instructor Walter Robinson and one of their students, Manuella Jackson. Fortunately, the Cub had a closed cockpit cabin, so the women were able to forgo heavy fur-lined flying clothes in favor of white coveralls Janet had designed herself.

Tuskegee was an adventure from start to finish. On the flight down, having to fight against a strong headwind meant they burned fuel more quickly than planned, and the trio were forced to land in a field in Boaz, Alabama, drawing a crowd. Thanks to the fuel coupons, they were able to refuel, but it was getting dark. In hope of finding a place to spend the night, Janet and Walter walked to a local gas station, where Janet asked a young white man she found there, "Are there any colored people living nearby?"

The young man was holding a big stick that he was using to strike at the ground. "Naw," he replied, "we are pretty tough on niggers around here."

Being from Georgia, Janet was familiar with this treatment. But for her northern copilot, it was an eye-opener. Janet hustled Walter back to Manuella and the plane. Huntsville—a bigger town where they could undoubtedly find a place to stay—was a five-minute flight away. But it was dark, and Walter was well aware they were not equipped for a night flight.

"Janet, are we going to take off?" he asked.

Janet replied, "Hell, yes!"

They took off and lucked into finding an Army Air Forces emergency landing strip. Although the man in charge of the little field was white, Janet said he was "exceptionally nice" and even directed them to the home of James Smith, a local widower, who happily put them up for the night and fed them "real Southern cooking" to boot.

When they finally arrived in Tuskegee, Chief Anderson was waiting for them—a sight for sore eyes.

Unfortunately, the misadventures did not end there. Janet bumped into more southern prejudice at Dorothy Hall, the guest house where Chief had booked rooms for them. While having breakfast in the dining hall with a white guest, they were told, "White folks and colored folks don't eat together in Alabama."

Janet tried to articulate her disillusionment. "All of a sudden, Dorothy Hall disappeared. The beauty of the place was gone. It took on a sad look. The old dining-room matron became an ugly ol' witch." But her anger soon turned to pity. Janet and Manuella left the dining room without eating. "Manuella was so confused she went back to our room. I went downstairs and, just as I got to the outer door, an Air Corps cadet squadron passed by, singing the Air Corps song about the 'wild blue yonder' and keeping in step as they sang. It was a beautiful sight to me. They looked so happy and proud to be in the Air Corps. As I stood there I almost said aloud, 'Do they know what a struggle, what a fight, what insults we have gone through for them to be air cadets, even though on a segregated basis?'"

Janet felt ready to pack it in and go back to Chicago. But it wasn't in her nature to quit.

Instead, she spent the month training at Tuskegee, and getting into trouble of the fun sort.

Macon County, where Tuskegee sits, was a "dry" county, meaning you could not legally buy or sell alcohol there.

"The fellows would drive to Uniontown, a small farming community west of Selma, to get their 'spirits,'" Janet recalled. "If they were caught with whiskey in their cars they were fined heavily."

So Janet became an amateur bootlegger. In her spare time, she'd fly a group of instructors down to friends in Georgia. The men would fill the baggage compartment with whiskey, and Janet would fly back to Tuskegee, checking for a pre-arranged "all-clear" or "keep-away" signal. If the coast was clear, she would land. If it wasn't, she was instructed to dump her contraband in a nearby pond.

"Fortunately, it was never necessary to dump the bottles," Janet said, "as I don't know how I would have gotten them out of the baggage compartment while flying the plane."

The exploits earned her the nickname "The Flying Bootlegger." In

Janet's memoir, she confessed that Chief Anderson never knew about these shady jaunts.

" 'Chief, I want to apologize to you for doing this," she wrote. "The fellows were so kind and helpful to me, I had to show them my appreciation. Forgive me."

With her flight training done, Janet discovered that her commercial pilot's written exam had lapsed. She would need to take it again before she could take the flight test at Tuskegee. So Janet took the bus to Birmingham, Alabama, to resit the exam. She passed once again and returned the same day back to Tuskegee.

"Then the day arrived when 'the man' came," Janet recalled, meaning the federal flight examiner, a white man named T.K. Hudson. "It was just after a rain. That afternoon the air was smooth, just like silk."

Janet was well prepared. She'd had the best teachers, and they knew what Hudson looked for in a pilot. Janet delivered.

"It was really beautiful," Janet said. "After each maneuver, Hudson gave me the okay signal with his hand. I really was relaxed.

"The plane's performance was magnificent, almost as if the little Piper were saying, 'I'll do this flight test myself.' "

Janet brought the plane in for a perfect landing. Chief Anderson and Janet's other instructors rushed up to meet them.

"How did she do, Mr. Hudson?" one of them, George Allen, asked.

"Well, George," Hudson replied, "she gave me a good flight. I will put her up against any of your flight instructors. But I've never given a colored girl a commercial license, and I don't intend to now."

He left the group standing in stunned silence.

"I looked at 'Chief,' " Janet recalled, "and tears were in his eyes. Allen was nauseated. The others just walked away, dejected. Finally, I came out of my shocked daze and said, 'Don't worry. We will find some way.'"

The way she saw it, "Every defeat was a challenge." Fortunately, she was a lifelong Challenger.

Janet returned to Chicago five weeks after her departure, and made arrangements to take the flight test for her commercial license once again. As luck would have it, this time her inspector was a white Texan.

"When he spoke with that Texas drawl, I thought, 'Oh my God, here we go again.'"

Janet took him up, but even as she flew well, she decided enough was enough. "It really didn't make any difference anymore if I passed or failed. But guess what? The man shook my hand, congratulated me, and told me to pick up my license on Wednesday," Janet later recalled. "How about those apples!"

——

As the year changed to 1944, so did the war, on all its fronts.

In the Pacific theater, U.S. forces were now close enough to Japan that they began running bombing raids on Japanese cities.

In Europe, the Axis nation of Italy had surrendered to Allied forces in September 1943. By the summer of 1944, a major Allied invasion of France on the beaches of Normandy, known as Operation Overlord, would lead to the liberation of that nation as well.

With these successes in the field, the War Department was seriously reevaluating the amount of money it was spending on civilian pilot training.

In 1944, both the Navy and the Army withdrew from the War Training Service, having reached their pilot-training goals. Existing training would wrap up by the end of the year, even though the war wouldn't end until 1945.

Possibly as a result of this change, Johnny Robinson finally fulfilled the old dream that the Challenger aviators had back in 1935: he pulled together a group of aviation mechanics from Chanute, and took them to Ethiopia "to instruct Ethiopian youths in the art of flying from the ground up," as the *Chicago Defender* put it.

After the invasion that had sent Johnny fleeing for his life in 1936, Italy occupied Ethiopia into the start of the second World War, declaring it, along with Eritrea and part of Somalia, to be "Italian East Africa." In 1942, British troops at war with Italy finally drove the Italians from Ethiopia and restored Haile Selassie to the imperial throne there. Johnny was welcomed back to his adopted country with open arms.

As for the Coffey School, it was able to offer flight training via the CPTP/WTS throughout the program's existence, and managed to keep offering independent flight training until 1945. In February of that year, Coffey enrolled in a flight instrument course at the Lewis School of Aeronautics on the outskirts of Chicago. Instrument flying, in which a pilot navigates and changes height and attitude (the relationship between the aircraft's nose and the horizon) using only the indications of the flight instruments on the dashboard instead of visual references, is considered a "use it or lose it" skill. Commercial pilots today train regularly to stay on top of the necessary skills for safe flight in all kinds of weather conditions, including zero visibility. Four months into the course, the Lewis School hired Coffey as a flight and Link simulator instructor.

By then, the Allies were gaining major ground against the Nazis in the European theater, and the Japanese Imperial Army in the East. The war would soon be over.

———

On May 8, 1945, Nazi Germany surrendered in Europe.

"Negro America Hails V-E Day!" the *Chicago Defender* headline declared.

V-E meant "Victory in Europe." It would be three more months before "V-J Day" could be proclaimed, when American planes dropped atomic bombs on Nagasaki and Hiroshima, effectively ending the war with Japan.

By the end of August 1945, World War II had ended. There was no longer an urgent need for training new pilots, and the Coffey School couldn't survive without government funding. After years of striving and climbing, Coffey sold the school in 1945. Ten years later, Fred and Eleanor Schumacher would lose the lease on Harlem Airport, and the land would be developed into housing.

During their existence, the Civilian Pilot Training Program and the War Training Service had operated at 1,132 colleges and universities and at 1,460 flight schools, training over 435,000 pilots. The Coffey School had trained approximately five hundred of those pilots.

Mild-mannered Coffey was proud of what he had achieved, for both the United States and for Black aviation.

"We never[,] in our whole operation, we never injured a student, we never wrecked an airplane," Coffey said. Sometimes a student would bend or break a propeller, but it was never anything that the Coffey School mechanics couldn't mend. Years later, when asked what he was most proud of during his CPTP/WTS work, Coffey answered, "I'm proud of the fact that I was a part of the training that finally got to be the 99[th. They] proved themselves what I knew all along."

During the war years, practically every Black student who completed the flight course at Harlem Airport ended up at Tuskegee and became one of the legendary Tuskegee Airmen.

Cornelius Coffey, the uppity little Black kid with his pocket money and his belief that he should be allowed to fly, had given America—and the world—a lasting legacy.

CHAPTER 12

TOUCHING DOWN, 1946 AND BEYOND

Oh! I have slipped the surly bonds of Earth
And danced the skies on laughter-silvered wings;
Sunward I've climbed, and joined the tumbling
   mirth
of sun-split clouds,—and done a hundred things
You have not dreamed of—

—John Gillespie Magee, Jr., "High Flight," 1941

WORLD WAR II ended in 1945. But it took longer to win the Double Victory—freedom at home as well as freedom abroad.

In 1948, Harry Truman had a problem. Once a mere senator from Missouri—in fact, the same senator who met with Dale White and Chauncey Spencer on their Goodwill Tour to Washington, D.C., and helped the cause of Black Civilian Pilot Training Programs—Truman was now the thirty-third president of the United States. It had been a rough arrival to the seat of power. He'd been elected as vice president to an ailing Franklin D. Roosevelt in 1944, in the midst of World War II. Less than three months later, Roosevelt had unexpectedly died of a cerebral hemorrhage, and Truman had suddenly become president of a nation at war.

"I felt like the moon, the stars, and all the planets had fallen on me," he said at the time.

Under Truman's leadership, the United States had won the war, but at a terrible cost. Truman had been the one to give the final order to use atomic weapons on the people of Japan, causing devastating casualties. The cities of Nagasaki and Hiroshima had been demolished, with estimates of up to two hundred thousand dead, and the health of survivors irrevocably damaged.

On the home front, the shift to peacetime had been a rocky one, as a new version of America—one where women worked in traditional men's roles, and minorities had moved closer to equal citizenship— attempted to make room for returning veterans.

Now, three years later, Harry Truman was up for reelection, and he was expected to lose. Unless . . .

Truman needed the Black vote, just as surely as African Americans had needed his support for the CPTP nine years earlier.

But did he deserve it?

The end of the war had threatened to be the end of opportunity for Black pilots in the United States. Soon the nation would have a surplus of pilots—more men and women aviators than ever before, and a limited number of civilian flying jobs. Coffey's older brother, Vernon, had seen firsthand the plight of Black veterans after the first World War. Black soldiers returning home had been met with the violence and hatred of the Red Summer in 1919. Men who had served bravely in Europe had been feared and reviled by many white Americans, who saw their military skills as a threat. At best, they were forced to return to the segregated restrictions of Jim Crow America. At worst, the losses of jobs, homes, and lives were their rewards. Would the same thing happen following the close of the second World War?

When World War II ended, Vernon Coffey became the chairman for the Post-War Planning Committee of Colored Veterans. He was determined to see that they were better provided for this time. Aviation seemed a perfect place to start.

On June 6, 1945, Vernon wrote to the World War Veterans Legislation committee, singing the praises of the teachers and facilities of the Coffey School of Aeronautics, and asking for a meeting with the president to discuss postwar aviation training for returning Black veterans. The Coffey group hoped to present "a concise plan for serving these veterans and which will contribute much toward protecting lives and property of these United States."

Despite support from other members of the government, the response to his request, which came a few months later from President Truman's secretary, was a polite but definitive, "No." Truman was simply too busy.

But in the halls of Washington, civil rights activists were also making noises of discontent. Why should Black Americans fight for a country that continued to refuse them a place at the table? Lack of support from the Black population could be devastating for the U.S. military, which, despite its discriminatory practices, had relied on Black soldiers since the dawn of the nation. But for Black Americans, it was much worse to love and bleed for a nation that did not love them back.

With the upcoming election hanging in the balance, President Truman recognized an opportunity—one that would secure Black military participation, make some concessions toward the civil rights movement, and perhaps win him the votes he needed to win a second term in office.

On July 26, 1948, given the track record of the Black graduates of the CPTP/WTS and the stellar performance of the Tuskegee Airmen—not to mention that it would be an election-winning move for himself—Truman signed Executive Order 9981, a law that would officially end segregation throughout the armed forces.

It was a huge success for civil rights.

The law might not have been the long-sought Double Victory African Americans had worked for, with the promise of peace in the world and equality at home. It was not able to end prejudice or outright racism in America or in the military. But it was a step in the right direction, one that would begin to open doors to Black aviators in the newly formed United States Air Force.

It could not have happened without the Harlem aviators.

———

When Johnny went to Ethiopia in 1935, he gave his friend Dale White an impressive business card embossed with the Ethiopian Lion of Judah and the simple legend, "Col. J.C. Robinson—Imperiale Ethiopienne Air Force." He scrawled a message across the card.

"To Dale—Say How is the old Chrysler—Hope to get a ride in it again—If I don't go West—Johnny"

"Going West" was a euphemism for death—probably associated with heading toward the setting sun, but popularized among the soldiers and pilots of World War I.

Johnny knew he might not make it back from Ethiopia during that year of dodging Italian bullets and fighter aircraft. Indeed, he had some close calls, but that didn't stop him from returning to Ethiopia the moment he was able in 1944, even before World War II had ended. This time, Johnny stayed there for ten years.

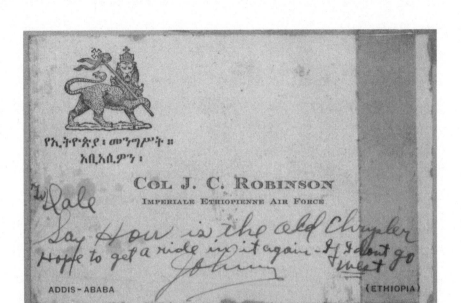

Johnny Robinson's business card while in the Imperial Ethiopian Air Force, 1935–1936
SMITHSONIAN NATIONAL AIR AND SPACE MUSEUM (NASM 9A16697-16B)

He had returned to help train young Ethiopians in aviation mechanics, but he continued to be involved in Ethiopian aviation even after the war was over. In 1948, Johnny teamed up with the Duke of Harar, Haile Selassie's second son, and established a private airline using Douglas DC-3s, a stalwart plane that first flew in 1935 and that continues to see active service even in the twenty-first century.

"It is our intention to link the world by air . . . anytime, anywhere and under any conditions with freight or passengers or both," Johnny said proudly.

It was an endeavor Coffey would have admired.

In March of 1954, Johnny was taking off in a trainer plane with an aircraft engineer as his passenger. The engine failed as they lifted off from the airport at Addis Ababa. Johnny's passenger was killed in the crash that followed, and Johnny himself suffered severe burns. When

Emperor Haile Selassie learned of the crash, he went to visit Johnny in the hospital.

But two weeks later, Johnny died of his injuries.

One last time, Johnny was celebrated in grand fashion. His funeral in Addis Ababa was conducted in Amharic and English at a church so packed that the mourners couldn't all fit in the building, and his funeral procession to Gulalle Cemetery stretched for miles across the city. In the crowd at the cemetery, among other government officials and dignitaries, stood Johnny's friend the Duke of Harar, while Haile Selassie's personal secretary represented the emperor.

Colonel John C. Robinson had flown West in style. He was not quite fifty years old.

A studio portrait of Johnny Robinson, dapper and dashing, inscribed "To Mother and Dad"

FROM THE COLLECTION OF YAHOSHUAH ISRAEL, AUTHOR OF THE LION AND THE CONDOR

Seven years earlier, in 1947, a seemingly small incident occurred that would change the course of Janet Harmon Waterford's life.

It happened when Johnny Robinson was back in Ethiopia assisting the Imperial Air Force to recover from the Italian invasion and ravages of World War II. In an attempt to rebuild Ethiopia's educated class—many of whom had been killed during the Italian occupation—the Ethiopian government was selecting promising students to send abroad for further studies. Two students were headed to Illinois Wesleyan University, in central Illinois. Johnny suggested the two men contact Janet when they arrived in Chicago.

"Johnny's description of me must have been enthusiastic," Janet later wrote.

She met the students at the train station, where they presented what Janet described as a "grimy" little note of introduction from Johnny that read: "Take care of these boys like they were your own."

Janet did just that, and then some.

Over the years, she would play "mother" to dozens of Ethiopian students (although the boys took to calling her "Sister"). The students traveled "in twos and threes," but over school holidays, Janet said, "sometimes I had as many as ten or fifteen staying with me." Her apartment, filled with sleeping bags, became a happy second home.

Janet's family situation changed again in 1951, when she got married for a second time, to a man named Sumner Bragg. This time, it was a match that would last a lifetime. Now known as Janet Harmon Bragg, she and her husband expanded the nursing home business that Janet had established, and eventually sold her last airplane, though Janet continued to fly into the 1970s.

In 1954, Janet received a surprising phone call. The emperor of Ethiopia was on a diplomatic tour of the United States, and her reputation had preceded her.

"His Majesty wishes an audience with you when he comes to Chicago," the caller said.

Janet, along with twenty-five Ethiopian students, met the emperor's party at the airport. The next day, the emperor met Janet in person. He thanked her for the help she had given to so many Ethiopian students, and invited her to visit him in Ethiopia.

The following year, she took him up on his offer. She spent some of that time settling Johnny Robinson's affairs following his tragic death the year before. But she also attended the celebration marking the twenty-fifth anniversary of Haile Selassie's reign, was received as a visitor to the imperial palace, and met the Crown Prince and Johnny's friend the Duke of Harar. It was the trip of a lifetime as, twenty years after Johnny first became the head of the Imperial Ethiopian Air Force, Janet became the only one of the other original Challenger pilots to actually make it to Ethiopia.

After years of little recognition, in September 1982, the aviators of the Challenger Air Pilots' Association and the National Airmen's Association of America, among others, were celebrated in a traveling exhibit called "Black Wings," curated by the National Air and Space Museum of the Smithsonian Institution. Janet helped to develop the exhibit, which is still touring as part of the Smithsonian's permanent collection today. Janet reunited with Coffey, Chauncey Spencer, and Charles "Chief" Anderson for the exhibit's opening.

In an interview for the Smithsonian a few years later, Janet was asked what she would want people to remember about the Black experience in aviation in a hundred years.

Janet said she wanted people to know "that we've laid a foundation for them, our Black kids, and even for any other kids who have had the same trouble that Black children have had. That the only thing you have to do now ... the foundation is there, is to keep building on that foundation because it isn't going to sink. It stayed up." As a result, she said, "There's so many opportunities for them now that we didn't have."

Janet Harmon Bragg flew West in April 1993. She was eighty-six years old.

———

Willa Brown wasn't going to let the closure of Harlem Airport stop her from attempting one more moonshot. Soon after the war ended, in the spring of 1946, she ran for Congress. Though she didn't win, she was probably the first Black woman to run.

When flight training tapered off at Harlem Airport, Willa took a job at the Great Lakes Naval Training Base in 1950 and moved to Waukegan, Illinois, where Johnny Robinson had taken his first flying lessons over twenty years earlier. The 1950 Census lists Willa as the head of her own household with her marital status as "separated," her marriage to Coffey having come undone along with their business endeavors, and during that time, she also let her pilot's license lapse. She spent five years in Waukegan, where she met and married the Reverend J.H. Chappell, the minister of her church. Now known as Willa B. Chappell, she and her husband moved back to Chicago in 1955 where, always the educator, Willa went back to work as a teacher of shorthand and typing, just as she'd done when she first finished college.

Then, in 1971, after she'd retired from teaching, Willa came across a slender history of the Civilian Pilot Training Program called *The Putt-Putt Air Force*. Written by Patricia Strickland and published by the Federal Aviation Administration (FAA) in 1970, the book included a chapter titled "Negro Pilots," singing Willa's praises for her work at Harlem Airport. It even included a photograph of Willa in the 1940s, posing by an Army training aircraft with four handsome young pilots who appear to be hanging on her every word as she points to the sky.

"The story inspired me so[,] until I decided I wanted to become more active in flying again," Willa wrote in a letter to the FAA.

She passed her medical certificate, and on May 17, 1972, at the age of sixty-six, Willa Brown Chappell was once again certified with a pilot's license and ready to take to the skies.

Never one to do things by half, Willa did more than just renew her license. In 1972 she became the first Black woman appointed to the FAA's Women's Advisory Committee on Aviation. She served on the committee for several years.

In a speech at the fourth annual National Convention of Tuskegee Airmen in 1975, Willa said, "Every time I see and hear one of those huge jetliners moving across my Chicago South Side home on its way to O'Hare airport, I know it just could be one of our Black airline pilots at the controls—and a little bit of me floats up heavenly towards that plane to rendezvous with another little part of me that was left in flying more than thirty years ago."

After a lifetime of striving, Willa lived in quiet retirement for the last few years of her old age. In 1992, at eighty-six, Willa Brown Chappell flew West.

In a large folder in the Coffey family archives at the University of Kansas in Lawrence, there is a sheet of ivory paper, creased across its middle. At the top in gold is embossed the seal of the United States of America—a bald eagle, wings spread, clutching an olive branch of peace in one set of talons, a fletch of arrows in the other. The body of the eagle is a striped shield. In its beak it holds a ribbon that reads, "E. Pluribus Unum," or "out of many, one." Overhead a sunburst features thirteen stars, one for each of the original thirteen colonies that became the United States of America.

The document reads: "The War Department expresses its appreciation for patriotic service in a position of trust and responsibility to Captain C.R. Coffey, Civil Air Patrol. For meritorious achievement as squadron commander in the Illinois Wing, for devoting his effort in time of national need to the leadership, recruitment, and training of civilian volunteers for wartime flying missions, and for contributing to the building of present and future air power."

Dated April 30, 1946, it is signed by a brigadier general, the commanding general of the Army Air Forces, and the secretary of war.

For Coffey, the war was over. He'd sold his flight school. But he did not want to see Black pilots bypassed yet again, and had visions of starting a freight flying service—harkening back to his earliest days as a delivery messenger on his old motorcycle. Commercial aviation was on the rise, and it was safe to assume that it would be the sole provenance of white pilots; Jim Crow would no doubt rule the airlines the way it did other forms of transportation, with restrictions in place for Black pilots and travelers alike. Freight, on the other hand, was behind-the-scenes work, and Coffey sensed an opportunity for growth there so that Black pilots, newly returned home from war, could make a decent living.

Unfortunately, luck was against the venture. On May 23, 1946, a railroad strike brought the usual method of freight delivery to a halt after a week of failed negotiations between railroad workers, management, and the U.S. government. New and existing airlines were quick to seize the opportunity. Coffey had been correct—there was money to be made in air freight, as evidenced by such major shipping conglomerates as Federal Express and DHL today—but Black flyers were once again squeezed out of an aviation opportunity, as white veteran pilots took civilian flying jobs in both freight and commercial airlines.

But he was not one to give up on a dream. Coffey had begun as a teacher—first for himself, then for others. In 1949, Coffey received a teacher's certificate from the Chicago Board of Education, enabling him to teach aviation and aviation mechanics in trade schools until he retired in 1969. As luck would have it, one of those schools was Dunbar Vocational High School, whose director, Clifford Campbell, had been the assistant principal at Wendell Phillips High School when Coffey took him for his first plane ride in 1940, back when the Coffey School of Aeronautics first got involved in the Civilian Pilot Training Program.

As Coffey liked to say, "I tell students there's no limit to what they can accomplish if they try."

On July 31, 1954, Coffey married for the final time, to Anna Mae Henderson. As with Janet's and Willa's postwar partners, this marriage would prove to be a match that would last to the end. Notably, none of the three, nor Johnny, appears to have had any children. Their legacy would live on through the young people they taught and inspired with their work.

In later years, Coffey earned some recognition for his huge contribution to aviation, and to the cause of Black flyers. He was the first

African American to receive the FAA's Charles Taylor Master Mechanic Award, given to aircraft mechanics with at least fifty years' experience under their belts. He reunited with Janet for the opening of the Smithsonian Institution's traveling exhibit "Black Wings." An approach to Midway Airport on the South Side of Chicago was named after him; to fit the five-letter limit, it is called the "Cofey" fix. In 2013, the Curtiss-Wright Aeronautical University Building was placed on the National Register of Historical Places because of its association with Coffey, Johnny, and those early classes for Black American flyers. And in 2023, Coffey was inducted into the National Aviation Hall of Fame.

In Coffey's 1990 interview with the Smithsonian Videohistory Program, the interviewer, Theodore Robinson, asked, "What message would you want to give people who might look at this tape fifty to one hundred years from now?"

After a moment of thought, Coffey replied, "Well, the message I would try to give to them, regardless of how hard it might seem, if you try hard enough, you'll succeed. I have been fortunate enough all the way through, as I said before. Every step that I took [that] I had blocked backwards, I had somebody to come to my rescue and move me ahead a step forward. So if you make up your mind and if you try hard enough, you'll succeed."

He told another reporter, "Flying is hard to give up, because up there in the skies you never know from one minute to the next which part of your wit and energy you're going to have to draw on. So as long as I can hold onto a wrench, I'm going to hang on to my license."

Coffey was eighty-nine at the time of the interview. He flew West in 1994 at the age of ninety-one.

One day back in the midst of World War II, a white teenaged paperboy named Tom Forys was hanging out at Harlem Airport. The young man's big brother Harry was a Navy pilot, and Tom himself was crazy about aviation. Overhead, airplanes buzzed, boldly announcing man's dominion over the air.

One of the planes, an ex-Army Fairchild PT-19, came in for a landing. Then, to Tom's delight, instead of taxiing past him, the plane stopped.

"Hey, Kid, wanna ride?"

Tom jumped at the chance.

The pilot was a Black man. He gave the kid his helmet and goggles, then took Tom for a quick spin over the airfield. The record doesn't show if he tried to scare the boy with loops and rolls, the way the barnstormer had tried to scare Coffey all those years ago.

What it does show is that a Black student from Cornelius Coffey's own flight school gave the white teenaged Tom Forys his first airplane ride.

And Tom had the feel for it, just like Coffey as a kid. Tom would one day learn to fly at Harlem Airport, and make a career of aviation, becoming known to his friends as "Tailspin Tommy."

Later in life, long after the war was over and the former Challenger pilots had all flown West, Tom Forys would organize a program to help out the Tuskegee Airmen's Association by giving free plane rides to elementary school–aged underprivileged children, many of them Black, at the former Meigs Field Airport on the Chicago lakefront—paying forward a dream that had begun in a farmer's field in Omaha more than a lifetime ago.

EPILOGUE

TO THE STARS

This generation does not intend to founder in the
backwash of the coming age of space. We mean to be
a part of it—we mean to lead it. For the eyes of the
world now look into space, to the moon and to the
planets beyond, and we have vowed that we shall not
see it governed by a hostile flag of conquest, but by a
banner of freedom and peace.

—President John F. Kennedy, Address at Rice University
on the Nation's Space Effort, September 12, 1962

In 1965, a young woman named Nichelle Nichols landed the role that
would define much of her life, that of communications officer Lieutenant Uhura on Gene Roddenberry's new science fiction TV show,
Star Trek. The show, chronicling the voyages of an imaginary research
vessel through deep space, was unique at the time for its diverse cast
and vision of cooperation. But it wasn't exactly a hit when it was first
broadcast. In fact, Nichols decided to quit.

Then one night she had a conversation with a fan at an NAACP
event in Beverly Hills, California. That fan was civil rights leader Reverend Dr. Martin Luther King, Jr.

"He said, 'We admire you greatly, you know,'" Nichols recalled years
later. When she said she was leaving the show, he told her, "You cannot.
You cannot."

Actress Nichelle Nichols, daughter of the mayor of Robbins, Illinois, as Lieutenant Uhura in Star Trek

*CBS/*CONTRIBUTOR

Nichols was one of the few Black women on television performing in a non-subservient role. She was an officer on the flagship craft of a future organization. It was an inspiration that the cause of Black excellence should not go without.

Needless to say, Nichols stayed with the show. After five seasons, it ended, only to be resurrected with multiple movies and spin-off shows for future generations. Today, *Star Trek* has a global fan base.

But what few people know is that Nichols was born in Robbins, Illinois, in 1932, just as the Challenger pilots were taking to the skies there. She was the daughter of Samuel Nichols, the mayor who gave the Challengers their first airfield.

Some dreams don't die. Instead, they multiply. Because of her fame as Lieutenant Uhura, in 1977, Nichelle Nichols became a representative for the National Aeronautics and Space Administration (NASA). Thanks to her recruitment efforts, for the first time in history, the fol-

Actress and spokesperson Nichelle Nichols at NASA's Kennedy Space Center in Cape Canaveral, Florida, 2010

NASA/Bill Ingalls

lowing year's class of astronaut candidates included both women and minorities.

In 1987, Nichols reached out to a former applicant who had been rejected by NASA and asked if she'd like to apply again.

That applicant was Mae Jemison. She went on to become the world's first Black female astronaut, thanks to the runway paved by Bessie Coleman, Cornelius Coffey, Johnny Robinson, Willa Brown Chappell, Janet Harmon Bragg, and so many others.

In fact, Jemison carried a picture of Bessie Coleman with her on her first space shuttle mission.

So the dream continues, to the stars and beyond.

Mae Jemison, the first Black woman to become an astronaut, aboard the space shuttle Endeavor
NASA

AUTHORS' NOTE

IN our parallel lives before we decided to collaborate on *American Wings*, we'd both written novels about young people taking to the skies. Sherri is the author of *Flygirl* and *The Blossom and the Firefly*, and Elizabeth of *Code Name Verity* and, most recently, *Stateless*. We'd also both written nonfiction for young people about flying in World War II, in Sherri's *Who Were the Tuskegee Airmen?* and Elizabeth's *A Thousand Sisters*. Sherri grew familiar with Cornelius Coffey and Willa Brown while doing research on *Flygirl* and the Tuskegee Airmen; Elizabeth included a fictional version of Johnny Robinson in her book *Black Dove, White Raven*. Both of us were curious to learn more about Chicago's amazing pioneering Black aviators. We decided to put our heads together and share the work, just as they had done.

We presented our idea to Stephanie Pitts, Sherri's editor at Putnam, in the fall of 2019. Our plan was to divide and conquer the material—each of us took on a couple of different aviators to research. Sherri, who lives in California, applied for and was awarded a grant to visit the University of Kansas Kenneth Spencer Research Library, in Lawrence, Kansas, where the Coffey family papers are kept. Elizabeth, who lives in Scotland, made plans for a trip to Chicago to check out the Betty Gubert Collection focusing on Willa Brown's life. And suddenly it was the middle of 2020.

Pandemic. Lockdown. The George Floyd and Black Lives Matter protests. The world erupted throughout that terrible year. Neither of our planned trips happened. We weren't able to visit our local libraries, let alone travel the States. Instead, we diligently bought used books and watched videos, sharing the information we found on the Internet and elsewhere, but *American Wings* took much longer to put together than we had hoped.

Now that it's finally finished, we are proud of the work we've done here. We believe it is one of the most comprehensive and detailed studies to date about the original Chicago Challenger pilots and their journey. But we know that there is always room for a more accurate picture. One thing we discovered as we worked is that there are always at least three sides to every story—as Sherri put it, "History seems to be a moving target." Almost all of our primary sources were memoirs written, or interviews given, at least thirty years after the events occurred. And nearly every one of the individuals remembering the past had conflicting memories and dates. Sometimes official records or newspaper reports helped us to pin things down. Other times, we had to make guesses about history. We have tried our best to keep clear in the text what we know for sure, and what we do not.

One thing that we discovered as we began to uncover our story from the isolation of our locked-down homes was that there are a lot of people out there who are *delighted* to share information from afar. The Federal Aviation Administration (FAA) proved to be a fantastic resource, with Mary Snyder of the FAA Airmen Certification Branch and Dr. Theresa L. Kraus, the FAA Agency Historian, both digging up obscure licensing dates and documents and answering a variety of questions. So did Indiana State University. So did Charla Wilson, Archivist for the Black Experience at Northwestern University. Jeanie Loiacono, Thomas Simmons's agent, generously sent us copies of Simmons's personal collection of photographs of Johnny Robinson; Elizabeth C. Borja, the Reference Services Archivist of the National Air and Space Museum, pointed us to online links where we could peruse

Dale White's scrapbook and pilot's logbook in the Smithsonian's collection. Yehoshuah Israel sent us pictures of Johnny Robinson's pilot's logbooks, which are in his personal possession, and has become a faithful correspondent. Jim Miller and Joe Tomasovsky at the Mississippi Gulf Coast Museum of History enthusiastically shared photos from Johnny's youth, and Suzy Quick at the Vigo Museum of History in Indiana did the same with photos of Willa Brown. Chauncey Spencer II shared his collection of essays and photos of the Challengers, and Regina Rush at the University of Virginia sent readable scans of one of Anne Spencer's lightly penciled notebooks. Hannah Byrne at the Smithsonian Institution Archives enthusiastically sent to us both, at no cost, hours of digital videos (and their transcripts) containing interviews with Charles "Chief" Anderson, Janet Harmon Bragg, Cornelius Coffey, Harold Hurd, and Lewis Jackson. We're indebted to Cian O'Day, who helped us in our Herculean task of hunting for photographs. To these enthusiasts and all the others who contributed pieces of this history, thank you so much!

Other online sources we've used include the Hathi Trust Digital Library at hathitrust.org, Newspapers.com, Ancestry.com, and the Golden Age of Flying Register at airhistory.org.uk. But of all these, nothing was as informative or indispensable as the electronic resources offered by the National Library of Scotland. There is no doubt in our minds that this book could not have been written without the NLS's unwitting assistance. Their free membership allowed us invaluable digital access to the *Chicago Defender* archives, as well as to those of the *Atlantic Daily World*; the *Baltimore Afro-American*; the Norfolk, Virginia, *New Journal and Guide*; the *New York Amsterdam News*; the *Pittsburgh Courier*; and other Black newspapers of the early twentieth century. We are eternally grateful for the National Library of Scotland's generosity.

Although our initial (and final) research was online, we are happy to say that we were both eventually able to make our planned research trips in person—in 2021, two years after we'd proposed the project! Sherri's trip to Kansas was funded thanks to Sandra Gautt and the Alyce Hunley Whayne Visiting Researcher Travel Award, allowing her to dive into the Coffey family archive at the Kenneth Spencer Research Library, where she worked under the gracious guidance of the African American Experience Collections Field Archivist and Curator Deborah Dandridge. Additional support came from Associate Dean of Distinctive Collections Beth Whittaker, Dean of Libraries Kevin L. Smith, and staff members Emily Beran, Molly Herring, Shannon Rover, Shelby Schellenger, and Jane Wilkerson—along with some incredible sandwiches from Wheatfields Bakery. Sitting in the reading room holding Coffey's handwritten notes and diplomas felt like an open doorway to the past.

Elizabeth's visit to the Betty Gubert Collection, in the Vivian G. Harsh Research Collection, was facilitated by Cynthia Fife-Townsel and the staff at Woodson Regional Library (a branch of the Chicago Public Library system), who made her very welcome. We are also deeply grateful to Tyrone Haymore, curator of the Robbins History Museum, which is located in his stepfather's former grocery store in Robbins, Illinois. After an impromptu interview, during which Mr. Haymore thrilled Elizabeth with memories of his friendship with Cornelius Coffey and his personal encounter with Janet Harmon Bragg, he drove her in his own car to Lincoln Cemetery in Blue Island, Illinois, to visit Bessie Coleman's grave—and also Robert S. Abbott's and Willa Brown's, and Janet Bragg's memorial stone—finishing off with a guided tour of Robbins and a visit to the original site of the Challenger aviators' airfield there. We are also immensely grateful to Mr. Haymore for vetting our newly completed manuscript.

Indeed we find ourselves grateful for so many things and to so many people—from Ethel Gordon, Elizabeth's Uber driver in Chicago, to our Feline Writing Group (Leo, Persephone, Pan, and Sneezy), to Kate Adams, who put up with us occupying the dining room table in Elizabeth's family home in Pennsylvania for a week in 2022, to Elizabeth's son Mark—who, in addition to providing us with digital access to the Claude Barnett Collection through his account with the University of Aberdeen library, emailed us photographs from Scotland of pages we were missing during our week in Pennsylvania (even though we'd both traveled thousands of miles each with a suitcase full of books)—to Anne Bain, who let Elizabeth isolate with Covid in her house in Shetland for another week while we frantically put together the last big revision of the manuscript early in 2023. To Hedgebrook, for a residency with a desk big enough to hold all of Sherri's timelines. And to each of us for shoring up the other through bouts of Covid and piles of research. This sort of time travel is easier with a friend.

Of course we could not even have started this project without the support of Sherri's agent, Kirby Kim, and Elizabeth's agent, Ginger Clark, who helped us pull together our original proposal, and of our editor Stephanie Pitts, who has worked nonstop to help us pull off the project in a timely manner. And we'd be nowhere without our long-suffering partners, Sherri's husband, Kelvin, and Elizabeth's husband, Tim.

Finally, we are grateful to the amazing men and women we have tried to pay tribute to in this book, whose incredible patience, persistence, and determination in the face of prejudice and inequality continues to help make our present America a better place. They have given us all the gift of wings.

Sherri L. Smith
Elizabeth Wein

Source Notes

All direct quotations are as faithfully transcribed as our typists' hands and editors' eyes were able, though we have made some light amendments here and there to conform to modern spelling, capitalization, and punctuation standards.

EPIGRAPH

ix • **"I shall never be satisfied":** Bessie Coleman, quoted in the *Chicago Defender*, October 8, 1921, 2.

PROLOGUE: A DREAM TAKES FLIGHT

1 • **It was going to cost three dollars:** $3 in 1919 = $47.36 in 2021; https://www .dollartimes.com/inflation/inflation.php?amount=3&year=1919 (accessed April 12, 2023).

1 • **Cornelius Robinson Coffey had the money:** Allen, September 26, 1979.

1 • **. . . today's barnstormer:** Hartzell Propeller, July 4, 2017.

1 • **His Curtiss JN-4:** Fort Vancouver Historic Site, "The JN-4," n.d.

2 • **His home state of Nebraska:** History Nebraska, "Nebraska's First Aviation Meet," n.d.

2 • **"When I get through with him . . .":** Grossman, July 25, 1993, 6.

2 • **The Jenny was built:** National Air and Space Museum, "Curtiss JN-4 Jenny," n.d.

2 • **Coffey most likely rode:** A pilot flying alone in a two-cockpit biplane usually flew from the rear cockpit for reasons of weight and balance; logically, "The front cockpit that was normally for the student in military training was usually used for passengers in postwar joy rides, so that the pilot could keep an eye on his paying customer/s." Winchester, 2004, 89.

3 • **"I think it was rougher . . .":** Allen, September 26, 1979.

3 • **"Well, you know . . .":** Cornelius Coffey, Smithsonian Videohistory Program, *African-American Aviation Pioneers*, Session Two, 1990, minute 00:01:14, transcript 1.

3 • **Coffey had the feel . . . :** Grossman, July 25, 1993, 6.

CHAPTER 1: PRE-FLIGHT, DETROIT, 1927

5 • **"Detroit Bound Blues":** Blind Blake, 1928, available at https://genius.com /Blind-blake-detroit-bound-blues-lyrics (accessed April 11, 2023).

5 • **. . . it was a bad day for Dr. Sweet:** Cornelius Coffey, business card in the Coffey family papers, Kenneth Spencer Research Library, Box 2, Folder 21.

5 • **Sweet had the car towed:** Cornelius Coffey, Smithsonian Videohistory Program, *African-American Aviation Pioneers*, Session Two, 1990, minute 00:21:18, transcript 9.

5 • **The mechanic on duty:** Simmons, 2013, 16–17; Tucker, 2012, 13–14; Waterford, April 4, 1936, 2.

6 • **He was a graduate:** Tucker, 2012, 16.

6 • **Coffey was the youngest:** US Census, 1910, https://www.ancestry.com/discovery -ui-content/view/571729:7884?tid=&pid=&queryId=469669bea7419bbf50ad 730c4a239316&_phsrc=Yps95&_phstart=successSource (accessed April 12, 2023).

6 • **Henry was a railroad man:** Grossman, July 25, 1993, 6.

7 • **The Model T, created by Henry Ford:** Ford Motor Company, "The Model T," n.d.

7 • **"I'd climb up on the crank":** Grossman, July 25, 1993, 6.

7 • **Coffey's older sister, Vida:** Arkansas US County Marriages Index 1837–1957.

7 • **Coffey's older brother:** Cornelius Coffey, Smithsonian Videohistory Program, *African-American Aviation Pioneers*, Session Two, 1990, minute 00:10:20, transcript 5.

7 • **There, in 1917:** ibid., minute 00:04:05, transcript 2.

8 • **Black men had served:** Rawn, 2013, 8, 11.

8 • **That policy changed:** Rawn, 2013, 29; Williams, 2010, 6.

8 • **One major reason:** Rawn, 2013, 27–28.

8–9 • **In Houston, Texas:** ibid., 31–35.

9 • **After the United States:** Murray, 1971, 58.

9 • **Black combat units:** Rawn, 2013, 56–57.

9–10 An estimated twenty-one million: https://www.britannica.com/question /How-many-people-died-during-World-War-I (accessed April 12, 2023).

10 • **Vernon returned:** https://exhibits.lib.ku.edu/exhibits/show/world-war-one /case-2 (accessed April 12, 2023).

10 • **Across the country:** Rawn, 2013, 79.

10 • **". . . men and women of my race":** Johnson, 1919, 242.

10–11 • **That September:** Menard, 2019.

11 • **"Why don't you go" . . . "auto mechanic":** Cornelius Coffey, Smithsonian Videohistory Program, *African-American Aviation Pioneers*, Session Two, 1990, minute 00:04:05, transcript 2.

11 • **So, in 1921:** ibid., minute 00:05:05, transcript 3.

11 • **He returned to Omaha:** Cornelius Coffey, Vocational Teacher's Record Card, n.d. Coffey family papers, Kenneth Spencer Research Library, Box 3, Folder 8.

11 • **By then, in a move:** Cornelius Coffey, Smithsonian Videohistory Program, *African-American Aviation Pioneers*, Session Two, 1990, minute 00:05:05, transcript 3.

11 • **A Frenchman named George Keon:** ibid., minute 00:09:00, transcript 4.

12 • **Coffey finished the course:** Cornelius Coffey, diploma from the Ogden Davis & Co. School of Automotive Engineering, May 17, 1926, in the Coffey family papers, Kenneth Spencer Research Library, "Oversized" box, Folder 3; Cornelius Coffey, Smithsonian Videohistory Program, *African-American Aviation Pioneers*, Session Two, 1990, minute 00:10:20, transcript 5.

12 • **He called the director:** Cornelius Coffey, Smithsonian Videohistory Program, *African-American Aviation Pioneers*, Session Two, 1990, minute 00:10:20 , transcript 5.

13 • **"It isn't that":** ibid., minute 00:23:00, transcript 10.

14–15 • **Born in Texas:** Freydberg, 1993, 262; Gubert et al, 2002, 78.

16 • **Abbott and the *Defender*:** Rich, 1993, 27–32.

16 • **On June 15, 1921:** ibid., 53.

16 • **In fact, she was the first:** Freydberg, 1993, 262.

16 • From the moment Queen Bess: Rich, 1993, 53; Cornelius Coffey, Smithsonian Videohistory Program, *African-American Aviation Pioneers*, Session Two, 1990, minute 00:03:30, transcript 2.

16–17 • Unfortunately, before that dream: Rich, 1993, 108–110.

17 • Bessie's body was returned: ibid., 112–113.

17 • "I wrote to two or three places": Cornelius Coffey, Smithsonian Videohistory Program, *African-American Aviation Pioneers*, Session Two, 1990, minute 00:22:00, transcript 10.

17 • John Charles Robinson: Gubert et al, 2002, gives 1903 as the year of Johnny's birth on 251–252; 1904 is listed in the FAA Airmen Certification Branch records and is implied in the 1940 Census.

17 • His father was killed: Tucker, 2012, 2.

18 • Charles Cobb was warm: Simmons, 2013, 10–11; Tucker, 2012, 5.

18 • By the time Johnny: Simmons, 2013, 12.

18 • Johnny got his first sight: As told by Katie Booth to Kat Bergeron, "Brown Condor: Gulfport aviation pioneer broke color barriers." *Sun Herald*, Biloxi, Ms., Mar. 15, 2002, A1.

18 • That plane was a Curtiss: Tucker, 2012, 3–5.

19 • "I'm gonna fly": Bonner, 2021, https://msaviationmuseum.org/blog/the-brown -condor-of-ethiopia-the-determination-of-john-c-robinson-hero-of-gulfport (accessed April 12, 2023).

19 • "Johnny designed a kite": Harvey Todd, quoted in Simmons, 2013, 12.

19 • Like Coffey, Johnny was: Simmons, 2013, 16–17; Tucker, 2012, 13–14.

19 • "We didn't know how": Henry Tartt, quoted in Tucker, 2012, 14.

19 • Johnny graduated in 1919: Tucker, 2012, 10, 15.

19–20 • Johnny's older sister: ibid., 16.

20 • The Tuskegee Institute: Jakeman, 1992, 2; https://www.tuskegee.edu/about-us /history-and-mission (accessed April 12, 2023); https://en.wikipedia.org/wiki /Tuskegee_University (accessed April 12, 2023).

20 • In 1921 at barely sixteen: Simmons, 2013, 24; Tucker, 2012, 22.

21 • But, in 1922: Simmons, 2013, 25.

21 • So, again like Cornelius Coffey: Gubert et al, 2002, 252; Simmons, 2013, 26.

21 • "Not a chance": Simmons, 2013, 34.

21–22 • Next, Johnny tried: ibid., 35.

22 • So Johnny began: *Atlanta Daily World*, "Life Story of Colonel John C. Robinson," June 2, 1936, 2; Simmons, 2013, 36, 40.

22 • The Waco 9: Johnsen, 2019, https://generalaviationnews.com/2019/03/07 /the-waco-model-9-and-10/ (accessed April 12, 2023).

22 • Johnny knew he was likely: Simmons, 2013, 39–42; Tucker, 2012, 25.

23 • Johnny—again like Coffey—was into motorcycles: *Chicago Defender*, April 3, 1954, 1; *Los Angeles Sentinel*, April 1, 1954, A4; *Philadelphia Tribune*, April 3, 1954, 1; *Pittsburgh Courier*, April 10, 1954, 31.

23 • Now, as the Waco 9 took off, he was experiencing: Simmons, 2013, 46.

23 • When his feet were back: Simmons, 2013, 50; Tucker, 2012, 25.

24 • **Johnny liked the idea:** Gubert et al, 2002, 252–253; *New York Amsterdam News*, April 3, 1954, 1; Tucker, 2012, 26–28.

24 • **"You know, Bessie Coleman":** John C. Robinson as quoted by Cornelius Coffey, Smithsonian Videohistory Program, *African-American Aviation Pioneers*, Session Two, 1990, minute 00:22:00, transcript 10.

24 • **"If you ever come back":** ibid., minute 00:24:00, transcript 11.

CHAPTER 2: GROUND SCHOOL, 1927–1929

25 • **Hog Butcher for the World:** Carl Sandburg, "Chicago," 1914, available at *Poetry Foundation*, https://www.poetryfoundation.org/poetrymagazine /poems/12840/chicago (accessed April 4, 2023).

25 • **Nicknamed for its historical status:** *New York Times*, April 8, 1984, 27.

25 • **Chicago had a population:** http://physics.bu.edu/~redner/projects/population /cities/chicago.html (accessed April 12, 2023).

25 • **From 1915 on:** Rawn, 2013, 23, 82–83.

26 • **He first found a job:** *New York Amsterdam News*, April 3, 1954, 1.

26 • **He applied:** *New Journal and Guide*, "Tried 7 Times To Enter Air School; Refused; Accepted," December 5, 1931, A7; *Philadelphia Tribune*, December 3, 1931, 12.

26 • **It must have been frustrating:** *Chicago Defender*, January 22, 1927, A3.

26 • **The aviation industry:** Federal Aviation Administration, "A Brief History of the FAA," n.d., https://www.faa.gov/about/history/brief_history (accessed April 12, 2023).

26 • **The first federal pilot's license:** Federal Aviation Administration, "The First U.S. Federal Pilot License," n.d., https://www.faa.gov/about/history/milestones /media/first_pilots_license.pdf (accessed April 12, 2023).

27 • **The new Aeronautics Branch:** ibid.

27 • **Before 1927 was over:** Jakeman, 1992, 63; Scott & Womack, 1998 (1992), 43; Tucker, 2012, 31.

27 • **Coffey would drive over:** Simmons, 2013, 58; Janet Harmon Bragg, Smithsonian Videohistory Program, *African-American Aviation Pioneers*, Session One, 1989, minute 00:04:50, transcript 3.

27 • **... an eloquent young Black man named William J. Powell:** Hardesty & Pisano, 1983, 7; National Air and Space Museum, 2016, https://airandspace .si.edu/stories/editorial/black-wings-life-african-american-aviation-pioneer- william-powell (accessed April 12, 2023); *New York Amsterdam News*, December 12, 1928, 3.

28 • **Meanwhile, the non-flying citizens:** *Chicago Defender*, September 15, 1928, 5.

28 • **... the Cooperative Business League donated:** *Chicago Defender*, June 9, 1928, A12; *New Journal and Guide*, June 16, 1928, 9; *Pittsburgh Courier*, May 26, 1928, 12, and June 9, 1928, A1.

28 • **A flashy Black aviator:** *Baltimore Afro-American*, June 9, 1928, 1.

29 • **Born in Trinidad in 1897:** Shaftel, 2008.

29 • **Julian had made a name:** Gubert et al, 2002, 184.

29 • **The audience, tired of waiting:** *Baltimore Afro-American*, June 9, 1928, 1.

30 • "Hey, your job's waiting": Emil Mack as quoted by Cornelius Coffey, Smithsonian Videohistory Program, *African-American Aviation Pioneers*, Session Two, 1990, minute 00:28:00, transcript 13.

30 • Coffey was immediately rehired: Scott & Womack, 1998 (1992), 43; Cornelius Coffey, Smithsonian Videohistory Program, *African-American Aviation Pioneers*, Session Two, 1990, minute 00:28:00, 00:34:00, transcript 13, 15; Tucker, 2012, 29.

30–31 • Created by the E.B. Heath: Museum of Flight, 2023; *Pleasant Hill Times*, November 21, 1930, 1; https://www.britannica.com/technology/parasol-wing (accessed April 3, 2023).

31 • Coffey and Johnny pooled their money: Cornelius Coffey, Smithsonian Videohistory Program, *African-American Aviation Pioneers*, Session Two, 1990, minute 00:26:30, transcript 11.

31 • . . . the two men visited the plant: ibid., minute 00:27:00, transcript 12.

31 • . . . over the next six months: Tucker, 2012, 29, 31.

31 • . . . northern Indiana was the Las Vegas: Mitchell, July 7, 2019, 2A.

32 • . . . Jennie B. Davis with the same birthdate: Ancestry.com.

32 • She was probably Dora Earnize Tate: Tate, D.E., birth certificate, 1942.

32 • She's referred to as "Mrs. Robinson": *Chicago Defender*, January 2, 1932, 20.

32 • Johnny came across an ad: Cornelius Coffey, Smithsonian Videohistory Program, *African-American Aviation Pioneers*, Session Two, 1990, minute 00:29:00, transcript 12.

32–33 • The plane was a Humming Bird: *Des Moines Tribune*, June 28, 1926, 2, April 11, 1927, 4, and August 11, 1931, 13; Cornelius Coffey, Smithsonian Videohistory Program, *African-American Aviation Pioneers*, Session Two, 1990, minute 00:30:00, transcript 13.

33 • Johnny just happened to have a Hudson: Cornelius Coffey, Smithsonian Videohistory Program, *African-American Aviation Pioneers*, Session Two, 1990, minute 00:29:00, transcript 15.

33 • With Johnny's car: ibid., minute 00:29:00, transcript 13.

33 • Located at Grand Avenue: ibid., minute 00:34:00, transcript 15.

33 • "When they found out": ibid., minute 00:31:00, transcript 13–14.

33 • Every weekend, Coffey and Johnny: Scott & Womack, 1998 (1992), 43; Tucker, 2012, 29; Waterford, April 4, 1936, 2.

34 • When Johnny insisted: Cornelius Coffey, Smithsonian Videohistory Program, *African-American Aviation Pioneers*, Session Two, 1990, minute 00:36:13, transcript 16–17.

34 • Coffey began taking expensive: Cornelius Coffey, pilot's license application, United States Department of Commerce, September 10, 1936. Coffey family papers, Kenneth Spencer Research Library Box 3, Folder 5, 2.

34 • "Back in those days": Cornelius Coffey, Smithsonian Videohistory Program, *African-American Aviation Pioneers*, Session Two, 1990, minute 00:53:28, transcript 23.

34 • $10 an hour was on the cheap end: Lewis Jackson, Smithsonian Videohistory Program, *African-American Aviation Pioneers*, Session One, 1989, minute 00:43:12, transcript 23.

34 • **That was twice:** Cornelius Coffey, Smithsonian Videohistory Program, *African-American Aviation Pioneers*, Session Two, 1990, minute 00:53:28, transcript 23.

34 • **"Hey, you guys are":** ibid., minute 00:34:00, transcript 15.

34 • **"That made sense to us":** ibid., minute 00:34:00, transcript 16.

34 • **Coffey moved out of the Y:** ibid., minute 00:34:00, transcript 16.

35 • **"You know, I got a Waco 9":** Alex Sergeyev as quoted by Cornelius Coffey, Smithsonian Videohistory Program, *African-American Aviation Pioneers*, Session Two, 1990, minute 00:38:00, transcript 17–18.

35 • **So in 1928, Cornelius Coffey:** Cornelius Coffey, Smithsonian Videohistory Program, *African-American Aviation Pioneers*, Session Two, 1990, minute 00:36:13, 00:54:00, transcript 16, 23.

35 • **The only things Coffey:** ibid., minute 00:55:00, transcript 24.

35 • **But he knew:** ibid., minute 00:54:00, transcript 23–24.

36 • **Johnny had already received:** *New Journal and Guide*, "Tried 7 Times To Enter Air School; Refused; Accepted," December 5, 1931, A7; *Philadelphia Tribune*, December 3, 1931, 12.

36 • **One Miss Hazel V. Pleasant:** *Chicago Defender*, May 11, 1929, A1, and May 18, 1929, 3; *Pittsburgh Courier*, May 4, 1929, 1.

36 • **They both passed:** Scott & Womack, 1998 (1992), 44.

37 • **... Chicago's downtown area:** https://www.britannica.com/place/the-Loop (accessed April 12, 2023).

37 • **"Got to be some mistake":** Lewis Churbuck as quoted by Cornelius Coffey, Smithsonian Videohistory Program, *African-American Aviation Pioneers*, Session Two, 1990, minute 00:38:00, transcript 18.

37 • **"Unless we go through":** Cornelius Coffey, Smithsonian Videohistory Program, *African-American Aviation Pioneers*, Session Two, 1990, minute 00:39:00, transcript 18.

37 • **Churbuck was worried:** ibid., minute 00:38:00, transcript 18.

37 • **They'd paid their fees:** Kellum, May 30, 1936, 2; Scott & Womack, 1998 (1992), 44.

37–38 • **On their way out:** Diakite, 2021; Haymore, July 21, 2021; Simmons, 2013, 57; Tucker, 2012, 34.

38 • **"Always cleaning classroom floors":** Henry Tartt, quoted in Tucker, 2012, 36.

38 • **For five months, Johnny:** *New Journal and Guide*, "Laudatory Determination," December 5, 1931, A6; *Philadelphia Tribune*, December 3, 1931, 12; William Scott, 1972, 16; Simmons, 2013, 62.

38 • **"Isn't that right, Mr. Robinson?":** Jack Snyder as quoted by Tyrone Haymore, July 21, 2021.

38 • **The students, too, began to interact:** Prattis, October 26, 1935, 5; Simmons, 2013, 57–58; Tucker, 2012, 34–37.

39 • **Finally, Emil Mack:** Cornelius Coffey, Smithsonian Videohistory Program, *African-American Aviation Pioneers*, Session Two, 1990, minute 00:41:55, transcript 18.

39 • **"I understand you" ... "buy your own school":** Galanis, 1939, 10; conversation

with Emil Mack as quoted by Cornelius Coffey, Smithsonian Videohistory Program, *African-American Aviation Pioneers*, Session Two, 1990, minute 00:41:55, transcript 19.

39 • **At a Christmas party:** Gubert et al, 2002, 74; Tucker, 2012, 32; Waterford, April 11, 1936, 6.

40 • **"But will it fly?":** Haymore, July 21, 2021.

40 • **Johnny got the idea:** Gubert et al, 2002, 253; Haymore, July 21, 2021.

40 • **"What's this strange-lookin' engine?"** ... **"We want you to fly it!":** conversation as quoted by Tyrone Haymore, July 21, 2021.

40–41 • **The plane was loaded:** Diakite, 2021; Haymore, July 21, 2021.

41 • **The entire Brown Eagle Aero Club:** *Atlanta Daily World*, June 2, 1936, 2; Simmons, 2013, 62–65.

41 • **Snyder gave the plane:** This story is according to Cornelius Coffey as narrated by Tyrone Haymore, July 21, 2021.

41 • **The seasoned pilot:** Simmons, 2018, 66–68; Tucker, 2012, 31.

41 • **He offered to try:** Simmons, 2013, 69.

41 • **"If we don't teach them":** Jack Snyder as quoted by Tyrone Haymore, July 21, 2021.

41 • **"Get 'em in here":** [Lewis Churbuck] as quoted by Tyrone Haymore, July 21, 2021.

41–42 • **"You're going to be on your own":** Lewis Churbuck as quoted by Cornelius Coffey, Smithsonian Videohistory Program, *African-American Aviation Pioneers*, Session Two, 1990, minute 00:44:00, transcript 19.

42 • **The school would accept:** Haymore, July 21, 2021.

42 • **They aced the exam:** Tucker, 2012, 37.

CHAPTER 3: TAKING OFF, 1929-1933

43 • **Ours is the commencement:** Amelia Earhart, 1928, 180.

43 • **Every Monday:** Cornelius Coffey, Smithsonian Videohistory Program, *African-American Aviation Pioneers*, Session Two, 1990, minute 00:46:00, 00:57:00, transcript 20, 25.

43 • **... in October 1929:** https://www.britannica.com/event/Great-Depression (accessed April 12, 2023).

43–44 • **"When we would go":** Cornelius Coffey, Smithsonian Videohistory Program, *African-American Aviation Pioneers*, Session Two, 1990, minute 00:45:00, transcript 20.

44 • **But their instructor, Jack Snyder:** ibid., minute 00:45:00, transcript 20.

44 • **One day, Snyder:** Scott & Womack, 1998 (1992), 44.

44 • **"You know something?":** Jack Snyder as quoted by Cornelius Coffey, Smithsonian Videohistory Program, *African-American Aviation Pioneers*, Session Two, 1990, minute 00:46:46, transcript 20.

44 • **"Now, I'm going to tell you":** ibid., minute 00:47:00, transcript 20–21.

44 • **... in an Alexander Eaglerock:** *Belvedere Daily Republican*, May 1, 1929, 3; *Chicago Defender*, May 30, 1936, 2; Kellum, May 30, 1936, 1, 2; Cornelius Coffey, Smithsonian Videohistory Program, *African-American Aviation Pioneers*, Session

Two, 1990, minute 00:56:00, transcript 25; *Waukegan News-Sun*, August 29, 1929, 1, and October 8, 1935, 2.

45 • "Hey, they['re] flying": Jack Snyder as quoted by Cornelius Coffey, Smithsonian Videohistory Program, *African-American Aviation Pioneers*, Session Two, 1990, minute 00:56:00, transcript 25.

45 • "After that lecture": Cornelius Coffey, Smithsonian Videohistory Program, *African-American Aviation Pioneers*, Session Two, 1990, minute 00:48:00, transcript 21.

45 • "They wouldn't let you buy nothing": ibid., minute 00:48:00, transcript 21.

45 • Johnny finally soloed: ibid., minute 00:55:00, transcript 25.

45 • A Polish flight instructor: Kellum, May 30, 1936, 2; Tucker, 2012, 29–30.

45 • He took off: *Pittsburgh Courier*, February 1, 1930, 2; Tucker, 2012, 30; Waterford, April 4, 1936, 2.

45–46 • . . . Johnny got permission: Tucker, 2012, 31; Waterford, April 11, 1936, 6.

46 • Johnny's hands: Tucker, 2012, 32; Waterford, April 11, 1936, 6.

46 • Coffey and Johnny completed: Tucker, 2012, 39.

46 • Johnny doesn't seem: Powell 1994 (1934), 149.

46 • "I wanted to trade": Cornelius Coffey, Smithsonian Videohistory Program, *African-American Aviation Pioneers*, Session Two, 1990, minute 00:54:00, transcript 23.

46 • . . . within two weeks he had received: Powell 1994 (1934), 149; Cornelius Coffey, Smithsonian Videohistory Program, *African-American Aviation Pioneers*, Session Two, 1990, minute 00:52:00, transcript 23.

46–47 • "Now you two fellows": Lewis Churbuck as quoted by Cornelius Coffey, Smithsonian Videohistory Program, *African-American Aviation Pioneers*, Session Two, 1990, minute 00:48:00, transcript 21.

47 • It was an almost unbelievable: *Chicago Tribune*, February 26, 1932, 6; Tucker, 2012, 39; Waterford, April 18, 1936, 3.

47 • They accepted the offer: Cornelius Coffey, Smithsonian Videohistory Program, *African-American Aviation Pioneers*, Session Two, 1990, minute 00:50:00, 02:01:55, transcript 21–22, 53; Tucker, 2012, 41.

48 • She was originally named: Bragg & Kriz, 1996, 3.

49 • . . . she taught herself . . . "Don't you ever do that again": ibid. 5–6.

49 • As a little girl: ibid., 8.

50 • But Samuel Harmon wanted: ibid., 9.

50 • It was "something I needed very badly": ibid., 10.

50 • She graduated from high school: ibid., 12.

50 • With twelve other young women: ibid., 13.

50 • The training was excellent: ibid., 15–16.

51 • . . . her older sister Viola: ibid., 16.

51 • . . . married a man: ibid., 26.

51 • Janet's childhood fascination: ibid., 26–27.

51–52 • "I didn't know one instrument": Janet Harmon Bragg, Smithsonian Videohistory Program, *African-American Aviation Pioneers*, Session One, 1989, minute 00:01:15, transcript 1.

52 • "I didn't know it was going": ibid., minute 00:01:15, transcript 1.

52 • **Fortunately, she'd always been:** Bragg & Kriz, 1996, 9.

52 • **"After the classwork":** Janet Harmon Bragg, Smithsonian Videohistory Program, *African-American Aviation Pioneers*, Session One, 1989, minute 00:01:15, transcript 1–2.

52 • **The class moved on:** Bragg & Kriz, 1996, 29.

52 • **The Curtiss-Wright students:** Speedy, July 22, 1933, A3.

53 • **Coffey and Johnny had very different:** Janet Harmon Bragg, Smithsonian Videohistory Program, *African-American Aviation Pioneers*, Session One, 1989, minute 00:09:31, transcript 5.

53 • **But they both knew their business:** Waterford, April 18, 1936, 3.

53 • **"I didn't know what tool"** . . . **"I became very, very independent":** Janet Harmon Bragg, Smithsonian Videohistory Program, *African-American Aviation Pioneers*, Session One, 1989, minute 02:37:00, transcript 81.

53 • **"One night after school":** ibid., minute 02:40:00, transcript 81.

54 • **"She encouraged me, too":** ibid., minute 02:40:15, transcript 81.

54 • **. . . a holiday dance:** *Chicago Defender*, December 24, 1932, 6.

54 • **"Opportunities for young":** *Negro World*, December 26, 1931, 2.

54 • **But after a while:** Bragg & Kriz, 1996, 29.

54 • **"When do we do":** Janet Harmon Bragg, Smithsonian Videohistory Program, *African-American Aviation Pioneers*, Session One, 1989, minute 00:02:00, transcript 2.

54 • **"That's the question":** ibid., minute 00:02:00, transcript 2.

54 • **He brought Janet:** Bragg & Kriz, 1996, 29.

54 • **"And he was dynamite":** Janet Harmon Bragg, Smithsonian Videohistory Program, *African-American Aviation Pioneers*, Session One, 1989, minute 00:03:20, transcript 1–2.

55 • **"He was a good instructor":** Bragg & Kriz, 1996, 29.

55 • **In 1931, Akers Airport:** Scott & Womack, 1998 (1992), 45; Smith, 2014; Cornelius Coffey, Smithsonian Videohistory Program, *African-American Aviation Pioneers*, Session Two, 1990, minute 01:01:57, transcript 28.

55 • **"We were told":** Harold Hurd, Smithsonian Videohistory Program, *African-American Aviation Pioneers*, Session Two, 1990, minute 02:05:00, transcript 56.

55 • **Hurd had moved:** Carter, 353; *Chicago Sun-Times*, September 10, 2002, 64; Harold Hurd, speaking in *Willa Beatrice Brown: An American Aviator*, 2009, minute 00:05:10; Speedy, July 22, 1933, A3.

55 • **The student pilots who'd been learning:** Haymore, July 21, 2021.

56 • **"They had a colored mayor":** Cornelius Coffey, Smithsonian Videohistory Program, *African-American Aviation Pioneers*, Session Two, 1990, minute 01:01:57, transcript 28.

56 • **Robbins was thriving:** Haymore, July 21, 2021.

56 • **When the men approached Mayor Nichols:** Haymore, 1989, 2.

56 • **There was a grassy stretch:** Bragg & Kriz, 1996, 29.

56 • **Neither Johnny nor Coffey:** Waterford, April 18, 1936, 3.

56 • **. . . the final expenses of its policyholders:** Bragg & Kriz, 1996, 23.

56 • **The group settled on a site:** *Chicago Defender*, June 4, 1932, A1; Haymore, 1989, 2; Robbins Historical Society and Museum, 2017, 22.

56 • "It had a few trees in there": Cornelius Coffey, Smithsonian Videohistory Program, *African-American Aviation Pioneers*, Session Two, 1990, minute 01:03:10, transcript 28.

57 • Robbins local Floyd Canter: Haymore, 1989, 2.

57 • "At times it seemed": Bragg & Kriz, 1996, 30.

57 • There was only room: ibid., 29.

57 • "... hot dogs, which we cooked": ibid., 29.

57 • "... let it fall into the hole": Cornelius Coffey, Smithsonian Videohistory Program, *African-American Aviation Pioneers*, Session Two, 1990, minute 01:03:15, transcript 28.

57 • Once it was in the hole: Cornelius Coffey as quoted by Tyrone Haymore, July 21, 2021; Harold Hurd, Smithsonian Videohistory Program, *African-American Aviation Pioneers*, Session Two, 1990, minute 02:03:00, transcript 54.

57 • After the holes were filled: Waterford, April 18, 1936, 3; Robbins Historical Society and Museum, 2017, 19.

57–58 • "We used the cinders": Bragg & Kriz, 1996, 30.

58 • "It was backbreaking work": ibid., 30.

58 • "... a biplane, painted red": ibid., 30.

58 • "It was a glorious day": ibid., 30.

58 • The coming winter also meant: Tucker, 2012, 46; Waterford, April 18, 1936, 3.

59 • The group scrounged for lumber: Cornelius Coffey, Smithsonian Videohistory Program, *African-American Aviation Pioneers*, Session Two, 1990, minute 01:03:00, transcript 28–29.

59 • "We built the hangar": ibid., minute 01:04:20, transcript 29.

59 • The hangar faced westward: Haymore, 1989, 3.

59 • Though the old Heath Parasol: Cornelius Coffey, Smithsonian Videohistory Program, *African-American Aviation Pioneers*, Session Two, 1990, minute 01:04:47, transcript 29.

59 • From now on they would be known: Haymore, July 21, 2021; Tucker, 2012, 47; *Pittsburgh Courier*, January 13, 1940, 12; Harold Hurd, Smithsonian Videohistory Program, *African-American Aviation Pioneers*, Session Two, 1990, minute 02:01:55, transcript 53.

59 • An inspector flew out: Speedy, July 22, 1933, A3.

59–60 • Johnny told him humbly ... "What a narrow escape": Waterford, April 18, 1936, 3.

60 • It was official: Waterford, April 18, 1936, 3.

60 • That tribute to the L.A. club's namesake: *Chicago Defender*, September 26, 1931, 2; Oxford African American Studies Centre, 2022.

60 • So on Memorial Day in 1932: *Chicago Defender*, June 4, 1932, A1; narration in *Willa Beatrice Brown: An American Aviator*, 2009, minute 00:06:30.

61 • "I finally really learned to fly": Bragg & Kriz, 1996, 30; Cornelius Coffey, Smithsonian Videohistory Program, *African-American Aviation Pioneers*, Session Two, 1990, minute 00:59:45–01:08:00, transcript 27–30. In her memoir, Janet gives the year as 1934, but records indicate it was 1932.

61 • "We started out in full force": Bragg & Kriz, 1996, 31.

61 • **Eight students in Coffey and Johnny's class:** Willa Brown, 1943, 13; Tucker, 2012, 41, 42.

61 • **That same year, Chinese students:** *Chicago Tribune*, February 26, 1932, 6; Tucker, 2012, 42.

61 • **"... an aviation enthusiast":** *New York Amsterdam News*, May 16, 1936, 13.

62 • **"The joy of being a licensed pilot":** *Chicago Defender*, January 2, 1932, 20.

62 • **Johnny probably received:** Federal Aviation Administration, communication from Mary Snyder, June 2, 2022; Powell, 1994 (1934), 148.

62 • **"J.C. Robinson—U.S. Government":** Dale L. White Scrapbook in the Dale L. White, Sr., papers, Accession 2013-0050, National Air and Space Museum, Smithsonian Institution, NASM-9A16697-001.tif, Box 3, Folder 1.

62 • **"Now that we have an approved"... "not passably, but well":** Waterford, April 25, 1936, 12.

62 • **In the warm summer weather:** *Chicago Defender*, June 4, 1932, A1; Cornelius Coffey, Smithsonian Videohistory Program, *African-American Aviation Pioneers*, Session Two, 1990, minute 01:02:00, transcript 28; Waterford, May 2, 1936, 12.

62 • **The Challenger pilots also:** Haymore, July 21, 2021.

62 • **The airfield was owned:** Lambertson, March 2010; Harold Hurd, Smithsonian Videohistory Program, *African-American Aviation Pioneers*, Session Two, 1990, minute 02:03:00, transcript 54.

62–63 • **Beacon Airport in Gary:** *Atlanta Daily World*, September 5, 1932, 1.

63 • **"As usual, I was wearing":** Bragg & Kriz, 1996, 31.

64 • **Coffey watched from the ground:** ibid., 31.

64 • **In September, she flew:** *Chicago Defender*, September 10, 1932, 15.; Speedy, July 22, 1933, A3.

64 • **By the end of the year:** Powell, 1994 (1934), 143–150.

64 • **After a little over a year:** Cornelius Coffey, Board of Examiners (Chicago) record update, in the Coffey family papers, Kenneth Spencer Research Library Box 2, Folder 12, 4.

64 • **Coffey still didn't have:** Churbuck, December 22, 1933, 3; Cornelius Coffey notes for speech, n.d., Coffey family papers, Kenneth Spencer Research Library Box 2, Folder 22; Cornelius Coffey, Smithsonian Videohistory Program, *African-American Aviation Pioneers*, Session Two, 1990, minute 01:06:00, transcript 30.

64 • **... Jennie B. Davis living in Detroit:** Ancestry.com.

64 • **In the meantime, there were now ten:** Bragg & Kriz, 1996, 31.

64–65 • **Janet and Johnny were the only:** according to Appendix in William Powell, 1994 (1934), 148, Department of Commerce list of licensed Black aviators in the US as of December 31, 1932.

65 • **"Johnny Robinson was in charge":** Janet Harmon Bragg, Smithsonian Videohistory Program, *African-American Aviation Pioneers*, Session One, 1989, minute 00:09:31, transcript 5.

65 • **... the Robbins runway "was usable":** Bragg & Kriz, 1996, 31.

65 • **Landing was just as much:** Janet Harmon Bragg, Smithsonian Videohistory

Program, *African-American Aviation Pioneers*, Session One, 1989, minute 00:04:50, transcript 3.

65 • "Our white neighbors to the south": Bragg & Kriz, 1996, 31.

66 • Charges were brought: Janet Harmon Bragg, Smithsonian Videohistory Program, *African-American Aviation Pioneers*, Session One, 1989, minute 00:04:50, transcript 3.

66 • Even the mayor of Midlothian: Galanis, 1989, 10.

66 • More than once, white policemen: Haymore, 1989, 3; Scott & Womack, 1998 (1992), 45; Tucker, 2012, 50; Waterford, April 18, 1936, 3.

66 • In December 1932: *Chicago Defender*, December 24, 1932, 6.

67 • Webster had a student: Speedy, July 22, 1933, A3.

67 • Doris Murphy Tanner, a Tuskegee: Beneš, 2017, 124; Jakeman, 1992, 10; Tucker, 2012, 58.

68 • Harold Hurd and Dale White: Cornelius Coffey, Smithsonian Videohistory Program, *African-American Aviation Pioneers*, Session Two, 1990, minute 00:50:00, 02:01:55, transcript 21–22, 53; Tucker, 2012, 41.

68 • Last but not least is Johnny Robinson: identification of the aviators in this photo as given by Cornelius Coffey in the Smithsonian Videohistory Program, *African-American Aviation Pioneers*, Session Two, 1990, minute 01:06:00, transcript 30; with the exception of Gerald Reed, identified by Tyrone Haymore via one of the Tuskegee Airmen, according to Haymore's interview with Stephanie Pitts on June 22, 2023.

68 • On Monday, May 1, 1933: Beneš, 2017, 137; Bragg & Kriz, 1996, 32; *Chicago Defender*, May 6, 1933, 3; Haymore, July 21, 2021; *Pittsburgh Courier*, May 13, 1933, 2; Tucker, 2012, 51.

68 • "It was our mistake": Harold Hurd, speaking in *Willa Beatrice Brown: An American Aviator*, 2009, minute 00:06:50.

68–69 • The storm apparently lifted: *Chicago Defender*, May 6, 1933, 3.

69 • Incredibly, though Janet's International: Cornelius Coffey, Smithsonian Videohistory Program, *African-American Aviation Pioneers*, Session Two, 1990, minute 01:05:00, transcript 29.

69–70 • Dale White, who served: *Pittsburgh Courier*, May 13, 1933, 2.

70 • A handsome man with a friendly smile: *Aerotech News*, 2021; Dale L. White, Sr., Papers, biographical note at https://sova.si.edu/record/NASM.2013.0050 (accessed April 12, 2023).

70 • Optimistically, Dale told: Speedy, July 22, 1933, A3.

70 • "... constantly molested by the police": Harold Hurd, speaking in *Willa Beatrice Brown: An American Aviator*, 2009, minute 00:07:10.

CHAPTER 4: CLIMB, 1933–1934

71 • Tuskegee, thou pride of the swift: Paul Lawrence Dunbar, "The Tuskegee Song," 1909, available at https://www.tuskegee.edu/student-life/student-organizations/choir/the-tuskegee-song (accessed April 11, 2023).

71 • "A pilot, without a thorough": *Atlanta Daily World*, September 5, 1932, 5.

72 • Fred was a taxi driver: Wilbur Bohl, interviewed by Gordon Welles, December 18, 1979, transcript 33–34.

72 • **His brother Bill had purchased:** Selig, 2013, 96; Lamberton, 2010.

72 • **... the airport was named:** Cornelius Coffey, Smithsonian Videohistory Program, *African-American Aviation Pioneers*, Session Two, 1990, minute 01:09:00, transcript 32.

72 • **He also knew that Oak Lawn:** ibid., minute 01:06:00, transcript 30.

72 • **"Don't bother to try to rebuild":** Fred Schumacher as quoted by Tyrone Haymore, July 21, 2021.

72 • **Founded in the early 1800s:** https://www.oaklawn-il.gov/about-oak-lawn (accessed April 12, 2023).

72 • **... the village had a population:** "Oak Lawn, IL," in the *Encyclopedia of Chicago*, http://www.encyclopedia.chicagohistory.org/pages/916.html (accessed April 12, 2023).

72 • **Oak Lawn frequently held minstrel shows:** Oak Lawn Public Library Programs, https://olpl.pastperfectonline.com/Search?search_criteria=minstrel &onlyimages=false (accessed April 12, 2023).

72 • **"Look, fellows," Fred told the Challengers:** Fred Schumacher as quoted by Harold Hurd, Smithsonian Videohistory Program, *African-American Aviation Pioneers*, Session Two, 1990, minute 01:57:00, transcript 54.

72 • **"We went out there":** Janet Harmon Bragg, Smithsonian Videohistory Program, *African-American Aviation Pioneers*, Session One, 1989, minute 00:12:31, transcript 7.

73 • **But that didn't stop:** Cornelius Coffey, Smithsonian Videohistory Program, *African-American Aviation Pioneers*, Session Two, 1990, minute 01:09:00, transcript 32.

73 • **"We didn't care":** Janet Harmon Bragg, Smithsonian Videohistory Program, *African-American Aviation Pioneers*, Session One, 1989, minute 00:12:31, transcript 7.

73 • **"Don't worry about it":** Fred Schumacher as quoted by Tyrone Haymore, July 21, 2021.

74 • **A connection with a Black parachutist:** *Chicago Defender*, September 30, 1933, 4.

74 • **Major Fisher was part:** Scott & Womack, 1998 (1992), 49, note 69, interview with Harold Hurd; Cornelius Coffey and Harold Hurd in conversation, Smithsonian Videohistory Program, *African-American Aviation Pioneers*, Session Two, 1990, minute 02:13:06, transcript 60–62.

74 • **So the Challenger Aero Club pursued:** *Atlanta Daily World*, May 17, 1934, 1; Beneš, 2017, 141; Cornelius Coffey and Harold Hurd in conversation, Smithsonian Videohistory Program, *African-American Aviation Pioneers*, Session Two, 1990, minute 02:12:00–02:20:00, transcript 60–62; Speedy, July 22, 1933, A3.

74 • **... both Coffey and Johnny were given:** Speedy, July 22, 1933, A3.

74 • **Nash was Harold Hurd's:** Harold Hurd, Smithsonian Videohistory Program, *African-American Aviation Pioneers*, Session Two, 1990, minute 02:23:35, transcript 65.

74 • **Born in Dry Branch, Georgia:** Gubert et al, 2002, 217; Waterford, May 21, 1938, 2.

75 • **Once inducted:** Tucker, 2012, 61.

75 • **... they were allowed to display:** Scott & Womack, 1998 (1992), 48–49.

75 • **The male members:** Scott & Womack, 1998 (1992), 49, according to an interview with Cornelius Coffey; Tucker, 2012, 61.

75 • **The Challenger Aero Club moved:** Bragg & Kriz, 1996, 32; Tucker, 2012, 51.

75 • **Meanwhile, probably with Earnize's help:** *Chicago Tribune*, May 25, 1936, 3; Haymore, July 21, 2021; Tucker, 2012, 28.

75 • **He converted it:** Simmons 2013, 56.

75 • **"They were doing some auto repair":** Cornelius Coffey, Smithsonian Videohistory Program, *African-American Aviation Pioneers*, Session Two, 1990, minute 01:10:00, transcript 32.

75 • **"It was a new beginning":** Bragg & Kriz, 1996, 32.

75 • **Nash's Buhl Pup:** Gubert et al, 2002, 217; Speedy, July 22, 1933, A3.

76 • **"This school makes no discrimination":** Churbuck, December 22, 1933, 3.

76 • **The Curtiss-Wright company realized:** Scott & Womack, 1998 (1992), 46.

76 • **Coffey shared Johnny's ambition:** Cornelius Coffey, Smithsonian Videohistory Program, *African-American Aviation Pioneers*, Session Two, 1990, minute 01:13:00, transcript 34.

77 • **In 1934, Tuskegee seemed:** Jakeman, 1992, 2.

77 • **Schools like New York University:** Eberhardt & Komerath, 2009, 14.

77 • **"They taught everything else":** Cornelius Coffey, Smithsonian Videohistory Program, *African-American Aviation Pioneers*, Session Two, 1990, minute 01:12:30, transcript 33–34.

77 • **So through Neely:** Bragg & Kriz, 1996, 32; Prattis, October 12, 1935, 4; Prattis, October 26, 1935, 1A; Scott & Womack, 1998 (1992), 46.

77 • **Though there's no record:** Department of Commerce, "Negro Aviators," July 1935; Tucker 2012, 53.

77 • **Coffey and Johnny would fly:** Cornelius Coffey, Smithsonian Videohistory Program, *African-American Aviation Pioneers*, Session Two, 1990, minute 01:14:00, transcript 32.

78 • **Grover Nash would also go along:** Scott & Womack, 1998 (1992), 46; Cornelius Coffey, Smithsonian Videohistory Program, *African-American Aviation Pioneers*, Session Two, 1990, minute 01:14:00, transcript 34; Tucker, 2012, 51.

78 • **He had a Curtiss-Wright Aeronautical:** Gubert et al, 2002, 217.

78 • **Their planned route:** *Atlanta Daily World*, May 17, 1934, 1.

78 • **So early in the morning:** ibid., 1.

78 • **But just before the International:** Waterford, May 2, 1936, 12.

78 • **This wasn't the first time:** Tucker, 2012, 53.

79 • **Nash's little plane:** Cornelius Coffey, Smithsonian Videohistory Program, *African-American Aviation Pioneers*, Session Two, 1990, minute 01:14:00, transcript 34.

79 • **... but the fifty gallons:** Scott & Womack, 1998 (1992), 46.

79 • **Unfortunately, the extra tank:** ibid., 47.

79 • **"Now, on our route down":** Cornelius Coffey, Smithsonian Videohistory Program, *African-American Aviation Pioneers*, Session Two, 1990, minute 01:14:00, transcript 34.

79 • **... it seems that Nash:** *Atlanta Daily World*, May 17, 1934, 1.

79 • **"There was no airport there":** Cornelius Coffey, Smithsonian Videohistory Program, *African-American Aviation Pioneers*, Session Two, 1990, minute 01:14:30, transcript 34.

79 • Both planes landed: *Chicago Defender*, May 26, 1934, 1.

79–80 • "We'll walk over the area": Johnny Robinson as quoted by Cornelius Coffey in Smithsonian Videohistory Program, *African-American Aviation Pioneers*, Session Two, 1990, minute 01:15:00, transcript 35.

80 • "Look. With that extra gas": Cornelius Coffey, Smithsonian Videohistory Program, *African-American Aviation Pioneers*, Session Two, 1990, minute 01:15:00, transcript 35.

80 • He stuck a wooden stick: Scott & Womack, 1998 (1992), 47; Cornelius Coffey, Smithsonian Videohistory Program, *African-American Aviation Pioneers*, Session Two, 1990, minute 01:15:30, transcript 35.

80 • From the front seat: Cornelius Coffey, Smithsonian Videohistory Program, *African-American Aviation Pioneers*, Session Two, 1990, minute 01:15:30, transcript 35.

80–81 • Coffey spun ... "This is going to be good": ibid., minute 01:16:00, transcript 35.

81 • He hauled the plane: ibid., minute 01:16:30, transcript 36.

81 • "If we'd attempted a turn": ibid., minute 01:16:00, transcript 36.

81 • "I never will forget": ibid., minute 01:16:30, transcript 36.

82 • Coffey loosened ... slender guide wire: ibid., minute 01:17:00, transcript 36.

82 • Miraculously, the International: Scott & Womack, 1998 (1992), 47.

82 • Coffey pointed ... safe crash landing: Scott & Womack, 1998 (1992), 47; their source is an interview with Cornelius Coffey.

82 • "I saw this cotton patch": Cornelius Coffey, Smithsonian Videohistory Program, *African-American Aviation Pioneers*, Session Two, 1990, minute 01:24:00, transcript 37.

82 • ... they realized there was a tree: *Chicago Defender*, "'Good Will' Flyers Crash," May 26, 1934, 1; Scott & Womack, 1998 (1992), 47.

82 • "We almost cleared that tree": Cornelius Coffey, Smithsonian Videohistory Program, *African-American Aviation Pioneers*, Session Two, 1990, minute 01:25:00; transcript 37.

82 • Their left wheel snagged: ibid., minute 01:25:00, transcript 37.

83 • The International lost: *Decatur Daily*, May 26, 1934, 1.

83 • Nash had watched helplessly: Scott & Womack, 1998 (1992), 48.

83 • But when the dust settled: Cornelius Coffey, Smithsonian Videohistory Program, *African-American Aviation Pioneers*, Session Two, 1990, minute 01:25:00, transcript 37.

83 • "People come across there": ibid., minute 01:25:00, transcript 37.

83 • After a couple of days: John C. Robinson, pilot's log book (1934–1935).

83 • ... dealing with the fallout: Cornelius Coffey, Smithsonian Videohistory Program, *African-American Aviation Pioneers*, Session Two, 1990, minute 01:26:00, transcript 38.

83–84 • He and Coffey would make: *Chicago Defender*, June 2, 1934, 2; *Decatur Daily*, May 26, 1934, 1; Scott & Womack, 1998 (1992), 48; Tucker, 2012, 52–53; Waterford, May 9, 1936, 12.

84 • On Tuesday, May 22, 1934: *Chicago Defender*, May 26, 1934, 22; Jakeman, 1992, 2.

84 • **The coverage of his eventful trip:** Stewart, 1934, 18.

84 • **In addition to talking:** Jakeman, 1992, 1, 6.

85 • **"It might have been different":** Cornelius Coffey, Smithsonian Videohistory Program, *African-American Aviation Pioneers*, Session Two, 1990, minute 02:32:00, transcript 70.

85 • **... he picked up his next airplane:** ibid., minute 01:32:00, transcript 41.

86 • **He set his sights:** Bragg & Kriz, 1992, 32.

86 • **"I have no money!"... he paid off the debt:** Tucker, 2012, 59, quoting Henry Tartt's story of John C. Robinson at the Brown Condor Symposium, March 15, 2002.

86 • **Her father and mother:** *Daily Challenge*, 1992, 2, in the Betty Gubert Collection of African Americans in Aviation, Box 2, Folder 19.

86–87 • **... Willa graduated:** Freydberg, "Willa Beatrice Brown," in Hine et al, 1993, Vol. A–L, 184–186; National Airmen's Association of America, "Willa B. Brown, Personal History," in *Who's Who in Aviation* [1941?], in the Betty Gubert Collection of African Americans in Aviation, Box 2, Folder 20.

87 • **... standing only five foot one:** Willa Brown, pilot's license application to the U.S. Department of Commerce dated Oct. 30, 1938, in the Records of the Federal Aviation Administration, National Archives Record Group 237, 1922–1992, supplied by Dr. Theresa Kraus.

87 • **Beacon Airport hosted:** *Lake County Times*, June 6, 1930, 1.

87 • **"Here's Your Chance":** *Gary American*, June 7, 1929, in the Betty Gubert Collection of African Americans in Aviation, Box 2, Folder 22.

88 • **... commuting back to Terre Haute:** Gubert et al, 2002, 49.

88 • **... she met one of Indiana's first:** *Gary American*, April 19, 1929, 4, in the Betty Gubert Collection of African Americans in Aviation, Box 2, Folder 22.

88 • **"... a likeable fella":** Simeon Brown, speaking in *Willa Beatrice Brown: An American Aviator*, 2009, minute 00:04.00.

88 • **In a race between eight:** Gladys Ingram, November 29, 1929, 1, in the Betty Gubert Collection of African Americans in Aviation, Box 2, Folder 22.

88 • **... having completed her college degree:** Indiana State University Public Records, Correspondence with the Office of General Counsel, Indiana State University, October 25, 2021.

88 • **The fabulous new Roosevelt:** *Gary American*, "Roosevelt High School Dedicated," April 5, 1931, 1, in the Betty Gubert Collection of African Americans in Aviation, Box 3, Folder 2.

88 • **... three hundred of them studied:** *Gary American*, "Students Are Given Training," April 25, 1931, 1, in the Betty Gubert Collection of African Americans in Aviation, Box 3, Folder 2.

89 • **Wilbur used his position:** *Gary American*, "Protest Building of Roosevelt School," June 28, 1930, 1, in the Betty Gubert Collection of African Americans in Aviation, Box 3, Folder 1.

89 • **He was known as "The Fighting Alderman":** *Gary American*, December 31, 1932, 1, in the Betty Gubert Collection of African Americans in Aviation, Box 3, Folder 3.

89 • **... once he even took a swing:** *Lake County Times*, May 3, 1932, 11.

89 • **"We wrecked our apartment":** Willa Brown as quoted by Enoch Waters, 1987, 197.

89 • **"We fought like dogs":** Willa Brown as quoted by Chauncey Spencer. From Betty Gubert's transcript of her interview with Spencer, April 20, 1995, in the Betty Gubert Collection of African Americans in Aviation, Box 3, Folder 15.

89 • **After Wilbur gave her a punch:** Copy of Court Order, "Willa B. Hardaway vs. Wilbur J. Hardaway, No. 21901," Lake County, Indiana, November 17, 1931; *Gary American*, November 7, 1931, 1, in the Betty Gubert Collection of African Americans in Aviation, Box 3, Folder 2.

90 • **On the drive back to Chicago:** *Atlanta Daily World*, May 6, 1962, A2.

90 • **A local boy watched:** *Chicago Defender*, May 19, 1934, 2; *Gary American*, May 19, 1934, 1, in the Betty Gubert Collection of African Americans in Aviation, Box 3, Folder 4.

90 • **The Walgreens drugstore:** *Chicago Tribune*, July 10, 1938, 31.

91 • **Since John McClellan's death:** *Chicago Defender*, May 19, 1934, 1; *Chicago Tribune*, July 10, 1938, 31; Haymore, July 21, 2021; Scott & Womack, 1998 (1992), 62; Waters, September 26, 1942, B15.

91 • **In January 1935, she would enroll:** Willa Brown, pilot's license applications with the United States Department of Commerce, April 23, 1938, in the Records of the Federal Aviation Administration, National Archives Record Group 237, 1922–1992, supplied by Dr. Theresa Kraus; *Chicago Tribune*, July 10, 1938, 31; Washington, 1972, in Collection No. 3, "Frederick D. Patterson," Archives and Special Collections, Tuskegee University, Tuskegee, AL, 59.

91 • **... its population speaks:** https://www.britannica.com/place/Ethiopia/Ethnic-groups-and-languages (accessed April 12, 2023).

92 • **... in the four years since:** https://www.britannica.com/place/Ethiopia/The-rise-and-reign-of-Haile-Selassie-I-1916-74 (accessed April 12, 2023).

CHAPTER 5: ETHIOPIA, 1935

93 • **I am glad to know:** John C. Robinson interviewed by J.A. Rogers, in Rogers, January 4, 1936, 1.

93 • **One of these was Liberia:** https://www.britannica.com/place/Liberia (accessed April 12, 2023).

94 • **Booker T. Washington, none other:** https://www.biography.com/scholars-educators/booker-t-washington (accessed April 12, 2023); confirmed in Charles Rivers Editors, 2018, Kindle edition location 200–203.

94 • **Pan-Africanism, the idea:** https://www.britannica.com/topic/Pan-Africanism (accessed April 12, 2023).

94 • **He argued that Black people:** Lewis, 1981, 7.

95 • **... Marcus Garvey offered a third path:** https://www.britannica.com/biography/Marcus-Garvey (accessed April 12, 2023).

95 • **Born Marcus Mosiah Garvey:** https://www.archives.gov/research/african-americans/individuals/marcus-garvey (accessed April 12, 2023).

95 • **Garvey traveled and worked:** Nnuriam, 2018, 13–21.

95 • **When he returned to Jamaica:** https://www.archives.gov/research

/african-americans/individuals/marcus-garvey (accessed April 12, 2023);
https://www.britannica.com/biography/Marcus-Garvey (accessed April 12, 2023).

95 • **The NAACP, the Urban League:** David Robinson, April 6, 1935, 14; William R. Scott, 1978, 118, 120, 122.

95 • **In the spring of 1935:** *New York Amsterdam News*, March 2, 1935, 3.

96 • **"Italy would be whipped":** *Pittsburgh Courier*, July 20, 1935, 5.

96 • **Smitten with the idea of flight:** Marcus, 1987, 50.

97 • **One of Julian's earlier:** Gubert et al, 2002, 184–185.

97 • **The Prince Regent wanted:** ibid., 185.

98 • **But his jump was even bigger:** Shaftel, 2008.

98 • **During the rehearsal:** ibid., 2008.

98 • **Julian was ejected:** Shaftel, 2008; Tucker, 2012, 66–67.

98 • **Haile Selassie had built:** Tucker, 2012, 65.

98 • **"Look, here's Hubert Julian":** John C. Robinson as quoted by Cornelius Coffey, Smithsonian Videohistory Program, *African-American Aviation Pioneers*, Session Two, 1990, minute 01:54:31, transcript 42.

99 • **... he was a licensed mechanic:** Cornelius Coffey, Smithsonian Videohistory Program, *African-American Aviation Pioneers*, Session Two, 1990, minute 01:54:31, transcript 42.

99 • **In New York, a group:** *Baltimore Afro-American*, August 3, 1935, 2.

99 • **They started to make plans:** Scott & Womack, 1998 (1992), 32; Tucker, 2012, 173.

99 • **Feeling that Johnny:** Hardesty & Pisano, 1983, 14; Scott & Womack, 1998 (1992), 50, according to interviews with Cornelius Coffey and Harold Hurd; Tucker, 2012, 89.

99 • **"I am going to try to get jobs":** John C. Robinson writing as Wilson James, "Whites Poisons Minds of Ethiopians" in the Kansas City *Plaindealer*, July 12, 1935, 2.

99 • **"I told my fellow pilots":** Robinson to Barnett, November 21, 1935, Claude A. Barnett papers, Box 170, Folder 9.

99 • **"I sold my garage in Detroit":** Cornelius Coffey, Smithsonian Videohistory Program, *African-American Aviation Pioneers*, Session Two, 1990, minute 01:36:00, transcript 42.

99 • **"We are willing to fight":** *Pittsburgh Courier*, July 20, 1935, 1.

99–100 • **But a national radio commentator:** *Chicago Defender*, July 20, 1935, 5.

100 • **In the summer of 1935:** https://history.state.gov/milestones/1921-1936 /neutrality-acts (accessed April 12, 2023).

100 • **"... the establishment of a course":** *Chicago Defender*, August 25, 1934, 5.

100 • **Early in 1935 came a change:** Jakeman, 1992, 4, 6.

101 • **In the spring of 1935:** ibid., 23.

101 • **"... deeply influenced by the self-help":** *Encyclopedia of Chicago*, https:// encyclopedia.chicagohistory.org/pages/1734.html (accessed April 12, 2023).

101 • **In January 1935, Johnny spoke:** Tucker, 2012, 69.

101 • **Barnett heard him speak:** Beneš, 2017, 155; Jakeman, 1992, 21; Tucker, 2012, 70.

101–102 • **Malaku did a bit of checking:** Claude A. Barnett to Malaku Bayen,

January 8, 1935; Claude A. Barnett to Jesse O. Thomas, May 11, 1936; Malaku Bayen to Claude A. Barnett, January 3, 1935, all in the Claude A. Barnett papers, Box 170, Folder 9.

102 • . . . in April 1935, Johnny received: Tucker, 2012, 70–71.

102 • Now Johnny had to choose: Prattis, October 12, 1935, 4.

102 • He asked George L. Washington: Jakeman, 1992, 23.

102 • Johnny got a passport: Hardesty & Pisano, 1983, 14; Tucker, 2012, 89.

102 • Earnize Tate would take care: Claude A. Barnett to John C. Robinson, October 19, 1935, April 22, 1936, and May 9, 1936, in the Claude A. Barnett papers, Box 170, Folder 9; *Chicago Tribune*, August 28, 1935, 5; *New York Amsterdam News*, May 16, 1936, 13; *New York World-Telegram*, May 19, 1936, in the Claude A. Barnett papers, Box 171, Folder 5; Prattis, October 12, 1935, 4.

102 • Coffey would stand in: *Pittsburgh Courier*, January 18, 1936, 5.

102 • Johnny left Chicago by rail: Malaku Bayen to Claude A. Barnett, May 6, 1935, in the Claude A. Barnett papers, Box 170, Folder 9; Tucker, 2012, 90.

102–103 • He'd broken his arm: *Pittsburgh Courier*, January 4, 1936, 4; Prattis, October 12, 1935, 4; Tucker, 2012, 90; Waterford, May 9, 1936, 12; White, [June 4, 1936], in the Claude A. Barnett papers, Box 171, Folder 5.

103 • At Dire Dawa, one of the dusty stops: Tucker, 2012, 92; White, [June 4, 1936], in the Claude A. Barnett papers, Box 171, Folder 5.

103 • Johnny arrived there on May 29, 1935: Jakeman, 1992, 22; William R. Scott, 1972, 61–62, in the Betty Gubert Collection of African Americans in Aviation, Box 7, Folder 16.

103 • His arm was still healing: *Pittsburgh Courier*, January 4, 1936, 4; Prattis, October 12, 1935, 4; Tucker, 2012, 90; Waterford, May 9, 1936, 12; White, [June 4, 1936], in the Claude A. Barnett papers, Box 171, Folder 5.

104 • "I arrived here last [Wednesday]" . . . "Know his line of work": John C. Robinson to Claude A. Barnett, June 3, 1935, in the Claude A. Barnett Papers, Box 170, Folder 9.

104 • Johnny felt that: John C. Robinson writing as Wilson James, September 7, 1935, 10.

104 • Malaku also cautioned: Malaku Bayen to Claude A. Barnett, May 6, 1935, in the Claude A. Barnett papers, Box 170, Folder 9.

104–105 • "Robinson has slipped quietly": Office of Claude Barnett to E.G. Roberts, July 17, 1935, in the Claude A. Barnett papers, Box 170, Folder 9.

105 • Although Johnny's arm kept him: *Baltimore Afro-American*, May 23, 1936, 13; *Philadelphia Tribune*, May 21, 1936, 19; Tucker, 2012, 107.

105 • Wary of his own reception: John C. Robinson to Claude A. Barnett, June 3, 1935, in the Claude A. Barnett papers, Box 170, Folder 9; John C. Robinson writing as Wilson James in the Kansas City *Plaindealer*, July 12, 1935, 2; Tucker, 2012, 95.

105 • It wasn't until three weeks: Tucker, 2012, 97; White, [June 4, 1936], in the Claude A. Barnett papers, Box 171, Folder 5.

106 • "This year the club boasts": *Baltimore Afro-American*, June 15, 1935, 3.

106 • The count likely included: Cornelius Coffey, Smithsonian Videohistory

Program, *African-American Aviation Pioneers*, Session Two, 1990, minute 02:15:47, transcript 61.

106 • Coffey led the Memorial Day flight: *Atlanta Daily World*, June 14, 1935, 2; *Baltimore Afro-American*, June 15, 1935, 3; *Chicago Defender*, June 8, 1935, 12; *Washington Tribune*, June 22, 1935, 3.

106–107 • "... junior birdmen": *Chicago Defender*, May 16, 1936, 15.

107 • Willa was also working: Willa Brown, pilot's license applications/licenses with the U.S. Department of Commerce, 1935–1939, in the Records of the Federal Aviation Administration, National Archives Record Group 237, 1922–1992, supplied by Dr. Theresa Kraus; see also Gubert et al, 2002, 48.

107 • ... she'd been taking flying: Willa Brown, application and license dated March 6, 1935, and application for pilot's license dated December 15, 1938, both with the US Department of Commerce, 1935–1939, in the Records of the Federal Aviation Administration, National Archives Record Group 237, 1922–1992, supplied by Dr. Theresa Kraus; see also *Chicago Tribune*, July 10, 1938, 31.

108 • "Negro women are proving": Lillian Johnson, May 25, 1935, 9.

108 • She wrote a weekly series: *Baltimore Afro-American*, May 23, 1936, 12; Lillian Johnson, May 25, 1935, 9; *Pittsburgh Courier*, October 9, 1937, 3.

108 • Janet churned out a series: Waterford in the *Chicago Defender*, April 13, 1935, 15; May 4, 1935, 16; May 25, 1935, 15.

108 • Janet would soon set about: *Pittsburgh Courier*, April 11, 1936, 2; June 4, 1938, 3; January 13, 1940, 12.

108 • ... Janet also seems: *Chicago Defender*, July 27, 1935, 20.

109 • Right from the beginning: Claude A. Barnett to John C. Robinson, October 19, 1935; John C. Robinson to Claude A. Barnett, June 3, 1935; Percival L. Prattis to Claude A. Barnett, July 15, 1935, all in the Claude A. Barnett papers, Box 170, Folder 9.

109 • This seems to have been Barnett's idea: Claude A. Barnett to E.G. Roberts, July 17, 1935, in the Claude A. Barnett papers, Box 170, Folder 9.

109 • Tuskegee Institute took in: Claude A. Barnett to John C. Robinson, October 19, 1935, Box 170, Folder 9; see also Jakeman, 1992, 22.

109 • The press, both Black and white: Jakeman, 1992, 22; *New York Times*, August 23, 1935, 10.

110 • "... because of his reputation": Harold Hurd, Smithsonian Videohistory Program, *African-American Aviation Pioneers*, Session Two, 1990, minute 02:11:00, transcript 59.

110 • "... had never seen him before": John C. Robinson to Claude A. Barnett, June 3, 1935, in the Claude A. Barnett papers, Box 170, Folder 9.

110 • By August 1935, Johnny had: Jakeman, 1992, 22; William R. Scott, 1972, 62–63, in the Betty Gubert Collection of African Americans in Aviation, Box 7, Folder 16.

110 • Now when Johnny wrote: John C. Robinson to Claude A. Barnett, June 3, 1935, in the Claude A. Barnett papers, Box 170, Folder 9.

110 • "I wish you would write": ibid.

111 • **Barnett published this exposé:** John C. Robinson writing as Wilson James in the *Philadelphia Tribune*, July 11, 1935, 1.

111 • **On August 8, 1935:** *Cincinnati Enquirer*, August 23, 1935, 3.

111 • **Julian confronted Johnny:** Claude Barnett to John C. Robinson, August 28, 1935, in the Claude A. Barnett papers, Box 170, Folder 9; Tucker, 2012, 98–99.

111 • **Julian shoved copies:** *Chicago World*, August 17, 1935, 5; *Plaindealer*, August 16, 1935, 8.

111 • **"You, you dirty so-and-so":** *Philadelphia Tribune*, August 15, 1935, 1.

111 • **... took a swing at Johnny:** *Cincinnati Enquirer*, August 23, 1935, 3.

111 • **Hubert Julian, once again in disgrace:** *Cincinnati Enquirer*, August 23, 1935, 3; *New York Times*, August 23, 1935, 10; Tucker, 2012, 99.

111 • **He left Ethiopia a few months:** John C. Robinson to Claude A. Barnett, November 21, 1935, in the Claude A. Barnett papers, Box 170, Folder 9.

112 • **So as the head of Ethiopia's:** *Baltimore Afro-American*, May 23, 1936, 13; Fleming, May 23, 1936, 13; Jakeman, 1992, 23; *Philadelphia Tribune*, May 21, 1936, 19.

112 • **Once his arm healed:** John C. Robinson, pilot's log book entries for 1935.

112 • **"There were no war maps":** Rogers, February 1, 1936, 6.

112 • **... Joel Augustus Rogers, who worked:** Fleming, May 23, 1936, 13; *Pittsburgh Courier*, January 4, 1936, 1; Dale L. White, Scrapbook, 3, in the Dale L. White, Sr., papers, Accession 2013-0050, National Air and Space Museum, Smithsonian Institution, NASM-9A16697-001.tif, Box 3, Folder 1.

112 • **"There are no towns":** Rogers, February 1, 1936, 6.

112 • **Toward the end of September:** Beneš, 2017, 172; *Philadelphia Tribune*, May 21, 1936, 19; Tucker, 2012, 130.

112–113 • **"Everyone here is of the opinion":** *Baltimore Afro-American*, October 12, 1935, 4.

113 • **Four large Italian planes:** *Time*, October 14, 1935.

113 • **Johnny was one of thousands:** *Pittsburgh Press*, October 6, 1935, 7.

113 • **"They were mistaken about":** *Time*, October 14, 1935.

114 • **"I will never forget that day":** John C. Robinson to Claude A. Barnett, November 21, 1935, in the Claude A. Barnett papers, Box 170, Folder 9.

114 • **Johnny couldn't take off ... outmaneuver them:** *New York Times*, October 5, 1935, 2; Tucker, 2012, 131.

114 • **Now Johnny's flight experience:** Tucker, 2012, 131.

115 • **"One part of the wing":** John C. Robinson to Claude A. Barnett, November 21, 1935, in the Claude A. Barnett papers, Box 170, Folder 9.

115 • **"Every red-blooded Negro":** *Pittsburgh Courier*, October 19, 1935, 12.

116 • **In Chicago, at a conference:** *Philadelphia Tribune*, October 17, 1935, 5.

116 • **... it was illegal for any:** https://history.state.gov/milestones/1921-1936/neutrality-acts (accessed April 12, 2023).

116 • **"He was able to escape":** Rogers, December 14, 1935, 1; see also *Plaindealer*, December 13, 1935, 1.

116 • **He put in an order:** *Atlanta Daily World*, December 26, 1935, 1; John C.

Robinson to Claude A. Barnett, November 21, 1935, in the Claude A. Barnett papers, Box 170, Folder 9.

116–117 • To his dismay, the British: John C. Robinson to Claude A. Barnett, November 28, 1935, in the Claude A. Barnett papers, Box 170, Folder 9.

117 • "I shall stay here and deliver": *New Journal and Guide*, October 12, 1935, 1.

117 • Oddly, when Johnny's own warnings: John C. Robinson to Claude A. Barnett, November 28, 1935, in the Claude A. Barnett papers, Box 170, Folder 9.

117 • "Every one [of the Challenger group]": John C. Robinson to Claude A. Barnett, November 21, 1935, in the Claude A. Barnett papers, Box 170, Folder 9; Tucker, 2012, 147.

117–118 • . . . his own letters sometimes: Claude A. Barnett to John C. Robinson, April 16, 1936, in the Claude A. Barnett papers, Box 170, Folder 9.

118 • He'd mailed a letter: *Chicago Tribune*, August 28, 1935, 5.

118 • Coffey had applied for: Department of Commerce, list of "Negro Aviators," August 1936.

118 • ". . . all togged out in aviator's togs": Claude A. Barnett to John C. Robinson, January 22, 1936, in the Claude A. Barnett papers, Box 170, Folder 9.

118 • "Wants To Fight Italian Bombers": *Pittsburgh Courier*, January 13, 1936, 1.

118 • Though Claude Barnett pulled: Claude A. Barnett to John C. Robinson, December 31, 1935, in the Claude A. Barnett papers, Box 170, Folder 9.

118 • "I came within six months": Cornelius Coffey in the afterword to Bragg & Kriz, 1996, 111.

CHAPTER 6: THE AIRWAYS PART, 1936–1937

119 • "We'll sing Ethiopia": William Lloyd Imes, "We'll Sing Ethiopia," [1936], in the Claude A. Barnett papers, Box 171, Folder 5.

119 • "Please let Mr. Washington": John C. Robinson to Claude A. Barnett, November 28, 1935, in the Claude A. Barnett papers, Box 170, Folder 9.

119 • "renounced his American": *New Journal and Guide*, October 19, 1935, 1.

119 • "Don't be afraid about": Claude A. Barnett to John C. Robinson, December 31, 1935, in the Claude A. Barnett papers, Box 170, Folder 9.

120 • "he was interested in pushing": Claude A. Barnett to John C. Robinson, January 22, 1936, in the Claude A. Barnett papers, Box 170, Folder 9.

120 • Ideally, the program: G.L. Washington to Claude A. Barnett, April 10, 1935, in the Claude A. Barnett papers, Box 170, Folder 9.

120 • Barnett was aware: Office of Claude Barnett to E.G. Roberts, July 17, 1935, in the Claude A. Barnett papers, Box 170, Folder 9.

120 • . . . formerly the Bessie Coleman: *Pittsburgh Courier*, May 16, 1936, A8.

120 • "It occurred to me": Claude A. Barnett to Frederick Douglass Patterson, May 9, 1936, in the Claude A. Barnett papers, Box 170, Folder 9.

120 • Tuskegee was enthusiastic: Claude A. Barnett to John C. Robinson, December 31, 1935, January 22, 1936, and April 16, 1936, in the Claude A. Barnett papers, Box 170, Folder 9; Jakeman, 1992, 23.

120 • As 1936 began: Norman, May 28, 1936, 10; *Toledo News Bee*, May 22, 1936, in the Claude A. Barnett papers, Box 171, Folder 5; Tucker, 2012, 109, 138.

120 • Adorned with the red: *Atlanta Daily World,* June 2, 1936, 2; *Philadelphia Tribune,* May 21, 1936, 19; Tucker, 2012, 98, 103–104.

121 • The Italian forces in Ethiopia: Tucker, 2012, 142.

121 • . . . Johnny endured three attacks: *Baltimore Afro-American,* May 30, 1936, 8; Fleming, May 23, 1936, 13; *New York Times,* May 19, 1936, 6; *Philadelphia Tribune,* May 21, 1936, 19.

121 • Johnny rightly guessed: *Atlanta Daily World,* June 2, 1936, 2; *Philadelphia Tribune,* May 21, 1936, 19.

121 • . . . the Challenger pilots ran: Beneš, 2017, 188.

121–122 • . . . they appeared on a weekly: Waterford, Apr 4 1936, 1, 2; April 11, 1936, 6; April 18, 1936, 3; April 25, 1936, 12; May 2, 1936, 12; May 9, 1936, 12.

122 • Up until nearly the last: *Chicago Defender,* April 25, 1936, 1.

122 • On May 1, 1936, Johnny Robinson: *New York Times,* May 19, 1936, 6; Jakeman, 1992, 23; Tucker, 2012, 184–185.

122 • The emperor would spend: Sbacchi, 1977, 503.

122 • ". . . I got a cable from Johnny" . . . "to come home on": Cornelius Coffey, Smithsonian Videohistory Program, *African-American Aviation Pioneers,* Session Two, 1990, minute 01:36:00, transcript 42.

123 • "Mrs. John C. Robinson, wife": *Baltimore Afro-American,* May 2, 1936, 3.

123 • "While she has shrunk": Kansas City *Plaindealer,* May 1, 1936, 2.

123 • Indeed, Claude Barnett had been: Claude A. Barnett to John C. Robinson, August 28, 1935 and October 19, 1935, in the Claude A. Barnett papers, Box 170, Folder 9.

123 • She confided to Barnett: Claude A. Barnett to Frederick Douglass Patterson, May 9, 1936, in the Claude A. Barnett papers, Box 170, Folder 9.

123 • ". . . may become an instructor": *Baltimore Afro-American,* May 2, 1936, 3.

123 • Other newspapers, including: *Baltimore Afro-American,* May 30, 1936, 8; *New York Amsterdam News,* May 16, 1936, 13; *New York Times,* May 19, 1936, 6.

123 • Claude Barnett knew: Jakeman, 1992, 23.

123 • In May 1936, he contacted: ibid., 25.

124 • . . . *Waukegan News-Sun* in Wisconsin: Claude A. Barnett to Jesse O. Thomas, May 11, 1936, in the Claude A. Barnett papers, Box 170, Folder 9; Jakeman, 1992, 25; *Waukegan News-Sun,* October 8, 1935, 2.

124 • Now the *New York Amsterdam News* along: Scott & Womack, 1998 (1992), 65.

124 • "Robinson is not spectacular": Claude A. Barnett to Frederick Douglass Patterson, May 9, 1936, in the Claude A. Barnett papers, Box 170, Folder 9.

124 • To make the most: Jakeman, 1992, 26, 27.

124 • On Monday, May 18, 1936: S.S. *Europa* passenger list, May 13, 1936, from Ancestry.com; *New York Amsterdam News,* May 16, 1936, 1; *New York Times,* May 19, 1936, 6; *New York World-Telegram,* May 19, 1936, in the Claude A. Barnett papers, Box 171, Folder 5; Robinson, telegram dated May 11, 1936, in the Claude A. Barnett papers, Box 170, Folder 9.

124 • The ship flew the flag: Fleming, May 23, 1936, 13; *Philadelphia Tribune,* May 21, 1936, 1.

124 • David W. Kellum: *Chicago Defender,* May 30, 1936, 5; Kellum, May 23, 1936, 1; *New Journal and Guide,* May 30, 1936, 18.

124–125 • Johnny looked smart and official: Norman, May 28, 1936, 10.

125 • "Everybody there has a beard": *New York World-Telegram*, May 19, 1936, in the Claude A. Barnett papers, Box 171, Folder 5.

125 • The poison gas had left him: *Baltimore Afro-American*, May 30, 1936, 8; Fleming, May 23, 1936, 13; *New York Times*, May 19, 1936, 6; *Philadelphia Tribune*, May 21, 1936, 19.

126 • "Johnny looked like he had": Percival L. Prattis to Claude A. Barnett, May 28, 1936, 1, in the Claude A. Barnett papers, Box 170, Folder 9.

126 • The moment Johnny set foot: Fleming, May 23, 1936, 1, 13; *Philadelphia Tribune*, May 21, 1936, 1.

126 • An air show was held: *New York Amsterdam News*, December 18, 1937, 11.

126 • *Five thousand* people welcomed him: Scott & Womack, 1998 (1992), 66; Kellum, May 23, 1936, 2.

126 • The event was hosted: P.H.M. Savory to Claude A. Barnett in a telegram, May 14, 1936, in the Claude A. Barnett papers, Box 170, Folder 9.

126 • When he arrived, they cheered: *Atlanta Daily World*, June 2, 1936, 2; Jakeman, 1992, 27; Tucker, 2012, 193; White, [June 4, 1936], in the Claude A. Barnett Papers, Box 171, Folder 5.

126 • Johnny made a heartfelt plea: Kellum, May 23, 1936, 2; Scott & Womack, 1998 (1992), 66.

127 • . . . she and the Challenger pilots: Cornelius Coffey, Smithsonian Videohistory Program, *African-American Aviation Pioneers*, Session Two, 1990, minute 01:40:00, transcript 44; Scott & Womack, 1998 (1992), 66.

127 • "When he took the ocean liner": Cornelius Coffey, Smithsonian Videohistory Program, *African-American Aviation Pioneers*, Session Two, 1990, minute 01:37:00, transcript 43.

127 • So on Sunday, May 24, 1936: *New Journal*, May 30, 1936, 10.

127 • "Heads swing upwards!": Slaughter, May 30, 1936, 7.

127 • Three thousand people of all races: Claude A. Barnett to James Boyack, May 28, 1936, in the Claude A. Barnett papers, Box 170, Folder 9; *New Journal and Guide*, May 30, 1936, 1; *Pittsburgh Courier*, June 6, 1936, 3; Slaughter, May 30, 1936, 7.

128 • Challenger club member Earl Renfroe: *Baltimore Afro-American*, May 23, 1936, 12; Department of Commerce, list of "Negro Aviators," 1936.

128 • Renfroe flew over from Harlem Airport: *Chicago Defender*, May 30, 1936, 7; *Washington D.C. Star*, May 25, 1936, in the Claude A. Barnett papers, Box 171, Folder 5.

128 • They posed with Johnny: *Chicago Defender*, May 30, 1936, 7; Kellum, May 30, 1936, 1; *New Journal*, May 30, 1936, 10.

128 • Congressmen, members of the Chicago: Kellum, May 30, 1936, 2.

128 • "This daring young man . . .": *New Journal and Guide*, May 30, 1936, 10.

128–129 • After forty-five minutes of interviews: Claude A. Barnett to James Boyack, May 28, 1936, in the Claude A. Barnett papers, Box 170, Folder 9; Jakeman, 1992, 27; Kellum, May 30, 1936, 1, 2; *New Journal and Guide*, May 30, 1936, 1; Slaughter, May 30, 1936, 7; Tucker, 2012, 195–197; Scott & Womack, 1998 (1992), 66.

129 • **"I'm simply overwhelmed":** Kellum, May 30, 1936, 2.

130 • **By the end of the day:** *New Journal and Guide*, May 30, 1936, 10; *Pittsburgh Courier*, June 27, 1936, A1.

130 • **Census records and a much:** 1950 Census, Cook County, Illinois, "Dora E. Tate," at Ancestry.com.

130 • **He gave a speech:** *Chicago Defender*, May 30, 1936, 20.

130–131 • **"Now Willa Brown, she had":** Cornelius Coffey, Smithsonian Videohistory Program, *African-American Aviation Pioneers*, Session Two, 1990, minute 01:40:00, transcript 44.

131 • **... new young Black pilot:** *Chicago Defender*, January 18, 1936, 5; Department of Commerce, list of "Negro Aviators," 1935.

131 • **Meanwhile, Claude Barnett:** *New Journal and Guide*, May 30, 1936, 10.

131 • **In June, soon after Johnny's return:** Jakeman, 1992, 29.

131 • **Tuskegee did not own:** *Baltimore Afro-American*, May 30, 1936, 6; Frederick Douglass Patterson to Claude A. Barnett, May 13, 1936, in the Claude A. Barnett papers, Box 170, Folder 9.

131 • **Johnny visited Tuskegee in July:** *Chicago Defender*, July 11, 1936, 24; Jakeman, 1992, 29; Tucker, 2012, 202–203.

131 • **The Challenger Air Pilots' Association:** *Chicago Defender*, June 13, 1936, 24.

131 • **... he was traveling all over:** *Cleveland Call and Post*, August 20, 1936, 2; Jakeman, 1992, 29.

132 • **Johnny complained to Barnett:** *Baltimore Afro-American*, May 30, 1936, 6; Jakeman, 1992, 30; John C. Robinson to Claude A. Barnett, July 1, 1936, in the Claude A. Barnett papers, Box 171, Folder 1.

132 • **... he wanted Tuskegee:** Jakeman, 1992, 30.

132 • **... suggestion of Clarence Wilson:** Fleming, May 23, 1936, 13.

132 • **Johnny's demands proved:** Jakeman, 1992, 31; Tucker, 2012, 208–211.

133 • **With Willa in charge:** John C. Robinson to Claude A. Barnett, July 1, 1936, in the Claude A. Barnett papers, Box 171, Folder 1.

133 • **Mrs. Annie Malone, one of the guests:** Bragg & Kriz, 1996, 33.

133 • **... had been a neighbor:** 1940 Census at Ancestry.com.

133 • **Malone had built:** "Fast Facts" at the Annie Malone Historical Society, https://www.anniemalonehistoricalsociety.org/fast-facts.html (accessed April 12, 2023).

133 • **Annie Malone and Johnny:** *New Journal and Guide*, May 30, 1936, 10; see also the 1940 Census reports for 1935, available at Ancestry.com.

133 • **Annie was nearly forty:** *Chicago Defender*, September 17, 1938, 7; *Pittsburgh Courier*, September 5, 1936, 5.

133–134 • **"... under the supervision of":** *Pittsburgh Courier*, September 5, 1936, 5.

134 • **"Every student will be required":** *New York Amsterdam News*, October 3, 1936, 24.

134 • **Johnny told his friend Joel:** Rogers, September 5, 1936, A2.

134 • **Cornelius Coffey was listed:** *Chicago Defender*, October 10, 1936, 11.

134 • **"This has been my whole":** ibid., 11.

134 • **The school received additional:** Bragg & Kriz, 1996, 33.

134 • **In November 1936, he wrote:** Frederick Douglass Patterson to John C.

Robinson, November 4, 1936, in the Claude A. Barnett papers, Box 171, Folder 1; Tucker, 2012, 221.

134–135 • Heavy rains in January: "Flood of 1937," *Encyclopedia of Arkansas*, https://encyclopediaofarkansas.net/entries/flood-of-1937-4878/ (accessed April 12, 2023).

135 • The *Chicago Defender* hired: Cornelius Coffey, Smithsonian Videohistory Program, *African-American Aviation Pioneers*, Session Two, 1990, minute 01:51:41, transcript 49; see also Beneš, 2017, 203 ff.

135 • . . . touring in a new Curtiss Robin C: Cornelius Coffey, Smithsonian Videohistory Program, *African-American Aviation Pioneers*, Session Two, 1990, minute 01:47:00, transcript 48.

135 • . . . owned by the *Defender*: Ellis, February 20, 1937, 1.

135 • When Johnny returned: Cornelius Coffey, Smithsonian Videohistory Program, *African-American Aviation Pioneers*, Session Two, 1990, minute 01:52:00, transcript 48.

135–136 • The new plane ran into trouble: ibid., minute 01:51:00, transcript 49.

136 • He'd spent the past year: *Chicago Tribune*, July 10, 1938, 31.

136 • The full commercial license: Cornelius Coffey, Smithsonian Videohistory Program, *African-American Aviation Pioneers*, Session Two, 1990, minute 01:44:00, transcript 46.

136 • He even invented and patented: Arkansas Aviation Historical Society, 2018; Davis, 2023.

136 • "They said to me": ibid., minute 1:42:50, transcript 45.

136 • "If I went up there": ibid., minute 1:44:00, transcript 46.

137 • "When you get your transport" . . . as his first student: Conversation with Charles Ecker as quoted by Cornelius Coffey, Smithsonian Videohistory Program, *African-American Aviation Pioneers*, Session Two, 1990, minute 02:56:00, transcript 81.

138 • Malone and forty-five: *Chicago Defender*, July 24, 1937, 9; Kansas City *Plaindealer*, July 8, 1937, 4.

138 • Johnny knew a good opportunity: Cornelius Coffey, Smithsonian Videohistory Program, *African-American Aviation Pioneers*, Session Two, 1990, minute 01:46:00, transcript 47.

138 • These were typically: Wegg, 1990, 131–137.

138 • "I never questioned Johnny": Cornelius Coffey, Smithsonian Videohistory Program, *African-American Aviation Pioneers*, Session Two, 1990, minute 01:47:00, transcript 47–48.

138 • Although, likely inspired by Coffey: Cornelius Coffey, Smithsonian Videohistory Program, *African-American Aviation Pioneers*, Session Two, 1990, minute 01:47:00, transcript 47–48; see also Scott & Womack, 1998 (1992), 69.

139 • "You know, people get so excited": Cornelius Coffey, Smithsonian Videohistory Program, *African-American Aviation Pioneers*, Session Two, 1990, minute 01:52:00, transcript 49.

139 • Coffey tells one story: ibid., minute 01:53:00, transcript 50.

139–140 • "I'm going to have to repair" . . . uppity ideas, too: Cornelius Coffey,

Smithsonian Videohistory Program, *African-American Aviation Pioneers*, Session Two, 1990, minute 01:52:00–02:00:00, transcript 50–52.

140 • **Four days later, with the plane:** Cornelius Coffey, Smithsonian Videohistory Program, *African-American Aviation Pioneers*, Session Two, 1990, minute 01:58:00, transcript 53; see also Scott & Womack, 1998 (1992), 68–70.

140 • **By the fall of 1937:** Department of Commerce, "Negro Statistical Bulletin No. 3: Negro Aviators," October 1, 1937, in the Records of the Federal Aviation Administration, National Archives Record Group 237, 1922–1992, supplied by Dr. Theresa Kraus; *Pittsburgh Courier*, October 16, 1937, 12.

140 • **Willa's skills as a secretary:** *Chicago Defender*, September 18, 1937, 13.

140 • **...then as a lab technician:** *Pittsburgh Courier*, September 25, 1937, 24.

140 • **In September 1937:** Gubert et al, 2002, 48; Elmo Paul Hohman, *Instructor's Semestral Report of Grades*, Northwestern University, School of Commerce, 1938, supplied by Charla Wilson, May 2022; "Who's Who in Aviation: Willa B. Brown, Personal History," 1, in the Betty Gubert Collection of African Americans in Aviation, Box 2, Folder 20. There is no evidence Willa completed this degree.

140–141 • **When the pilots hanging out:** *Cleveland Call and Post*, August 22, 1941, 2B; Gubert et al, 2002, 50; Peck, April 6, 1940, 6; *Time*, September 25, 1939.

141 • **Willa's younger brother Simeon:** Interview with Rachel Carter Ellis by Betty Gubert, July 22, 1995, transcript in the Betty Gubert Collection of African Americans in Aviation, Box 3, Folder 13.

141 • **"I spent about ten years":** Simeon Brown, speaking in *Willa Beatrice Brown: An American Aviator*, 2009, minute 00:08:15.

141 • **Under Fred Schumacher's tutelage:** Willa Brown, application for pilot's license with the Department of Commerce dated December 15, 1938, in the Records of the Federal Aviation Administration, National Archives Record Group 237, 1922–1992, supplied by Dr. Theresa Kraus.

142 • **"We put it into service":** Cornelius Coffey, Smithsonian Videohistory Program, *African-American Aviation Pioneers*, Session Two, 1990, minute 01:41:00, transcript 44.

142 • **Banking on Johnny's fame:** ibid., minute 02:41:14, transcript 75.

142 • **"...he couldn't explain it":** ibid., minute 02:42:00, transcript 75.

142 • **Since it was founded in 1967:** Chan, July 9, 2013.

143 • **"...ten most frequent causes":** The quotation and the list that follows are quoted from the FAA Aeronautical Information Manual (AIM), [2023], "Safety of Flight. Section 6: Potential Flight Hazards. 7-6-1, Accident Cause Factors."

143 • **Unfortunately, flight recorders:** Paur, March 17, 2010.

144 • **Years later, Coffey still:** Cornelius Coffey writing in letters in the Coffey family papers, Kansas Collection, Kenneth Spencer Research Library.

CHAPTER 7: THE *DEFENDER* FLYERS, 1938

145 • **Lift every voice and sing:** James Weldon Johnson, "Lift Every Voice and Sing," 1900, available at https://www.poetryfoundation.org/poems/46549 /lift-every-voice-and-sing (accessed April 11, 2023).

145 • **While Johnny struck out:** Cornelius Coffey, notes for speech, n.d. Coffey family papers, Kenneth Spencer Research Library, Box 2, Folder 22.

145 • **He invested in a yellow-and-red J-3:** Cornelius Coffey, biography in *OX-5 Aviation Pioneers*, edited by Robert F. Lang et al, 1985, 113, in the Coffey family papers, Kenneth Spencer Research Library, Box 3, Folder 2; also mentioned by Cornelius Coffey in the Smithsonian Videohistory Program, *African-American Aviation Pioneers*, Session Two, 1990, minute 02:48:32, transcript 77.

145–146 • **"a brand-new Piper Cub":** Bragg & Kriz, 1996, 33.

146 • **. . . in May of 1938, Grover Nash:** Waterford, May 21, 1938, 2.

146 • **". . . nowhere did anyone seem":** Waterford, May 28, 1938, 2.

147 • **Of course, Nash also flew:** ibid.

147 • **The Chicago Girls' Flight Club:** *Pittsburgh Courier*, June 4, 1938, 3, and January 13, 1940, 12.

147–148 • **In the past year, Willa:** Willa Brown, applications and licenses with the U.S. Department of Commerce, 1935–1939, in the Records of the Federal Aviation Administration, National Archives Record Group 237, 1922–1992, supplied by Dr. Theresa Kraus.

148 • **On June 22, 1938, Willa Brown:** Willa Brown, pilot's license application with the Department of Commerce, dated April 26, 1938 and approved June 22, 1938, in the Records of the Federal Aviation Administration, National Archives Record Group 237, 1922–1992, supplied by Dr. Theresa Kraus; this event and date was widely reported in Black newspapers around the nation.

148 • **She took the written test:** *Atlanta Daily World*, June 27, 1938, 1; *Chicago Tribune*, July 10, 1938, 31; *New York Amsterdam News*, July 23, 1938, 4; *Pittsburgh Courier*, July 2, 1938, 11.

148 • **. . . Willa and Coffey beamed:** *Chicago Defender*, July 2, 1938, 1.

148 • **"I shall work next fall":** *Atlanta Daily World*, June 27, 1938, 1.

148 • **Now she had a fantastic:** See *Baltimore Afro-American*, July 9, 1938, 2; *New Journal and Guide*, July 9, 1938, 1; *Philadelphia Tribune*, July 14, 1938, 6.

148 • **Donning this striking aviator's outfit:** Waters, 1987, 195–196. In his 1987 memoir, Waters dates this visit to 1936, but the date on Willa Brown's license and Waters's own subsequent coverage of the Challenger pilots confirm that it was 1938. She could not legally have given him a public flight without a full license!

149 • **"I'm Willa Brown":** Waters, 1987, 195.

150 • **"I wasn't convinced":** Waters, 1987, 196; see also Spencer, 1975, 30, and the Appendix in Powell, 1994 (1934).

150 • **But by the end of the day:** Scott & Womack, 1998 (1992), 64.

150 • **The "Mammoth Air Show":** Gubert et al, 2002, 180.

150–151 • **. . . they staged the event:** Gubert et al, 2002, 180; *New Journal and Guide*, September 3, 1938, 1.

152 • **In addition to this showstopper:** *Chicago Defender*, September 3, 1938, 1 and 2; *New Journal and Guide*, September 3, 1938, 1, 10; *New York Amsterdam News*, September 3, 1938, 5.

152 • **Around a hundred flyers:** *Chicago Defender*, October 1, 1938, 1.

152 • **". . . to develop interest in flying":** *Chicago Defender*, September 24, 1938, 4.

152 • **. . . by September of 1938:** ibid., 4.

152 • Now the white chairman: *Baltimore Afro-American*, September 17, 1938, 23; *Chicago Defender*, September 24, 1938, 4; *New Journal and Guide*, September 24, 1938, 2.

153 • When the big day came: *Atlanta Daily World*, October 2, 1938, 1; *California Eagle*, October 6, 1938, 10; *Chicago Defender*, October 1, 1938, 1.

153 • "Our family was not poor": Spencer, 1975, 13.

153 • "Oh, you came at the wrong time": ibid., 28.

154 • "I went to visit the John Robinson": ibid., 29.

154 • "I finally persuaded the administrator": ibid., 29.

154 • "If they would give me": ibid., 29–30.

155 • Chauncey secured a dishwashing job: Spencer, 1975, 28–30. This was probably in 1936, despite the earlier date Spencer gives in his memoir. The *Chicago Defender*, August 17, 1940, 8, Anne Spencer's notebook entry of October 18, 1936, and Chauncey Spencer's description of his arrival at Robinson's flight school all bear this out.

155 • . . . he earned the nickname: *Pittsburgh Courier*, May 20, 1939, 1; Spencer, 1975, 36.

155 • "You could hear them say": Chauncey Spencer, speaking in *Willa Beatrice Brown: An American Aviator*, 2009, minute 00:11:55.

155 • In the Harlem air show: *Atlanta Daily World*, October 2, 1938, 1; Spencer, 1975, 30–31.

155 • "The pilot took us up": Spencer, 1975, 31.

155–156 • "Spectators held their breaths": *Chicago Defender*, October 1, 1938, 2.

156 • . . . the two competing young men: ibid., 1.

156 • "The crowd loved us all the same": Spencer, 1975, 31.

156 • When he touched down: *Chicago Defender*, October 1, 1938, 2.

157 • "I did my snap rolls": Lola Jones, speaking in *Willa Beatrice Brown: An American Aviator*, 2009, minute 00:11:35.

157 • Willa, Coffey, and Dale White: *Atlanta Daily World*, October 2, 1938, 1; *California Eagle*, October 6, 1938, 10.

157 • There were even students participating: *Chicago Defender*, October 1, 1938, 2.

157 • Enoch Waters kept on: *Chicago Defender*, November 12, 1938, 5, November 12, 1938, 10, and November 19, 1938, 1.

CHAPTER 8: THE MOONSHOT, 1939

158 • We choose to go to the moon: John F. Kennedy, September 12, 1962.

159 • In 1933, the National Socialist German: http://www.history.com/topics /world-war-ii/nazi-party (accessed April 12, 2023).

159 • . . . in 1937, the War Department: *Baltimore Afro-American*, April 22, 1939, 4.

159 • The new Protective Mobilization Plan: Scott & Womack, 1998 (1992), 77.

159 • "The Marines and the Air Corps": Napier, July 1, 2021.

159 • In the event of the U.S. going: Scott & Womack, 1998 (1992), 79–81.

160 • In 1925, the United States: Jakeman, 1992, 53; Scott & Womack, 1998 (1992), 78.

160 • The renowned white aviator: Charles A. Lindbergh, November 1939, 64–68.

161 • New pilots couldn't qualify: Craft, 2012, 6.

161 • **On September 17, 1938:** *New Journal and Guide*, April 22, 1939, 10; Scott & Womack, 1998 (1992), 85–86; Selig, 2013, 8.

161 • **A training prototype:** Broadnax, 2007, 41; Kraus, "The CAA Helps America Prepare for World War II," n.d., 1; Scott & Womack, 1998 (1992), 102.

162 • **There was no provision:** Scott & Womack, 1998 (1992), 79.

162 • **"why colored men are not":** Claude A. Barnett to Frederick Douglass Patterson, May 12, 1936, in the Claude A. Barnett papers, Box 170, Folder 9.

162 • **Several important national:** Civilian Pilot Training Act, 27 June, 1939 (H.R. 5619); Public Law 18, 3 April 1939 (H.R. 3791).

163 • **So Waters appealed:** Scott & Womack, 1998 (1992), 68.

163 • **If they could put together:** Waters, September 26, 1942, B15; Waters, 1987, 201.

164 • **Waters was the catalyst:** Harold Hurd, Smithsonian Videohistory Program, *African-American Aviation Pioneers*, Session Two, 1990, minute 02:34:00, transcript 71.

164 • **"We've got to give Mr. Waters credit":** Cornelius Coffey, Smithsonian Videohistory Program, *African-American Aviation Pioneers*, Session Two, 1990, minute 02:33:00, transcript 70.

164 • **Also invaluable was the support:** *Chicago Defender*, June 17 1939, 2.

164 • **She was working on:** Willa Brown, pilot's license applications/licenses with the United States Department of Commerce, 1935–1939, in the Records of the Federal Aviation Administration, National Archives Record Group 237, 1922–1992, supplied by Dr. Theresa Kraus.

164 • **"President Roosevelt will name":** *Pittsburgh Courier*, January 28, 1939, 13.

164 • **. . . Coffey wrote to Tuskegee's President:** Jakeman, 1992, 112, per Cornelius Coffey to Frederick Douglass Patterson, 27 January 1939, in Collection No. 3, "Frederick D. Patterson," Archives and Special Collections, Tuskegee University, Tuskegee, AL, Co–Cy folder, GC 1939.

164–165 • **"Now is the time for":** Earl Renfroe, *Pittsburgh Courier*, February 25, 1939, 3.

165 • **On Friday, March 17, 1939:** *Chicago Defender*, March 18, 1939, 7, and June 29, 1940, 13; *Cleveland Call and Post*, August 22, 1941, 2B. There is some scholarly confusion about the original founding of the National Airmen's Association of America, which seems to be entirely due to Enoch Waters erroneously dating it to 1937 in his 1987 memoir. Contemporary newspaper reports, the copy of the charter in Chauncey Spencer's autobiography, Willa Brown in her "Wings Over Jordan" speech, and Waters himself in his "Black Wings" article of September 26, 1942, all consistently place this organization's roots firmly in 1939. It is correctly dated 1939 in the Smithsonian's *Black Wings* exhibit.

165 • **"The first name that we thought":** Chauncey Spencer, speaking in *Willa Beatrice Brown: An American Aviator*, 2009, minute 00:14.20.

165 • **But under the guidance:** McRae, 1995.

165 • **"We are fighting segregation":** Chauncey Spencer, speaking in an interview with Betty Gubert, April 20, 1995, transcript in the Betty Gubert Collection of African Americans in Aviation, Box 3, Folder 15; see also Chauncey Spencer, speaking in *Willa Beatrice Brown: An American Aviator*, 2009, minute 00:14.20.

165 • **In this first official meeting:** *Chicago Defender*, March 18, 1939, 7.

166 • **". . . that at least one colored":** Lautier, March 18, 1939, 1.

166 • No school had been selected: Jakeman, 1992, 98–99.

166 • In their new roles: *Chicago Defender,* April 1, 1939, 6.

166 • The idea of Chicago: *Atlanta Daily World,* March 29, 1939, 1; Edgar Brown, March 10, 1939, 157–162.

166 • "... a tense, stern-visaged man": Waters, 1987, 205.

166–167 • "... designated by the Civil Aeronautics": *Chicago Defender,* April 8, 1939, 1; also quoted in Jakeman, 1992, 101.

167 • "Whether or not colored youths": *New Journal and Guide,* April 22, 1939, 10.

167 • Such academic affiliations: Strickland, 1970, 3–4.

167 • Without the backing: Cornelius Coffey, Smithsonian Videohistory Program, *African-American Aviation Pioneers,* Session Two, 1990, minute 02:36:00, transcript 71–72.

167–168 • "He being in Washington": ibid., minute 02:35:32, transcript 72.

168 • Edgar Brown also advised: *Chicago Defender,* June 29, 1940, 13.

168 • "... the training school be interracial": *Chicago Defender,* March 29, 1939, 1.

168 • Willa, too, threw body and soul: *Chicago Defender,* May 6, 1939, 13.

168 • One of the NAAA's schemes: *Chicago Defender,* April 22, 1939, 7.

168 • Meanwhile, Waters mailed: Waters, 1987, 202–203.

168 • "As an administrator": Cornelius Coffey, Smithsonian Videohistory Program, *African-American Aviation Pioneers,* Session Two, 1990, minute 03:11:00, transcript 90.

169 • At the insistence of Edgar Brown: *New York Amsterdam News,* April 29, 1939, 1.

169 • "... none of the benefits": *New Journal and Guide,* April 29, 1939, 1.

169 • Despite opposition: *Baltimore Afro-American,* April 29, 1939, 5; Lautier, April 29, 1939, 1, 4.

169 • Waters made a suggestion: Waters, 1987, 205.

169 • The National Airmen's Association had already: *Atlanta Daily World,* May 1, 1939, 1, and May 12, 1939, 1; *Chicago Defender,* April 29, 1939, 1.

170 • He'd been the Challenger: Tucker, 2012, 222.

170 • Dale and Chauncey had become: *Chicago Defender,* October 1, 1938, 2; *Pittsburgh Courier,* October 9, 1937, 3; Spencer, 1975, 29–30.

171 • "... message of appreciation": *Chicago Defender,* April 29, 1939, 1.

171 • "What about fuel": Bragg & Kriz, 1996, 37.

171 • "Chauncey, with tears in his eyes": ibid., 37.

171 • By this point, Dale: Bragg & Kriz, 1996, 37; Spencer, 1975, 34.

171 • Queenie came up with: Bragg & Kriz, 1996, 37.

172 • The Jones brothers ... "winning big": WTTW, 2022.

172 • In 1938, a local Chicago: ibid.

172 • Sure enough, the Jones brothers: Spencer, 1975, 32.

172 • The sky was overcast: *Pittsburgh Courier,* May 20, 1939, 1; Spencer, 1975, 22–32.

172 • The words "National Airmen": *Chicago Defender,* May 13, 1939, 4; Peck, May 20, 1939, 1, 4.

172–173 • Almost right away, in Avilla: Telegram from Dale White to Enoc[h] Waters in the Dale L. White Scrapbook, May 8, 1939, in the Dale L. White, Sr., papers, Accession 2013-0050, National Air and Space Museum, Smithsonian Institution, NASM-9A16697-001.tif, Box 3, Folder 1.

173 • After only twenty minutes: *Chicago Defender*, May 13, 1939, 1; Peck, May 20, 1939, 1, 4; Scott & Womack, 1998 (1992), 91; Dale L. White, log book, May 8, 1939, in the Dale L. White, Sr., papers, Accession 2013-0050, National Air and Space Museum, Smithsonian Institution, NASM-9A12585-49-50.tif.

173 • This time when they took off: Dale L. White log book, May 8, 1939, in the Dale L. White, Sr., papers, Accession 2013-0050, National Air and Space Museum, Smithsonian Institution, NASM-9A12585-49-50.tif.

173 • "The plane started bucking": Spencer, 1975, 32.

173 • "We swerved and slid": ibid., 32.

173 • "Where were you going?" ... "Can I have a ride?": ibid., 32.

173 • Dale and Chauncey climbed: *Chicago Defender*, May 13, 1939, 1; Peck, May 20, 1939, 1, 4; Dale L. White, log book, May 8, 1939, in the Dale L. White, Sr., papers, Accession 2013-0050, National Air and Space Museum, Smithsonian Institution, NASM-9A12585-49-50.tif.

173–174 • "... a gracious group of people": *Chicago Defender*, November 4, 1939, 13; Spencer, 1975, 32.

174 • Dale and Chauncey sent: Spencer, 1975, 33.

174 • "It took two days": ibid., 33.

174 • Coffey and another man: *Chicago Defender*, May 27, 1939, 4; Cornelius Coffey, Smithsonian Videohistory Program, *African-American Aviation Pioneers*, Session Two, 1990, minute 02:28:00, transcript 67–68.

174 • Three days after they started: *Chicago Defender*, May 13, 1939, 1; Peck, May 20, 1939, 1, 4.

175 • Now the airfield staff: Peck, May 20, 1939, 1.

175 • "You can't stay here overnight": Dale L. White log book, May 11, 1939, in the Dale L. White, Sr., papers, Accession 2013-0050, National Air and Space Museum, Smithsonian Institution, NASM-9A12585-49-50.tif; Peck, May 20, 1939, 1, 4; Spencer, 1975, 33.

175 • They spent the night in Pittsburgh: *Chicago Defender*, May 20, 1939, 6; Spencer, 1975, 33.

176 • He also made a generous: Waters, 1987, 206.

176 • The unlucky duo: Peck, May 20, 1939, 4.

176 • On Sunday afternoon: *Baltimore Afro-American*, May 20, 1939, 6; *Chicago Defender*, May 20, 1939, 6; *New Journal and Guide*, May 20, 1939, 1; Dale L. White, log book, May 12, May 13, and May 14, 1939, in the Dale L. White, Sr., papers, Accession 2013-0050, National Air and Space Museum, Smithsonian Institution, NASM-9A12585-49-50.tif.

176 • In 1790, the bordering states: Pollack, February 21, 2019; see also https://en .wikipedia.org/wiki/District_of_Columbia_retrocession (accessed April 12, 2023).

177 • "... were assured that the plane": *Chicago Defender*, May 20, 1936, 6.

177 • "As we were getting off": Spencer, 1975, 33–34.

177 • Brown introduced Dale: Jakeman, 1992, 109; Waters, 1987, 206.

177–178 • "Why aren't you in the Air Corps?" ... "he didn't want a plane ride": The encounter and conversation with Truman as described here is from Spencer, 1975, 34.

178 • **"If you had guts enough":** Paraphrased in Spencer, 1975, 34, and quoted fully, 143; also quoted fully in Waters, 1987, 206.

179 • **Dale and Chauncey left:** *Chicago Defender*, May 27, 1939, 11; Spencer, 1975, 35.

179 • **The two flyers spent the rest:** Dale L. White, log book, May 18, 1939, in the Dale L. White, Sr., papers, Accession 2013-0050, National Air and Space Museum, Smithsonian Institution, NASM-9A12585-49-50.tif.

180 • **... the *Pittsburgh Courier* pushed:** *Pittsburgh Courier*, June 3, 1939, 1.

180 • **Edgar Brown made an impassioned:** Edgar Brown, May 26, 1939, 339.

180 • **In Chicago, the Harlem aviators:** Dale L. White, log book, May 30, 1939, in the Dale L. White, Sr., papers, Accession 2013-0050, National Air and Space Museum, Smithsonian Institution, NASM-9A12585-49-50.tif.

180 • **Then on Friday, June 16, 1939:** *Chicago Defender*, April 29, 1939, 7.

181 • **Waters used the *Defender*:** *Chicago Defender*, 1939: June 24, 11; July 1, 15; July 8, 15; July 15, 24; July 22, 15.

181 • **Dale White would plan:** *Chicago Defender*, August 12, 1939, 4.

181 • **"... mark the beginning":** *Chicago Defender*, June 17, 1939, 24.

181 • **Earlier that same day:** Willa Brown, pilot's license application dated December 15, 1938, and licensed June 16, 1939, with the U.S. Department of Commerce, in the Records of the Federal Aviation Administration, National Archives Record Group 237, 1922–1992, supplied by Dr. Theresa Kraus.

182 • **Only four other Black pilots:** Department of Commerce, "Negro Statistical Bulletin No. 3: Negro Aviators," January 1939, in the Records of the Federal Aviation Administration, National Archives Record Group 237, 1922–1992, supplied by Dr. Theresa Kraus.

182 • **... on June 19, 1939, the Civilian Pilot:** *Baltimore Afro-American*, June 24, 1939, 19; *Chicago Defender*, June 24, 1939, 2; Jakeman, 1992, 110, per *Congressional Record*, 76th Congress, 1st session, 7504, June 19, 1939; *New Journal and Guide*, June 24, 1939, 4.

182 • **The following week, on June 27, 1939:** Jakeman, 1992, 101, 110; Kraus, "The CAA Helps America Prepare for World War II," n.d., 1.

183 • **"A throng of over two thousand":** *Chicago Defender*, August 12, 1939, 11.

183 • **... that same month, August 1939:** Bragg & Kriz, 1996, 36; Willa Brown, January 30, 1943, 10, 13; *Chicago Defender*, August 26, 1939, 1; Spencer, 1975, 148–149.

183 • **"... to further stimulate":** Gubert et al, 2002, 75.

183 • **The initial members:** Spencer, 1975, 29, 148–149.

183 • **They used the *Defender*'s offices:** Bragg & Kriz, 1996, 36; Gubert et al, 2002, 50; Spencer, 1975, 140; Chauncey Spencer, interviewed by Betty Gubert, April 20, 1995, from her transcript in the Betty Gubert Collection of African Americans in Aviation, Box 3, Folder 15.

183–184 • **Like Coffey, Johnny had written:** Jakeman, 1992, 113, per a letter from John C. Robinson to Frederick Douglass Patterson, 1 April 1939, in Collection No. 3, "Frederick D. Patterson," Archives and Special Collections, Tuskegee University, Tuskegee, AL, Civil Aeronautics Authority folder, GC 1939; also Jakeman, 1992, 114, per John C. Robinson to G.L. Washington, 23 May 1939, and John C.

Robinson to Frederick Douglass Patterson, 29 May 1939, also in Collection No. 3, "Frederick D. Patterson," Archives and Special Collections, Tuskegee University, Tuskegee, AL, Ro–Ry folder, GC 1939.

184 • **He'd even gone so far:** Jakeman, 1992, 116, per John C. Robinson to Frederick Douglass Patterson, 29 May 1939, in Collection No. 3, "Frederick D. Patterson," Archives and Special Collections, Tuskegee University, Tuskegee, AL, Ro–Ry folder, GC 1939.

184 • **"Under the ruling of the War":** *Atlanta Daily World*, May 13, 1939, 5.

184 • **". . . a well-known man of question":** [John C. Robinson], "It Didn't Work Out," circa May 1939, 1, in the Betty Gubert Collection of African Americans in Aviation, Box 7, Folder 16.

184 • **". . . trained practically every":** ibid., 2.

184 • **"No one seems to know":** Edgar Brown, "Recent Article On Aviation Activities In Chicago Overlook Established Aviation School," circa May 1939, in the Betty Gubert Collection of African Americans in Aviation, Box 7, Folder 16.

184 • **Aircraft began to touch down:** *Chicago Defender*, September 2, 1939, 3; *New Journal and Guide*, September 9, 1939, 3.

185 • **The final program for the three-day:** *Chicago Defender*, August 26, 1939, 1.

185 • **"This air meet has fulfilled":** Galbreath, September 2, 1939, 16.

185 • **That is exactly what . . . in the new training program:** Adams, September 3, 1939, 31; *Baltimore Afro-American*, September 2, 1939, 5; *Chicago Defender*, September 2, 1939, 1; *New Journal and Guide*, September 9, 1939, 3.

185–186 • **. . . the Chicago hosts awarded:** *Chicago Defender*, August 12, 1939, 4.

186 • **Dr. A. Porter Davis of Kansas City:** *Chicago Defender*, September 2, 1939, 1.

186 • **Davis, who'd earned his license:** A. Porter Davis as described in the National Air & Space Museum Udvar-Hazy Center in Chantilly, VA, in a biography on their Honor Wall.

186 • **Donated by Illinois's governor:** *Chicago Defender*, September 20, 1941, 1.

186 • **"outstanding contribution":** *Baltimore Afro-American*, September 2, 1939, 5; *Chicago Defender*, September 2, 1939, 3; *New Journal and Guide*, September 9, 1939, 3.

187 • **"outstanding flight":** *New Journal and Guide*, September 9, 1939, 3.

187 • **The awards were presented:** *Chicago Defender*, September 2, 1939, 1; Galbreath, September 2, 1939, 16.

CHAPTER 9: THE LOVE STORY OF CORNELIUS R. COFFEY, 1939–1940

188 • **Blivens—I see Miss Headstrong:** James M. Harrison, "Stray Thoughtlets," Norfolk *New Journal and Guide*, January 14, 1922, 4.

188 • **"Business increased to the point":** Waters, 1987, 204.

189 • **"I put it that way":** ibid., 204.

190 • **. . . Courthouse records show:** Cornelius Coffey and Willa Brown, certified copy of marriage certificate, February 7, 1947. In the Betty Gubert Collection of African Americans in Aviation, Box 4, Folder 10.

190 • **The good news:** Kraus, "The CAA Helps America Prepare for World War II," n.d., 2; Strickland, 1970, 10.

191 • **The first two awards:** *Chicago Defender*, September 30, 1939, 5.

191 • ... they were directly responsible: Earl Brown, "Credits the Chicago Defender With Getting Air School At West Va. State," October 21, 1939, 6; *Chicago Defender*, "Defender's Goodwill Flyers Inspired 'Wings' At West Virginia State," October 21, 1939, 6.

191 • The CPTP initially consisted: Civil Aeronautics Authority, [1940], in the Claude A. Barnett papers, Box 9, Folder 769; Strickland, 1970, 3–4.

191 • ... and the government would foot: Strickland, 1970, 10.

191–192 • A minimum of thirty-five hours: Kraus, "The CAA Helps America Prepare for World War II," n.d., 1.

192 • ... the schools had to be within: ibid.

192 • ... even instructors had to undergo: Selig, 2013, 9.

192 • ... and all CPTP facilities required: Cornelius Coffey, Smithsonian Videohistory Program, *African-American Aviation Pioneers*, Session Two, 1990, minute 02:49:00, transcript 77.

192 • ... article appeared in *Time* magazine: *Time*, September 25, 1939.

192 • They'd have to upgrade: Cornelius Coffey, Smithsonian Videohistory Program, *African-American Aviation Pioneers*, Session Two, 1990, minute 02:49:00, transcript 77–78; Gubert et al, 2002, 171.

192 • Like so many aviators, Lewis: CAF Rise Above, November 6, 2018; Federal Aviation Administration, Airmen Inquiry and Archives, https://amsrvs.registry.faa.gov/airmeninquiry/ (accessed April 12, 2023); Gubert et al, 2002, 171.

192–193 • "... taxied a great deal": Lewis Jackson quoted in Gubert et al, 2002, 171.

193 • By 1939, still in his twenties: Gubert et al, 171.

193 • One fateful day that same year: Lewis Jackson, Smithsonian Videohistory Program, *African-American Aviation Pioneers*, Session One, 1989, minute 00:57:00, transcript 29.

193 • "Mr. Coffey, I understand" ... "become a part of it": Cornelius Coffey describing conversation with Lewis Jackson, Smithsonian Videohistory Program, *African-American Aviation Pioneers*, Session Two, 1990, minute 02:51:00, transcript 78.

193 • The program allowed ten: Cornelius Coffey, Smithsonian Videohistory Program, *African-American Aviation Pioneers*, Session Two, 1990, minute 02:51:00, transcript 78; Strickland, 1970, 9.

193 • "Lewis, they will require": Cornelius Coffey, Smithsonian Videohistory Program, *African-American Aviation Pioneers*, Session Two, 1990, minute 02:51:00, transcript 78–79.

193 • Fred Schumacher wasn't part: Cornelius Coffey, Smithsonian Videohistory Program, *African-American Aviation Pioneers*, Session Two, 1990, minute 02:51:30, transcript 79; Lewis Jackson, Smithsonian Videohistory Program, *African-American Aviation Pioneers*, Session One, 1989, minute 00:47:00, transcript 29.

193 • Glenview had been: Naval Air Station Museum, Glenview, IL https://www.thehangarone.org/ (accessed April 12, 2023).

194 • But the hangar that Fred: Cornelius Coffey, Smithsonian Videohistory Program, *African-American Aviation Pioneers*, Session Two, 1990, minute 02:49:00, transcript 77.

194 • Once those requirements: Cornelius Coffey, Smithsonian Videohistory Program, *African-American Aviation Pioneers*, Session Two, 1990, minute 02:49:00, transcript 78; Waters, 1987, 204.

194 • Finally, on October 16, 1939: *Baltimore Afro-American*, October 21, 1939, 5; *Chicago Defender*, October 28, 1939, 19; *Pittsburgh Courier*, October 21, 1939, 3.

194 • "The CAA air pilot course": *Baltimore Afro-American*, October 21, 1939, 5.

194 • Ultimately, the CPTP would: Department of Commerce, "Negro Statistical Bulletin No. 3: Negro Aviators," September 1940, 1, in the Records of the Federal Aviation Administration, National Archives Record Group 237, 1922–1992, supplied by Dr. Theresa Kraus; Kraus, "The CAA Helps America Prepare for World War II," n.d., 2; *New Journal and Guide*, October 21, 1939, 4; Strickland, 1970, 39.

194 • The Coffey School of Aeronautics was the only: Cornelius Coffey, Smithsonian Videohistory Program, *African-American Aviation Pioneers*, Session Two, 1990, minute 02:33:00, transcript 71.

194 • Johnny Robinson's school: *Atlanta Daily World*, October 21, 1939, 1; *Baltimore Afro-American*, October 21, 1939, 5; *Chicago Defender*, "Col. Robinson Named Aviation Consultant," October 21, 1939, 5.

195 • . . . Rose Agnes Rolls, a senior: *Chicago Defender*, December 23, 1939, 7.

195 • . . . the CAA and the Air Corps: *Atlanta Daily World*, December 28, 1939, 1–2; *Baltimore Afro-American*, December 30, 1939, 2; *Cleveland Call and Post*, December 28, 1939, 1; Jakeman, 1992, 161; *New York Age*, January 6, 1940, 3; *New York Amsterdam News*, December 30, 1939, 1; *Pittsburgh Courier*, February 3, 1940, 10; John C. Robinson, "Memorandum," circa January 1940, 1, in the Claude A. Barnett Papers, Box 171, Folder 1.

195 • "I did not want to go": John C. Robinson, "Memorandum," circa January 1940, 2, in the Claude A. Barnett Papers, Box 171, Folder 1.

195–196 • Dr. Midian Othello Bousfield: Jakeman, 1992, 161; https://www .encyclopedia.com/african-american-focus/news-wires-white-papers-and-books /bousfield-midian-o (accessed April 12, 2023).

196 • "I know as much about": John C. Robinson, "Memorandum," circa January 1940, 2, in the Claude A. Barnett Papers, Box 171, Folder 1.

196 • Major Webster went on: Jakeman, 1992, 162.

196 • By the end of the day: Willa Brown to John Green, March 22, 1940, in the Betty Gubert Collection of African Americans in Aviation, Box 3, Folder 7; *Chicago Defender*, January 20, 1940, 1; Jakeman, 1992, 162–163.

196 • The ground school classes: Jakeman, 1992, 163; *Pittsburgh Courier*, February 3, 1940, 10.

196 • Harlem Airport wasn't equipped: *Chicago Defender*, November 29, 1941, 5.

197 • The Bousfields gave Coffey: Cornelius Coffey, Smithsonian Videohistory Program, *African-American Aviation Pioneers*, Session Two, 1990, minute 02:58:00, transcript 81–82.

197 • "I tried to sell him": ibid., minute 02:59:00, transcript 82.

197 • And so, on February 5, 1940: *Chicago Bee*, February 1940, in the Betty Gubert Collection of African Americans in Aviation, Box 3, Folder 7; *Chicago Defender*, March 16, 1940, 5; *New York Amsterdam News*, April 6, 1940, 7; Peck, April 3, 1940, 1.

197 • ... three hours a night: *Chicago Tribune*, July 7, 1940, part 3, 2.

197 • By the middle of February: Willa Brown to Dr. M.O. Bousfield, "Memorandum," February 19, 1940, in the Claude A. Barnett papers, Box 9, Folder 769.

197 • Later that month, Robert S. Abbott: *Chicago Defender*, March 9, 1940, 1.

198 • "Thirty Flight Scholarships": *Atlanta Daily World*, February 14, 1940, 3; [Willa Brown] [?], leaflet, "Thirty Flight Scholarships Offered Negro Pilots by United States Government," [January 1940], in the Oak Lawn Public Library Archives, Willa B. Brown Records, Accession No. 2020.224.001; *Pittsburgh Courier*, February 17, 1940, 11.

198 • Of the forty-seven students: *Chicago Defender*, June 15, 1940, 12; *Chicago Tribune*, July 7, 1940, part 3, 2.

198 • The top ten candidates: [Willa Brown] [?], leaflet, "Thirty Flight Scholarships Offered Negro Pilots by United States Government," [January 1940], in the Oak Lawn Public Library Archives, Willa B. Brown Records, Accession No. 2020.224.001; Kraus, "The CAA Helps America Prepare for World War II," n.d., 2; *Chicago Defender*, March 22, 1940, 5; Civil Aeronautics Authority, [1940], 2, in the Claude A. Barnett papers, Box 9, Folder 769; Strickland, 1970, 9.

198 • "... to prove their worth in the field": *Chicago Tribune*, July 7, 1940, part 3, 1.

198 • From the start, the section: [Willa Brown] [?], leaflet, "Thirty Flight Scholarships Offered Negro Pilots by United States Government," [January 1940], in the Oak Lawn Public Library Archives, Willa B. Brown Records, Accession No. 2020.224.001; Howe, January 27, 1940, 14.

198 • "[The] purpose of the demonstration": *Chicago Tribune*, July 7, 1940, part 3, 1.

198 • "Every ten students that I took": Cornelius Coffey, Smithsonian Videohistory Program, *African-American Aviation Pioneers*, Session Two, 1990, minute 02:55:00, transcript 80.

198 • "They had no excuse": ibid., minute 02:56:00, transcript 81.

198–199 • The first non-college group: *Detroit Tribune*, January 25, 1941, 6.

199 • "The field is not and never": Howard D. Gould to William L. Hastie, November 15, 1940, in the Claude A. Barnett papers, Box 3, Folder 865.

199–200 • In June 1940, the CAA sent officials: *Baltimore Afro-American*, June 22, 1940, 23; *New York Amsterdam News*, June 22, 1940, 3.

200 • The CAA inspector was impressed: *Atlanta Daily World*, June 23, 1940, 6.

200 • Willa organized an open house: *Chicago Defender*, July 6, 1940, 8, and July 13, 1940, 6.

200 • When the second round: *Chicago Defender*, August 17, 1940, 8.

200 • "... went through that program": Cornelius Coffey, Smithsonian Videohistory Program, *African-American Aviation Pioneers*, Session Two, 1990, minute 02:52:00, transcript 79.

CHAPTER 10: THE TUSKEGEE TUSSLE, 1940-1941

201 • We do feel that if you will: J. Finley Wilson, May 26, 1939, 341.

201 • The Danish military: https://www.annefrank.org/en/timeline/61/the -german-invasion-of-denmark-and-norway/ (accessed April 12, 2023).

201–202 • In the French coastal town: https://www.english-heritage.org.uk

/visit/places/dover-castle/history-and-stories/fall-of-france/ (accessed April 12, 2023).

202 • **When Tuskegee had joined:** Jakeman, 1992, 118–119; George L. Washington, 1972, in Collection No. 3, "Frederick D. Patterson," Archives and Special Collections, Tuskegee University, Tuskegee, AL, 6.

202 • **"I had heard much about"... "She impressed me"** Frederick Douglass Patterson, quoted in George L. Washington, 1972, in Collection No. 3, "Frederick D. Patterson," Archives and Special Collections, Tuskegee University, Tuskegee, AL, 58.

203 • **As well as providing:** Strickland, 1970, 11, 22.

203 • **Back in Tuskegee:** Jakeman, 1992, 142.

203 • **It was no secret:** *New York Amsterdam News,* June 22, 1940, 3.

203 • **"it could, as a partner":** George L. Washington, 1972, in Collection No. 3, "Frederick D. Patterson," Archives and Special Collections, Tuskegee University, Tuskegee, AL, 66.

204 • **In July 1940, Tuskegee:** Jakeman, 1992, 143; Strickland, 1970, 12.

204–205 • **...Charles Alfred Anderson had been:** Gubert et al, 2002, 9.

205 • **...buying a plane and teaching:** Charles Alfred Anderson, Smithsonian Videohistory Program, *African-American Aviation Pioneers,* Session One, 1989, minute 00:24:00, transcript 16; Broadnax, 2007, 19; Gubert et al, 2002, 9.

205 • **In 1932, Anderson became:** *Philadelphia Tribune,* February 25, 1932, 1.

205 • **Anderson went on to teach:** Hardesty, 2008, 52.

205 • **...who was a Tuskegee alum:** Jakeman, 1992, 7.

205 • **Washington made phone calls:** Jakeman, 2002, 144; George L. Washington, 1972, 164, in Collection No. 3, "Frederick D. Patterson," Archives and Special Collections, Tuskegee University, Tuskegee, AL.

206 • **Apparently Johnny *still* didn't:** George L. Washington to John C. Robinson, May 22, 1941, 1, in the Claude A. Barnett Papers, Box 171, Folder 1.

206 • **And it appears he did get it:** Communication with Dr. Theresa Kraus, archivist for the Records of the Federal Aviation Administration, June 2, 2022. She had evidence John C. Robinson received his commercial license around July 30, 1940, but was unsure of the exact date.

206 • **But when Washington wrote:** George L. Washington to John C. Robinson, May 22, 1941, 1, in the Claude A. Barnett papers, Box 171, Folder 1.

206 • **The man who drew his attention:** Jakeman, 1992, 145.

206 • **"That is when Willa":** Cornelius Coffey, Smithsonian Videohistory Program, *African-American Aviation Pioneers,* Session Two, 1990, minute 02:52:00, transcript 79.

206 • **"Lewis got a little bit anxious":** ibid., minute 02:52:00, transcript 79.

207 • **To qualify as a secondary:** George L. Washington, 1972, 93, in Collection No. 3, "Frederick D. Patterson," Archives and Special Collections, Tuskegee University, Tuskegee, AL.

207 • **But he stayed with the Coffey:** Jakeman, 1992, 149.

207 • **He started at Tuskegee:** George L. Washington, 1972, 150, in Collection No. 3, "Frederick D. Patterson," Archives and Special Collections, Tuskegee University, Tuskegee, AL.

207 • **Willa made a trip:** Cornelius Coffey, Smithsonian Videohistory Program, *African-American Aviation Pioneers*, Session Two, 1990, minute 02:52:00, transcript 79.

207 • **"Fifty-six pilots":** Waters, 1987, 206.

207 • **And what a month:** *Chicago Defender*, August 31, 1940, 12.

208 • **Anna Howard was a vibrant:** *Chicago Defender*, August 31, 1940, 10; Chauncey Spencer Jr. interview with The HistoryMakers, June 9, 2010.

208 • **. . . the college students in their:** Jakeman, 1992, 163.

208 • **In October, the CAA made plans:** *Chicago Defender*, September 14, 1940, 4.

208 • **. . . by now there were over 150:** *Chicago Defender*, September 21, 1940, 7.

208 • **". . . without regard to race, creed, or color":** Edgar Brown, September 28, 1940, 349.

208 • **"We must have done a pretty":** Cornelius Coffey, Smithsonian Videohistory Program, *African-American Aviation Pioneers*, Session Two, 1990, minute 02:52:00, transcript 79.

208–209 • **In addition to the aerobatic:** ibid., minute 02:59:44, transcript 82.

209 • **Writing to another interested:** Cornelius Coffey to Wesley Hudson, January 22, 1942, 1–2, in the Coffey family papers, Kenneth Spencer Research Library, Box 2, Folder 5.

210 • **Transportation to the airfield:** Waters, February 22, 1941, 15.

210 • **With two aerobatic planes:** Cornelius Coffey, Smithsonian Videohistory Program, *African-American Aviation Pioneers*, Session Two, 1990, minute 03:02:47, transcript 85.

210 • **"Mr. Coffey, I understand":** Homer Carrick, quoted by Cornelius Coffey, Smithsonian Videohistory Program, *African-American Aviation Pioneers*, Session Two, 1990, minute 03:03:30, transcript 86.

210 • **"In two weeks' time":** Cornelius Coffey, Smithsonian Videohistory Program, *African-American Aviation Pioneers*, Session Two, 1990, minute 03:04:00, transcript 86.

211 • **When William Paris and Charles Johnson:** Bourne, August 24, 1940, 3; *Chicago Defender*, August 24, 1940, 8; *New York Amsterdam News*, August 17, 1940, 9.

211 • **"In Pennsylvania, over":** *New York Amsterdam News*, August 24, 1940, 12.

211 • **The eventful flight:** *New York Amsterdam News*, August 31, 1940, 13.

211 • **. . . her mother now:** Bragg & Kriz, 1996, 34.

211–212 • **Janet's latest endeavor:** ibid., 39, 40.

212 • **"Chicago's winter weather":** ibid., 39.

212 • **In the early days of Tuskegee's flight:** Jakeman, 1992, 118.

212 • **By the spring of 1940:** ibid., 127–128.

212 • **But the institute:** ibid., 132.

212–213 • **Both Janet and Johnny spoke . . . "all phases of American democracy":** *Atlanta Daily World*, November 17, 1940, 1.

213 • **What's more, none of the recent:** Jakeman, 1992, 160.

213 • **Roderick Williams, the African American:** Scott & Womack 1998 (1992), 95; George L. Washington, 1972, 114, in Collection No. 3, "Frederick D. Patterson," Archives and Special Collections, Tuskegee University, Tuskegee, AL.

213 • **"Shall we ever be given":** Peck, December 7, 1940, 3.

214 • **Williams was a twenty-four-year-old:** Jakeman, 1992, 204.

214 • "...appropriate Air Corps units": Jakeman, 1992, 205, quoting Major Floyd
W. Ferree to Yancey Williams, November 23, 1940, U.S. Army Air Corps, Yancey
Williams Case, 1940–1941 folder, Series IIB, NAACP Papers, Library of Congress.

214 • After several appeals: Jakeman, 1992, 205.

214 • The 1937 mobilization plan: Scott & Womack, 1998 (1992), 77; "Characteristics of the Population" Table 7, 1940 and 1930, US Census 22, available at
https://www.census.gov/library/publications/1943/dec/population-vol-2.html
(accessed April 12, 2023).

214 • The Army had been working: Broadnax, 2007, 30.

215 • The plan was made public: Jakeman, 1992, 223.

215 • The Army Air Corps considered: George L. Washington, 1972, 101–102, in
Collection No. 3, "Frederick D. Patterson," Archives and Special Collections,
Tuskegee University, Tuskegee, AL.

215 • Nevertheless, on January 16, 1941: *Baltimore Afro-American,* January 25, 1941,
1; *Chicago Defender,* January 25, 1941, 6; George L. Washington, 1972, 103–105, 118,
in Collection No. 3, "Frederick D. Patterson," Archives and Special Collections,
Tuskegee University, Tuskegee, AL.

215 • So was the NAACP: *Chicago Defender,* February 15, 1941, 2.

215 • That the Air Corps training: George L. Washington, 1972, 133, in Collection
No. 3, "Frederick D. Patterson," Archives and Special Collections, Tuskegee
University, Tuskegee, AL.

215 • When Willa was twenty-one: James B. Lane, 1978, 141–144, in the Betty
Gubert Collection of African Americans in Aviation, Box 3, Folder 12.

216 • ...known as the Roosevelt Annex: https://en.wikipedia.org/wiki/Theodore
_Roosevelt_College_and_Career_Academy (accessed April 12, 2023).

216 • Three senior girls: James B. Lane, 1978, 146–147, in the Betty Gubert
Collection of African Americans in Aviation, Box 3, Folder 12.

216 • "...discriminatory, un-American": Isaac James Quillen, 1986, 438–440,
quoting "Petition from Committee Representing Colored Citizens," October 3,
1927 (in drawer labelled "Council Misc., May 1928–December 1930" in vault of
Gary city clerk's office), in the Betty Gubert Collection of African Americans in
Aviation, Box 3, Folder 12.

216 • The city agreed to spend: Isaac James Quillen, 1986, 438–440, in the Betty
Gubert Collection of African Americans in Aviation, Box 3, Folder 12.

217 • "Here we have what we": Claude A. Barnett to Frederick Douglass Patterson,
January 18, 1941, in the Claude A. Barnett papers, Box 239, Folder 7.

217 • Barnett tried to calm Willa down: Claude A. Barnett to Frederick
Douglass Patterson, January 20, 1941, Box 239, Folder 7; *Detroit Tribune,*
January 25, 1941, 1.

217 • "A strong resolution condemning": *Detroit Tribune,* January 25, 1941, 1;
Waters, January 25, 1941, 1.

217 • Equally outrageous: *Detroit Tribune,* January 25, 1941, 6.

217 • Even during World War I: Rawn, 2013, 74–75.

217–218 • "Our fight for entrance": Cornelius Coffey, quoted in the *Detroit Tribune,*
January 25, 1941, 6, and in Waters, January 25, 1941, 1.

218 • **A photograph in the:** *Baltimore Afro-American*, February 8, 1941, 23.

218 • **"There is no segregation":** *Detroit Tribune*, January 25, 1941, 6; Waters, *Chicago Defender*, January 25, 1941, 1.

218 • **Claude Barnett worked hard:** Claude A. Barnett to Frederick Douglass Patterson, January 26, 1941, in the Claude A. Barnett papers, Box 239, Folder 7.

218 • **Meanwhile, Dr. Patterson managed:** George L. Washington, 1972, 127, in Collection No. 3, "Frederick D. Patterson," Archives and Special Collections, Tuskegee University, Tuskegee, AL.

218 • **On March 19, 1941, the 99th:** Strickland, 1970, 45.

219 • **That same spring, Mrs. Roosevelt:** George L. Washington, 1972, 175, in Collection No. 3, "Frederick D. Patterson," Archives and Special Collections, Tuskegee University, Tuskegee, AL.

219 • **"She said, 'I'm going to take'":** Charles Alfred Anderson, Smithsonian Videohistory Program, *African-American Aviation Pioneers*, Session One, 1989, minute 01:52:15, transcript 57.

219 • **She also insisted that:** George L. Washington, 1972, 187, in Collection No. 3, "Frederick D. Patterson," Archives and Special Collections, Tuskegee University, Tuskegee, AL.

219 • **"Mrs. Roosevelt was willing":** Gubert et al, 2002, 11.

220 • **Mrs. Roosevelt's stamp of approval:** Jakeman, 1992, 248.

220 • **Construction began on July 23:** George L. Washington, 1972, 251, in Collection No. 3, "Frederick D. Patterson," Archives and Special Collections, Tuskegee University, Tuskegee, AL.

221 • **He'd been elected president:** *Chicago Defender*, January 11, 1941, 8.

221 • **"I am opposed to segregation":** John C. Robinson quoted in Faulkner, January 29, 1941, 1.

221 • **"small group of Negroes":** Robinson, February 4, 1941, 1.

221 • **. . . Johnny had been encouraging:** *Chicago Defender*, March 29, 1941, 8; Jakeman, 1992, 260–262.

221 • **". . . plans for courses in aviation":** *Chicago Defender*, April 26, 1941, 2.

221–222 • **In May, Johnny called up . . . a constant lack, it seemed:** John C. Robinson to George L. Washington, May 20, 1941, and George L. Washington to Claude A. Barnett, May 22, 1941, in the Claude A. Barnett papers, Box 171, Folder 1.

222 • **Johnny didn't take Barnett:** Jakeman, 1992, 262–264.

222 • **Even institute administrators:** George L. Washington, 1972, 131–132, in Collection No. 3, "Frederick D. Patterson," Archives and Special Collections, Tuskegee University, Tuskegee, AL.

223 • **Now that they had been granted:** *Baltimore Afro-American*, April 5, 1941, 6; Cornelius Coffey, Smithsonian Videohistory Program, *African-American Aviation Pioneers*, Session Two, 1990, minute 03:04:46, transcript 86; the course terms are defined in Strickland, 1970, 18–19.

223 • **Willa and Coffey flew:** *Chicago Defender*, June 14, 1941, 4.

223 • **She was also now president:** *Chicago Defender*, February 15, 1941, 9.

223 • **"She had a sternness too":** Rachel Carter Ellis, speaking in an interview by

Betty Gubert, July 22, 1995, transcript in the Betty Gubert Collection of African Americans in Aviation, Box 3, Folder 15.

223 • **And Willa found:** *Chicago Defender*, August 16, 1941, 5, and September 20, 1941, 1; *New Journal and Guide*, June 21, 1941, 5; Marie St. Clair Trottman, speaking in *Willa Beatrice Brown: An American Aviator*, 2009, minute 00:13.50.

223 • **"She was a mentor to me":** Marie St. Clair, speaking in an interview by Betty Gubert, May 9, 1996, transcript in the Betty Gubert Collection of African Americans in Aviation, Box 3, Folder 15.

223–224 • **She'd gone to Washington:** *Chicago Defender*, April 5, 1941, 5.

223–224 • **". . . that members of our race":** *Baltimore Afro-American*, April 5, 1941, 6.

224 • **On August 17, 1941, Willa:** *Baltimore Afro-American*, August 9, 1941, 13; *Chicago Defender*, August 9. 1941, 8; Waters, 1987, 207.

224 • **. . . the show, based in Cleveland:** Waters, 1987, 207.

224 • **. . . aired Sunday mornings:** ibid., 208.

224–225 • **". . . we flew back to Oberlin":** ibid., 208.

225 • **"It was sensational":** ibid., 208.

225 • **"Those who had worked hardest":** Willa Brown, August 22, 1941, 2B.

225 • **". . . dismayed as we gradually":** Waters, 1987, 208.

226 • **In September 1941, a hundred:** *Pittsburgh Courier*, September 13, 1941, 11.

226 • **This time, it was Cornelius Coffey:** *Chicago Defender*, September 20, 1941, 1; *Pittsburgh Courier*, September 13, 1941, 13.

226 • **"On the strength of his having":** *Chicago Defender*, September 6, 1941, 2.

226 • **In November, at a meeting:** *Baltimore Afro-American*, November 22, 1941, 6.

227 • **The group also began to plan:** *Daily Press*, November 16, 1941, 6D.

227 • **A highlight of the year:** *Chicago Defender*, November 29, 1941, 5.

227–228 • **Less than two weeks later . . . "too great for me to master":** Willa Brown to Eleanor Roosevelt, December 6, 1941, in the Betty Gubert Collection of African Americans in Aviation, Box 2, Folder 20.

228 • **Back in July, Japan had:** National World War II Museum, "The Path to Pearl Harbor," n.d., https://www.nationalww2museum.org/war/articles/path-pearl-harbor (accessed April 12, 2023).

228 • **On December 7, 1941:** https://www.britannica.com/event/Pearl-Harbor-attack (accessed April 12, 2023).

228 • **Battleships in the harbor:** National World War II Museum, "Remembering Pearl Harbor: A Pearl Harbor Fact Sheet," n.d., https://www.census.gov/history/pdf/pearl-harbor-fact-sheet-1.pdf (accessed April 12, 2023).

228 • **". . . a date which will live in infamy":** Franklin D. Roosevelt, 1941, https://www.loc.gov/item/afccal000483/ (accessed April 12, 2023).

CHAPTER 11: WINGS OF WAR, 1941–1945

230 • **The negro does not perform:** U.S. Army War College, 1925, in Collection No. 259, "Negroes in Military," Archives and Special Collections, Tuskegee University, Tuskegee, AL.

230 • **. . . over 3,500 people killed:** National World War II Museum, "Remembering

Pearl Harbor: A Pearl Harbor Fact Sheet," n.d., https://www.census.gov/history/pdf /pearl-harbor-fact-sheet-1.pdf (accessed April 12, 2023).

231 • **"When I first heard":** Unnamed counter boy interviewed by Alan Lomax, in Lomax et al, December 8, 1941, AFC 1941/004: AFS 6358, side b, minute 00:09:01–00:09:10, 00:10:21–00:10:36, https://www.loc.gov/item/afc1941004_sr02/ (accessed April 12, 2023). Transcript available at https://tile.loc.gov/storage-services/service/ afc/afc1941004/afc1941004_sr02b/afc1941004_sr02b.pdf (accessed April 12, 2023).

231 • **"Would it be demanding":** James G. Thompson, January 31, 1942, 3.

231 • **Because he was Black:** https://www.blackpast.org/african-american-history /events-african-american-history/the-double-v-campaign-1942-1945/ (accessed April 12, 2023).

231 • **"... lose sight of our fight":** James G. Thompson, *Pittsburgh Courier*, January 31, 1942, 3.

232 • **"Those who perpetuate":** ibid.

232 • **Thompson suggested a name:** Rawn, 2013, 141–142.

232 • **"The 'Double V' stands for victory":** *Pittsburgh Courier*, March 21, 1942, 12.

233 • **Late one night at a small:** Neprud, 1948, 24.

233 • **He was also Ohio's State:** *Cincinnati Enquirer*, December 21, 1941, 28.

233 • **He loaded his own plane:** United States Civil Air Patrol, "History of Civil Air Patrol," available at Homeland Security Digital Library, n.d., 8.4, https://www.hsdl .org/c/view?docid=456489 (accessed April 12, 2023).

234 • **Single-handedly, Johnson:** ibid., 8.5.

234 • **For his part, Johnson:** *Cincinnati Enquirer*, December 21, 1941, 28.

234 • **The CAA immediately brought:** United States Civil Air Patrol, "History of Civil Air Patrol," available at Homeland Security Digital Library, n.d., 8.5, https://www.hsdl.org/c/view?docid=456489 (accessed April 12, 2023).

234 • **Everyone had to file:** Selig, 2013, 114–115.

234 • **"After Pearl Harbor, every":** Cornelius Coffey, Smithsonian Videohistory Program, *African-American Aviation Pioneers*, Session Two, 1990, minute 03:13:00, transcript 91.

234 • **Now if a careless Coffey:** ibid., minute 03:14:00, transcript 91.

235 • **And thus the Civil Air:** *Chicago Defender*, March 7, 1942, 1; United States Civil Air Patrol, "History of Civil Air Patrol," available at Homeland Security Digital Library, n.d., 8.1, 8.3, 8.4, https://www.hsdl.org/c/view?docid=456489 (accessed April 12, 2023).

235 • **Less than a year later:** Department of Commerce, "Negro Statistical Bulletin No. 3: Negro Aviators," April, 1942, 1, in the Records of the Federal Aviation Administration, National Archives Record Group 237, 1922–1992, supplied by Dr. Theresa Kraus; *Victory*, March 31, 1942, 2.

235 • **... by the end of the war:** United States Civil Air Patrol, "History of Civil Air Patrol," available at Homeland Security Digital Library, n.d., 8.7, https://www.hsdl .org/c/view?docid=456489 (accessed April 12, 2023).

235 • **Further inland they were:** Selig 2013, 10–11.

236 • **Within a week of the United States:** Strickland, 1970, 13.

236 • **On December 13, 1941:** Strickland, 1970, iii; Kraus, "The CAA Helps America Prepare for World War II," n.d., 2–3.

236 • Women would no longer: Strickland, 18; Kraus, "The CAA Helps America Prepare for World War II," n.d., 3.

236 • On behalf of the NAAA: *Chicago Defender*, March 7, 1942, 12.

236 • Their officers were sworn: *Chicago Defender*, March 21, 1942, 7.

236 • . . . Cornelius Coffey as the squadron: *Baltimore Afro-American*, September 19, 1942, 23; Paulson, [2016], 14.

236 • The squadron was expected: *Chicago Defender*, March 7, 1942, 1.

236–237 • Group 613-6 pilots: Paulson, [2016], 9, 14, 16, 18.

237 • The group, including Willa: *Cleveland Call and Post*, June 12, 1943, 11B.

237–238 • The War Department had called it: *Chicago Defender*, March 7, 1942, 1.

238 • Harlem Airport was shut down: *Chicago Defender*, June 20, 1942, 5; *Chicago Defender*, June 27, 1942, 13; *New Journal and Guide*, June 27, 1942, 3.

238 • Storck had flown over Harlem: *Chicago Defender*, June 27, 1942, 13.

238 • . . . Fred Schumacher, who was: *Chicago Defender*, June 20, 1942, 5.

238 • Schumacher brought the entire: *Chicago Defender*, June 27, 1942, 13.

238 • If the Japanese Imperial: National World War II Museum, "The Battle of Midway," n.d., https://www.nationalww2museum.org/war/articles/battle-midway (accessed April 12, 2023).

239 • But with its new war footing: Strickland, 1970, 19.

239 • "Because of the reorganization": *New Journal and Guide*, August 1, 1942, 2.

239 • She begged McKeough: *Chicago Defender*, August 1, 1942, 3.

239 • "Only one Negro school is left": *New Journal and Guide*, August 1, 1942, 2.

239–240 • In the summer of 1942 . . . and instrument training: *Chicago Defender*, September 12, 1942, 5; *New Journal and Guide*, August 15, 1942, A11.

240 • In August 1942, Willa proudly: Grossman, July 25, 1991, 65; *New Journal and Guide*, August 15, 1942, A11, and September 5, 1942, 20; O'Brien, August 29, 2022, https://exploreblackheritage.com/list-of-tuskegee-airmen/ (accessed April 12, 2023).

240 • ". . . in freeing the bottleneck": *Philadelphia Tribune*, September 12, 1942, 20.

240–241 • . . . the U.S. military decided: Scott & Womack, 1998 (1992), 168, 172, 199.

241 • "The funny thing about that": Cornelius Coffey, Smithsonian Videohistory Program, *African-American Aviation Pioneers*, Session Two, 1990, minute 02:35:00, transcript 71.

241 • "When we finished the first": ibid., minute 03:03:00, transcript 86.

241 • Willa's brother Simeon: Federal Aviation Administration, Airmen Certification Branch, Airmen Inquiry and Archives, https://amsrvs.registry.faa.gov /airmeninquiry/Main.aspx (accessed April 12, 2023).

241 • "We had to come up": Cornelius Coffey, Smithsonian Videohistory Program, *African-American Aviation Pioneers*, Session Two, 1990, minute 03:06:56, transcript 88.

242–243 • "We not only got uniforms": ibid., minute 03:11:23, transcript 89.

243 • The Coffey program used: ibid., minute 03:12:00, transcript 89, 90.

243 • In July of 1942, a law: Kraus, "The CAA Helps America Prepare for World War II," n.d., 3.

243 • Johnny Robinson, who'd been: *Cleveland Call and Echo*, September 5, 1942, 12; *New Journal and Guide*, September 5, 1942, 2.

243 • **The technical school at Chanute:** Waters, January 30, 1943, 13.

243–244 • **The school even boasted five:** *Pittsburgh Courier*, December 5, 1942, 10.

244 • **... featured in a couple of national:** Waters, December 5, 1942, 13.

244 • **"... for the moment unaware":** Waters, January 30, 1943, 13.

244 • **"Exactly what will happen":** ibid.

244 • **... in December 1942, the War:** *Chicago Defender*, December 19, 1942, 1.

244–245 • **Undeterred as 1943 began:** Rawn, 2013, 123.

245 • **In this time of opportunity:** Willa Brown, January 30, 1943; National Airmen's Association of America, February 3, 1943, 9, both in the Oak Lawn Public Library Archives, courtesy of the National Archives and Records Administration 1940–1943, Accession No. 2020.224.001.

245 • **The bid was rejected:** L.S. Smith, memorandum to Truman K. Gibson, March 8, 1943, 2, in the Oak Lawn Public Library Archives, courtesy of the National Archives and Records Administration 1940–1943, Accession No. 2020.224.001.

245 • **However, in the same month, the CAA:** *Chicago Defender*, March 6, 1943, 1.

245 • **"... at least until the end":** ibid.

245–246 • **"I want you to fill this out":** Bragg & Kriz, 1996, 40.

246 • **"When he saw me":** ibid.

247 • **"Are you Janet Harmon Waterford?" ... Janet assured her:** ibid.

247 • **"Oh no! I don't know what to do":** Janet Harmon Bragg, Smithsonian Videohistory Program, *African-American Aviation Pioneers*, Session One, 1989, minute 00:17:00, transcript 10.

247 • **"I've never interviewed a colored girl":** Bragg & Kriz, 1996, 40.

247 • **"Whatever Mrs. Sheehy told":** ibid.

247 • **The white student who:** Janet Harmon Bragg, Smithsonian Videohistory Program, *African-American Aviation Pioneers*, Session One, 1989, minute 00:17:00, transcript 10–11.

247 • **When her mother pointed out:** Bragg & Kriz, 1996, 40–41.

248 • **"Now I had made two attempts":** ibid., 41.

248 • **"I thought, 'I will never get them'":** ibid., 41.

248 • **"Dear Janet," he replied:** Charles Alfred Anderson as quoted in Bragg & Kriz, 1996, 43.

249 • **"I told them I wanted":** Bragg & Kriz, 1996, 44.

249 • **"They gave me gas coupons":** ibid., 44.

249 • **"Tuskegee, here I come!":** ibid., 44.

249 • **On a cold February morning:** ibid., 45.

249 • **On the flight down:** ibid., 45.

249 • **"Are there any colored":** ibid., 45.

250 • **"Naw," he replied:** ibid., 45.

250 • **"Janet, are we going" ... "Hell, yes!":** ibid., 46.

250 • **"... real Southern cooking":** ibid., 46.

250 • **"White folks and colored folks":** ibid., 47.

250–251 • **"All of a sudden, Dorothy Hall":** ibid., 47–48.

251 • **"The fellows would drive":** ibid., 49.

251 • **"Fortunately, it was never":** ibid., 49–50.

252 • "'Chief,' I want to apologize": ibid., 50.

252 • "Then the day arrived": ibid., 50.

252 • "It was really beautiful": ibid., 50–51.

252 • "How did she do, Mr. Hudson?" ... "I don't intend to now": ibid., 51.

252–253 • "I looked at 'Chief'": ibid., 51.

253 • "Every defeat was a challenge": ibid., 51.

253 • "When he spoke with that": ibid., 52.

253 • "It really didn't make": ibid., 52.

253 • In 1944, both the Navy: Pisano, 1993, 86; Strickland, 1970, 19.

253–254 • Existing training would wrap up: Strickland, 1970, 83.

254 • "to instruct Ethiopian youths": *Chicago Defender*, November 3, 1945, 12.

254 • Italy occupied Ethiopia: https://www.britannica.com/event/North-Africa-campaigns (accessed April 12, 2023).

254 • ... the Lewis School hired Coffey: Cornelius Coffey, Instructor's Record Card, n.d., in the Coffey family papers, Kenneth Spencer Research Library, Box 3, Folder 8.

255 • "Negro America Hails V-E Day!": *Chicago Defender*, May 12, 1945, 1.

255 • Ten years later, Fred and Eleanor: Selig, 2013, 98.

255 • During their existence: Kraus, "The CAA Helps America Prepare for World War II," n.d., 3.

255 • The Coffey School had trained: Cornelius Coffey, Smithsonian Videohistory Program, *African-American Aviation Pioneers*, Session Two, 1990, minute 03:20:30, transcript 94.

255 • "We never[,] in our whole operation": ibid., minute 03:14:30, transcript 91.

256 • "I'm proud of the fact": ibid., minute 03:23:00, transcript 95.

CHAPTER 12: TOUCHING DOWN, 1946 AND BEYOND

257 • Oh! I have slipped: John Gillespie Magee, Jr., "High Flight," 1941, available at *Poetry Foundation*, https://www.poetryfoundation.org/poems/157986/high-flight-627d3cfb1e9b7 (accessed April 11, 2023).

257 • He'd been elected as vice president: https://www.history.com/topics/us-presidents/harry-truman (accessed April 12, 2023).

257 • "I felt like the moon": https://www.whitehouse.gov/about-the-white-house/presidents/harry-s-truman/ (accessed April 12, 2023).

258 • ... with estimates of up to: Wellerstein, August 4, 2020, available at https://thebulletin.org/2020/08/counting-the-dead-at-hiroshima-and-nagasaki/ (accessed April 12, 2023).

259 • "...a concise plan for serving": Vernon Coffey to Errett P. Scrivener, June 6, 1945, in the Coffey family papers, Kenneth Spencer Research Library, Box 1, Folder 25.

260 • ... an impressive business card ... "If I don't go West—Johnny": John C. Robinson, business card, [circa 1935/1936], in the Dale L. White Scrapbook in the Dale L. White, Sr., papers, Accession 2013-0050, National Air and Space Museum, Smithsonian Institution, NASM-9A16697-001.tif, Box 3, Folder 1.

261 • "It is our intention to link": *Baltimore Afro-American*, February 7, 1948, 5; Hall, February 14, 1948, 19.

261 • In March of 1954, Johnny: *Atlanta Daily World*, March 18, 1954, 1.

261 • **The engine failed as they lifted:** *Chicago Defender*, April 3, 1954, 1.

261–262 • **When Emperor Haile Selassie:** Hall, *Baltimore Afro-American*, April 3, 1954, 3.

262 • **But two weeks later, Johnny:** *New York Amsterdam News*, April 3, 1954, 1.

263 • **Two students were headed:** Bragg & Kriz, 1996, 61.

263 • **"Johnny's description of me" ... "like they were your own":** ibid., 62.

263 • **Over the years ... "fifteen staying with me":** ibid., 62.

263 • **... in 1951, when she got married:** ibid., 55.

263 • **... Janet continued to fly:** *Jet*, May 10, 1993, 36, in the Betty Gubert Collection of African Americans in Aviation, Box 2, Folder 15.

264 • **"His Majesty wishes an audience":** Bragg & Kriz, 1996, 67.

264 • **She spent some of that time:** *Baltimore Afro-American*, October 22, 1955, 9.

265 • **"... that we've laid a foundation":** Janet Harmon Bragg, Smithsonian Videohistory Program, *African-American Aviation Pioneers*, Session One, 1989, minute 02:24:26, transcript 74.

265 • **Janet Harmon Bragg flew West:** *Jet*, May 10, 1993, 36, in the Betty Gubert Collection of African Americans in Aviation, Box 2, Folder 15.

265 • **... in the spring of 1946, she ran:** *Chicago Defender*, February 2, 1946, 12.

265 • **... Willa took a job at the Great Lakes:** Waters, August 24, 1960, 2.

265 • **The 1950 Census lists Willa:** Ancestry.com.

265 • **She spent five years in Waukegan:** *Atlanta Daily World*, May 6, 1962, A2; J. H. Chappell and Willa B. Brown, certificate of marriage, September 12, 1955, in the Records of the Federal Aviation Administration, National Archives Record Group 237, 1922–1992, supplied by Dr. Theresa Kraus.

266 • **"The story inspired me so":** Willa Brown to Department of Transportation, July 6, 1971, in the Records of the Federal Aviation Administration, National Archives Record Group 237, 1922–1992, supplied by Dr. Theresa Kraus.

266 • **... on May 17, 1972, at the age of sixty-six:** Willa Brown, letters to Department of Transportation, July 6, 1971 & July 20, 1971, in the Records of the Federal Aviation Administration, National Archives Record Group 237, 1922–1992, supplied by Dr. Theresa Kraus; FAA Airmen Certification Branch, Airmen Inquiry and Archives, https://amsrvs.registry.faa.gov/airmeninquiry/ (accessed April 12, 2023).

266 • **"Every time I see and hear":** Willa Brown, speech, August 1975, 5, supplied to Betty Gubert by Chauncey Spencer, May 1, 1995. In the Betty Gubert Collection of African Americans in Aviation, Box 3, Folder 17.

267 • **"The War Department expresses":** [United States] War Department, Certificate of Appreciation, April 30, 1946, in the Coffey family papers, Kenneth Spencer Research Library, Box 2, Folder 6.

267 • **Jim Crow would no doubt rule:** Bay, March 23, 2021.

268 • **On May 23, 1946, a railroad strike:** National World War II Museum, May 28, 2021.

268 • **Coffey had been correct:** Cornelius Coffey, Smithsonian Videohistory Program, *African-American Aviation Pioneers*, Session Two, 1990, minute 03:24:00, transcript 95–96.

268 • **In 1949, Coffey received:** Grossman, July 25, 1993, 6.

268 • **As luck would have it:** Cornelius Coffey, Smithsonian Videohistory Program, *African-American Aviation Pioneers*, Session Two, 1990, minute 03:24:30, transcript 96.

268 • **"I tell students there's no limit":** Golab, July 14, 1993, 24, in the Betty Gubert Collection of African Americans in Aviation, Box 4, Folder 10.

268 • **On July 31, 1954, Coffey married:** Ancestry.com.

268–269 • **He was the first African American:** Arkansas Aviation Historical Society, 2018.

269 • **In 2013, the Curtiss-Wright:** African American Heritage Sites, n.d.

269 • **And in 2023, Coffey was:** National Aviation Hall of Fame, February 21, 2023.

269 • **"What message would you" . . . "Well, the message":** Theodore Robinson interviewing Cornelius Coffey, Smithsonian Videohistory Program, *African-American Aviation Pioneers*, Session Two, 1990, minute 03:36:00, transcript 100.

269 • **"Flying is hard to give up":** Grossman, July 25, 1993, 6.

270 • **One day back in the midst . . . quick spin over the airfield:** Selig, 2013, 86.

270 • **Tom would one day . . . a lifetime ago:** ibid., 82, 87.

EPILOGUE: TO THE STARS

271 • **This generation does not intend:** John F. Kennedy, September 12, 1962.

271–273 • **In 1965, a young woman . . . both women and minorities:** Weber, August 1, 2022, D-8.

273 • **In 1987, Nichols reached out:** Milner, August 1, 2022.

273 • **In fact, Jemison carried a picture:** Lauria-Blum, June 7, 2019.

RESOURCES

COLLECTIONS

Barnett, Claude A., papers. Chicago History Museum, Chicago, IL. Accessed online via the Melville J. Herskovits Library of African Studies, Northwestern University.

Betty Gubert Collection of African Americans in Aviation. Vivian G. Harsh Research Collection of Afro-American History and Literature, Chicago Public Library.

Black Wings: American Dreams of Flight. Smithsonian Institution Traveling Exhibition Service and the National Air and Space Museum. Exhibit on national tour 2011–2016; donated to the Kalamazoo Air Zoo, Kalamazoo, MI, 2016. Viewed March 2018.

Coffey family papers. Kansas Collection, RH MS 692. Kenneth Spencer Research Library, University of Kansas, Lawrence, KS.

John C. Robinson "Brown Condor" Association. Gulfport, MS.

Local History Online Collections Database, Oak Lawn Public Library, Oak Lawn, IL. Accessed May 26, 2023. https://olpl.pastperfectonline.com

Mississippi Gulf Coast Museum of Historical Photography. Accessed April 12, 2023. http://www.msmohp.com/john-c-robinson.html

Robbins Historical Society and Museum. 3644 W. 139th St., Robbins, IL.

Spencer, Chauncey Edward, papers. Bentley Historical Library, University of Michigan Library, Ann Arbor, MI.

Tuskegee University Archives and Special Collections. Tuskegee, AL.

White, Dale L., Sr., papers. Accession 2013-0050, National Air and Space Museum, Smithsonian Institution. Accessed April 5, 2023. https://sova.si.edu/record/NASM.2013.0050

FILM AND VIDEO

African-American Aviation Pioneers. Session One. November 27, 1989. Interviewer: Theodore Robinson. Participants: Charles Alfred Anderson, Janet Harmon Bragg, Lewis A. Jackson. Site: National Air & Space Museum, Washington, D.C. Smithsonian Institution Archives, Record Unit 9545, Black Aviators Videohistory Collection. Transcript: *Black Aviators Session One.*

African-American Aviation Pioneers. Session Two. March 14, 1990. Interviewer: Theodore Robinson. Participants: Cornelius Coffey, Harold Hurd. Site: Carter G. Woodson Library, Chicago, IL. Smithsonian Institution Archives, Record Unit 9545, Black Aviators Videohistory Collection. Transcript: *Black Aviators Session Two.*

Barrow-Murray, Barbara, and Tanya Hart, directors. *Flyers In Search of a Dream.* Philip Hart, UCLA Center for Afro-American Studies, and WGBH, 1986. PBS Home Video, 1988.

Davis, Yaw, director. *The Emperor's Aviator: The Story of the African-American Commander of Ethiopia's First Air Force.* Pan African Technical Association, 2014.

Hardesty, Von. "Black Wings: African American Pioneers." "Ask an Expert" lecture series, National Air and Space Museum, Smithsonian Institution, February 9, 2011. Accessed April 12, 2023. https://www.youtube.com/watch?v=HY6lvYzGovY

The HistoryMakers. "Interview with Chauncey E. Spencer II on the National Airmen's Association of America," Parts 1–5. Interviewer: Larry Crowe. The HistoryMakers, June 9, 2010. Uploaded May 24, 2022.
https://www.youtube.com/watch?v=IQ-S3COkIM4
https://www.youtube.com/watch?v=hyJtIy1-2uw
https://www.youtube.com/watch?v=gPAlMVlfFEI
https://www.youtube.com/watch?v=fcfe8Qqoax8
https://www.youtube.com/watch?v=p9z6v9C-aRI

O'Derek, Keith, director. *Black Aviation Museum: American History on Wheels.* Featuring Umberto Ricco. Upfront Productions, 2019. Accessed May 28, 2023. https://www.youtube.com/watch?v=ai9Mzx8zqEo

Perez, Severo, director. *Willa Beatrice Brown: An American Aviator.* Script and Post-Script, 2006. Transcript by Alexander Street Press.

MEMOIRS

Bragg, Janet Harmon, as told to Marjorie M. Kriz. *Soaring Above Setbacks: The Autobiography of Janet Harmon Bragg, African American Aviator.* Washington, D.C.: Smithsonian Institution Press, 1996.

Powell, William J. *Black Aviator: The Story of William J. Powell.* Los Angeles: Ivan Deach, Jr., 1934. Reprinted with an introduction by Von Hardesty. Washington, D.C.: Smithsonian Institution Press, 1994.

Spencer, Chauncey E. *Who Is Chauncey Spencer?* Detroit: Broadside Press, 1975.

Waters, Enoch P., Jr. *American Diary: A Personal History of the Black Press.* Chicago: Path Press, Inc., 1987.

OTHER PRIMARY SOURCES

16th Census of the United States 1940, Cook County, Illinois, Sheet No. 7B, "Residence April 1, 1935," available at https://www.ancestry.com/discoveryui -content/view/142809956:2442?_phsrc=Yps25&_phstart=successSource&gsfn =John+C&gsln=Robinson&ml_rpos=2&queryId =bcd44d39d895490af8bc1d13ce727072 (accessed April 12, 2023).

Arkansas US County Marriages Index 1837–1957, available at https://www.ancestry .co.uk/search/collections/2548/ (accessed April 12, 2023).

Barnett, Claude. Letter to Malaku Bayen, January 8, 1935 [erroneously dated 1934] (unsigned carbon). Claude A. Barnett papers (Chicago History Museum), Box 170, Folder 9, "ETHIOPIA (Incl. John C. Robinson), 1930, '33, Feb. 1935–May 1936."

Barnett, Claude. Letter to John C. Robinson, August 28, 1935 (unsigned carbon). Claude A. Barnett papers (Chicago History Museum), Box 170, Folder 9, "ETHIOPIA (Incl. John C. Robinson), 1930, '33, Feb. 1935–May 1936."

Barnett, Claude. Letter to John C. Robinson, October 19, 1935 (unsigned carbon). Claude A. Barnett papers (Chicago History Museum), Box 170, Folder 9, "ETHIOPIA (Incl. John C. Robinson), 1930, '33, Feb. 1935–May 1936."

Barnett, Claude. Letter to John C. Robinson, December 31, 1935 (unsigned carbon). Claude A. Barnett papers (Chicago History Museum), Box 170, Folder 9, "ETHIOPIA (Incl. John C. Robinson), 1930, '33, Feb. 1935–May 1936."

Barnett, Claude. Letter to John C. Robinson, January 22, 1936 (unsigned carbon). Claude A. Barnett papers (Chicago History Museum), Box 170, Folder 9, "ETHIOPIA (Incl. John C. Robinson), 1930, '33, Feb. 1935–May 1936."

Barnett, Claude. Letter to John C. Robinson, April 16, 1936 (unsigned carbon). Claude A. Barnett papers (Chicago History Museum), Box 170, Folder 9, "ETHIOPIA (Incl. John C. Robinson), 1930, '33, Feb. 1935–May 1936."

Barnett, Claude. Letter to John C. Robinson, April 22, 1936 (unsigned carbon). Claude A. Barnett papers (Chicago History Museum), Box 170, Folder 9, "ETHIOPIA (Incl. John C. Robinson), 1930, '33, Feb. 1935–May 1936."

Barnett, Claude. Letter to Frederick Douglass Patterson, May 9, 1936 (unsigned carbon). Claude A. Barnett papers (Chicago History Museum), Box 170, Folder 9, "ETHIOPIA (Incl. John C. Robinson), 1930, '33, Feb. 1935–May 1936."

Barnett, Claude. Letter to Jesse O. Thomas, May 11, 1936. Claude A. Barnett papers (Chicago History Museum), Box 170, Folder 9, "ETHIOPIA (Incl. John C. Robinson), 1930, '33, Feb. 1935–May 1936."

Barnett, Claude. Letter to Frederick Douglass Patterson, May 12, 1936. Claude A. Barnett papers (Chicago History Museum), Box 170, Folder 9, "ETHIOPIA (Incl. John C. Robinson), 1930, '33, Feb. 1935–May 1936."

Barnett, Claude. Letter to James E. Boyack, May 28, 1936. Claude A. Barnett papers (Chicago History Museum), Box 170, Folder 9, "ETHIOPIA (Incl. John C. Robinson), 1930, '33, Feb. 1935–May 1936."

Barnett, Claude. Letter to Scipio A. Jones, July 4, 1936. Claude A. Barnett papers (Chicago History Museum), Box 171, Folder 1.

Barnett, Claude. Letter to Frederick Douglass Patterson, January 18, 1941. Claude A. Barnett papers (Chicago History Museum), Box 239, Folder 7, "TUSKEGEE 1940–41."

Barnett, Claude. Letter to Frederick Douglass Patterson, January 20, 1941. Claude A. Barnett papers (Chicago History Museum), Box 239, Folder 7, "TUSKEGEE 1940–41."

Barnett, Claude. Letter to Frederick Douglass Patterson, January 26, 1941. Claude A. Barnett papers (Chicago History Museum), Box 239, Folder 7, "TUSKEGEE 1940–41."

Bayen, Malaku E. Letter to Claude Barnett, January 3, 1935. Claude A. Barnett papers (Chicago History Museum), Box 170, Folder 9, "ETHIOPIA (Incl. John C. Robinson), 1930, '33, Feb. 1935–May 1936."

Bayen, Malaku E. Letter to Claude Barnett, May 6, 1935. Claude A. Barnett papers

(Chicago History Museum), Box 170, Folder 9, "ETHIOPIA (Incl. John C. Robinson), 1930, '33, Feb. 1935–May 1936."

Bohl, Wilbur. Oral History interview. Interviewer: Gordon Welles. Oak Lawn, IL: Oak Lawn Public Library, December 18, 1979, available at https://olpl .pastperfectonline.com/Archive/399BA31B-4CA5-4CD0-AD90-365148012175 (accessed April 12, 2023).

Brown, Edgar G. "Statement" representing the United Government Employees' Union and the National Airmen's Association of America, made on March 10, 1939, in "Construction of Certain Public Works," U.S. Congress Committee on Appropriations Hearings, Seventy-Sixth Congress, First Session. Washington, D.C.: United States Government Printing Office, 1939, 157–162, available at https://hdl.handle.net/2027/mdp.35112104251741?urlappend =%3Bseq=491%3Bownerid=34704964-496 (accessed April 12, 2023).

Brown, Edgar G. "Statement" on "Training of Negro Air Pilots," made on May 26, 1939, in "Supplemental Military Appropriation Bill, 1940." U.S. Congress Committee on Appropriations Hearings, Seventy-Sixth Congress, First Session. Washington, D.C.: United States Government Printing Office, 1939, 339–341, available at https://hdl.handle.net/2027/mdp.39015035795627?urlappend =%3Bseq=349%3Bownerid=13510798900837950-415 (accessed April 12, 2023).

Brown, Edgar G. "Recent Article On Aviation Activities In Chicago Overlook Established Aviation School." Circa May 1939. Betty Gubert Collection of African Americans in Aviation, Box 7, Folder 16 ("Robinson, John C."), Vivian G. Harsh Research Collection of Afro-American History and Literature, Chicago Public Library.

Brown, Edgar G. "Statement" on "To Provide Training for Negro Pilots," made on August 3, 1939, in "Third Deficiency Appropriation Bill, 1939." U.S. Congress Committee on Appropriations Hearings, Seventy-Sixth Congress, First Session. Washington, D.C.: United States Government Printing Office, 1939, 113, available at https://hdl.handle.net/2027/mdp.35112104251550?urlappend =%3Bseq=1575%3Bownerid=32706990-1574 (accessed April 12, 2023).

Brown, Edgar. "Statement" on "Airfields for Training of Negro Air Pilots Under Civil Aeronautics Administration," made on September 28, 1940, in "First Supplemental Civic Functions Appropriation Bill, 1941." U.S. Congress Committee on Appropriations Hearings, Seventy-Sixth Congress, Third Session. Washington, D.C.: United States Government Printing Office, 1940, 348–349, available at https://hdl.handle.net/2027/mdp.39015035798761?urlappend =%3Bseq=352%3Bownerid=2153688-336 (accessed April 12, 2023).

Brown, Willa. Pilot's license applications/licenses. United States Department of Commerce, 1935–1939, in the Records of the Federal Aviation Administration, National Archives Record Group 237, 1922–1992. Supplied by Dr. Theresa Kraus, historian at the Federal Aviation Administration.

[Brown, Willa] [?]. Leaflet: "Thirty Flight Scholarships Offered Negro Pilots by United States Government." Chicago, [January 1940]. Oak Lawn Public Library

Archives, Willa B. Brown Records, courtesy of the National Archives and Records Administration 1940–1943, Accession No. 2020.224.001, available at https://cdn .olpl.org/documents/BrownWilla.pdf and https://catalog.archives.gov/id/631274 (accessed April 12, 2023).

Brown, Willa. Map sketch attachment to letter to Grove Webster, February 10, 1940. Claude A. Barnett papers (Chicago History Museum), Box 9, Folder 769, "Brown, Willa B. / Coffey School of Aeronautics."

Brown, Willa B. Memorandum to M.O. Bousfield, February 19, 1940. Claude A. Barnett papers (Chicago History Museum), Box 9, Folder 769, "Brown, Willa B. / Coffey School of Aeronautics."

Brown, Willa. Letter to Eleanor Roosevelt, December 6, 1941. Negroes in Defense; General Correspondence, 5/1941–5/1942; Records of the Office of Civilian Defense, Record Group 171; National Archives at College Park, College Park, MD, available at https://www.docsteach.org/documents/document/brown -roosevelt (accessed April 12, 2023).

Brown, Willa. "A Request for $750,000.00 Federal Funds for an Airport at Chicago, Illinois Is Prepared for Presentation based on the Following Facts and Figures." January 30, 1943. Oak Lawn Public Library Archives, Willa B. Brown Records, courtesy of the National Archives and Records Administration 1940–1943, Accession No. 2020.224.001, available at https://cdn.olpl.org/documents /BrownWilla.pdf (accessed April 12, 2023).

Brown, Willa (Chappell). Letter to the Department of Transportation, Federal Aviation Administration, July 6, 1971, in the Records of the Federal Aviation Administration, National Archives Record Group 237, 1922–1992. Supplied by Dr. Theresa Kraus, historian at the Federal Aviation Administration.

Brown, Willa (Chappell). Letter to the Department of Transportation, Federal Aviation Administration, July 20, 1971, in the Records of the Federal Aviation Administration, National Archives Record Group 237, 1922–1992. Supplied by Dr. Theresa Kraus, historian at the Federal Aviation Administration.

Brown, Willa (Chappell). Speech delivered at the Fourth National Convention of Tuskegee Airmen, Detroit, MI, July 31–August 3, 1975. Supplied to Betty Gubert by Chauncey Spencer, May 1, 1995. Betty Gubert Collection of African Americans in Aviation, Box 3, Folder 17 ("Brown, Willa—OBITS"), Vivian G. Harsh Research Collection of Afro-American History and Literature, Chicago Public Library.

Chappell, J. H., and Willa B. Brown. Certificate of marriage for J.H. Chappell and Willa B. Brown, September 12, 1955. Application No. B 73949, Cook County, IL Registry Office, 1955. In the Records of the Federal Aviation Administration, National Archives Record Group 237, 1922–1992. Supplied by Dr. Theresa Kraus, historian at the Federal Aviation Administration.

Civil Aeronautics Authority. "Civilian Pilot Training Program: Non-College Phase." Washington, D.C., [1940]. Claude A. Barnett papers (Chicago History Museum),

Box 9, Folder 769, "Brown, Willa B. / Coffey School of Aeronautics."

Coffey, Cornelius. Business card. Coffey family papers, Kansas Collection, RH MS 692, Kenneth Spencer Research Library, University of Kansas, Box 2, Folder 21.

Coffey, Cornelius. Diploma from the Ogden Davis & Co. School of Automotive Engineering, Chicago, IL, May 17, 1926. Coffey family papers, Kansas Collection, RH MS 692, Kenneth Spencer Research Library, University of Kansas, "Oversized" box, Folder 3.

Coffey, Cornelius. Pilot's license application. United States Department of Commerce, September 10, 1936. Coffey family papers, Kansas Collection, RH MS 692, Kenneth Spencer Research Library, University of Kansas, Box 3, Folder 5.

Coffey, Cornelius. Board of Examiners (Chicago) record update, November 12, 1941. Coffey family papers, Kansas Collection, RH MS 692, Kenneth Spencer Research Library, University of Kansas, Box 2, Folder 12.

Coffey, Cornelius. Instructor's Record Card. State of Illinois, Office of the Superintendent of Public Instruction, n.d. Coffey family papers, Kansas Collection, RH MS 692, Kenneth Spencer Research Library, University of Kansas, Box 3, Folder 8.

Coffey, Cornelius. Letter to Wesley Hudson, January 22, 1942. Coffey family papers, Kansas Collection, RH MS 692, Kenneth Spencer Research Library, University of Kansas, Box 2, Folder 5.

Coffey, Cornelius. Vocational Teacher's Record Card. n.d. Coffey family papers, Kansas Collection, RH MS 692, Kenneth Spencer Research Library, University of Kansas, Box 3, Folder 8.

Coffey, Cornelius R., and Willa B. Brown. Certified copy of marriage certificate for Cornelius R. Coffey and Willa B. Brown, February 7, 1947. Application No. 1954547, Cook County, IL, Registry Office, 1947. Betty Gubert Collection of African Americans in Aviation, Box 4, Folder 10 ("Coffey, Cornelius"), Vivian G. Harsh Research Collection of Afro-American History and Literature, Chicago Public Library.

Coffey, Cornelius. Notes for speech, n.d. Coffey family papers, Kansas Collection, RH MS 692, Kenneth Spencer Research Library, University of Kansas, Box 2, Folder 22.

Coffey, Vernon. Letter to Errett P. Scrivener, June 6, 1945. Coffey family papers, Kansas Collection, RH MS 692, Kenneth Spencer Research Library, University of Kansas, Box 1, Folder 25.

Department of Commerce. "Negro Aviators." Washington, D.C.: July 1, 1935; October 15, 1935; August 15, 1936; February 1, 1937, in the Records of the Federal Aviation Administration, National Archives Record Group 237, 1922–1992. Supplied by Dr. Theresa Kraus, historian at the Federal Aviation Administration.

Department of Commerce. "Supplement to Negro Aviators—October 15, 1935." Washington, D.C.: December 15, 1935, in the Records of the Federal Aviation Administration, National Archives Record Group 237, 1922–1992. Supplied by Dr. Theresa Kraus, historian at the Federal Aviation Administration.

Department of Commerce. "Negro Statistical Bulletin No. 3: Negro Aviators." Washington, D.C., October 1, 1937; January 1939; September 1940, in the Records of the Federal Aviation Administration, National Archives Record Group 237, 1922–1992. Supplied by Dr. Theresa Kraus, historian at the Federal Aviation Administration.

Ellis, Rachel Carter. Telephone interview conducted by Betty Gubert, July 22, 1995. Betty Gubert Collection of African Americans in Aviation, Box 3, Folder 15 ("Brown, Willa—Interviews, transcripts"), Vivian G. Harsh Research Collection of Afro-American History and Literature, Chicago Public Library.

S.S. *Europa*, List of United States Citizens, Tour List 45, May 13, 1936, available at https://www.ancestry.com/imageviewer/collections/7488/images /NYT715_5803-0090?treeid=&personid=&hintid=&queryId =172855aa499a13abfad0c4c22f934af6&usePUB=true&_phsrc=Yps28&_phstart =successSource&usePUBJs=true&pId=20395445 (accessed April 12, 2023).

Fauset, Crystal Bird. Letter to Willa B. Brown, December 17, 1941. Betty Gubert Collection of African Americans in Aviation, Box 3, Folder 7 ("Willa Brown: Biography, 1940–42"), Vivian G. Harsh Research Collection of Afro-American History and Literature, Chicago Public Library.

Federal Aviation Administration, Airmen Certification Branch, Airmen Inquiry and Archives. Available at https://amsrvs.registry.faa.gov/airmeninquiry/ (accessed April 9, 2023).

Federal Aviation Administration. *Aeronautical Information Manual.* "Safety of Flight. Section 6: Potential Flight Hazards. 7-6-1, Accident Cause Factors," [2023], available at https://www.faa.gov/air_traffic/publications/atpubs/aim_html /chap7_section_6.html (accessed April 7, 2023).

Gould, Harold D. Letter to William L. Hastie, November 15, 1940. Claude A. Barnett papers (Chicago History Museum), Box 3, Folder 865, "AIR CORPS—GENERAL."

Gubert, Betty. Handwritten notes from the Terre Haute City Directory, 1925 & 1927. Betty Gubert Collection of African Americans in Aviation, Box 2, Folder 19 ("Willa Brown: Biography 1 of 2"), Vivian G. Harsh Research Collection of Afro-American History and Literature, Chicago Public Library.

Harmon, Janet. Pilot's license applications/licenses. United States Department of Commerce, 1933–1945, in the Records of the Federal Aviation Administration, National Archives Record Group 237, 1922–1992. Supplied by Dr. Theresa Kraus, historian at the Federal Aviation Administration.

Haymore, Tyrone. Interview conducted by Elizabeth Wein, Robbins Historical Museum, Robbins, IL, July 21, 2021.

Haymore, Tyrone. Telephone interview conducted by Stephanie Pitts, June 22, 2023.

Hohman, Elmo Paul. "Instructor's Semestral Report of Grades, Elements of Economics II," first semester 1937–1938. Northwestern University, School of Commerce, 1938. Supplied by Charla Wilson, Archivist for the Black Experience, Northwestern University Libraries, May 2022.

Indiana State University Public Records, correspondence between Elizabeth Wein and the Office of General Counsel, Indiana State University, October 25, 2021.

Jennings, Leon Joy Gurley. Telephone interview conducted by Betty Gubert, August 13, 1995. Betty Gubert Collection of African Americans in Aviation, Box 3, Folder 15 ("Brown, Willa—Interviews, transcripts"), Vivian G. Harsh Research Collection of Afro-American History and Literature, Chicago Public Library.

Jennings, Leon Joy [Gurley]. Letter to Betty Gubert, September 12, 1995. Betty Gubert Collection of African Americans in Aviation, Box 3, Folder 15 ("Brown, Willa—Interviews, transcripts"), Vivian G. Harsh Research Collection of Afro-American History and Literature, Chicago Public Library.

Kennedy, John F. Address at Rice University on the Nation's Space Effort, September 12, 1962. John F. Kennedy Library, available at https://www.jfklibrary.org/learn/about-jfk/historic-speeches/address-at-rice-university-on-the-nations-space-effort (accessed April 8, 2023).

Lomax, Alan, Philip H. Cohen, and Jerome B. Weisner. "Man-on-the-Street," Washington, D.C., December 8, 1941. AFC 1941/004: AFS 6358, side b. Available at https://www.loc.gov/item/afc1941004_sr02/ Transcript available at https://tile.loc.gov/storage-services/service/afc/afc1941004/afc1941004_sr02b/afc1941004_sr02b.pdf (accessed April 10, 2023).

National Airmen's Association of America. "Willa B. Brown, Personal History," in *Who's Who in Aviation* [1941?] Betty Gubert Collection of African Americans in Aviation, Box 2, Folder 20 ("Willa Brown: Biography 2 of 2"), Vivian G. Harsh Research Collection of Afro-American History and Literature, Chicago Public Library.

National Airmen's Association of America. "Prospectus of a Project for Developing an Airport for Pilot Training under the War Department's C.A.A. War Training Service." February 3, 1943. Oak Lawn Public Library Archives, Willa B. Brown Records, courtesy of the National Archives and Records Administration 1940–1943, Accession No. 2020.224.001.

Norton, E. Miles. Copy of court order for Willa B. Hardaway vs. Wilbur J. Hardaway, No. 21901, November 17, 1931. Lake County, IN, 1931. Betty Gubert Collection of African Americans in Aviation, Box 3, Folder 2 ("Willa Brown: Biography, 1931"), Vivian G. Harsh Research Collection of Afro-American History and Literature, Chicago Public Library.

O'Brian, Margaret. "List of Tuskegee Airmen," *Black Heritage*, August 29, 2022. Accessed May 26, 2023. https://exploreblackheritage.com/list-of-tuskegee-airmen/

Office of Claude Barnett. Letter to E.G. Roberts, July 17, 1935 (unsigned carbon). Claude A. Barnett papers (Chicago History Museum), Box 170, Folder 9, "ETHIOPIA (Incl. John C. Robinson), 1930, '33, Feb. 1935–May 1936."

Patterson, Frederick Douglass. Letter to Claude A. Barnett, May 13, 1936. Claude A. Barnett papers (Chicago History Museum), Box 170, Folder 9, "ETHIOPIA (Incl. John C. Robinson), 1930, '33, Feb. 1935–May 1936."

Pentland, Andrew. "Aircraft Registers," Golden Years of Aviation. Accessed April 12, 2023. http://www.airhistory.org.uk/gy/index.html

Prattis, Percival L. Letter to Claude Barnett, July 15, 1935. Claude A. Barnett papers

(Chicago History Museum), Box 170, Folder 9, "ETHIOPIA (Incl. John C. Robinson), 1930, '33, Feb. 1935–May 1936."

Prattis, [Percival L.]. Letter to Claude Barnett, May 28, 1936. Claude A. Barnett papers (Chicago History Museum), Box 170, Folder 9, "ETHIOPIA (Incl. John C. Robinson), 1930, '33, Feb. 1935–May 1936."

Quinn, Patrick N. (University Archivist, Northwestern University). Letter to Betty Gubert, August 25, 1995. Betty Gubert Collection of African Americans in Aviation, Box 3, Folder 18 ("Willa Brown: Research Correspondence, 1 of 3"), Vivian G. Harsh Research Collection of Afro-American History and Literature, Chicago Public Library.

Robinson, John C. Business card. [c. 1935–1936]. In the Dale L. White, Sr., Scrapbook: *African Americans in Aviation (1933–1939)*, Dale L. White, Sr., Papers Collection, Accession 2013-0050, National Air and Space Museum, Smithsonian Institution. NASM-9A16697-001.tif, Box 3, Folder 1, available at https://edan.si.edu/slideshow/viewer/?eadrefid=NASM.2013.0050_ref36 (accessed April 12, 2023).

Robinson, John C. Pilot's Log Book (1934–1935). Photographs in the Robbins Historical Society and Museum, courtesy of Yehoshuah Israel.

Robinson, John C. Letter to Claude Barnett, June 3, 1935. Claude A. Barnett papers (Chicago History Museum), Box 170, Folder 9, "ETHIOPIA (Incl. John C. Robinson), 1930, '33, Feb. 1935–May 1936."

Robinson, John C. Letter to Claude Barnett, November 21, 1935. Claude A. Barnett papers (Chicago History Museum), Box 170, Folder 9, "ETHIOPIA (Incl. John C. Robinson), 1930, '33, Feb. 1935–May 1936."

Robinson, John C. Letter to Claude Barnett, November 28, 1935. Claude A. Barnett papers (Chicago History Museum), Box 170, Folder 9, "ETHIOPIA (Incl. John C. Robinson), 1930, '33, Feb. 1935–May 1936."

Robinson, John C. Telegram to Claude Barnett, May 11, 1936. Claude A. Barnett papers (Chicago History Museum), Box 170, Folder 9, "ETHIOPIA (Incl. John C. Robinson), 1930, '33, Feb. 1935–May 1936."

Robinson, John C. Letter to Claude Barnett, July 1, 1936. Claude A. Barnett papers (Chicago History Museum), Box 171, Folder 1.

Robinson, John C. Letter to Claude Barnett, July 6, 1936. Claude A. Barnett papers (Chicago History Museum), Box 171, Folder 1.

[Robinson, John C.] "It Didn't Work Out." Circa May 1939. Betty Gubert Collection of African Americans in Aviation, Box 7, Folder 16 ("Robinson, John C."), Vivian G. Harsh Research Collection of Afro-American History and Literature, Chicago Public Library.

[Robinson, John C.] "Memorandum." Circa January 1940. Claude A. Barnett papers (Chicago History Museum), Box 171, Folder 1.

Robinson, John C. Letter to G[eorge] L. Washington, May 20, 1941. Claude A. Barnett papers (Chicago History Museum), Box 171, Folder 1.

Robinson, John C. Letter to F[rederick] [Douglass] Patterson, April 3, 1942. Claude A. Barnett papers (Chicago History Museum), Box 171, Folder 1.

Roosevelt, Franklin D. "[Day of Infamy] Speech," 1941. Library of Congress, available at https://www.loc.gov/item/afccal000483/ (accessed April 10, 2023).

St. Clair, Marie. Telephone interview conducted by Betty Gubert, Colt, IL, May 9, 1996. Betty Gubert Collection of African Americans in Aviation, Box 3, Folder 15 ("Brown, Willa—Interviews, transcripts"), Vivian G. Harsh Research Collection of Afro-American History and Literature, Chicago Public Library.

Savory, P.H.M. Telegram to Claude Barnett. May 14, 1936. Claude A. Barnett papers (Chicago History Museum), Box 170, Folder 9, "ETHIOPIA (Incl. John C. Robinson), 1930, '33, Feb. 1935–May 1936."

Smith, L. S. Memorandum for Truman K. Gibson, Jr., on the Coffey School of Aeronautics. March 8, 1943. Oak Lawn Public Library Archives, Willa B. Brown Records, courtesy of the National Archives and Records Administration 1940–1943, Accession No. 2020.224.001.

Snyder, Mary, archivist, Airmen Certification Branch. Personal emails with Elizabeth Wein dated April 26, May 27, and June 2, 2022.

Spencer, Anne. Notebook, October 18, 1936. Papers of Anne Spencer and the Spencer Family, 1829, 1864–2007, #14204, Special Collections, University of Virginia Library, Charlottesville, VA. Supplied by Regina Rush.

Spencer, Chauncey E. Interview conducted by Betty Gubert, Lynchburg, VA, April 20, 1995. Transcript. Betty Gubert Collection of African Americans in Aviation, Box 3, Folder 15 ("Willa Brown—Interviews, Transcripts"), Vivian G. Harsh Research Collection of Afro-American History and Literature, Chicago Public Library.

Tate, Dora Earnize. Certificate used for birth which occurred prior to 1914 for Dora Earnize Tate, November 27, 1906. No. 239, Philips County, AR, State of Arkansas, State Board of Health, Bureau of Vital Statistics, May 20, 1942, available at https://www.ancestry.co.uk/imageviewer/collections/61774/images/61774 _01_00338-00251?usePUB=true&_phsrc=llN66&_phstart=successSource &usePUBJs=true&pId=597763 (accessed May 26, 2023).

United States Army War College. "Notes on Proposed Plan for Use of Negro Manpower," 1925, in Collection No. 259, "Negroes in Military," Archives and Special Collections, Tuskegee University, Tuskegee, AL, available at https://tuskegeeairmen.org/wp-content/uploads/2020/11/TAI_Resources _Negro-Manpower-In-War.pdf (accessed April 10, 2023).

[United States] War Department. Certificate of Appreciation to Cornelius R. Coffey. Washington, D.C., April 30, 1946. Coffey family papers, Kansas Collection, RH MS 692, Kenneth Spencer Research Library, University of Kansas, Box 2, Folder 6.

Washington, G[eorge] L. Letter to Claude Barnett, April 10, 1935. Claude A. Barnett papers (Chicago History Museum), Box 170, Folder 9, "ETHIOPIA (Incl. John C. Robinson), 1930, '33, Feb. 1935–May 1936."

Washington, G[eorge] L. Letter to John C. Robinson, May 22, 1941. Claude A. Barnett papers (Chicago History Museum), Box 171, Folder 1.

Washington, George L. *The History of Military and Civilian Pilot Training of Negroes at Tuskegee, Alabama, 1939–1945.* Washington, D.C.: George L. Washington, 1972. Collection No. 339, George L. Washington, Archives and Special Collections, Tuskegee University, AL, available at http://archive.tuskegee.edu/repository /wp-content/uploads/2021/01/History-of-Military-and-Civilian-Pilot -Training-of-Negroes-at-Tuskegee-1939-1945.pdf (accessed April 10, 2023).

Waters, Enoch P. *Black Wings* exhibit speech, Lynchburg, VA, August 24, 1984. Betty Gubert Collection of African Americans in Aviation, Box 8, Folder 2 ("Spencer, Chauncey"), Vivian G. Harsh Research Collection of Afro-American History and Literature, Chicago Public Library.

White, Dale L., Sr. Scrapbook: *African Americans in Aviation (1933–1939)*, Dale L. White, Sr., Papers Collection, Accession 2013-0050, National Air and Space Museum, Smithsonian Institution. NASM-9A16697-001.tif, Box 3, Folder 1, available at https://edan.si.edu/slideshow/viewer/?eadrefid=NASM.2013.0050 _ref36 (accessed April 12, 2023).

White, Dale L., Sr. Pilot's Log Books (1933–1940), Dale L. White, Sr., Papers Collection, Accession 2013-0050, National Air and Space Museum, Smithsonian Institution. NASM-9A12585-49-50.tif, available at https://edan.si.edu/slideshow /viewer/?eadrefid=NASM.2013.0050_ref554 (accessed April 12, 2023).

Williams, Daniel T. (Archivist). "Registrars at Tuskegee Institute." In *Positions At Tuskegee Institu[t]e: Names and Tenure*, n.d. Collection No. 93, "Daniel T. Williams," Archives and Special Collections, Tuskegee University, Tuskegee, AL, 9.

Wilson, J. Finley. "Statement" on "Training of Negro Air Pilots" made on May 26, 1939, in "Supplemental Military Appropriation Bill, 1940." U.S. Congress Committee on Appropriations Hearings, Seventy-Sixth Congress, First Session. Washington, D.C.: United States Government Printing Office, 1939, 341, available at https://babel.hathitrust.org/cgi/pt?id=mdp.39015035795627 &view=1up&seq=351&q1=finley%20wilson (accessed April 11, 2023).

NEWSPAPER AND MAGAZINE ARTICLES 1919–1962

Adams, Oscar W. "What Negroes Are Doing." *Birmingham News.* September 3, 1939, 31.

Atlanta Daily World. "James, Dead Flyer, Had 'Nerve': Money Kept Aviator From Using Best of Airplanes." September 5, 1932, 1, 5.

Atlanta Daily World. "Flyers Plan Flight to Tuskegee: Chicago Aviators to Make Goodwill Trip: To Reach Institute on Saturday." May 17, 1934, 1.

Atlanta Daily World. "Tuskegee Alumni Hold Convention in Chicago: Tuskegee's Alumni Meet; Establishment of $10,000 Scholarship Fund is Aim of Alumni Association." August 27, 1934, 1.

Atlanta Daily World. "Aviatrix." March 11, 1935, 1.

Atlanta Daily World. "Flyers Pay Tribute To Pal: Bessie Coleman Gets Memorial Honor in Big Air Pageant In Windy City." June 14, 1935, 2.

Atlanta Daily World. "Col. Robinson Orders New Planes For Chicago Flyers As Ethiopia Becomes Air Minded; Whites Beg For Jobs." December 26, 1935, 1.

Atlanta Daily World. "Former Tuskegee Flying Ace Back From Ethiopia." June 2, 1936, 2.

Atlanta Daily World. "Hail Colonel John C. Robinson, 'Brown Condor,' As He Returns From Ethiopia With Thrilling Tales Of Why Haile Selassie Lost War." June 2, 1936, 2.

Atlanta Daily World. "Life Story of Colonel John C. Robinson, Brown Condor." June 2, 1936, 2.

Atlanta Daily World. "'Brown Condor' To Visit Nashville." September 1, 1936, 5.

Atlanta Daily World. "Race Flyers For First Time Enter Air Show." October 2, 1938, 1.

Atlanta Daily World. "Kelly Aids Air School Movement." March 29, 1939, 1, 6.

Atlanta Daily World. "Chicago Pilots Plan Tour Of Ten Cities." May 1, 1939, 1.

Atlanta Daily World. "As Final Checkup Was Made." May 12, 1939, 1.

Atlanta Daily World. "Edgar Brown Claims 'No Selfish Interest' In Aviation School Fight." May 13, 1939, 1, 5.

Atlanta Daily World. "Ethiopian Air Ace Named Ill. Aviation Consultant." October 21, 1939, 1.

Atlanta Daily World. "Approve 2 Air Schools For Negroes." December 28, 1939, 1, 6.

Atlanta Daily World. "Gov't Offers Thirty Flight Scholarships." February 14, 1940, 3.

Atlanta Daily World. "Aviation Course To Open." March 15, 1940, 1.

Atlanta Daily World. "Willa Brown Praised By CAA Chiefs Visiting Air School." June 23, 1940, 6.

Atlanta Daily World. "She's Adjutant." March 8, 1942, 1.

Atlanta Daily World. "Willa Brown Is Considered For Flying Command." December 7, 1942, 1.

Atlanta Daily World. "The Color Guard . . . lt. Willa Brown." February 27, 1944, 6.

Atlanta Daily World. "'Brown Condor' Injured In Ethiopian Air Crash." March 18, 1954, 1.

Atlanta Daily World. "Famous Aviatrix Willa Brown Now Teaches School in Chicago." May 6, 1962, A2.

Baltimore Afro-American. "Julian Disappoints Memorial Day Crowd." June 9, 1928, 1.

Baltimore Afro-American. "Girl Flyer Heads Aero Club." November 10, 1928, 2.

Baltimore Afro-American. "Two Get Pilot's License in New York." March 9, 1935, 17.

Baltimore Afro-American. "West Family Points to Honors, Denies Abyssinian Rumors." July 13, 1935, 6.

Baltimore Afro-American. "Air Squadron Flies in Memorial Service." June 15, 1935, 3.

Baltimore Afro-American. "Watch Out, Duce!" August 3, 1935, 2.

Baltimore Afro-American. "United States Flier with Selassie Does Not Fear Italians: Italian Planes Ineffective in Ethiopian Hills." October 5, 1935, 4.

Baltimore Afro-American. "Ethiopian Air Unit Hopeless, Says U.S. Pilot: Robinson Says Plane Combat with Italy Would Be Murder." October 12, 1935, 3.

Baltimore Afro-American. "Robinson May Return to U.S. as Rains Start." April 11, 1936, 3.

Baltimore Afro-American. "Mrs. Robinson Glad Hubby Is Coming Home From War." May 2, 1936, 3.

Baltimore Afro-American. "Ethiopia Not Subdued, Says Black [sic] Condor." May 23, 1936, 13.

Baltimore Afro-American. "Dentist and Wife Expert Flyers." May 23, 1936, 12.

Baltimore Afro-American. "Tuskegee May Buy Plane for Robinson." May 30, 1936, 6.

Baltimore Afro-American. "Ethiop Clouds Save Life of Black [sic] Condor." May 30, 1936, 8.

Baltimore Afro-American. "Woman Flyer Gets Private Pilot's OK." July 2, 1938, 8.

Baltimore Afro-American. "Gets a Private Pilot's License." July 9, 1938, 2.

Baltimore Afro-American. "Pilots Receive Air Show Bids." September 17, 1938, 23.

Baltimore Afro-American. "Air Expansion Bill to Serve Dual Purpose." April 22, 1939, 4.

Baltimore Afro-American. "Civilian Air Bill Provides Equality." April 29, 1939, 5.

Baltimore Afro-American. "Aviators Visit." May 20, 1939, 6.

Baltimore Afro-American. "Air Tour Delayed." May 20, 1939, 15.

Baltimore Afro-American. "It Wasn't Engine Trouble." May 27, 1939, 20.

Baltimore Afro-American. "Senate Passes Civilian Pilot Training Bill." June 24, 1939, 19.

Baltimore Afro-American. "Davis Wins Air Trophy at First Birdmen's Meet." September 2, 1939, 5.

Baltimore Afro-American. "CAA Gives Ill. Private Air School." October 21, 1939, 5.

Baltimore Afro-American. "Own Race Will Train Pilots in Ill." December 30, 1939, 2.

Baltimore Afro-American. "Airmen's Body Is Organized at West Va. State." February 10, 1940, 2.

Baltimore Afro-American. "CAA's Woman Flight Director Is Praised." June 22, 1940, 23.

Baltimore Afro-American. "Million for Airfield Okeyed [sic]." January 25, 1941, 1.

Baltimore Afro-American. "Proof That Races Can Mix in Aviation Training." February 8, 1941, 23.

Baltimore Afro-American. "U.S. May One Day Welcome Any Pilots." March 29, 1941, 1, 2.

Baltimore Afro-American. "U.S. Air Official Promises Full Expansion in CAA." April 5, 1941, 6.

Baltimore Afro-American. "Queen of the Air to Discuss Aviation." August 9, 1941, 13.

Baltimore Afro-American. "Association of CAA Aviation Schools Formed." November 22, 1941, 6.

Baltimore Afro-American. "Willa Brown named to Ill. Civil Air Patrol." March 7, 1942, 1.

Baltimore Afro-American. "Lino Operator at Work." September 19, 1942, 23.

Baltimore Afro-American. "Racial Bias Keeps Balto. Man Out of CAA Pilot Course." October 24, 1942, 21.

Baltimore Afro-American. "Lt. Willa Brown Confers in D.C." June 12, 1943, 5.

Baltimore Afro-American. "New Airline in Ethiopia Headed by Col. Robinson." February 7, 1948, 5.

Baltimore Afro-American. "American aviatrix arrives in Ethiopia." October 22, 1955, 9.

Belvedere Daily Republican. "Waukegan Establishing Airport and School." May 1, 1929, 3.

Best, Edwin L. "No U.S. Race Aviators." *Chicago Defender,* November 24, 1934, A2.

Bourne, St. Clair. "Texas Ace Here; Urges Greater Interest in Flying." *New York Amsterdam News,* August 24, 1940, 1, 3.

Brown, Earl W. "Credits The Chicago Defender With Getting Air School At West Va. State." *Chicago Defender,* October 21, 1939, 6.

Brown, Willa. "Speech Delivered Sunday, August 17th at Cleveland, Ohio." *Cleveland Call and Post,* August 23, 1941, 2B.

Burley, Dan. "Brown Condor Lands Plane In Memphis." *Chicago Defender,* March 6, 1937, 6.

California Eagle. "Negro Flyers Participate in Air Show." October 6, 1938, 10.

Carr, J.D. "Flyer Burns To Death In Plane Crash." *Chicago Defender,* September 4, 1932, 1.

Carter, Elmer Anderson (editor). "Survey of the Month." *Opportunity: Journal of Negro Life,* vol. 7. New York: National Urban League, 1929, 352–353, available at https://archive.org/details/sim_opportunity-a-journal-of-negro-life_1929-11_7_11 /page/352/mode/2up?view=theater (accessed April 7, 2023).

Chicago Bee. "Aviatrix-Instructor." February 1940. Betty Gubert Collection of African Americans in Aviation, Box 3, Folder 7 ("Brown, Willa: Biography, 1940–1942"), Vivian G. Harsh Research Collection of Afro-American History and Literature, Chicago Public Library.

Chicago Defender. "Aviatrix Must Sign Away Life to Learn Trade." October 8, 1921, 2.

Chicago Defender. "Future Flyer." January 22, 1927, A3.

Chicago Defender. "Chicagoans Unveil Monument to Bessie Coleman." June 9, 1928, A12.

Chicago Defender. "Bessie Coleman Charity Club." September 15, 1928, 5.

Chicago Defender. "Girl Upsets Florida Contest: 'Passes' For White; Joins Flying Club." May 11, 1929, A1.

Chicago Defender. "Upsets Nordics." May 18, 1929, 3.

Chicago Defender. "Pretty 'Billie' Lawson Weds Earl Renfroe." July 13, 1929, 5.

Chicago Defender. "Eight Licensed Pilots." September 14, 1920, A2.

Chicago Defender. "Aviator James Has Sunday Air Circus." May 10, 1930, 11.

Chicago Defender. "Give Air Circus as a Tribute to Bessie Coleman." September 26, 1931, 2.

Chicago Defender. "Just Landed." January 2, 1932, 20.

Chicago Defender. "Future Aces at Grave of Bess Coleman." June 4, 1932, A1.

Chicago Defender. "Air Exhibition Planned." August 13, 1932, 22.

Chicago Defender. "Trio Fly to Cleveland to Attend Air Races." September 10, 1932, 15.

Chicago Defender. "Beautiful Dancing Party of Challenger Aero Club." December 24, 1932, 6.

Chicago Defender. "Tornado Plays Prank With Airplane." May 6, 1933, 3.

Chicago Defender. "Large Crowd Sees Stunts Done in Air." September 30, 1933, 5.

Chicago Defender. "Plenty Of Thrills Here." September 30, 1933, 4.

Chicago Defender. "Teacher at Philips is Auto Victim." May 19, 1934, 1.

Chicago Defender. "'Good Will' Flyers Crash: Chicago Pilots En Route to Tuskegee on Southern Tour Smash Up at Decatur, Ala." May 26, 1934, 1, 2.

Chicago Defender. "53d Commencement at Tuskegee Inst." May 26, 1934, 22.

Chicago Defender. "Aviators Drop in on Commencement at Tuskegee Inst." June 2, 1934, 2.

Chicago Defender. "Tuskegee Alumni Map $10,000 Endowment Plan: Aviation School Seen." August 25, 1934, 5.

Chicago Defender. "To Fly Soon." March 9, 1935, 13.

Chicago Defender. "Let's Go! Janet Harmon Waterford." March 28, 1936, 1.

Chicago Defender. "Noted Aviatrix To Teach Kiddies How To Fly Planes: Janet Harmon Waterford Writes Very Interesting Article." April 13, 1935, 15.

Chicago Defender. "Hundreds Join In Memorial To Bessie Coleman." June 8, 1935, 12.

Chicago Defender. "Volunteers For Ethiopian War Are Condemned: Says Citizenship Should Be Revoked By U.S." July 20, 1935, 5.

Chicago Defender. "Rockford, Ill." July 27, 1935, 20.

Chicago Defender. "Attend Inauguration." November 16, 1935, 7.

Chicago Defender. "Brown Condor: Col. John C. Robinson." April 4, 1936, 3.

Chicago Defender. "Leading Mountain Attack." April 25, 1936, 1.

Chicago Defender. "To Help Us" and "To Organize Junior Birdmen." May 16, 1936, 15.

Chicago Defender. "A Defender Man Gets First Story From Col. Robinson." May 30, 1936, 5.

Chicago Defender. "Aviatrices Welcome Col. John Robinson." May 30, 1936, 7.

Chicago Defender. "Col. Robinson Speaker At Du Saible [sic]." May 30, 1936, 20.

Chicago Defender. "Rally To Buy Col. Robinson A New Plane." June 13, 1936, 24.

Chicago Defender. "'Brown Condor' At Tuskegee Institute." July 11, 1936, 24.

Chicago Defender. "Students Enroll In Brown Condor's Air College." October 10, 1936, 5.

Chicago Defender. "Aviation College Is Opened Here By Col. John Robinson." October 10, 1936, 11.

Chicago Defender. "Mme. Malone, Poro Head, Takes To Air." July 24, 1937, 9.

Chicago Defender. "In Which The Sky's The Limit, With The Earth Below, And All Of Its Fabulous Delights Wedged In!" September 18, 1937, 13.

Chicago Defender. "Congratulations!" July 2, 1938, 1.

Chicago Defender. "Plans Coast To Coast Flight." July 23, 1938, 1, 2.

Chicago Defender. "Youngest Flier." August 13, 1938, 4.

Chicago Defender. "'Cuts Capers' In Air." September 3, 1938, 1.

Chicago Defender. "Leaping to Fame." September 3, 1938, 1.

Chicago Defender. "Willie 'Suicide' Jones Breaks Air-Leap Record." September 3, 1938, 1.

Chicago Defender. Display Ad 14, no title. September 17, 1938, 7.

Chicago Defender. "12 Race Pilots Invited To Participate In Air Show." September 24, 1938, 4.

Chicago Defender. "Spencer Thrills Huge Crowd With 2-Mile Air Leap." October 1, 1938, 1, 2.

Chicago Defender. "Features Of Sunday's Air Show." October 1, 1938, 4.

Chicago Defender. "Wins Air Show Award." November 12, 1938, 5.

Chicago Defender. "Community Crusaders And Fliers Spread Goodwill Message." November 12, 1938, 10.

Chicago Defender. "Fliers Who Scattered Leaflets On Chicagoans." November 19, 1938, 1.

Chicago Defender. "Local Fliers Organize To Foster Meet: New Organization To Map Plans For August Confab." March 18, 1939, 7.

Chicago Defender. "City Fliers Make Appeal To Mayor Kelly." April 1, 1939, 6.

Chicago Defender. "F.D.R. Signs Air Corps Bill At Warm Springs." April 8, 1939, 1.

Chicago Defender. "Free Flights Make Chicago Air Conscious: Pilots Move To Arouse Local Interests In Civilian Flying." April 22, 1939, 7.

Chicago Defender. "Local Flyers Plan 3,000-Mile Hop." April 29, 1939, 1, 2.

Chicago Defender. "House Puts Its O.K. On Aviation Training Bill." April 29, 1939, 2.

Chicago Defender. "Prepare For Flight." April 29, 1939, 3.

Chicago Defender. "Check Air Meet Questionnaire." April 29, 1939, 7.

Chicago Defender. "Jam Airports As Spring Revives Interest In Aviation." May 6, 1939, 13.

Chicago Defender. "Flyers Are Grounded By Motor Fault." May 13, 1939, 1.

Chicago Defender. "Motor Trouble Interrupts 3,000-Mile Flight." May 13, 1939, 4.

Chicago Defender. "Flyers Visit Pittsburgh Courier and Editor Vann." May 20, 1939, 6.

Chicago Defender. "N.A.A.-Defender Flyers Visit Nation's Capital." May 20, 1939, 6.

Chicago Defender. "Back Home And Happy." May 27, 1939, 4.

Chicago Defender. "Goodwill Flyers End 3,000-Mile Epoch [sic] Hop." May 27, 1939, 4.

Chicago Defender. "N.A.A. Defender Flyers Welcomed Home After 3,000-Mile Tour." May 27, 1939, 11.

Chicago Defender. "'Air' School Assured For Race Pilots." June 17, 1939, 2.

Chicago Defender. "Coffey Named Chairman For National Air Meet." June 17, 1939, 24.

Chicago Defender. "Civil Pilots Air Bill Gets O.K. From Senate: Race Schools Will Share In Appropriation." June 24, 1939, 2.

Chicago Defender. "Those Who Fly: Perry H. Young." June 24, 1939, 11.

Chicago Defender. "Those Who Fly: Perry H. Young [sic; the article is about John Delton Reed]." July 1, 1939, 15.

Chicago Defender. "Those Who Fly: Abram D. Jackson." July 8, 1939, 15.

Chicago Defender. "Those Who Fly: George W. Allen." July 15, 1939, 24.

Chicago Defender. "Those Who Fly: Walter Caldwell Jr." July 22, 1939, 15.

Chicago Defender. "'Derbytown' Awaits Happy Landing Of Aviatrix." July 29, 1939, 2.

Chicago Defender. "Airmen To Swoop On City For First Confab: Flyer Slated In Exhibition Over Airport." August 12, 1939, 4.

Chicago Defender. "Louisville Fetes Chicago Woman Flyer." August 12, 1939, 11.

Chicago Defender. "President Puts O.K. On Air Pilot Training Bill." August 19, 1939, 1.

Chicago Defender. "Flyers Open Air Confab: Chicago Set For Meeting Of Aviators." August 26, 1939, 1.

Chicago Defender. "Doctor Wins Aviation Award." September 2, 1939, 1.

Chicago Defender. "Aviators From Six States Hold Chicago Meet." September 2, 1939, 3.

Chicago Defender. "Hampton Is Named Base For Air Training." September 30, 1939, 5.

Chicago Defender. "Col. Robinson Named Aviation Consultant." October 21, 1939, 5.

Chicago Defender. "Defender's Goodwill Flyers Inspired 'Wings' At West Virginia State." October 21, 1939, 6.

Chicago Defender. "Harlem Airport Chosen For CAA Pilot School." October 28, 1939, 19.

Chicago Defender. "Local Flyers Feted In All White Town." November 4, 1939, 13.

Chicago Defender. "Name School To Train Flyers For U.S. Army." December 2, 1939, 1.

Chicago Defender. "Defender Sports Editor Inspects W. Va. State's Air Pilots' Program." December 23, 1939, 7.

Chicago Defender. "U.S. To Train Thirty Air Pilots In Chicago." January 20, 1940, 1.

Chicago Defender. "Win Long, Hard Fight." January 27, 1940, 3.

Chicago Defender. "Chicago's Last Goodbye To Robert S. Abbott: Fliers Drop Flowers On Editor's Grave." March 9, 1940, 1, 9.

Chicago Defender. "Instructs Aviation Class." March 16, 1940, 5.

Chicago Defender. "Handpicked Aviation Students Learn About Parachutes." May 18, 1940, 6.

Chicago Defender. "30 Taking Government Air Training In Chicago." June 15, 1940, 12.

Chicago Defender. "This Organization Has Made Sky The Limit For Negro Youth." June 29, 1940, 13, 15.

Chicago Defender. "Flyers Plan Open House At Airport." July 6, 1940, 8.

Chicago Defender. "Poses With Admirers." July 13, 1940, 6.

Chicago Defender. "Anonymous Source Honors Flyers White And Spencer." August 17, 1940, 8.

Chicago Defender. "Over 100 Seek Civilian Pilot Training." August 17, 1940, 8.

Chicago Defender. "Clevelanders Welcome Race Flyers' Derby." August 24, 1940, 8.

Chicago Defender. "Spencer And White Get 1939 Aviation Trophy." August 31, 1940, 12.

Chicago Defender. "Weds Aviator." August 31, 1940, 10.

Chicago Defender. "75 Flight Students To Get CAA Certificates." September 14, 1940, 4.

Chicago Defender. "Aviation Unit Scores High In Theory Test." September 21, 1940, 6.

Chicago Defender. "Aviator New Head Of Tuskegee Club." January 11, 1941, 8.

Chicago Defender. "Scholarships Available In Flight School." January 25, 1941, 6.

Chicago Defender. "Jim Crow Air Squadron Hit In NAACP Attack." February 15, 1941, 2.

Chicago Defender. "Willa Brown Made Airmen's Leader." February 15, 1941, 9.

Chicago Defender. "No Army Air Training For Race Until October—Then It'll Be Jim Crow." March 29, 1941, 3.

Chicago Defender. "Band Leader's Check Aids Airport Fund." March 29, 1941, 8.

Chicago Defender. "Plan Air Training Expansion." April 5, 1941, 5.

Chicago Defender. "Seven Pilots Get License In Illinois Area." April 5, 1941, 5.

Chicago Defender. "Local Pilot Gets Instructor Rating." April 19, 1941, 8.

Chicago Defender. "Plan Aviation Mechanics At Tuskegee." April 26, 1941, 2.

Chicago Defender. "Coffey Air School Buys 10th Plane." June 14, 1941, 4.

Chicago Defender. "Willa Brown, 'Air Queen,' On Wings Program, Aug. 17." August 9, 1941, 8.

Chicago Defender. "Flight Student." August 16, 1941, 5.

Chicago Defender. "Award Coffey Dwight Green Flyer Trophy." September 6, 1941, 1, 2.

Chicago Defender. "Flyer Gets Coveted Award." September 20, 1941, 1.

Chicago Defender. "Dr. Bethune Visits Phillips Aviation Shops." November 29, 1941, 5.

Chicago Defender. "Airmen Launch Seventh Pilot Training Course." January 10, 1942, 13.

Chicago Defender. "Civil Air Patrol Does The Impossible." March 7, 1942, 1, 12.

Chicago Defender. "CAP Flyers Sworn In For Duty." March 21, 1942, 7.

Chicago Defender. "Harlem Airport Is Closed By U.S." June 20, 1942, 5.

Chicago Defender. "Airport is Reopened By CAA Order." June 27, 1942, 13.

Chicago Defender. "Move To Save Air School In Chicago." August 1, 1942, 3.

Chicago Defender. "Chicago Air School Gets $25,000; RFC Loan For Expansion, Training." September 12, 1942, 5.

Chicago Defender. "Flying 99th Anxious To Clash With Foe." December 19, 1942, 5.

Chicago Defender. "Negro America Hails V-E Day!" May 12, 1945, 1.

Chicago Defender. "Col. John Robinson Nears End Of Air Mission In Ethiopia." November 3, 1945, 12.

Chicago Defender. "Willa Brown Files For Congress Race." February 2, 1946, 12.

Chicago Defender. "Crash Injuries Fatal To Ace John Robinson." April 3, 1954, 1.

Chicago Tribune. "Flying Instructions Will Begin Monday For Chinese Youths." February 26, 1932, 6.

Chicago Tribune. "Wife of Ethiopia Air Leader Runs Chicago Garage." August 28, 1935, 5.

Chicago Tribune. "Miss Willa Brown." July 10, 1938, 31.

Chicago Tribune. "Negro Youths Win Chance to Demonstrate Ability as Flyers." July 7, 1940, Part 3, 2.

Chicago Tribune. "Negro Aviatrix Wins Place in Skies for Race." July 7, 1940, Part 3, 1, 2.

Chicago Tribune. "Starts New Aviation Term." September 7, 1941, Part 3, 2.

Chicago Tribune. "Air Corps Board Accepts 11 Negro Flying Cadets." June 21, 1942, 1.

Chicago World. "Chicagoan Gives The 'Black Eagle' A Black Eye In Abyssinia." August 17, 1935, 5.

Childress, Lucile. "At Checkerboard Field." *Chicago Defender,* August 31, 1929, A2.

Churbuck, Lewis M. "Aviation, Coming Mode of Travel, Opens New Vistas for Race Youth." *Abbott's Weekly and Illustrated News,* Chicago, December 22, 1933, 2–3.

Cincinnati Enquirer. "Italian Consul Is Wounded In Jungles Of Ethiopia; Says It Was An Accident. Robinson Has Ability." August 23, 1935, 3.

Cincinnati Enquirer. "The *Enquirer* Reviews the Week's News: Ohio Valley." December 21, 1941, 28.

Cleveland Call and Post. "'Brown Condor' Makes His First Visit To This City." August 13, 1936, 1, 2.

Cleveland Call and Post. "Elks Fete Brown Condor." August 20, 1936, 2.

Cleveland Call and Post. "Two Negro Women Get Solo Licenses." July 28, 1938, 6.

Cleveland Call and Post. "To Carry Fight for Negroes in U.S. Air Corps to Senate Finance Comm." July 6, 1939, 7.

Cleveland Call and Post. "2 Civilian, Army Air Schools To Open January 15." December 28, 1939, 1.

Cleveland Call and Post. "Clevelanders Greet Feminine Flyer at Cleveland Airport." August 23, 1941, 2A.

Cleveland Call and Post. "Biographical Sketch of Willa Brown." August 23, 1941, 2B.

Cleveland Call and Post. "Col. Robinson Named Instructor In Aviation at Chanute Field." September 5, 1942, 12.

Cleveland Call and Post. Photo Standalone 35, no title. June 12, 1943, 11B.

Daily Press. "Negro Fliers Will Sponsor Air Contest." Newport News, VA. November 16, 1941, 6D.

Decatur Daily. "Plane Crashes In Field Here: Negroes Escape Unhurt As Ship Is Badly Wrecked." May 19, 1934, 1.

Des Moines Tribune. "'Humming Bird', First Airplane Built Here, Scores Triumph in Maiden Flight." June 28, 1926, 2.

Des Moines Tribune. "Des Moines To Have Airplane Service." April 11, 1927, 4.

Des Moines Tribune. "Burd S. White Rites Pending." August 11, 1931, 13.

Dismond, Dr. H. Binga. "Negroes, Despite Handicaps, Make Rapid Progress in Various Fields of Aviation." *New York Amsterdam News*, November 9, 1935, 3.

Ellis, Jack. "Col. Robinson Flies Defender Mercy Plane To Flood Area." *Chicago Defender*, February 20, 1937, 1, 4.

Evening Times. "American Flier For Selassie Is Attack Witness." Sayre, PA, October 5, 1935, 1.

Faulkner, Daniel J. "Patterson Pleads For New Airport." *Atlanta Daily World*, November 17, 1940, 1.

Faulkner, Daniel J. "Tuskegee Air Unit Praised." January 29, 1941, 1.

Fleming, G. James. "Ethiopia War Ace Captures Harlem." *New York Amsterdam News*, May 23, 1936, 1, 13.

Galbreath, Elizabeth. "Typovision." *Chicago Defender*, September 2, 1939, 16.

Gary American. "No Clowns In The City Council." April 19, 1929, 4. Betty Gubert Collection of African Americans in Aviation, Box 2, Folder 22 ("Willa Brown: Biography, 1929"), Vivian G. Harsh Research Collection of Afro-American History and Literature, Chicago Public Library.

Gary American. "Here's Your Chance To Go Skylarking For $5 If You Like Airplanes!" June 7, 1929. Betty Gubert Collection of African Americans in Aviation, Box 2, Folder 22 ("Willa Brown: Biography, 1929"), Vivian G. Harsh Research Collection of Afro-American History and Literature, Chicago Public Library.

Gary American. "Jumping From Parachute Is Not Easy Job." June 28, 1930, 1. Betty Gubert Collection of African Americans in Aviation, Box 3, Folder 1 ("Willa Brown: Biography, 1930"), Vivian G. Harsh Research Collection of Afro-American History and Literature, Chicago Public Library.

Gary American. "Protest Building of Roosevelt School: Mass Meeting Protests Gary School Plans." June 28, 1930, 1. Betty Gubert Collection of African Americans in Aviation, Box 3, Folder 1 ("Willa Brown: Biography, 1930"), Vivian G. Harsh Research Collection of Afro-American History and Literature, Chicago Public Library.

Gary American. "Roosevelt High School Dedicated: Gary's New Million Dollar High School Dedicated This Week." April 25, 1931, 1. Betty Gubert Collection of African Americans in Aviation, Box 3, Folder 2 ("Willa Brown: Biography, 1931"), Vivian G. Harsh Research Collection of Afro-American History and Literature, Chicago Public Library.

Gary American. "Students Are Given Training In Office Work." April 25, 1931, 1. Betty Gubert Collection of African Americans in Aviation, Box 3, Folder 2 ("Willa Brown: Biography, 1931"), Vivian G. Harsh Research Collection of Afro-American History and Literature, Chicago Public Library.

Gary American. "Wife Is Granted Divorce From Gary Alderman." October 31, 1931, 1. Betty Gubert Collection of African Americans in Aviation, Box 3, Folder 2 ("Willa Brown: Biography, 1931"), Vivian G. Harsh Research Collection of Afro-American History and Literature, Chicago Public Library.

Gary American. "Mrs. Hardaway Asks Protection From Husband." November 7, 1931, 1. Betty Gubert Collection of African Americans in Aviation, Box 3, Folder 2 ("Willa Brown: Biography, 1931"), Vivian G. Harsh Research Collection of Afro-American History and Literature, Chicago Public Library.

Gary American. "The Fighting Alderman Dances And Battles." December 31, 1932, 1. Betty Gubert Collection of African Americans in Aviation, Box 3, Folder 3 ("Willa Brown: Biography, 1933"), Vivian G. Harsh Research Collection of Afro-American History and Literature, Chicago Public Library.

Gary American. "Victim Badly Injured; Companion Killed, in Weekend Accident." May 19, 1934, 1. Betty Gubert Collection of African Americans in Aviation, Box 3, Folder 4 ("Willa Brown: Biography, 1934–1936"), Vivian G. Harsh Research Collection of Afro-American History and Literature, Chicago Public Library.

Hall, Chatwood. "'Brown Condor' Tells Side Of Ethiop Brawl." *Atlanta Daily World,* September 13, 1947, 1.

Hall, Chatwood. "Col. Robinson Launches East African Airlines." *Chicago Defender,* February 14, 1948, 19.

Hall, Chatwood. "Colonel Robinson, veteran flyer, fights for life after plane crash in Ethiopia." *Baltimore Afro-American,* April 3, 1954, 3.

Hall, Chatwood. "'Brown Condor' Rests: Large Crowds view Robinson's funeral." *Baltimore Afro-American,* April 17, 1954, 7.

Hall, Chatwood. "Robinson's unmarked grave marked—by American Friends." *Baltimore Afro-American,* April 16, 1955, 5.

Harrison, James M. "Stray thoughtlets." *New Journal and Guide.* Norfolk, VA, January 14, 1922, 4.

Howe, David Ward. "The Observation Post: Daring Young Woman Wins Fight For Race Pilots." *Chicago Defender,* January 27, 1940, 14.

Imes, William Lloyd. "We'll Sing Ethiopia." [1936]. Claude A. Barnett papers (Chicago History Museum), Box 171, Folder 5, "AFRICA—JOHN C. ROBIN-SON—SCRAPBOOK."

Ingram, Gladys. "Romance of Popular Gary Couple Culminates in Wedding: 35 Witness." *Gary American,* November 29, 1929, front page. Betty Gubert Collection of African Americans in Aviation, Box 2, Folder 22 ("Willa Brown: Biography, 1929"), Vivian G. Harsh Research Collection of Afro-American History and Literature, Chicago Public Library.

James, Wilson [John C. Robinson]. "Cite Julian (Almost Spanned Harlem River) Fakir On Abyssinian War Front: Tells Natives Of 60 Planes, $60,000 In Bank." *Philadelphia Tribune,* July 11, 1935, 1, 10.

James, Wilson [John C. Robinson]. "Whites Poison Minds Of Ethiopians Aainst [sic]

Negroes, Says Writer: Hubert Julian Reported To Owe Big Debt; Beats His Servants Daily." *Plaindealer*, Kansas City, KS, July 12, 1935, 2.

James, Wilson [John C. Robinson]. "Col. Julian Beat Up by Police in Africa: Julian Charged With Deceiving Abyssinians; Helps To Create Lack of Faith In U.S. Negroes." *New Journal and Guide*, Norfolk, VA, July 13, 1935, 1, 8. [These last three stories are essentially the same, reprinted with variations in three different papers.]

James, Wilson [John C. Robinson]. "Leave A Bad Impression In Ethiopia: American 'Negroes', And Thus Play Right Into The Hands Of Prejudiced Whites, Their Enemies. 'Negro' Aviator, Hubert Julian, Now In Abyssinia, Said to Be Creating a Bad Impression—Not His First Trip to Addis Ababa—Little Known Facts." *Cleveland Gazette*, July 20, 1935, 1.

James, Wilson [John C. Robinson]. "Japan Ready for Import of Fire Arms." *Plaindealer*, Kansas City, KS, September 6, 1935, 2.

James, Wilson [John C. Robinson]. "Report Japan Will Furnish Ethiopia Arms: Country To Have Aid In Preparing For War." *New Journal and Guide*, Norfolk, VA, September 7, 1935, 10.

Johnson, James Weldon. "The Riots," *The Crisis*, Vol. 18, No. 5 (September 1919), 241–243, available at https://library.brown.edu/pdfs/1295988909203125.pdf (accessed April 3, 2023).

Johnson, Lillian. "The Feminine Viewpoint: Women In The Air." *New Journal and Guide*, Norfolk, VA, May 25, 1935, 9.

Kellum, David W. "Defender Scribe Greets Robinson: War Ace Is Welcomed By Harlemites." *Chicago Defender*, May 23, 1936, 1, 2.

Kellum, David W. "Twenty Thousand Greet 'Brown Condor' On Return: Local Flyer In Ethiopian War Lauded." *Chicago Defender*, May 30, 1936, 1, 2.

Lake County Times. "Air Tour Hits Gary June 19." Hammond, IN, June 6, 1930, 1.

Lake County Times. "Co. Organization Formed." Hammond, IN, October 13, 1930, 6.

Lake County Times. "Frenzied Campaign Conducted Fruitless: One Stabbed To Death." Hammond, IN, May 3, 1932, 11.

Lautier, L. R. "Army To Train Race Aviators: Courier Drive For Government Recognition Brings Senate Action." *Pittsburgh Courier*, March 18, 1939, 1.

Lautier, L. R. "Air Bill Bans Discrimination." *Pittsburgh Courier*, April 29, 1939, 1, 4.

Layne, Lou. "Girl Operates Realty Office, Flies As Hobby: Lola Jackson Only Negro Aviatrix in the East." *New York Amsterdam News*, December 18, 1937, 11.

Lindbergh, Charles A. "Aviation, Geography, and Race." *Reader's Digest*, Vol. 35, November 1939, 64–68, available at http://reparti.free.fr/lindbergh39.pdf (accessed April 7, 2023).

Los Angeles Sentinel. "Col. Robinson Dies of Injuries in Ethiopia." April 1, 1954, A4.

Negro World. "Future in Air Bright for Race: Youth Urged to Train for Service by Negro Mechanic." New York, NY, December 26, 1931, 2.

New Journal and Guide. "To the Memory of A Pioneer Aviatrix." Norfolk, VA, June 16, 1928, 9.

New Journal and Guide. "Laudatory Determination." Norfolk, VA, December 5, 1931, A6.

New Journal and Guide. "Tried 7 Times To Enter Air School; Refused; Accepted." Norfolk, VA, December 5, 1931, A7.

New Journal and Guide. "Aviators Plan 65-Hour Round-Trip Flight Across U.S." Norfolk, VA, July 1, 1933, A8.

New Journal and Guide. "Flyers Fog Bound In Penn. Weather Is Bad On West-East Flight: Expect Foggy Weather To Keep Them At Pittsburgh 2 Days. Achievement Hailed. Invited To Return To Chicago For World Fair Special Day." Norfolk, VA, July 29, 1933, A1, 15.

New Journal and Guide. "'No Less Than Murder' To Meet Italy In Present Ethiopian Planes, Robinson Says In Exclusive Story." Norfolk, VA, October 12, 1935, 1, 10.

New Journal and Guide. "Brown Condor Prepares For Flight." Norfolk, VA, October 19, 1935, 1.

New Journal and Guide. "Chicago Turns Out To Greet Brown Condor: Leaders Lavish Praises On Head of Daring Young Aviator." Norfolk, VA, May 30, 1936, 1, 10.

New Journal and Guide. "Gangway For the 'Brown Condor.'" Norfolk, VA, May 30, 1936, 18.

New Journal and Guide. "Revolt, Not Italy, Caused Ethiopia's Downfall, Says Flyer." Norfolk, VA, May 30, 1936, 18.

New Journal and Guide. "Pretty Aviatrix Sets Pace." Norfolk, VA, July 9, 1938, 1.

New Journal and Guide. "Three Women Have Pilots' Licenses." Norfolk, VA, July 30, 1938, 20.

New Journal and Guide. "Sets Parachute Jump Record." Norfolk, VA, September 3, 1938, 1, 10.

New Journal and Guide. "Invite Negro Flyers To Enter Air Show." Norfolk, VA, September 24, 1938, 2.

New Journal and Guide. "Passage of Aviation Bill Vital To Race." Norfolk, VA, April 22, 1939, 1, 10.

New Journal and Guide. "Air Bill Is Framed To Aid Race." Norfolk, VA, April 29, 1939, 1, 10.

New Journal and Guide. "Goodwill Flyers In Washington." Norfolk, VA, May 20, 1939, 1, 10.

New Journal and Guide. "Senate Passes Civilian Pilot Training Bill: Howard University To Participate In Program." Norfolk, VA, June 24, 1939, 4.

New Journal and Guide. "Chicagoans Heads [sic] National Airmen's Association." Norfolk, VA, September 9, 1939, 3.

New Journal and Guide. "Howard, Tuskegee To Share In Air Training Program." Norfolk, VA, October 21, 1939, 4.

New Journal and Guide. "Aviation Training Course To Begin April 15." Norfolk, VA, March 16, 1940, 11.

New Journal and Guide. "Statistics Show Negro Licensed Pilots Have Multiplied Five Times In Five Years." Norfolk, VA, September 28, 1940, 10.

New Journal and Guide. "Girl Wins Flying Scholarship." Norfolk, VA, June 21, 1941, 5.

New Journal and Guide. "No Armed Guards, U.S. Closes Harlem Airport." Norfolk, VA, June 27, 1942, 3.

New Journal and Guide. "Appeals For The Saving Of Pilot School." Norfolk, VA, August 1, 1942, 1, 2.

New Journal and Guide. "Speed Up Training At Coffey Air School." Norfolk, VA, August 15, 1942, A11.

New Journal and Guide. "'Brown Condor' Now Chanute Field Instructor." Norfolk, VA, September 5, 1942, 1, 2.

New Journal and Guide. "Miss Brown Sees Her Students Sworn Into Army." Norfolk, VA, September 5, 1942, 20.

New Journal and Guide. "Women In Uniform: Flier In D.C." Norfolk, VA, June 19, 1943, 9.

New York Age. "Doris H. Murphy." March 9, 1935, 5.

New York Age. "2 Civilian And Army Schools Will Train Negroes As Aviators." January 6, 1940, 3.

New York Age. "National Airmen's Association Scores Jim Crow Air Corps; Calls Proposal Ridiculous." February 22, 1941, 1.

New York Amsterdam News. "What Will the Negro Contribute to Aviation?" June 22, 1927, 13.

New York Amsterdam News. "Julian Still Plans Atlantic Flight." June 20, 1928, 3.

New York Amsterdam News. "No Negro Aviator Holds Commercial License." December 12, 1928, 3.

New York Amsterdam News. "Girl Wins Place In Flying Club." May 8, 1929, 1.

New York Amsterdam News. "Few Negro Youths Entering Aviation." September 11, 1929, 11.

New York Amsterdam News. "Aviators Abused." March 2, 1935, 3.

New York Amsterdam News. "Colonel Robinson In Harlem Monday: Hero of Ethiopian War Returning to U.S." May 16, 1936, 1, 13.

New York Amsterdam News. "Emperor and Air Hero Are Honored in Song." May 30, 1936, 11.

New York Amsterdam News. "Col. Robinson Starts Own Aviation College." October 3, 1936, 24.

New York Amsterdam News. "More Aviators Discovered By Federal Lists." October 23, 1937, 3.

New York Amsterdam News. "Solo Licenses Go To 2 Women." 23 July 1938, 4.

New York Amsterdam News. "Willie Jones Breaks World's Record for Parachute Jump." September 3, 1938, 5.

New York Amsterdam News. "Amends Pilots Training Bill." April 29, 1939, 1, 5.

New York Amsterdam News. "Three Pilots Begin Flight Next Monday." May 6, 1939, 16.

New York Amsterdam News. "Two Air Schools to Train Negro Pilots Open Jan. 15." December 30, 1939, 1.

New York Amsterdam News. "Appoint Chicago Aviatrix." April 6, 1940, 7.

New York Amsterdam News. "Willa Brown Earns Praise." June 22, 1940, 3.

New York Amsterdam News. "B.J. Strode, Tex. Aviator, Arrives." August 17, 1940, 9.

New York Amsterdam News. "Weary of Social Life, She Sought Kinship With Stars And Youthful Aviatrix Finds Thrills in Air." August 24, 1940, 12.

New York Amsterdam News. "Aviatrix Talks On Flying Experiences." August 31, 1940, 13.

New York Amsterdam News. "Ethiopia Honors Dead U.S. Flier." April 3, 1954, 1, 2.

New York Times. "Ethiopia Gets New Flier." August 23, 1935, 10.

New York Times. "American Negro Pilot Bests 2 Italian Planes." October 5, 1935, 2.

New York Times. "Selassie's Air Aide Back From Africa: Col. J.C. Robinson Returns to Teach Aviation at Tuskegee, His Alma Mater." May 19, 1936, 6.

New York World-Telegram. "Negro Flier to Keep Beard; Made Him Ethiopia's Hero." May 19, 1936. Claude A. Barnett papers (Chicago History Museum), Box 171, Folder 5, "AFRICA—JOHN C. ROBINSON—SCRAPBOOK."

Norman, Charles. "'Brown Condor,' Pilot Of Selassie, Feted As Harlem's Newest Hero." *Wausau [Wi.] Daily Herald*, May 28, 1936, 10; see also *Courier-News*, Bridgewater, NJ, June 5, 1936, 15, and *Daily Mail*, Hagerstown MD, June 12, 1936, 4.

Peck, James [L.H.] "Good-Will Aviators Run Into Plenty Of Trouble: Broken Crankshaft, Forced Night Landing, But White and Spencer Finally Get Into New York on 'Hedge-Hopping' Flight." *Pittsburgh Courier*, May 20, 1939, 1, 4.

Peck, James L.H. "Winsome First Lady Of Sky Named Flight Director." *Atlanta Daily World*, April 3, 1940, 1, 3.

Peck, James L.H. "ANP Aviation Editor Takes A Slant At Willa Brown, Race's 'Ladybird.'" *Chicago Defender*, April 6, 1940, 6.

Peck, James [L.H.] "Negro Aviator Accuses Army Air Officials Of Giving Negroes The Run Around In Pilot Training." *New York Age*, December 7, 1940, 3.

Philadelphia Tribune. "Brighter Future Seen For Negro Aviators." December 3, 1931, 12.

Philadelphia Tribune. "C. Alfred Anderson Receives Transport Pilot License." February 25, 1932, 1.

Philadelphia Tribune. "War Begins In Ethiopia—Between Two Americans, But It Is Only A Fist Fight." August 15, 1935, 15.

Philadelphia Tribune. "Brown Condor Of Ethiopia Hits War Scare." October 3, 1935, 1.

Philadelphia Tribune. "Brown Condor An Eye Witness At Aduwa Raid." October 10, 1935, 3.

Philadelphia Tribune. "'Brown Condor' Club Organized in 'Chi.'" October 17, 1935, 5.

Philadelphia Tribune. "Ethiopian Air Ace, Back From Battle Front, Hits War Tactics." May 21, 1936, 1, 19.

Philadelphia Tribune. "Young Aviatrix." July 14, 1938, 6.

Philadelphia Tribune. "75 Pilots To Train At Harlem Airport." September 12, 1942, 20.

Philadelphia Tribune. "Col. Robinson Dies, Crashed In Ethiopia." April 3, 1954, 1.

Pittsburgh Courier. "Monument To Late Aviatrix Ready." May 26, 1928, 12.

Pittsburgh Courier. "Monument To Bessie Coleman Unveiled In Chicago." June 9, 1928, A1.

Pittsburgh Courier. "Girl Wins Place in White Flying Club." May 4, 1929, 1.

Pittsburgh Courier. "Aero Club To Buy 100 Planes." May 11, 1929, 5.

Pittsburgh Courier. "Youthful Aviator Makes Flight." February 1, 1930, 2.

Pittsburgh Courier. "Aviation School Opens." May 17, 1930, 2.

Pittsburgh Courier. "Queen Of The Air: Mrs. Janet Harmon Waterford." June 11, 1932, 1.

Pittsburgh Courier. "Storm Destroys Airport." May 13, 1933, 2.

Pittsburgh Courier. "Stalled Plane Landed Safely In Chi Park." July 8, 1933, 3.

Pittsburgh Courier. "12 White American Aviators Ready To Fight For Ethiopia." July 20, 1935, 1.

Pittsburgh Courier. "U.S. Whites Volunteer For Ethiopian Service: Negro World Alliance Wins Many Recruits." July 20, 1935, 5.

Pittsburgh Courier. "An Appeal From Haile Selassie." October 19, 1935, 12.

Pittsburgh Courier. "American Correspondent And Pilot." November 16, 1935, 4.

Pittsburgh Courier. "Col. Robinson Orders Six New Planes For Chi Flyers To Fight For Ethiopia." January 4, 1936, 7.

Pittsburgh Courier. "Wants To Fight Italian Bombers." January 18, 1936, 1.

Pittsburgh Courier. "Robinson's Chi Air Ass'n Names Officers." January 18, 1936, 5.

Pittsburgh Courier. "Sponsor." April 11, 1936, 2.

Pittsburgh Courier. "Aviation Boom Sweeps West; 75 Now Pilots: Powell Leads Teaching Of Brown Airmen." May 16, 1936, A8.

Pittsburgh Courier. "Thousands Give 'Brown Condor' Of Ethiopia A Conquering Hero's Welcome On Return To Chi." June 6, 1936, 3.

Pittsburgh Courier. "They're All 'Air-Minded.'" June 6, 1936, 1.

Pittsburgh Courier. "Col. Robinson, Ethiopian Air Hero, Tells Story In Three Eastern Cities." June 27, 1936, A1.

Pittsburgh Courier. "Col. John Robinson Opens Aviation College: Ethiopia's 'Brown Condor' Founds Chicago School." September 5, 1936, 5.

Pittsburgh Courier. "The Brown And Jones Girls . . . First Sepia Airport Hostesses. Lola Jones and Willa Brown Delighted With New Duties. Receiving Practical Training Daily at Colonel J.C. Robinson's Flying Field." October 31, 1936, 8.

Pittsburgh Courier. "Professor's Secretary Now." September 25, 1937, 24.

Pittsburgh Courier. "Dentist Aviation Enthusiast." October 9, 1937, 3.

Pittsburgh Courier. "10 Race Women, 93 Men Qualify As Aviators." October 16, 1937, 12.

Pittsburgh Courier. "Chicago Aviation Enthusiasts To See Wedding In Clouds Soon." June 4, 1938, 3.

Pittsburgh Courier. "Young Woman Flyer Gets Pilot's License." July 2, 1938, 11.

Pittsburgh Courier. "Our Women Advancing In Aviation." July 23, 1938, 13.

Pittsburgh Courier. "Aviatrix In 'Tail Spins' Test Flight." January 28, 1939, 13.

Pittsburgh Courier. "Intrepid Chicago Aviators Pilot 'Old Faithful' In Cross Country Goodwill Tour." May 20, 1939, 1.

Pittsburgh Courier. "Spurned By Their Country's Armed Forces, These 'Forgotten Heroes' Carry On." May 20, 1939, 20.

Pittsburgh Courier. "Seek $10,000,000 To Train Race Pilots: Courier Fight To Gain Recognition Reaches New High." June 3, 1939, 1, 4.

Pittsburgh Courier. "Aviatrix Is Cited In 'Time.'" October 7, 1939, 13.

Pittsburgh Courier. "Airport For Pilots Named: Chicago Field Chosen By CAA." October 21, 1939, 3.

Pittsburgh Courier. "Chicago Will Have 2 U.S. Air Schools." February 3, 1940, 10.

Pittsburgh Courier. "Thirty Flight Scholarships For Government Training!" February 17, 1940, 11.

Pittsburgh Courier. "Chicago Tribune Backs Courier Air Fight." August 17, 1940, 1, 4.

Pittsburgh Courier. "Air Conference Held In Chicago." September 13, 1941, 11.

Pittsburgh Courier. "Receives Dwight Green Flyer Trophy Award." September 13, 1941, 13.

Pittsburgh Courier. "Nation-Wide Support Grows For 'Double V.'" March 14, 1942, 12.

Pittsburgh Courier. "Victory At Home, Victory Abroad Sweeps Nation." March 21, 1942, 12.

Pittsburgh Courier. "Pretty Aviatrix Puts Students Through Paces." March 21, 1942, 3.

Pittsburgh Courier. "Girl Instructors Accepted At Chanute Flying Field School." December 5, 1942, 10.

Pittsburgh Courier. "Air Crash in Ethiopia Fatal to Colonel Robinson." April 10, 1954, 31.

Pittsburgh Press. "Aviator Tells How Air Raiders Bombed Aduwa: John Robinson, Flying For Ethiopia, Says City Was Taken by Surprise." October 6, 1935, 7.

Pittsburgh Press. "Flier for Haile Selassie Thinks War Was 'Swell.'" June 12, 1936, 27.

Plaindealer. "Julian And Chicago Aviator Have Fist Fight At Ethiopia." Kansas City, KS, August 16, 1935, 8.

Plaindealer. "Col. Robinson Chased by Flyers." Kansas City, KS, December 13, 1935, 1.

Plaindealer. "Col. Robinson Ethiopian Air King Returns." Kansas City, KS, May 1, 1936, 2.

Plaindealer. "Mrs. Annie Malone Takes To The Air." Kansas City, KS, July 9, 1937, 4.

Pleasant Hill Times. "Works On Home-Made Plane." Pleasant Hill, MO, November 21, 1930, 1.

Powell, William [J.]. "Race Neglects Its Opportunities In Aviation." *Chicago Defender*, November 17, 1934, 10.

Prattis, P[ercival]. L. "Ethiopian Air Ace Outwits Italian Planes In Battle." *Pittsburgh Courier*, October 12, 1935, 4.

Prattis, P[ercival]. L. "Ethiopia's Black [sic] Condor: The Story of John C. Robinson, Who Set His Heart on Becoming an Aviator—by a Man Who Knows Him." *New York Amsterdam News*, October 26, 1935, 1A, 5.

Renfroe, Earl W. "Suggests Way To Open 'Closed Doors' Of Army: United Front Is Urged By Aviator." *Pittsburgh Courier*, February 25, 1939, 3.

Robinson, David. "Helping Abyssinia." *Chicago Defender*, April 6, 1935, 14.

Robinson, John C. "Robinson's Own Story Of Epic Flight: Pilot Describes Trip To Memphis In Plane; Tells Of Perils." *Chicago Defender*, March 6, 1937, 1, 2.

Robinson, John C. "Col. Robinson In Defense Of All-Negro Air Squadron." *Atlanta Daily World*, February 4, 1941, 1.

Rocky Mountain News. "Selassie's Air Aid." Denver, CO, May 23, 1936. Claude A. Barnett papers (Chicago History Museum), Box 171, Folder 5, "AFRICA—JOHN C. ROBINSON—SCRAPBOOK."

Rogers, J.A. "Col. Robinson Stages Air Duel In Clouds With Enemy Planes!" *Pittsburgh Courier*, December 14, 1935, 1.

Rogers, J.A. "J.A. Rogers Gets Exclusive Interview With Col. Robinson, Ethiopia's 'Brown Condor.'" *Pittsburgh Courier*, January 4, 1936, 1, 4.

Rogers, J.A. "Rogers Takes 'Death Ride' With Robinson: Flying Four Miles In Clouds, Writer Takes Perilous Trip Beyond Ethiopian War Zone." *Pittsburgh Courier*, February 1, 1936, 6.

Rogers, J.A. "Rogers Pays Tribute To Colonel Robinson: Believes 'Brown Condor' Is One Of World's Heroes." *Pittsburgh Courier*, September 5, 1936, A2.

Salt Lake Tribune. "Harlem's 'Black Eagle' Hotly Denies Story of Attempt to Kill Selassie." November 7, 1935, 8.

Service, Calvin. "'Brown Condor' Returns." *Cleveland Call and Post*, May 28, 1936, 2.

Slaughter, Vera B. "20,000 Greet 'Brown Condor' At Airport." *Chicago Defender*, May 30, 1936, 7.

Speedy, Nettie George. "Sepia Air Pilots Thrill World's Fair Visitors: Female Flyers And Instructor On Exhibition. Government-Controlled Aviation School Is Scene of Interesting Accomplishments By Negro Aviators—Familiar With Models of the Fledging [sic]." *Pittsburgh Courier*, July 22, 1933, A3.

Speedy, Nettie George. "One Girl And Three Men Graduated From Chicago Aeronautical College: Miss Doris Murphy, Dale L. White, Edward C. Anderson and Clyde B. Hampton Qualify to Become Flyers—Ceremonies Are Impressive." *Pittsburgh Courier*, March 2, 1935, 2.

Stewart, O. A. "Tuskegee Institute Graduates 183 At Its 53rd Commencement." *Montgomery Advertiser*, May 25, 1934, 18.

Thompson, James G. "Should I Sacrifice To Live 'Half-American'?" *Pittsburgh Courier*, January 31, 1942, 3.

Time Magazine. "The Front: Solemn Hours." Vol. 26, No. 16, October 14, 1935, available at https://content.time.com/time/subscriber/article/0,33009,755119,00 .html (accessed April 12, 2023).

Time Magazine. "National Affairs: School for Willa." Vol. 34, No. 13, September 25, 1939, 16.

Toledo News Bee. "Ethiopia's 'Back [sic] Condor', Back in U.S., Still Ducks When He Hears Airplane." May 22, 1936. Claude A. Barnett papers (Chicago History Museum), Box 171, Folder 5, "AFRICA—JOHN C. ROBINSON—SCRAPBOOK."

Victory: Official Weekly Bulletin of the Agencies in the Office for Emergency Management. "Johnson Succeeds Curry as Civil Air Patrol Commander." Washington, D.C. 3:13, March 31, 1942, 2, available at https://books.google.co.uk/books?id =9oxIAQAAIAAJ&pg=RA13-PA2&lpg=RA13-PA2&dq=%22hard-hitting+and +effective+organization%22&source=bl&ots=sM9pag0uvX&sig=ACfU3U3 _LQ98x_l2rej693paBRnEAF2YFg&hl=en&sa=X&ved=2ahUKEwiz0eTzs4z4Ah XYilwKHcDgByUQ6AF6BAgEEAM#v=onepage&q=%22hard-hitting%20 and%20effective%20organization%22&f=false (accessed April 12, 2023).

Ward, Stancil L. "The Typewriting Department." *Annex News*. East Roosevelt Annex, Roosevelt High School, Gary, IN, Vol. 1, No. 2, November 14, 1927, 5. Betty Gubert Collection of African Americans in Aviation, Box 3, Folder 12 ("Willa Brown: Gary Schools"), Vivian G. Harsh Research Collection of Afro-American History and Literature, Chicago Public Library.

Ward, Stancil L. "Typewriting Department." *Annex News*. East Roosevelt Annex, Roosevelt High School, Gary, IN, Vol. 1, No. 3, December 19, 1927, 2. Betty Gubert Collection of African Americans in Aviation, Box 3, Folder 12 ("Willa Brown: Gary Schools"), Vivian G. Harsh Research Collection of Afro-American History and Literature, Chicago Public Library.

Washington D.C. Star. "Colored U.S. Mechanic Hailed As Hero of Selassie's Pilots." May 25, 1936. Claude A. Barnett papers (Chicago History Museum), Box 171, Folder 5, "AFRICA—JOHN C. ROBINSON—SCRAPBOOK."

Washington Tribune. "Negro Squadron Flies In Memorial Rites: Chicago Airmen Pay Tribute to Bessie Coleman, Pioneer Woman Flyer." June 22, 1935, 3.

Waterford, Janet H[armon]. "The History of Aviation." *Chicago Defender*, April 13, 1935, 15.

Waterford, Janet H[armon]. "Noted Aviatrix To Teach Kiddies How To Fly Planes: Janet Harmon Waterford Writes Very Interesting Article [War and Aviation]." *Chicago Defender*, May 4, 1935, 16.

Waterford, Janet H[armon]. "Aeroplane Engines." *Chicago Defender*, May 25, 1935, 15.

Waterford, Janet Harmon. "Race Interest In Aviation In Actuality Begins With Advent Of Bessie Coleman: Deeds Of Intrepid Young Aviatrix Light Torch Of Black Flyers Here." *Chicago Defender*, March 28, 1936, 3.

Waterford, Janet [Harmon]. "The Real Story of Col. John Robinson Or How A Gulfport, Miss. Boy Grew To Be The No. 1 Flyer Of His Race: Ethiopian Flying Ace Was Circus Motorcycle Rider." *Chicago Defender*, April 4, 1936, 1, 2.

Waterford, Janet [Harmon]. "Robinson Organizes Brown Eagle Aero Club In Effort To Interest Race In Flying: Public Turns Deaf Ear To Plea Of Pilot; Lacks Funds." *Chicago Defender*, April 11, 1936, 6.

Waterford, Janet [Harmon]. "Robinson Arouses Race Interest In Aviation." *Chicago Defender*, April 18, 1936, 3.

Waterford, Janet [Harmon]. "Robinson Excelled as an Instructor in Aviation Because of his Keen Insistence on Real Discipline: 'Law of Gravity Makes No Provisions for First Offenders,' he declared." *Chicago Defender*, April 25, 1936, 12.

Waterford, Janet [Harmon]. "First Race Airport Was Destroyed In Big Storm." *Chicago Defender*, May 2, 1936, 12.

[Waterford], Janet [Harmon]. "John Robinson Wings His Way Down To Tuskegee." *Chicago Defender*, May 9, 1936, 12.

[Waterford], Janet [Harmon]. "The Race And Aviation." *Chicago Defender*, May 30, 1936, 5.

Waterford, Janet [Harmon]. "Race Aviator Flies U.S. Air Mail Route." *Chicago Defender*, May 21, 1938, 1, 2.

Waterford, Janet [Harmon]. "First Race Pilot To Fly U.S. Mail Relates Experiences During Flight." *Chicago Defender*, May 28, 1938, 2.

Waters, Enoc[h] P., Jr. "Airmen Oppose 'Jim Crow' Pursuit Squadron Ordered By Department." *Detroit Tribune*, January 25, 1941, 1, 6.

Waters, Enoc[h] P., Jr. "Nation's Flyers Blast Jim Crow Air Unit." *Chicago Defender*, January 25, 1941, 1, 2.

Waters, Enoc[h] P., Jr. "Peacetime Flyers." *Chicago Defender*, February 22, 1941, 13, 15.

Waters, Enoc[h] P., Jr. "Black Wings Over America." *Chicago Defender*, September 26, 1942, B15 & B27.

Waters, Enoc[h] P., Jr. "'Whites Only' In U.S. Bombers." *Chicago Defender*, December 19, 1942, 1.

Waters, Enoc[h] P., Jr. "Expert Negro Teachers Rank High At Chanute 'Ground Crew' School." *Chicago Defender*, January 30, 1943, 13.

Waters, Enoc[h] P., Jr. "Blazed Trail For Men In Flying: Aviatrix Willa Brown Moves From Clouds To Classroom And Church." *Atlanta Daily World*, August 24, 1960, 2.

Watson, Ted. "Colored Aviation As It Is Today In Chicago At Oak Hill's [sic] Harlem Airport." *Pittsburgh Courier*, January 13, 1940, 12.

Waukegan News-Sun. "Passes Test for Pilot's License." August 29, 1929, 1.

Waukegan News-Sun. "Former Local Flier On Duty In War Region." October 8, 1935, 2.

White, A.E. "Harlem In Wild Acclaim Over Return Of 'Brown Condor.'" n.p., [June 4, 1936], Claude A. Barnett papers (Chicago History Museum), Box 171, Folder 5, "AFRICA—JOHN C. ROBINSON—SCRAPBOOK."

Whiting Evening Times. "Colored People In Parade." Whiting, IN, 9 June 1930, 1.

OTHER SOURCES FOR THE CHICAGO AVIATORS

Aerotech News. "Black History Month: African American Pioneer Dale White and the 1939 Goodwill Flight." *The Lake Air Force Base Thunderbolt*, February 10, 2021. Accessed May 26, 2023. https://www.aerotechnews.com/lukeafb/2021/02/10 /black-history-month-african-american-pioneer-dale-white-and-the-1939 -goodwill-flight/

Allen, Henry. "To Fly, To Brave the Wind." *Washington Post*, September 26, 1979, available at https://www.washingtonpost.com/archive/lifestyle/1979/09/26 /to-fly-to-brave-the-wind/0fc63cd9-4464-4834-8f37-56c95759c5a6/ (accessed April 12, 2023).

Arkansas Aviation Historical Society. "Cornelius Robinson Coffey." 2018. Accessed June 23, 2023. https://www.arkavhs.com/cornelius-robinson-coffey

Beneš, Jan. "Writing in the Sky: Black Aviation in the Interwar Black Press." M.A. Thesis in English, Texas A&M University, May 2017, available at https://oaktrust .library.tamu.edu/bitstream/handle/1969.1/161521/BENES-THESIS-2017.pdf (accessed April 12, 2023).

Bergeron, Kat. "Brown Condor: Gulfport aviation pioneer broke color barriers." *Sun Herald*, Biloxi, MS, March 15, 2002, A1, A9.

Bonner, Michael. "The Brown Condor of Ethiopia: The Determination of John C. Robinson, Hero of Gulfport." Gulfport, MS: Mississippi Aviation Heritage Museum, February 28, 2021. Accessed on May 26, 2023. https://msaviationmuseum.org/blog/the-brown-condor-of-ethiopia-the -determination-of-john-c-robinson-hero-of-gulfport

Borja, Elizabeth. "The Dream of Abyssinia: Two Black Aviators and Ethiopia." National Air and Space Museum, 27 February 2021. Accessed May 26, 2023. https://airandspace.si.edu/stories/editorial/dream-abyssinia-two-black -aviators-and-ethiopia

Broadnax, Samuel L. *Blue Skies, Black Wings: African American Pioneers of Aviation.* Westport, CTA: Praeger Publishers, 2007.

CAF Rise Above. "Lewis A. Jackson, Ph.D: Aviation Pioneer—Innovator —Educator—Administrator." November 6, 2018. Accessed May 26, 2023. https://cafriseabove.org/lewis-a-jackson-ph-d/

Chicago Sun-Times. "Harold Hurd, 90, Pioneering Black Aviator." September 10, 2002, 64.

Daily Challenge. "Black Aviation Pioneer Dead at 86." New York, NY, July 21, 1992, 2. Betty Gubert Collection of African Americans in Aviation, Box 2, Folder 19 ("Willa Brown: Biography 1 of 2"), Vivian G. Harsh Research Collection of Afro-American History and Literature, Chicago Public Library.

Davis, Edmond. "Cornelius Robinson Coffey (1903–1994)." *Encyclopedia of Arkansas*, June 16, 2023. Accessed June 23, 2023. https://encyclopediaofarkansas.net/entries /cornelius-robinson-coffey-6940/

Diakite, Parker. "How The First Black-Owned Airport Gave Black Pilots Access To

The Skies." *Travel Noire*, May 14, 2021. Accessed April 12, 2023. https://travelnoire.com/black-owned-airport-black-pilots-access-to-the-skies

EAA Aviation Museum: Collections: Curtiss JN-4D "Jenny." Accessed May 26, 2023. https://www.eaa.org/eaa-museum/museum-collection/aircraft-collection-folder/1918-curtiss-jn4d-jenny

Galanis, Diane. "South suburban 'first': Robbins—first black village, first black-owned airport." *Southtown Star*, April 30, 1989, 10.

Gantt, Marlene. "Black female flyer gave life to aviation." *Dispatch*, Moline, IL, March 23, 1991, 4.

Gibson, Karen Bush. *Women Aviators: 26 Stories of Pioneer Flights, Daring Missions, and Record-Setting Journeys.* Chicago: Chicago Review Press, 2013.

Golab, Art. "Black Aviator Still Flies High: Pioneer Aids Students." *Chicago Sun-Times*, July 14, 1993, 24. Betty Gubert Collection of African Americans in Aviation, Box 4, Folder 10 ("Coffey, Cornelius"), Vivian G. Harsh Research Collection of Afro-American History and Literature, Chicago Public Library.

Grossman, Ron. "A Flight Against the Wind." *Chicago Tribune*, July 25, 1993, section 5, 1, 6, available at https://www.chicagotribune.com/news/ct-xpm-1993-07-25-9307250224-story.html (accessed April 3, 2023).

Gubert, Betty Kaplan, Miriam Sawyer, and Caroline M. Fannin. *Distinguished African Americans in Aviation and Space Science.* Westport, CT: Oryx Press, 2002.

Gubert, Betty Kaplan. *Invisible Wings: An Annotated Bibliography on Blacks in Aviation, 1916–1993.* Westport, CT: Greenwood Press, 1994.

Hardesty, Von. *Black Wings: Courageous Stories of African Americans in Aviation and Space History.* New York, NY: HarperCollins, 2008.

Hardesty, Von, and Dominick Pisano. *Black Wings: The American Black in Aviation.* Washington, D.C.: National Air and Space Museum, 1983.

Hart, Philip S. *Flying Free: America's First Black Aviators.* Minneapolis, MN: Lerner Publications Company, 1992.

Haymore, Tyrone. "Robbins Airport, 1930." In *The Story of Robbins*, Robbins Historical Society, No. 3, February 1989. Coffey family papers, Kansas Collection, RH MS 692, Kenneth Spencer Research Library, University of Kansas, Box 3, Folder 4.

Israel, Yahoshuah. *The Lion and the Condor: The Untold Story of Col. John C. Robinson and the Crippling of Ethiopia.* Addis Ababa, Ethiopia: International Council for the Commemoration of Col. John C. Robinson, 2015.

Jakeman, Robert J. *The Divided Skies: Establishing Segregated Flight Training at Tuskegee, Alabama, 1934–1942.* Tuscaloosa, AL: The University of Alabama Press, 1992.

Jennings, Michael. "A soar winner: Black aviatrix helped open sky to Tuskegee airmen." *Courier-Journal*, Louisville, KY, March 11, 1996, 1, 3.

Jet. "Janet H. Bragg, Pioneer Black Aviatrix, Succumbs at Age 86 ." May 10, 1993, 36. Betty Gubert Collection of African Americans in Aviation, Box 2, Folder 15 ("Bragg, Janet Harmon W."), Vivian G. Harsh Research Collection of Afro-American History and Literature, Chicago Public Library.

Lambertson, Giles. "The Other Harlem." *Smithsonian Air & Space Magazine*, March 2010, available at https://www.smithsonianmag.com/air-space-magazine /the-other-harlem-5922057/ (accessed April 12, 2023).

Locke, Theresa A. "Willa Brown-Chappell Mother of Black Aviation." *Negro History Bulletin*, Vol. 50, No. 1 (January, February, March 1987), 5–6. Association for the Study of African American Life and History, available at https://www.jstor.org /stable/44254446 (accessed April 12, 2023).

McRae, Bennie J., Jr. "National Airmen Association of America . . . before the Tuskegee Airmen." In *Lest We Forget* 3.3, LWF Publications, July 1995, available at http://lestweforget.hamptonu.edu/page.cfm?uuid=9FEC34DF-BD35-EC52 -06AC946C7292C6D8 (accessed April 12, 2023).

National Aviation Hall of Fame. "The National Aviation Hall of Fame Announces the Class of 2023." February 21, 2023. Accessed June 25, 2023. https://national aviation.org/the-national-aviation-hall-of-fame-announces-the-class-of-2023/

OX-5 Aviation Pioneers, Robert F. Lang, et al, editors. *OX-5 Aviation Pioneers*. Dallas, TX: Taylor Publishing, 1985. Coffey family papers, Kansas Collection, RH MS 692, Kenneth Spencer Research Library, University of Kansas, Box 3, Folder 2.

Oxford African American Studies Center. "Photo Essay—Early African American Aviators." Oxford University Press, 2022. Accessed May 26, 2023. https://oxfordaasc.com/page/photo-essay-early-african-american-aviators

Perez, Severo. *Willa Brown & The Challengers (The Challengers Aero Club)*. Los Angeles: Script & Post Script, 2012.

Powell, Murella. "'Brown Condor' takes a swim." *Sun Herald*, Biloxi, MS, May 12, 2002, 66.

Robbins Historical Society Museum. *Historic Robbins, Illinois, Souvenir Journal*. Country Club Hills, IL: J.V. Cook, Inc., 2017.

Scott, Lawrence P., and William M. Womack, Sr. *Double V: The Civil Rights Struggle of the Tuskegee Airmen*. East Lansing, MI: Michigan State University Press, 1998 (1992).

Scott, William R. "Colonel John C. Robinson: The Condor of Ethiopia." *Pan African Journal* Vol. 1 (Spring 1972), 59–69. Betty Gubert Collection of African Americans in Aviation, Box 7, Folder 16 ("Robinson, John C."), Vivian G. Harsh Research Collection of Afro-American History and Literature, Chicago Public Library.

Simmons, Thomas E. *The Man Called Brown Condor: The Forgotten History of an African American Fighter Pilot*. New York, NY: Skyhorse Publishing, 2013.

Smith, Bryan. "The Trouble with Robbins." *Chicago Magazine*, December 1, 2014, available at https://www.chicagomag.com/Chicago-Magazine/December-2014 /The-Trouble-with-Robbins/ (accessed April 12, 2023).

Tucker, Phillip Thomas. *Father of the Tuskegee Airmen, John C. Robinson*. Dulles, VA: Potomac Books, 2012.

THE TUSKEGEE AIRMEN

Caver, Joseph, et al. *The Tuskegee Airmen: An Illustrated History, 1939–1949.* Sydney, Australia: NewSouth Books, 2011.

Davis, Edmond, and Roscoe D. Draper. *Pioneering African-American Aviators: Featuring the Tuskegee Airmen of Arkansas.* Little Rock, AR: Aviate Through Knowledge Productions, 2012, available at https://www.researchgate.net/publication /271702221_Pioneering_African_American_Aviators_featuring_the _Tuskegee_Airmen_of_Arkansas_with_Foreword_by_Dr_Roscoe_D_Draper (accessed April 12, 2023).

Dryden, Charles W., and Benjamin O. Davis. *A-Train: Memoirs of a Tuskegee Airman.* Tuscaloosa, AL: University of Alabama Press, 2002 (1997).

Grossman, Ron. "Tuskegee Aces." *Chicago Tribune,* July 25, 1991, 65.

Moye, J. Todd. *Freedom Flyers: The Tuskegee Airmen of World War II.* New York, NY: Oxford University Press, 2012.

Rose, Robert A. *Lonely Eagles: The Story of America's Black Air Force in World War II.* Los Angeles, CA: Tuskegee Airmen Inc., 1976.

BESSIE COLEMAN

Freydberg, Elizabeth Hadley. "Bessie Coleman." In *Black Women in America,* Hine et al, 1993, 262–263.

Lauria-Blum, Julia. "Bessie Coleman: Pioneer Aviator." *Metropolitan Air News,* June 7, 2019. Accessed May 26, 2023. https://metroairportnews.com/bessie-coleman -pioneer-aviator/

Rich, Doris L. *Queen Bess: Daredevil Aviator.* Washington, D.C.: Smithsonian Institution Press, 1993.

MISCELLANEOUS AND GENERAL SOURCES

Atkins, Jeannine. Illustrated by Dušan Petričić. *Wings and Rockets: The Story of Women in Air and Space.* New York, NY: Farrar, Straus, and Giroux, 2003.

Bay, Mia. "What It Was Like to Fly as a Black Traveler in the Jim Crow Era." *Condé Nast Traveler.* March 23, 2021. Accessed May 26, 2023. https://www.cntraveler.com /story/how-black-travelers-fought-discrimination-while-flying-in-the-jim-crow-era

Chan, Wilfred. "Q&A: How does an air crash investigation work?" CNN, July 9, 2013. Accessed May 26, 2023. https://edition.cnn.com/2013/07/09/us/asiana-air-crash -investigation-explainer/index.html

Charles Rivers Editors. *The Harlem Renaissance: The History and Legacy of Early 20th Century America's Most Influential Cultural Movement.* North Charleston, SC: CreateSpace Independent Publishing Platform, 2018.

Civil Air Patrol. "History of Civil Air Patrol." Accessed April 12, 2023. https://www.gocivilairpatrol.com/about/history-of-civil-air-patrol

Craft, Stephen G. "Laying the Foundation of a Mighty Air Force: Civilian Schools and Primary Flight Training During World War II." *Air Power History* 59:3, Fall 2012, 4–13.

Eberhardt, Scott, and Narayanan Komerath. "The Guggenheim Schools of Aeronautics: Where Are They Today?" Paper given at the Annual Conference and Exposition of the American Society for Engineering Education, June 14, 2009, available at https://peer.asee.org/4835 (accessed May 12, 2023).

Edwards, Jim, and Wynette Edwards. *Chicago: City of Flight.* Mt. Pleasant, SC: Arcadia, 2003.

Federal Aviation Administration. "A Brief History of the FAA," n.d. Accessed January 19, 2023. https://www.faa.gov/about/history/brief_history

Federal Aviation Administration. "First U.S. Federal Pilot License," n.d. Accessed January 19, 2023. https://www.faa.gov/about/history/milestones/media/first _pilots_license.pdf

Ford Motor Company. "The Model T," n.d. Accessed April 7, 2023. https://corporate .ford.com/articles/history/the-model-t.html

Fort Vancouver National Historic Site. "The JN-4 Jenny: The Plane that Taught America to Fly." National Park Service, n.d. Accessed April 3, 2023. https://www.nps.gov/articles/jn-4.htm

Gates, Henry Louis, Jr., and Evelyn Brooks Higginbotham. "Faucet, Crystal Bird." In *African American Lives*. London: Oxford University Press, 2004, 292–294.

Goeres, Vince. *Wings over Nebraska: Historic Aviation Photographs.* Lincoln, NE: History Nebraska, 2010.

Guzman, Jessie Parkhurst. *Negro Year Book: A Review of Events Affecting Negro Life, 1941–1946.* Atlanta, GA: Tuskegee Institute Department of Records and Research, 1947, available at https://archive.org/stream/negroyearbook rev00guzmrich/negroyearbookrev00guzmrich_djvu.txt (accessed April 12, 2023).

Hartzell Propeller. "Hartzell History: The Fabulous History of Barnstorming," July 4, 2017. Accessed April 7, 2023. https://hartzellprop.com/hartzell-history -history-barnstorming/

Hine, Darlene Clark, Elsa Barkley Brown, and Rosalyn Terborg-Penn (editors). *Black Women in America: An Historical Encyclopedia*, Vol. A–L. Bloomington, IN: Indiana University Press, 1993.

Hine, Darlene Clark, Elsa Barkley Brown, and Rosalyn Terborg-Penn (editors). *Black Women in America: An Historical Encyclopedia*, Vol. M–Z. Bloomington, IN: Indiana University Press, 1993.

History Nebraska. "Nebraska's First Aviation Meet." Lincoln, NE: History Nebraska Publications, n.d. Accessed April 3, 2023. https://history.nebraska.gov /publications_section/nebraskas-first-aviation-meet/

Horton, Lucy. "1st Black Woman Commercial Pilot Joins FAA Panel." *Chicago Tribune*, February 27, 1972, Section 10, 8.

Johnsen, Frederick. "The Waco Model 9 and 10." *General Aviation News*, March 7, 2019, available at https://generalaviationnews.com/2019/03/07/the-waco -model-9-and-10/ (accessed January 19, 2023).

Kraus, Theresa L. "The CAA Helps America Prepare for World War II." Federal Aviation Administration, FAA Milestones and Events, n.d. Accessed April 12, 2023. https://www.faa.gov/about/history/milestones/media/The_CAA_Helps _America_Prepare_for_World_WarII.pdf

Lane, James B. *City of the Century: A History of Gary, Indiana.* Bloomington, IN: Indiana University Press, 1978. Betty Gubert Collection of African Americans in Aviation, Box 3, Folder 12 ("Willa Brown: Gary Schools"), Vivian G. Harsh Research Collection of Afro-American History and Literature, Chicago Public Library.

Lewis, David. *When Harlem Was in Vogue.* New York, NY: Oxford University Press, 1981.

Marcus, Harold G. *Haile Selassie: The Formative Years, 1892–1936.* Lawrenceville, NJ: Red Sea Press, 1987.

Menard, Orville D. "Lest We Forget: The Lynching of Will Brown, Omaha's 1919 Race Riot," *Nebraska History* 91, 2010, 152–165, available at https://history.nebraska.gov/wp-content/uploads/2022/10/NH2010Lynching.pdf (accessed April 7, 2023).

Milner, Richard. "*Star Trek* Star Nichelle Nichols' Dedication to NASA Was Nothing Short of Remarkable." *Grunge*, August 1, 2022. Accessed April 11, 2023. https://www.grunge.com/947535/star-trek-star-nichelle-nichols-dedication-to -nasa-was-nothing-short-of-remarkable/

Mitchell, Dawn. "Indiana was a scandalous marriage mill and Valentino took advantage." *Indianapolis Star*, July 7, 2019, 2A.

Murray, Paul T. "Blacks and the Draft: A History of Institutional Racism." *Journal of Black Studies* Vol. 2, No. 1 (September 1971), 57–76.

Museum of Flight. "Heath Parasol." Seattle, WA, 2023. Accessed May 26, 2023. https://www.museumofflight.org/exhibits-and-events/aircraft/heath-parasol #:~:text=The%20Museum's%20Heath%20Parasol%20was,%2C %20Washington%20during%201996%2D2008

Napier, Walt. "A Short History of Integration in the US Armed Forces." United States Air Force, July 1, 2021. Accessed May 26, 2023. https://www.af.mil/News /Commentaries/Display/Article/2676311/a-short-history-of-integration -in-the-us-armed-forces/

National Air and Space Museum. "Curtiss JN-4 'Jenny.'" Smithsonian, n.d. Accessed May 26, 2023. https://airandspace.si.edu/collection-objects/curtiss-jn-4d-jenny /nasm_A19190006000

National Air and Space Museum. "Black Wings: The Life of African American Aviation Pioneer William Powell." February 2, 2016. Accessed May 26, 2023. https://airandspace.si.edu/stories/editorial/black-wings-life-african-american -aviation-pioneer-william-powell

National World War II Museum. "The Battle of Midway." New Orleans, LA: National World War II Museum, n.d. Accessed May 26, 2023. https://www.national ww2museum.org/war/articles/battle-midway

National World War II Museum. "The Path to Pearl Harbor." New Orleans, LA: National World War II Museum, n.d. Accessed May 26, 2023. https://www.nationalww2museum.org/war/articles/path-pearl-harbor

National World War II Museum. "Remembering Pearl Harbor: A Pearl Harbor Fact Sheet." New Orleans, LA: National World War II Museum, n.d., available at https://www.census.gov/history/pdf/pearl-harbor-fact-sheet-1.pdf (accessed May 26, 2023).

National World War II Museum. "Wages and Working Conditions: The Railroad Strike of 1946." New Orleans, LA: National World War II Museum, May 28, 2021. Accessed May 26, 2023. https://www.nationalww2museum.org/war /articles/1946-railroad-strike

Neprud, Robert E. *Flying Minute Men: The Story of the Civil Air Patrol.* New York: Duell, Sloan, and Pearce, 1948.

New York Times. "Los Angeles Replaces Chicago as Second City." April 8, 1984, 27, available at https://timesmachine.nytimes.com/timesmachine/1984 /04/08/108108.html?pageNumber=27 (accessed May 26, 2023).

Nnuriam, Paul Chigozie. *The Influence of Pan Africanism on Africa's International Relations, 1945–1965.* Equatorial Journal of History and International Relations, 1(1), 2018, 13–21, available at https://papers.ssrn.com/sol3/papers.cfm?abstract _id=3130717 (accessed April 6, 2023).

Paulson, Jill (compiler). "Illinois Wing History 1942." Illinois Wing Civil Air Patrol, [2016], available at https://ilwg.cap.gov/media/cms/ILWIngHistory1942 _CD33884582172.pdf (accessed April 12, 2023).

Paur, Jason. "March 17, 1953: The Black Box is Born." *Wired*, March 17, 2010. Accessed April 7, 2023. https://www.wired.com/2010/03/0317warren-invents -airplane-black-box/

Peck, James L.H. *So You're Going to Fly.* New York, NY: Dodd, Mead & Co., 1943.

Pisano, Dominick A. *To Fill the Skies with Pilots: The Civilian Pilot Training Program, 1939–1946.* Urbana and Chicago, IL: University of Illinois Press, 1993.

Pollack, Theo Mackey. "The Broken Diamond of Washington, D.C." *Legaltowns*, February 21, 2019. Accessed April 8, 2023. https://www.legaltowns.com /2019/02/21/the-broken-diamond-of-washington-d-c/

Quillen, Isaac James. *Industrial City: A History of Gary, Indiana to 1929.* New York, NY: Garland Publishing, 1986, 438–440. Betty Gubert Collection of African Americans in Aviation, Box 3, Folder 12 ("Willa Brown: Gary Schools"), Vivian G. Harsh Research Collection of Afro-American History and Literature, Chicago Public Library.

Rawn, James, Jr. *The Double V: How Wars, Protest, and Harry Truman Desegregated America's Military.* New York, NY: Bloomsbury Press, 2013.

Redner, Sidney. "Population history of Chicago from 1840–1990," in "Distribution of City Populations." Boston University, November 6, 2003. Accessed January 20, 2023. http://physics.bu.edu/~redner/projects/population/cities/chicago.html

Sbacchi, Alberto. "Italian Colonization in Ethiopia: Plans and Projects, 1936–1940." *Africa: Rivista trimestrale di studi e documentazione dell'Istituto italiano per l'Africa e l'Oriente*, Vol. 32, No. 4 (December 1977), 503–516.

Scott, William R. "Black Nationalism and the Italo-Ethiopian Conflict 1934–1936." *Journal of Negro History*, 63:2 (April 1978), 118–134.

Selig, Nicholas C. *Lost Airports of Chicago*. Charleston, SC: The History Press, 2013.

Selig, Nicholas C. *Forgotten Chicago Airports*. Charleston, SC: The History Press, 2014.

Shaftel, David. "The Black Eagle of Harlem: The truth behind the tall tales of Hubert Fauntleroy Julian." *Smithsonian Air & Space Magazine*, December 2008, available at https://www.smithsonianmag.com/air-space-magazine/the-black-eagle-of -harlem-95208344/ (accessed April 12, 2023).

Sharpe, Michael. *Biplanes, Triplanes, and Seaplanes*. London: Grange Books, 2000.

Strickland, Patricia. *The Putt-Putt Air Force: The Story of The Civilian Pilot Training Program and The War Training Service (1939–1945)*. [Washington, D.C.]: Department of Transportation, Federal Aviation Administration, Aviation Education Staff, 1970, available at https://babel.hathitrust.org/cgi/pt?id=uc1.b3907789 &view=1up&seq=11 (accessed April 12, 2023).

Thompson, Lowell D. *African Americans in Chicago*. Mt. Pleasant, SC: Arcadia, 2012.

United States Civil Air Patrol. "History of Civil Air Patrol." Homeland Security Digital Library, n.d. Accessed April 10, 2023. https://www.hsdl.org/c/view?docid=456489

Watson, Tim, and Betsy Jacoway Watson. *Images of America*. Mt. Pleasant, SC: Arcadia, 2016.

Weber, Bruce. "Nichelle Nichols, Lieutenant Uhura on *Star Trek*, Dies at 89." *New York Times*, August 1, 2022, D-8, available at https://www.nytimes.com/2022/07/31 /obituaries/nichelle-nichols-dead.html (accessed April 11, 2023).

Wegg, John. *General Dynamics Aircraft and Their Predecessors*. London: Putnam Aeronautical Press, 1990.

Wellerstein, Alex. "Counting the Dead at Hiroshima and Nagasaki." Bulletin of the Atomic Scientists, August 4, 2020. Accessed April 11, 2023. https://thebulletin .org/2020/08/counting-the-dead-at-hiroshima-and-nagasaki/

Whitfield, John H. *"A Friend to All Mankind": Mrs. Annie Turnbo Malone and Poro College*. North Charleston, SC: CreateSpace Independent Publishing Platform, 2015.

Williams, Chad L. *Torchbearers of Democracy: African American Soldiers in the World War I Era*. Chapel Hill, NC: The University of North Carolina Press, 2010.

Winchester, Jim, ed. "Curtiss JN-4 'Jenny.'" *Biplanes, Triplanes and Seaplanes* (Aviation Factfile). London: Grange Books plc, 2004.

WTTW. "From Riots to Renaissance: Policy Kings." Chicago, 2022. Accessed April 8, 2023. https://interactive.wttw.com/dusable-to-obama/policy-kings

OTHER ONLINE SOURCES

African American Heritage Sites. "Curtiss-Wright Aeronautical University Building," n.d. Accessed June 24, 2023. https://africanamericanheritagesites.stqry.app/en /story/55603

Airtug. "A Brief History of Aerobatics." December 14, 2016. Accessed May 26, 2023. https://airtug.com/brief-history-aerobatics/

Anne Frank House. "Germany invades Denmark and Norway." Accessed May 26, 2023. https://www.annefrank.org/en/timeline/61/the-german-invasion-of -denmark-and-norway/

Annie Malone Historical Society. "Fast Facts." 2014. Accessed May 26, 2023. https://www.anniemalonehistoricalsociety.org/fast-facts.html

Biography. "Booker T. Washington." April 23, 2021. Accessed May 26, 2023. https://www.biography.com/scholars-educators/booker-t-washington

Bryan, Jami L. "Fighting for Respect: African-American Soldiers in WWI." The Army Historical Foundation. Accessed May 26, 2023. https://armyhistory.org /fighting-for-respect-african-american-soldiers-in-wwi/

Encyclopaedia Britannica Editors. "How many people died during World War I?" Britannica. Accessed May 26, 2023. https://www.britannica.com/question /How-many-people-died-during-World-War-I

Encyclopaedia Britannica Editors. "Marcus Garvey." Britannica, May 19, 2023. Accessed May 26, 2023. https://www.britannica.com/biography/Marcus-Garvey

Encyclopaedia Britannica Editors. "Pearl Harbor attack." Britannica, April 23, 2023. Accessed May 26, 2023. https://www.britannica.com/event/Pearl-Harbor-attack

Encyclopaedia Britannica Editors. "The Loop/area, Chicago, Illinois, United States." Britannica, March 26, 2023. Accessed May 26, 2023. https://www.britannica.com /place/the-Loop

Encyclopaedia Britannica Editors. "Wing/aircraft." Britannica, June 12, 2020. Accessed May 26, 2023. https://www.britannica.com/technology/wing-aircraft

Encyclopedia.com. "Midian O. Bousfield 1885–1948." 2019. Accessed May 26, 2023. https://www.encyclopedia.com/african-american-focus/news-wires-white -papers-and-books/bousfield-midian-o

English Heritage. "The Fall of France in the Second World War." Accessed May 26, 2023. https://www.english-heritage.org.uk/visit/places/dover-castle /history-and-stories/fall-of-france/

Foreign Service Institute, Office of the Historian. "The Neutrality Acts, 1930s." United States Department of State. Accessed May 26, 2023. https://history.state .gov/milestones/1921-1936/neutrality-acts

Gurlacz, Betsy. "Oak Lawn, IL." Encyclopedia of Chicago, 2005. Accessed May 26, 2023. http://encyclopedia.chicagohistory.org/pages/916.html

Hart, Basil Liddell. "North Africa campaigns." Britannica, May 6, 2023. Accessed May 26, 2023. https://www.britannica.com/event/North-Africa-campaigns

History.com Editors. "Harry S. Truman." *History*, January 8, 2021. Accessed May 26, 2023. https://www.history.com/topics/us-presidents/harry-truman

History.com Editors. "Nazi Party." *History*, October 4, 2022. Accessed May 26, 2023. https://www.history.com/topics/world-war-ii/nazi-party

Hogan, Lawrence Daniel. "Associated Negro Press." *Encyclopedia of Chicago*, 2005. Accessed May 26, 2023. https://encyclopedia.chicagohistory.org/pages/1734.html

Holsoe, Svend E., Donald Rahl Petterson, and Abeodu Bowen Jones. "Liberia." *Britannica*, May 25, 2023. Accessed May 26, 2023. https://www.britannica.com /place/Liberia

Kuryla, Peter. "Pan-Africanism." *Britannica*, January 27, 2023. Accessed May 26, 2023. https://www.britannica.com/topic/Pan-Africanism

Mehretu, Assefa, Donald Edward Crummey, and Harold Marcus. "Ethiopia/Ethnic groups and languages." *Britannica*, May 24, 2023. Accessed May 26, 2023. https://www.britannica.com/place/Ethiopia/Ethnic-groups-and-languages

Mehretu, Assefa, Donald Edward Crummey, and Harold Marcus. "Ethiopia/The rise and reign of Haile Selassie I (1916–74)." *Britannica*, May 24, 2023. Accessed May 26, 2023. https://www.britannica.com/place/Ethiopia/The-rise-and-reign -of-Haile-Selassie-I-1916-74

National Archives. "Marcus Garvey (August 17, 1887–June 10, 1940)." September 15, 2020. Accessed May 26, 2023. https://www.archives.gov/research/african -americans/individuals/marcus-garvey

Naval Air Station Museum Glenview. "A Global Legacy of Naval Aviation and Innovation." Hangar One Foundation, 2021. Accessed May 26, 2023. https://www.thehangarone.org/

Nielsen, Euell A. "The Double V Campaign (1942–1945)." *BlackPast*, July 1, 2020. Accessed May 26, 2023. https://www.blackpast.org/african-american-history /events-african-american-history/the-double-v-campaign-1942-1945/

Romer, Christina D., and Richard H. Pells. "Great Depression." *Britannica*, April 28, 2023. Accessed May 26, 2023. https://www.britannica.com/event/Great -Depression

Spurgeon, John. "Flood of 1937." *Encyclopedia of Arkansas*, March 16, 2023. Accessed May 26, 2023. https://encyclopediaofarkansas.net/entries/flood-of-1937-4878/

Tuskegee University. "History of Tuskegee University." Accessed May 26, 2023. https://www.tuskegee.edu/about-us/history-and-mission

United States Census Bureau. "1940 Census of Population." Vol. 2. 1943. Accessed May 26, 2023. https://www.census.gov/library/publications/1943/dec/population-vol-2.html

University of Kansas. "To Make the World Safe for Democracy: Kansas and the Great War/Those Who Served." 2018. Accessed May 26, 2023. https://exhibits.lib.ku .edu/exhibits/show/world-war-one/case-2

Village of Oaklawn. "About Oak Lawn." Oak Lawn, IL. 2023. Accessed May 26, 2023. https://www.oaklawn-il.gov/about-oak-lawn

White House Historical Association. "Harry S. Truman, the 33rd President of the United States." The White House. Accessed May 26, 2023. https://www.whitehouse.gov/about-the-white-house/presidents/harry-s-truman/

Wikipedia. "District of Columbia retrocession." Wikipedia: The Free Encyclopedia, March 29, 2023. Accessed May 26, 2023. https://en.wikipedia.org/wiki /District_of_Columbia_retrocession

Wikipedia. "Theodore Roosevelt College and Career Academy." Wikipedia: The Free Encyclopedia, March 28, 2023. Accessed May 26, 2023. https://en.wikipedia.org /wiki/Theodore_Roosevelt_College_and_Career_Academy

Wikipedia. "Tuskegee University." Wikipedia: The Free Encyclopedia, May 22, 2023. Accessed May 26, 2023. https://en.wikipedia.org/wiki/Tuskegee_University

INDEX